D0802803

As a frequent writer for Ain't It Cool News, VERN has gained notoriety for his unorthodox reviewing style and his expertise in "the films of Badass Cinema." His review of the slasher movie *Chaos* earned him a wrestling challenge from its director; his explosive essay on the PG-13 rating of the fourth *Die Hard* movie prompted Bruce Willis himself to walk barefoot across the broken glass of movie nerd message boards to respond. Guillermo Del Toro, the director of *Pan's Labyrinth*, called Vern "a National Treasure." He lives in Seattle.

SEAGALOGY

SEAGALOGY
A STUDY OF THE ASS-KICKING FILMS OF STEVEN SEAGAL

ISBN 1 84576 927 9
ISBN-13 9781845769277

Published by
Titan Books
A division of
Titan Publishing Group Ltd
144 Southwark St
London
SE1 0UP

First Titan edition May 2008
10 9 8 7 6 5 4 3 2 1

Cover design by Martin Stiff, with thanks to Bryan Thiess.

Visit our websites:
www.titanbooks.com
www.geocities.com/outlawvern/

Did you enjoy this book? We love to hear from our readers. Please e-mail us at:
readerfeedback@titanemail.com or write to Reader Feedback at the above address.

To receive advance information, news, competitions, and exclusive Titan offers online, please register as a
member by clicking the "sign up" button on our website: www.titanbooks.com

A CIP catalogue record for this title is available from the British Library.

Printed in the United States of America.

SEAGALOGY
[se-gal-uh-jee]:

A STUDY OF THE ASS-KICKING FILMS OF STEVEN SEAGAL

BY VERN

TITAN BOOKS

NOTE: Some portions of this book were written under the influence of Steven Seagal's Lightning Bolt Energy Drink (Cherry Charge flavor)

CONTENTS

INTRODUCTION by David Gordon Green i
INTRODUCTION 2: DARK TERRITORY v

GOLDEN ERA (1988-1991)
Chapter 1: **Above the Law** 3
Chapter 2: **Hard to Kill** 19
Chapter 3: **Marked For Death** 33
Chapter 4: **Out For Justice** 41

SILVER ERA (1992-1997)
Chapter 5: **Under Siege** 57
Chapter 6: **On Deadly Ground** 69
Chapter 7: **Under Siege 2: Dark Territory** 85
Chapter 7.5: **Executive Decision** 95
Chapter 8: **The Glimmer Man** 101
Chapter 9: **Fire Down Below** 109
interlude: My Giant 117

[transitional period] (1998-2002)
Chapter 10: **The Patriot** 123
Chapter 11: **Exit Wounds** 131
Chapter 12: **Ticker** 141
Chapter 13: **Half Past Dead** 151

DTV ERA (2003-present)
Chapter 14: **The Foreigner** 165
Chapter 15: **Out For a Kill** 175
Chapter 16: **Belly of the Beast** 185
interlude: Songs From the Crystal Cave 199
Chapter 16.5: **Clementine** 205
Chapter 17: **Out of Reach** 211
Chapter 18: **Into the Sun** 225

Chapter 19: **Submerged** 243
interlude: Steven Seagal's Lightning Bolt Energy Drink 251
Chapter 20: **Today You Die** 257
Chapter 21: **Black Dawn** 271
Chapter 22: **Mercenary For Justice** 283
interlude: Mojo Priest 291
Chapter 23: **Shadow Man** 295
Chapter 24: **Attack Force** 307
Chapter 25: **Flight of Fury** 315
Chapter 26: **Urban Justice** 325
Chapter 27: **Pistol Whipped** 335

CONCLUSION 353

APPENDIX I: Other Appearances and Productions 369
APPENDIX II: Hard To Film: The Ones That Never Made It 383
APPENDIX III:
My Review of Steven Seagal and Thunderbox Live in Seattle 387

AN INTRODUCTION TO A BOOK
By DAVID GORDON GREEN

It was the Spring of 1988. I was thirteen years old, growing up in Dallas, Texas and coming to terms with life as a pubescent movie junkie. A distinct memory I have is the weekend when the film *Above the Law* came to the local theaters. I had been primed for Steven Seagal through countless articles introducing him as the next great action hero. This was quite a claim. Could he top Chuck Norris in *Invasion U.S.A.*? Would he dethrone Charles Bronson from my favorite film *Murphy's Law*? Could he channel Sonny Chiba, Michael Dudikoff and Dolph Lundgren in the same roundhouse kick? Unlikely, but my anticipation could not be ignored. Fortunately, the release fell on the same day as the Lea Thompson vehicle *Casual Sex* and my erection was primed in two directions: sneak into a double feature – hopefully get my eyes on the boobies of the beauty I so admired from *All the Right Moves* and *Howard the Duck* and possibly get rocked by the next admiral of Aikido. The day did not disappoint.

Since that awakening as an audience member, I have had the privilege to cheer for Seagal as he dominated the genre. Who wants to see Jean Claude Van-Damme in *Death Warrant* or fucking *Cyborg* when you could witness the brutal human elegance of Seagal's *Marked For Death* or the astonishing *Hard to Kill*? His stretch of films that promoted themselves with three dramatic words was for me a trademark and a guarantee that

I would be getting my money's worth (though to be honest, I typically snuck into the movies in the first place – slipping past the "R" rating and ticket price). I suppose for the majority of the American public, Seagal truly arrived with mainstream muscle with *Under Siege* – Playboy Playmates jumping out of cakes and whatnot – but for me… it was all born in the early flicks, not quite a franchise, but his character was never too far a departure from the last.

A strange tide turned as his fame and fortune grew. Perhaps it was the dazzling spotlight of Tinseltown that prompted a shift in his work. He was no longer studying linguistics and martial arts in the Orient and making intimate action movies. Suddenly, I found myself sitting in front of a slew of message films. Beginning with *On Deadly Ground*, Seagal began to slip environmental themes, spiritual quests and politics into his films. Perhaps he had lost touch with reality and was living in a vacuum. Where was the soft spoken shitkicker that I gravitated toward in my youth? I was worried that soon I would experience the cramps I felt when I ended my affair with Tom Laughlin's *Billy Jack* during his two silly sequels.

Fortunately, as any true movie fanatic, I was able to grow to appreciate his personal crusade. I chose to accept this curveball and take my own enjoyment and expectations to the next level. I began waiting for his films to come out on video and watching them with friends, then soon had no option but to experience his series of foreign financed Direct to Video projects like *Black Dawn*. I felt obligated to talk to the screen during *Half Past Dead* and I'm optimistic that *Out For a Kill* will ferment with age like a fine wine. Through his prolific output, in some way he has become even more interesting. I have returned to watching his films back to back with other films, but strangely paired now with films along the lines of *The Kid with the 200 I.Q.*, *The Englishman Who Went Up a Hill, And Came Down a Mountain*, or frequently *Troop Beverly Hills*.

Through my studies of Seagal, I have come to understand why monks walk before this movie star and throw pebbles at his feet. He is a walking contradiction on a mythical path. Some say he is a douche, while others recognize and value him for his humanitarian work and charitable contributions. He holds the Dalai Lama close, while the mafia wanted to extort him, allegedly. He surrounds himself with German Shepherd attack dogs, but carries around bowls of candy for a sweet accent at the end of a hard day. These are genuine qualities that make this icon so complex. And it is exactly this searing mystique that inspires audiences to roll with his professional transitions and accept his body of work as the portfolio of a soldier lost and found. Seagal's actual stunt performance may be limited now as his age and death blows have taken their toll. His voice is sometimes dubbed and his silhouette not as sleek, but my enthusiasm for his efforts and entertainment perseveres.

— David Gordon Green, September 2007

David Gordon Green is the acclaimed director of George Washington, All the Real Girls, Snow Angels *and the action-comedy* The Pineapple Express.

INTRODUCTION 2:
DARK TERRITORY

"You are about to go on a sacred journey. This journey will be good for all people. But you must be careful."

"Bring people forward into contemplation." In interviews that's what Steven Seagal has often said is the goal of his movies. Contemplation. Now, a lot of people don't hold Steven Seagal or his movies in the same high regard that I do. So that may seem like a ridiculous statement to some people, especially everybody who is not Steven Seagal. I mean what is there to contemplate about a dude in a ponytail and shiny shirts going around breaking wrists and throwing people through windows? Well, I am not Steven Seagal, but I will try to tell you.

The French invented the auteur theory, the idea that the director can be considered the author of a movie, the one who puts his or her personal stamp on the thing and who deserves most of the credit and blame. But I invented the badass auteur theory. The badass auteur theory is the idea that in some types of action or badass pictures, it is the badass (or star) who carries through themes from one picture to the next.

I mean I agree with the French about the importance of the director, and they also make good bread and were right about Iraq. But in the type of picture we're going to be discussing in this book it is the star that connects the body of work more than the director. So it makes more sense to compare *Above the Law* to other movies starring Steven Seagal than to director Andrew Davis's later best picture nominee *The Fugitive*.

I think I first developed the theory in discussing the films of Charles Bronson, but I might as well have invented it for Seagal. More than any action star I know of, Seagal puts his imprint on every movie he makes, whether he's writing and producing it or just appearing in it. He brings a certain personality, formula and set of motifs to pretty much every picture he ever does. Most actors try to find scripts they can work with, Seagal seems to have scripts grow out of him. Seagal once said, "I haven't always been dealt scripts that were palatable and movies that I thought were even makable, and I think one of the secrets of my success is that I *changed* them into something that was almost watchable[1]." These scripts are written for him, or by him, or they are rewritten to fit him, so they always end up featuring some of his obsessions: enlightened men with shadowy CIA pasts, westerners with expertise in Asian ways (aikido, swords, herbology, Buddhism), various types of mafia (Italian-American, European, Asian), music (blues, bluegrass, reggae, much of it performed by or written by Seagal himself), the protection of animals or the environment.

And then there's his politics. From the very beginning his movies have had themes of an out of control CIA trafficking drugs into the country, rogue secret agents turning into terrorists, corporations pillaging the land and indigenous cultures... the types of things you didn't usually see in action movies at the time, and that you saw a lot more in real life as the years went on. Seagal has admitted that he hasn't had much control over his movies and has done many of them to fulfill contractual obligations. But he also talks proudly of an "environmental conscientiousness" and "political conscientiousness" he has been able to work into many of his films.

Seagal might be the first to admit that his pictures are often ridiculous, full of corny lines and silly ideas. If so, I would be the second. And I would add that in the case of some of the later films there are many laughable action scenes. Well, boo fucking hoo. I can still say I honestly admire Seagal's attempts to use his dumb action movies to glorify environmental protection, non-violence, indigenous cultures, intelligence agency reform, Chinese shirts and whatever other hobbies he picks up along the way. (Remember what a surprise it was the first time he picked

---

1 Choi, "Seagal flies East" in *Impact: The Action Movie Magazine*, May 1994, p. 26.

up a guitar in a movie?)

A lot of people don't understand how you can take the thematic business seriously when the movie itself is a cocky guy with a ponytail going around saying shit like, "What does it take to change the essence of a man?" But you know what, the Bible has some pretty corny parts in it too. The burning bush? What the fuck was *that* about? And I never got the part about crustaceans being an abomination. Despite those eccentricities, people still dig on that Bible. Because there's some good stuff in there and the part with the boat full of animals was awesome. Also the plagues. Yes, I am comparing the films of Steven Seagal to the Holy Bible. Sorry.

A lot of people don't remember it, or won't admit it, or most likely never noticed it, but Seagal's filmography is full of good parts too. If you retrace his footsteps you will find a trail of broken windows and bones. Along that trail will be a series of surprisingly entertaining b-movies and some inexplicably effective big time studio blow 'em up movies, sometimes in the *Die Hard* mold. You will find evidence of one-liners both wonderful and hilariously awful. Lines like "I'm gonna take you to the bank, Senator Trent. *To the blood bank*," are delivered with such sincerity that I don't even know anymore if it's so bad it's good or so good it's awesome. It's like on the old video games, if the score got high enough it would just flip back over to zero and start over. That might be what happened when he said that line in *Hard to Kill* – it was so bad it flipped over and became great. Or maybe it's the other way around. I don't know but the point is, I wish I said that shit to somebody. That was great. Good job Seagal.

Seagal has lived an interesting life. He was the first foreigner to run an aikido dojo in Japan, he broke Sean Connery's wrist teaching him martial arts for *Never Say Never Again*, he hosted *Saturday Night Live*, he was declared the reincarnation of a Buddhist lama, he was blackmailed by the mob and allegedly wiretapped by notorious private eye Anthony Pellicano. There are times when his biographical information has obvious parallels to his work, and is worth mentioning. But this will not be a biography. That is a task worthy of a greater writer than I, one who does interviews and research and crap. I am not that writer and this will not be that book. Instead, this will be a book about the deep study and analysis of the entire Seagal filmography. By watching each of Seagal's movies in chronological order, cross-referencing their plots and motifs, watching the themes build, the formulas evolve, and the hairline turn into a strange Eddie Munster style widow's peak, I believe I can come to understand *the essence of a man*. That is Seagalogy. Join me on this journey, etc.

A quick note before we get started: for better understanding, I have divided the filmography into a distinct set of eras. I got help in naming them from a comic book nerd friend who insisted the early ones had to be "the golden age." Feel free to define your own eras, but for the purposes of the book here's how it lays out:

GOLDEN ERA

Above the Law through *Out For Justice*
(1988-1991)
These four films represent Seagal's pinnacle as a serious action hero and all the qualities that made him a star. Even if you're not a serious Seagalogist you should see these films.

SILVER ERA

Under Siege through *Fire Down Below*
(1992-1997)
These six films (including *Executive Decision*, in which he takes a supporting role) represent Seagal's biggest success as a mainstream movie star and what he chose to do with that success. Beginning with the breakout hit *Under Siege* and continuing through his environmental thrillers *On Deadly Ground* and *Fire Down Below*, you get to see him at both his best and his most ridiculous, often at the same time. That's the yin and yang of Seagalogy.

[transitional period]

The Patriot through *Half Past Dead*
(1998-2002)
In this period, Seagal found himself making his first direct-to-video film (*The Patriot*), then triumphantly returning to the big screen with the sleeper hit *Exit Wounds*. Suddenly he was on video again with *Ticker* and theatrical again with *Half Past Dead*, which was not as big of a hit.

DTV ERA[2]

The Foreigner and beyond
(2003-present)
We can't read the future, but we can make a guess. This may turn out to be the longest and most productive era of Seagalogy. This is when Seagal made peace with his title as the king of straight to video action movies and let loose. He indulged his weirdest tendencies and made some of his most interesting (but not necessarily best) films. He also became far more prolific than before, releasing as many as 4 movies a year. Mainstream acceptance seemed unattainable, plagued as he was with criticisms of his weight gain, increasing reliance on stunt doubles and voiceovers. But he traveled around Europe and Asia making a series of highly distinctive, low budget movies, sometimes even with titles similar to those of his older films. And then he started drinking goji berry juice and playing the blues.

---

2 My comic book nerd friend wanted to call this "the Kal El Age," because "Kal El" is Superman's Christian name and he likes Superman a lot. I told him to go fuck himself.

GOLDEN ERA

1988-1991

CHAPTER 1:
ABOVE THE LAW

"Nico, why is the CIA calling you at 2 o'clock in the morning?"

Most of the big action heroes had to start out small and build their way up. A year before Rocky, Sylvester Stallone was still taking roles like "Young Man In Crowd" in scenes cut out of *Mandingo*. Arnold Schwarzenegger of course had *Hercules In New York* as well as bit parts like "Muscleman" in an episode of the TV show *San Pedro Beach Bums* and "Lars, Gym Instructor" in *Scavenger Hunt*. Jean Claude-Van Damme not only played an Ivan Drago knockoff in *No Retreat, No Surrender*, he can also be spotted as a background dancer in *Breakin'*. Chuck Norris didn't do much before co-starring with Bruce Lee in *Way of the Dragon*, but at least in that one he got his ass kicked. Seagal took the opposite route – he started as the star, in one of his best movies, with virtually all the elements of his later pictures already in place. In the martial arts he had climbed the ladder through years of training, but in movies he really was an overnight success.

Directed by future Academy Award nominee for best director Andrew Davis, *Above the Law* is the blueprint for the rest of Seagal's career. It lays out his typical storylines, motifs and characters, his *Billy Jack*-like knack for adding left-ish politics to action movies, his fascination with other cultures, and even the partly fictional backstory that he liked to promote as his public persona. On the other hand, he doesn't have a ponytail in this one. So in that sense it's completely different from most of his other movies.

Seagal plays ex-aikido instructor, ex-CIA Vietnam vet Chicago vice-sergeant turned vigilante Nico Toscani. Or, as the trailer narrator describes him, "Nico Toscani – he's a covert agent, trained to survive in Viet-Nam. He has a master's sixth degree black belt in aikido, and family in the mafia. He's a cop – *with attitude.*" This attitude of his will come in handy when he stumbles across a CIA drug smuggling operation that blows up the priest at his church and plans to assassinate a senator. Like many cops in movies of the '70s and '80s, Nico gets pulled off the case, but he pursues it anyway. *With attitude.*

So *Above the Law* is sort of a cop movie about the Iran-Contra scandal, but more than that it's about introducing the world to Steven Seagal. He'd been around Hollywood a little bit, choreographing fights for *The Challenge* and *Never Say Never Again*, and possibly teaching aikido to the powerful agent Michael Ovitz. But *Above the Law* was his first appearance in a movie, and he wasn't just starting out with a starring role – he was starting out with a vehicle. As much as the movie is about a story, it's about Steven Seagal.

With that in mind, the movie begins by explaining *the premise* of Steven Seagal. The first image is Seagal's actual baby photo. The movie opens with Seagal's gentle voice narrating over a photo montage, as if we're watching a Ken Burns documentary about his life. He explains that he was born in Sicily but his family emigrated to the US, he grew up patriotic, saw an aikido demonstration at a baseball game and "by the time I was 17 I was there [in Japan], studying with the masters." It shows real photos of a young Seagal training in Japan and we see that he eventually opened his own dojo.

So now that the movie has established the basic idea behind Seagal, it's time to demonstrate his abilities. The photo montage segues into new footage of Nico in his dojo, sparring with students. Years later, as Seagal was ridiculed for gaining weight and making silly direct-to-video movies, revisionists would claim that he was not the real deal, that he had never been a very good martial artist and that he only made it into movies because of his connection to Ovitz. But the opening credits alone of *Above the Law* put the lie to that one. It's maybe two minutes into the movie and he's already flipping guys over, waving his hands around at ridiculous speeds and even showing off by speaking Japanese[3].

Next the voiceover explains that Nico's skills and a chance meeting led to him doing work for the CIA, and there's a funny montage of the Vietnam War and peace marches with badly dubbed chanting and that type of electric guitar that is supposed to remind you enough of Jimi Hendrix that you know it's the '60s.

So there it is. The American so amazed by martial arts that he moves to Japan, trains for years and against all odds becomes a teacher himself, then starts freelancing for the CIA. This is Nico's backstory and it's similar to the background Seagal assigned to himself in interviews at the time. But like the '60s montage it's a combination of real and phony. Seagal is not from Sicily, he was born in Lansing, Michigan. But he really did go to Japan as a young man, he may have really hung around in the general vicinity of the founder of aikido, and later he definitely did run an aikido school, unheard of for a white man in Japan whether he has an attitude or not. However, Seagal's claims and innuendo about working for the CIA are at best unverifiable. Most tend to write that off as a promotional gimmick. Still, a good chunk of the character of Nico Toscani is the real Seagal, enough that they can share the same photo album on the opening credits. It's sort of like the approach they use now to turn non-actors like Eminem and 50 Cent into movie stars: create a character based on their real life, and a story based around their abilities, and treat it very seriously.

At the end of the credits sequence there's a clip of Richard Nixon quoting Lincoln as saying, "No one is above the law, no one is below the law, and we're going to enforce the law and Americans should remember that if we're going to have law and order." This cuts directly to the villain, Kurt Zagon (Henry Silva), on the border between Vietnam and Cambodia during the war, clearly not thinking about the importance of law and order. We don't know yet that he's a brutal interrogator and torturer, or that his mission is to get back some missing opium, or that

---

3 Other than explaining his fighting style in later action scenes, Nico's experiences in Japan are not necessary to the plot. In those naïve days, you had to *explain* why a dude in an action movie could do martial arts. We've come a long way, in my opinion.

in the future he'll still be in the CIA and using coke money to fund a secret invasion of Nicaragua. But we still know he's up to no good. And let's be honest, it's obvious that the CIA is corrupt if they're gonna hire a guy who looks like Henry Silva. I mean look at the guy's face. Don't tell me they didn't know that motherfucker was evil.

And there he is, Nico Toscani, the first ever Steven Seagal character. According to the script, "We see from Nico's gait that he is athletic, a born leader and totally at home in the jungle." I'm not sure I really got all that from his gait, but fair enough – he is totally at home in the jungle. He is not at home, however, with these crazy CIA bastards like Zagon. Nico is the naïve rookie who gets upset when he encounters Zagon and other agents doing "chemical interrogation" on some POWs, not for war purposes but to find out who fucked with their opium. At first Nico tries to play along, but his conscience won't let him. Like Billy Jack before him, he tries to intervene, yelling in outrage "What does this have to do with military intelligence?" and "You guys think you're soldiers? You're fucking barbarians!" Which is another way of saying, "Nobody is *above the law*!" Also he is wearing a cool scarf.

After a brief scuffle he runs off, declaring "I'm through!" as his buddy Nelson Fox (Chelcie Ross) buys him time.

Flash forward to the present day, where Nico is a Chicago cop with a sassy female partner named Jax (the great Pam Grier) and a crying wife (the crying Sharon Stone). Jax is in the middle of her last week on the job before becoming the D.A., so the whole time you're worried she's gonna die. And Sharon Stone spends the entire movie crying and whining and trying to get Nico to back down like a coward instead of do the right thing, so you wouldn't mind that much if she did die.

Like the wedding sequence in *The Godfather Part II* we meet the whole family because it's a christening ceremony for Nico's daughter, and then there's a big party. We learn that half of Nico's relatives are cops and the other half are mafia, so they don't mingle much at the barbecue. It's not clear in the movie why they included the mafia angle, except that Seagal has a fascination with the mafia. (Years later, ironically, alleged members of the Gambino crime family would try to extort him in real life.) With these connections established, you'd think after the police failed him Nico would go to his mafia relatives for help, but it never happens. The only person that seems to think the mafia relatives are important is the narrator of that trailer. More on this later.

During the party Nico's mom is crying because his teenage cousin is holed up doing drugs with her pimp boyfriend again. Nico leaves the party, taking Jax with him, telling the family he has to go to work. Then he tells Jax he has to take a piss and he goes into a bar, but instead of pissing he starts roughing up the dudes hanging out at the bar (including *Henry: Portrait of a Serial Killer's* Michael Rooker, who has one line) trying to find out where his cousin is. This is the first full-fledged Seagal fight scene, and the beginning of a tradition of fights in bars. The bartender (Ronnie Barron) is a memorable loudmouth asshole, yelling "Holy shit man, stop this motherfucker he's crazy!" But Nico scares him enough that he gives up which room the cousin and the pimp are coking out in. Nico kicks the door down and stages an intervention, shoving the pimp's face in a table of coke. The guy gets so desperate to not go to jail he tries to butter up Nico by telling him about the "big shipment" he heard about.

When Nico comes out dragging his cousin and the pimp, being yelled at by the bartender, Jax says, "Boy, you got some strange toilet habits!"[4]

Before long, Nico, Jax and cohorts are dressed up as meatpackers waiting to bust this shipment. After Seagal's first big car chase scene (where he holds onto the roof of a high speed car and punches through the side window to grab the driver) they open up the crates and discover that the shipment isn't drugs, but military explosives. Nico knows enough about explosives that he is able to sniff them and declare, "C-4, m'man."

Soon he finds himself following drug traffickers to his own church, but he has to let them go because Father Genarro (Joe Greco) starts talking to him and it would be socially awkward not to go into the basement with the man to find out what he has to say about the Nicaraguan, El Salvadoran and Chilean refugees he has stashed down there. Nico is guilted into coming to church the next Sunday, which is when he notices

---

4 Seagal characters will have strange toilet habits in other films too, most notably *The Foreigner*, where he'll be using a urinal when suddenly he'll jump out a window without washing his hands or, as far as we can tell, zipping his pants.

one of the people he followed is in the congregation, and she leaves a bomb. Not exactly the best Sunday to go back to church, in my opinion, but it was good to have Nico there to carry out the bodies.

Like most Seagal movies the plot gets pretty complicated, but unlike the later ones the story unfolds naturally enough that it's easy to follow. Father Genarro's friend Father Tomasino (Henry Godinez) has learned through the South American refugees about a CIA plan to kill the senator who's investigating their activities in Nicaragua. The woman who left the bomb was actually CIA, and she meant to get Thomasino but got Genarro instead. In other words our tax dollars are going to church bombings and they're not even killing the right padres.

Along the way Nico, of course, is told by his superiors to back off, so he gets mad and kicks a chair. When he stays on the case he gets suspended (a rare "I want your badge and your gun[5]" scene for Seagal) but gets out a stash of guns he has hidden somewhere and keeps investigating.

A reoccurring theme in Seagal movies, especially in the Golden and Silver eras, is the "old agency friend" who either gives him a tip or helps him break into government databases. *Above the Law* has both – Nelson Fox (despite being corrupt) tries to warn him that he's in trouble, and a computer expert named Watanabe helps him break into the CIA's computer files. Watanabe represents the kind of minimalism Seagal usually applies to these characters – we see that she works for some kind of corporate entity because she's working at an electronics conference, and we can assume since she knows Nico and knows how to break into the CIA's databases that she used to work for the CIA. But they don't bother to explain any details because, really, what difference does it make?

In an earlier screenplay some of these details *were* filled in. Watanabe indicates that she owes Nico because he saved her life once, referring to the time he "kept a few 'friendly' tribesmen from cutting my heart out and serving it up as Pad Thai." The scene is a lot less corny as filmed. Of course it helps that they also cut Watanabe's line, "If I can't crack that

---

5 In an earlier script his superior uses the more slangy "I want your tin… and your iron."

turkey's code, it's time to hang up my rock and roll shoes." The script even describes "Watanabe working two computers simultaneously, with the gusto of a rock keyboard player," which fortunately is not how the scene ended up being filmed. When you compare the finished film to the screenplay it emphasizes that *Above the Law* is so much better than it seems like it ought to be.

But even if it wasn't, the movie has many good fights and action scenes that helped Seagal to enter the popular consciousness. Seagal fights in a style never seen before on screen, not just because aikido had not been showcased in films like kung fu and karate had, but because he had developed his own system of aikido. According to Seagal student Kent Moyer, "Throughout the entire course of his training and teaching, Seagal's goal was to develop and refine the ultimate 'street style'; the most practical combative art for modern applications[6]." Seagal's fast, blunt style of fighting immediately stands out as an unusual approach to fight choreography. My favorite is the one where a bunch of dudes get out of a car and surround Nico with a gun, two machetes and a baseball bat. It takes Nico about three seconds to get rid of the gun, steal a machete and turn it into a sword fight. He beats them silly and chases the last guy down an alley, scaring the guy so badly he starts to cry and scream "Don't kill me!" Coincidentally, a very tall acquaintance of the crying man happens to be hanging out on the corner. He sees what's going on and says, "Hey, that's my buddy!" He runs over to kick Nico's ass but is taken down with one punch.

One of the weirdest aspects of the movie is Nico's relationships with his wife and his partner. In most respects the guy is a saint, looking after his relatives and his congregation, carrying mutilated bodies away from church bombings, hugging the crying women in the hospital, going on missions alone to keep his partner away from danger. On the other hand he seems like a real bad husband, always being cold to poor Sharon Stone unless she's crying on his shoulder. I haven't timed it but I bet Sharon

---

6 Moyer, *Martial Arts Legends Presents Shigemichi Take, Shihan Steven Seagal, The Spiritual Warrior Who Prospered on the Island of Budo*, p. 34. Moyer elaborates: "The Steven Seagal style has sometimes been criticized because it does not resemble the soft, impractical Aikido so often seen in America today. In fact, it is a very severe style by comparison."

spends more than 80% of her screen time either crying, pouting or cowering in fear, saying things like "I'm scared, Nico!" Maybe all that crying practice helped her get her Oscar nomination for *Casino*, I don't know. In one of the rare moments of happiness between the two, at the christening party, Nico jokes about Jax wearing lingerie to work, and Jax jokes "Don't tell her our secrets, she'll never let you go out with me again!"

For her part, Jax doesn't seem to have a more important man in her life – she turns down guys who hit on her and complains that she has turned down a hot date to go tail a suspect with Nico. They get dressed up and go to a restaurant and even refer to it as a date. Later in the picture, after Jax is shot in slow motion by Zagon and may die, Nico mourns in the usual movie fashion by looking at photos, including a family portrait of him, his wife, his baby, and Jax! Now think about it. All cops are gonna have close relationships with their partners, but do you think Danny Glover invites Mel Gibson to be in his family portraits? No, not until the end of part 4. I think we all know what is going on here. Nico is cheating on his wife. But maybe Seagal didn't want to make it too obvious since his real wife might get the wrong idea if she saw part of this movie on cable or something. It's one of those things you don't pick up on until you've seen the movie a couple times. Which you will.

Another weird aspect is this bartender character. Throughout his career, Seagal will have many fights in bars, but this is the only bartender who will hold a grudge against him and try to come after him. Usually there's a fight, maybe the bartender says something, but you never see the character again. This guy just keeps showing up. After the fight in his bar, he's outside trying to convince the other cops to arrest Nico. Later, after the cops have turned on Nico, he's in the police station filing a complaint about him, and he has a weird way of describing the bar brawl. "He starts doing all this outer space kinda stuff. Puttin my customers in orbit, even."

Okay so that much is unusual but when it gets really strange is at the end when Zagon gets out of a car with a bunch of dudes and one of them is the bartender! For some reason he gets to hang out and smile sadistically while Nico gets tortured, like he's getting off on it. I couldn't figure out how this guy convinced the corrupt CIA madman to let him come along. That outer space story is not gonna be enough, I don't think.

The only explanation is offered in the end credits. In the script he's called "Bad Dude," but in the credits he's "CIA bartender." I'm not sure how that works that the sleazy bartender is a spook, but there you go.

Seagal himself is not particularly strange in the movie. There is only one little scene late in the picture that gives an indication of what a great weirdo he'll grow into. He sits at the kitchen table, holding his baby daughter, as his wife and his mom cry and try to convince him that they need to leave town for their own safety. Instead of addressing their concerns, he just says quietly, "You ever notice how clean babies smell – like nothing in the world has ever touched them?" It's a line only Seagal, or possibly Marlon Brando, could get away with.

Some people have pointed to Seagal's running in the movie as stranger. There are scenes when he performs a physical activity commonly described as "running like a girl." I don't think it's that bad, though. He looks like he runs pretty fast, at least. You don't see him chasing guys anymore, so enjoy it while you can.

After you've seen the movie a few times, you might start to wonder why the hell they included the detail that Nico comes from a mafia family. They make a big deal about him coming from Sicily, you see his mafia relatives complaining about his cop friends at the christening party, and when he's being suspended the lieutenant mentions his family as if the apple doesn't fall too far from the tree. But it doesn't seem worth all this just as an explanation for why he has "attitude." Sure enough, the script contained an entire deleted sequence where it all fits together. In the scene where Nico's wife Sara whines about the need to run away, and Nico talks about the smell of babies, Sara was originally trying to convince him to go talk to his uncle Frederico Larusso in prison. Reluctantly, Nico goes to the prison under the assumed name "Mr. Carlucci." He confesses to his uncle that he has always hated the mafia but now realizes that they're not that different from the people he was working for. Uncle Frederico says he knew Nico would come for help and that he had planned not to, but he changes his mind and gives Nico an address to memorize. This cuts directly to the scene where Nico is on the roof and gets caught by Nelson Fox.

It's weird that they would cut this sequence without finding another story reason for Nico's mafia connections, but the sequence as it is is pretty useless. It's not really clear what the address was. If it's the address to the building he goes to, couldn't he have found out about the senator's public appearances and figured it out without the help of the mafia (as he apparently does in the finished film)? And how would his uncle know that address anyway? Not to mention the fact that his plan doesn't exactly work, he gets captured and tortured while on the rooftop. So even though everything works out in the end it's not really because of Uncle Frederico's mysterious tip.

To the Seagal illiterate, this picture is the best bet at explaining why he ever became popular. Although he is not as imposing as in his later, fatter pictures, he moves much faster, his aikido looks convincing and the quickness of the fights make them stand out from other action pictures of the time. The fights are also more raw and brutal than many martial arts films, especially American ones. His style is not as much about looking cool as it is about dispatching opponents as quickly as possible. There is some blood and some graphically broken bones. Nico himself gets pretty bloody too, which doesn't happen to Seagal much in later films.

In a scenario that would become very familiar over later films, Nico chases some guys into a mini-mart and ends up destroying every shelf or glass surface in the joint beating them down. There's a classic slo-mo shot where he jumps through the front window using a thug to shield him from the glass. Variations on this stunt will show up in many, many other Seagal films over the years. The scene is an insult to private business owners but a delight to action fans.

Of course, riding on top of cars, throwing guys through windows and turning in your gun and badge are things we've seen a million times before. And David M. Frank's typical '80s score (drum machines, guitar noodling and poppin' keyboard basslines) adds a certain level of cheesiness. But I would argue that, for the genre, this is a high-class affair, nicely directed by Andrew Davis. In the press kit Davis said he "wanted to use the full scope of Chicago as an actual character in the film." This is, of course, pretentious horse shit, unless he meant Chicago was a bit part character, like the "Hey that's my buddy!" guy or Michael

Rooker. That said, it is a nice setting for the movie and Davis gives the city a more realistic feel than almost any other Seagal film. The streets are always populated. Zagon can be walking into a place to do some business and you can hear some random guys having an unrelated argument across the street. Or Nico can get in a gunfight and you'll see all the neighbors looking down from the windows of nearby buildings wondering what the hell's going on.

A lot of the cops seem authentic, too (perhaps because some of them, like Joseph F. Kosala, are retired police officers). The scene where they come to the house to arrest Nico is especially believable. One guy tries to be nice about it, keeps apologizing and saying "we'll work this out." Other guys are being assholes and getting in Nico's face.

Unlike Seagal, Davis had already made a few movies, the most recent one having been the 1985 Chuck Norris vehicle *Code of Silence*. In 1992, he would raise Seagal briefly to the level of mainstream blockbuster movie star courtesy of the film *Under Siege*. The next year he'd get best picture and best director Oscar nominations for *The Fugitive*. I guess it probably made more sense at the time. Anyway, he's a pretty good director and this is undoubtedly one of his best.

Without a doubt, Davis played a hugely important role in Seagalogy. He is pretty much the mastermind of Chapter One. Not only did he direct, he co-wrote the script with Steven Pressfield, Ronald Shusett and an uncredited Seagal, which means he helped figure out exactly how to showcase Seagal for movies, creating a template for all of Seagalogy.

A good way to see what Seagal's contribution was is to compare *Above the Law* to *Code of Silence*. After all, both are about Chicago cops becoming isolated by institutional corruption while dealing with South American drug lords. Both star a martial artist turned actor and feature Henry Silva playing the main villain. Some of the same actors (like Ron Dean and Joseph F. Kosala) play cops, and even that asshole CIA bartender, Ronnie Barron, is in there playing another loudmouth criminal with a bad hair cut. They have similar Chicago shooting locations, similar Andrew Davis directing style and the same type of cheeseball '80s score by David M. Frank.

And yet they aren't exactly the same type of movie. *Code of Silence* does not feel like what would become a Seagal movie. *Above the Law* introduces a lot of new elements to the story that are unmistakably Seagal. First of all, the emphasis on the backstory. Not just because there's a flashback and semi-autobiographical narration, but because (like most Seagal characters) it's crucial that he has a past in the CIA. Adding the CIA into the picture is important in itself. The corruption in *Code of Silence* is isolated: a drunk fuckup cop shoots a kid by accident and plants a gun on him, and the other cops support him even if they know he's lying. Seagal's corruption tale is about a thousand times more ambitious since it reaches back to the Vietnam War and has the CIA involved in drug trafficking and plans to assassinate a senator. More novel and more relevant to the time it was made.

You gotta give some credit to Chuck Norris though, in his movie he teams up with a heavily armed police robot, which unfortunately does not happen in *Above the Law*.

While *Above the Law* is the template for all of Seagalogy, it is the very first try. So some of the motifs and concepts are in most Seagal pictures even to this day, while others continued for a while but were eventually abandoned. The CIA and aikido backgrounds, of course, turn up in almost every (but not quite every) Seagal film. They're so common that if a CIA past isn't mentioned in a Seagal film, you usually assume it's there anyway.

The theme of corrupt intelligence agencies and the complicated intrigue continue to this day, but the way they're presented is pretty different. In the early films, they tend to follow *Above the Law*'s lead by using a monologue or speech where Seagal lays out his feelings about the topic. In later films he still does that occasionally, but it always feels like an improvised bit of dialogue inserted by Seagal to put his fingerprints on the movie, and not a deliberate dramatic moment in the screenplay.

This film has a sense of outrage that eventually disappears from his work. Early on he was able to be more passionate about wrongdoing. Later he will mostly play cynical characters who have seen it all and are hard to surprise.

Above the Law goes out of its way to show Nico's close relationship to his family, and many of the early Seagal films will have sweet bonding moments to show how much he loves his son or his wife or whatever.

Family shit. In the later films, he mostly plays single loners who have little connection to other people, though he often hooks up briefly with a pretty younger woman by the end of the picture.

The vast destruction of glass and glass objects will continue throughout all his films, as will the fascination with Japanese culture. Fights in bars will seem like a requirement for a while but eventually he'll get tired of that motif and drop it. Same with the "old agency friend" who gives him a tip or helps him out. And speaking different languages. For a while he uses every chance he gets to speak Japanese or Spanish and to do Spanish pronunciations, like when he says "Nee-ca-lrauga." The hidden cache of weapons will show up a few more times too.

One thing that's a lot different from later films, he's much more American here. He's got the Japanese background but he lives a very American life. I think he was interested in mafia movies, so he put a strong emphasis on Catholicism – the christening, the two Fathers, the bombing in the church. He has a close relationship with the Father and tries to get him to call his mom to say hi. These days, with Seagal so involved in Buddhism, it's hard to imagine him playing a Catholic at all, let alone making it such a big part of the story.

Even his outfit is all-American: white button up shirt, black suit jacket, blue jeans[7]. No Asian shirts or robes. No Asian statues or shrines in his home. Not even decorative swords. Seventeen years later, on the *Making of Black Dawn* featurette, Seagal will sit in a throne wearing a shiny blue robe and say that his favorite place is Japan and that he considers himself "more Asian than American." But in *Above the Law*, Japan has not overwhelmed his identity as an American. It's just one of the things he's into. He's a Chicago cop who happens to know aikido.

Seagal took the politics of the movie seriously, saying in the press notes "This is not a martial arts film. [It] is based on a true story about CIA complicity in narcotics trafficking for the purpose of funding covert operations." From the opening credits on, it's clear that this is a political movie. It's hard to miss the irony of Richard "I am not a crook" Nixon

---

7 At one point the script describes Nico as "Educated, classy, an elegant dresser – yet underneath an out-and-out wild man." In other words, he wears a suit jacket with jeans.

saying that no one is above the law. This is a movie about abuse of power, about government corruption, as well as about shootouts and awesome car chases. I think the Nixon clip signals that it's a little more serious about its politics than your average action movie. A lot of people tend to lump Seagal in with Chuck Norris, Jean-Claude Van Damme, and maybe on a good day Arnold Schwarzenegger or Sylvester Stallone. But none of those guys were making movies quite like this, especially not with this point-of-view. If their pictures had a political edge, they tended to be about fighting communists, about re-winning the Vietnam War or about having to break through liberal bureaucracies to fight out of control urban crime. Those movies were part of the Reagan years, sharing the worldview of the administration. *Above the Law* was a response to the Reagan years, calling for an end to some of what was going on.

The screenwriters clearly wanted the audience to see the connection between the plot of the movie and the Iran-Contra scandal[8] that was brewing at the time. In the scene where the sleazy lawyer Salvano meets with FBI Agent Neeley and Neeley gets a call from the CIA to let Salvano's clients go, the script even specifies that "pictures of Reagan and Meese[9] are prominent on the wall." If you check the movie, sure enough, there is a photo of Ed Meese on the wall, although the photo of Reagan is cropped out of the shot.

Seagal's alleged CIA background, if it were verifiable, would've lent some extra weight to the movie's portrayal of a rogue agency. But that extra credibility wasn't really necessary considering how prominent the Iran-Contra Affair still was in the headlines. The movie was released less than five months after Congress released its final report on the scandal,

---

8 Brief explanation for the kids: members of the Reagan administration secretly sold weapons to Iran (our enemy) and then gave the money from the deal to the Contras, an army of terrorists in Nicaragua who the administration supported because they fought communists. That much everyone agrees on. It is also alleged, but not officially acknowledged, that the arms deal was made before Reagan was in office so that Iran would hold onto hostages until the election in order to hurt Carter's re-election chances. The part that *Above the Law* is most concerned with however is the still-controversial allegation that the CIA were complicit in drug trafficking as an additional source of funding for the Contras.

9 Edwin "Ed" Meese III was Attorney General under Reagan. The Final Report of the Independent Counsel For Iran/Contra Matters concluded that Meese knew that shipments authorized by Reagan and the CIA were illegal and just chose to ignore that fact. Also Meese was the asshole who tried to ban *Playboy* and *Penthouse* from convenience stores, but I'm not sure if the screenwriters really care about that or not. That might just be my thing. I mean how convenient is the store, really, if they can't even get you some mainstream porn?

and less than one month after Oliver North and John Poindexter were indicted on multiple charges.

Even so, the movie was ahead of its time. Most of the media attention revolved around the arms-for-hostages part of the scandal, and how the money from selling arms to Iran was used to fund the terrorist Contra army. It wasn't until 8 years later that investigative reporter Gary Webb's "Dark Alliance" series in the *San Jose Mercury News* revived talk about drug money funding Reagan's beloved Contra "freedom fighters." The article (later expanded into a book) didn't quite describe the scenario shown in *Above the Law*, with CIA agents themselves running drug empires to fund a secret invasion. Instead, Webb's work detailed exhaustive evidence of Nicaraguans coming to Los Angeles, supplying cocaine to the new crop of crack kingpins and funneling their profits to the Contras, possibly with the knowledge and wink wink nudge nudge of the CIA. Webb's series won a few awards but created a firestorm of criticism in the mainstream media. The *Mercury News* long defended the story but then suddenly turned tail and made a half-assed disavowal. Webb was transferred to a suburban bureau far from his home, effectively forcing him out of the paper. In 2004 Webb was found dead of an apparent suicide[10]. The CIA had conducted an investigation on itself and released a two-part report which initially denied any evidence of the claims but then on the other hand described how the CIA had protected more than 50 contras and drug traffickers from federal investigation in order to support the Contra war. Not surprisingly, the mainstream media interpreted the report to mean "innocent of all charges, but guilty of being 100% super awesome," so many of the newspaper obituaries stated that Webb had been proven wrong.

Above the Law, however, has never been disproven.

Above the Law (*Nico* in the U.K.), 1988
Directed by Andrew Davis
Written by Andrew Davis and Steven Pressfield (*King Kong Lives, The Legend of Bagger Vance*), story by Andrew Davis, Steven Seagal and Ronald Shusett (*Alien, Total Recall*)

---

10 I am no expert but I am guessing that a suicide where the guy supposedly shot himself in the head *twice* should be considered suspicious.

Distinguished co-stars: Pam Grier, Sharon Stone. Bit part by Michael Rooker (*Henry: Portrait of a Serial Killer*) as "Man in bar."

Seagal regulars: Miguel Nino (Chi Chi Ramon) plays a commando in *Under Siege*. Joseph Kosala (Lieutenant Strozah) plays "Engine Room Watch Officer" in *Under Siege*. Gene Barge, who plays Detective Harrison, plays one of the Fabulous Bail Jumpers in *Under Siege*. Admittedly those ones are really Andrew Davis regulars (he often re-uses the same bit players), but others are definitely affiliated with Seagal. Patrick Gorman, one of the CIA interrogators at the beginning, also plays an oil executive in *On Deady Ground*. Tom Muzila (one of the aikido fighters in the beginning) plays himself in *Hard to Kill* and Cates in *Under Siege*. Another one of the aikido fighters, Craig Dunn, played a liquor store punk in *Hard to Kill* and a commando in *Under Siege*. He also did stunts in *Out For Justice*, *On Deadly Ground* and *Executive Decision* and is in the Seagal aikido documentary *The Path Beyond Thought*. Haruo Matsuoka is the most impressive of the aikido fighters though because he was in *Hard to Kill*, did stunts in *The Glimmer Man*, and even did stunts with Seagal way back in 1982's *The Challenge*.

Title refers to: CIA, who think they are above the law.

Just how badass is this guy? In a scripted scene cut from the movie, Jax says, "You don't wanna catch him without no gun. 'Cause what he do with his hands... make bullet holes look pretty."

Adopted culture: Japanese.

Languages: English, Japanese, Spanish.

Improvised weapons:

Old friends: agency buddy Fox (turns out to be evil), cop buddy, computer lady who "has a guy at Princeton" so she can find important files Nico needs.

Fight in bar: yes.

Broken glass: head through cooler and man through window during mini-mart fight.

Innocent bystanders: Seagal punches out "buddy" who tries to intervene with a fight.

Family shit: tracks down cokehead girl to appease crying old Italian grandma, very close with priest, hugs crying wife and mother at hospital, random children wave to him on crosswalk right before shootout.

Infidelity: Closer to female partner than to his wife.

Political themes: CIA trafficking opium and torturing innocents during Vietnam War, police paid off, federal agencies cooperating with drug dealer in "ongoing investigation," Father Gennaro says in sermon that we need to investigate what our leaders do in our name, Iran-Contra style hearings expose "major intelligence agencies" trafficking drugs, Nico implies that CIA assassinated JFK and RFK, testifies that agencies "manipulate the press, judges and members of our Congress" and are in fact ABOVE THE LAW.

Cover accuracy: Very accurate. It's a dramatic posed photo of Seagal holding a gun in front of a black void. The tagline describes his background and re-iterates the trailer's claim that "He's a cop with an attitude."

CHAPTER 2:
HARD TO KILL

"You know they always said Storm was superhuman."

Seagal's second film rearranges the politics and action formula of *Above the Law* to create a little more of a mythic hero's journey type deal about a man almost killed who comes back years later to get his revenge. Seagal plays Mason Storm, an ex-LAPD coma victim "raised in the Orient" who is out to avenge those who killed his wife (Bonnie Burroughs) and tried to kill him and his son Sonny (Geoffrey Bara at age 5, later Zachary Rosencrantz).

The story opens in 1983 with Storm sneaking around a dock trying to videotape mobsters as a mysterious shadowy figure hires them to kill a senator. The picture's first line is, "Come on guys, I'm missin' the Oscars" (that would make it April 11th, 1983). He can't make out the face, but he gets it on tape before being found out and having to make a run for it. The shadowy figure turns out to be Assemblyman Vernon Trent (William Sadler, later of *Die Hard 2,* another guy you know is evil as soon as you see his face), who plans to use the senator's death to ascend to office and then maybe run for vice president. Before he can do that though he's got to stop this eavesdropper from getting the word out.

Luckily, Mason Storm happens to be hard to kill, so he escapes to his car, which by the way has Chuck Mangione's "Feels So Good" in the tape deck, in case you're wondering[11]. It's these little bits of character detail that elevate the movie above the level of a Steven Seagal movie where his character *doesn't* have Chuck Mangione's "Feels So Good" in the tape deck. Storm calls his deskbound partner Karl Becker (Lou Beatty Jr.) to tell him that he recorded the gangsters discussing a hit[12], then stops for champagne at a liquor store, where he is forced to beat four robbers who are armed with a shotgun, a knife and a baseball bat. This is in my opinion the best fight scene in the movie, and it's also the one that has no connection to the plot at all. He just happens to be in the store when it gets robbed. The fight includes a part where he puts his gun down and gets down on his knees to give his opponent more of a fair shot, and it ends with Storm twisting the poor bastard's leg in ungodly directions. As the thief screams in agony, we suddenly smash cut to a smiling Mason Storm out front shooting the shit with the cops who report to the scene. Then he drives away grooving to his Mangione. It *feels so good* when you've just hospitalized some armed robbers and you're unaware that corrupt cops listened in on your phone call and have been sent to eliminate you.

I guess in a way the fight is important to the plot, because he manages to leave with the champagne, which is intended for a romantic evening with his wife Felicia. She finds his advances irresistible, even after she notices that he has someone else's blood on his shirt. This is the rare Seagal picture where he gets two different sex scenes, with two different women. It's also the movie that debuted Seagal's iconic ponytail, which must've been impressive at the time judging by the way his wife lovingly fondles it. As Mr. and Mrs. Storm get it on to Johnny Carson's monologue, thugs in ski masks bust in. Storm whips a pistol off of the dresser and busts a guy's wrist, but the thugs kill his wife. For the second movie in a row he gets to yell "NOOOO!" after a loved one gets shot. Then they shoot him, chase his son out the window and plant cocaine all over the place so they can say *he* was the dirty cop. (This seems to

---

11 Also, having Chuck Mangione's "Feels So Good" in the tape deck was specified in the script, in case you were wondering about that as well.

12 He doesn't mention that the hit is on a senator, though. I guess after *Above the Law* senatorial assassination plots are old hat.

prove the wisdom of the old adage about "he who smelt it.")

Meanwhile, they kill his partner Karl, the only other person who knows about the tape. At the hospital we meet another cop buddy, internal affairs lieutenant O'Malley (Frederick Coffin, *Shoot to Kill*, *If Looks Could Kill*, the 1986 TV movie *Under Siege*), who calls Storm "the cleanest man I ever knew" and "most unstoppable sonofabitch I ever knew" and is real upset to hear that Storm is dead. But remember, Mason Storm is hard to kill, so his heart starts up again and O'Malley convinces the doctors not to tell anyone. As far as the rest of the world knows, Mason Storm is a dead, dirty, coke dealing cop. But really, he's a John Doe hidden away in a coma ward.

If he'd only been a little *harder* to kill maybe he would've escaped, at which point he would've learned that *Gandhi* had dominated the Oscars that night, winning 8 awards including best picture, director and actor. Another great icon of pacifism, E.T. The Extra-Terrestrial, had taken home 5. *Tron* had been nominated in 2 categories, but did not win either one. Not sure if that is relevant.

Now the movie skips ahead to "1990 – Seven years later." The first time I saw this I felt a little insulted that the filmatists did not trust me to subtract 1983 from 1990 and figure out the seven years later part myself, but then I remembered how *Halloween* tells me it's "October 31st – Halloween" and I realized this wasn't all that bad. Anyway now Storm has a cool Rip Van Winkle beard and he's in a coma center where a nurse named Andy (Seagal's real life wife at the time Kelly LeBrock) has a crush on him. When Storm miraculously wakes up, word spreads and a dirty cop assassin shows up disguised as a doctor. Storm makes a daring escape using a hospital bed and a mop. At one point the assassin, chasing after Storm, bumps into a janitor and falls down. This makes him so mad that he actually shoots the janitor two times in the chest. Can you believe that shit? The guy is just trying to mop the hallway so his family can keep the electricity on. That is the type of assholes we are dealing with here, killers of innocent janitors. So it's pretty easy to root against them.

Managing to escape, Andy brings Storm to a place where she is housesitting that luckily happens to be decorated with a distinctly Asian style and even has a shrine complete with huge Buddha statue. This is a good time for Seagal to start writing down the names of herbs in Chinese and announce, "When I was a kid, my father was a missionary. I was raised in the Orient. As a young white boy over there, I needed to learn how to fight, as you can imagine."

And he will learn to fight again, but first there are a few opportunities for *Planet of the Apes* type "holy shit what planet have I landed on?" moments. There's a part where he turns on the TV and sees Geraldo Rivera's infamous nose-breaking chair fight with the white supremacists. It really illustrates how much the world has changed while he was sleeping and growing a beard, but what makes it especially great is when he reads the name 'Geraldo' off the screen and rolls the 'r' to prove that he is familiar with Spanish. (This is another Seagal motif – he did the same thing with 'Nicaragua' in *Above the Law.*)

There is an awesome montage where he regains his muscles and fighting skills through self-acupuncture and training. Then he climbs up a little hill and you hear the sound of an eagle. This endorsement by an endangered species proves that he is now hard to kill again and, like the narrator of the trailer says, "now the climate is right for revenge." (See – Storm, climate. It is a play on words, I believe.) But this same climate is also right for sex with Kelly LeBrock. He takes care of that matter, then feels kinda bad about it because of his dead wife. But not that bad, probably.

By the way, Storm does shave off the beard (you can't rock the John Walker Lindh for a whole movie, I guess) and goes back to the ponytail. Just like the kids get rid of their little braid things when they become *Star Wars* Jedis, coma victims lose the beard and get a ponytail when they become badass again. There was a period there, while he was in the coma, that Mason Storm was fairly easy to kill. But now that he is awake and has regained the ability to walk and fight, he officially has hard to kill status again. And he's already gotten laid so the next highest priorities are to get his son back, clear his name, kill every last motherfucker who wronged him, etc. He tracks down his old buddy O'Malley, who is so loyal he has retired from the force, raised Storm's son for him, and brought him guns. You figure Storm better be planning a pretty fuckin good Christmas present for that guy this year. That's a good friend there.

When O'Malley suggests that he hasn't done enough, Seagal delivers his greatest inspirational monologue:

"No no no. You did the right thing. Then wasn't the time. Now's the time. We're outgunned and undermanned, but you know something? We're gonna win. And I'll tell you why: superior attitude, superior state of mind. We'll get 'em, buddy. Believe me. Every fuckin' one of 'em." Then he unloads his gun on an innocent woodpile[13].

The one thing Storm hasn't figured out, though, is the identity of the mysterious shadowy figure – i.e., the motherfucker he has to track down. But he remembers from the old tape that the guy said the phrase "and you can take that to the bank." And he eventually makes the connection that he also saw Senator Vernon Trent on TV saying, "No new taxes – and you can take that to the bank." This is the setup for my personal favorite one-liner in all of Seagalogy: "I'm gonna take *you* to the bank, Senator Trent. To the blood bank."

Now we see Senator Trent in a hot tub drinking champagne with some babe (Julia Stormson). Is this how our tax dollars are being spent? Maybe he's right about no new taxes. When Trent hears that Mason Storm is causing trouble he tells the babe, "Listen, we're not gonna make the ballet tonight. Take a hike. GET LOST!"

So if killing a senator, killing Mason Storm's wife and putting Storm himself in a 7-year coma wasn't enough to make you root against this guy, now you have this whole bad dating etiquette thing to hold against him. I mean come on, she probably was pretty excited about the ballet. He should at least let her go by herself. But he doesn't, so we're definitely rooting for him to make a large deposit at the bank. At the blood bank.

In the climax, Storm sneaks into Trent's mansion and he gets kind of sadistic. He basically stalks the corrupt police captain Holland (Andrew

---

13 If you are ever in need of a pep talk and you want to just skip straight to this part the chapter title on the DVD is "superior attitude."

Bloch) and Senator Trent. He writes threatening messages on the walls and toys with them before breaking bones and stuffing shotguns in mouths. Usually in an action movie the main villain that the hero fights at the end puts up the biggest fight, but in this movie we're dealing with a senator. Stripped of the mafia thugs and corrupt police that he used to destroy Storm's life, he's powerless and cowardly. Storm makes him think he's gonna blow his balls off, then makes fun of the alleged smallness of said balls. Ultimately he doesn't kill him because he has managed to get the tape to the media and the police and convince everyone that Trent had set up the death of Senator Caldwell. In other words, he decides that it would be in his best interest *not* to take Senator Trent to the blood bank. Maybe some day if we're lucky we will get a *Hard to Kill 2* but until then the blood bank will always be several quarts low of Storm's goal.

Hard to Kill is one of Seagal's most entertaining pictures. In many ways it's similar to *Above the Law:* he gets set up and isolated by corrupt cops, his family is in danger, a Senator is involved, etc. There's an attempt to show his family life – not in as much detail as the last movie, but much more than the later ones, where he's usually a loner. Like *Above the Law* he is shown to be Christian, saying the Lord's Prayer with his son (although later he knows his way around a Buddhist shrine). But the more mythic coma and revenge angle to the story makes the movie a little more fun and a lot more enjoyably silly than *Above the Law*.

The story of a victim coming out of a coma, regaining strength, training, then tracking down those responsible and killing them is always a lot of fun (see also Quentin Tarantino's *Kill Bill*). For Seagal it's a novelty because you don't often get to see him defeated. He fails to save his wife, he's almost killed himself, and he fails to prevent the assassination of the Senator. From that low point he rebuilds and strikes back. Also it's unusual because you get to see him with a beard and wearing pajamas.

The action is at times more sadistic and brutal than you expect, like in the liquor store scene when Seagal twists a young punk's foot in ways it clearly was not designed to be twisted, or when he stabs through a guy's neck with a broken pool stick. There are also plenty of those little Seagalian touches that literally no other action star would include in their movies, the best being the majestic scoring as a beautiful white horse escapes to freedom through a fence damaged in a thrilling Jeep chase. Would Jean-Claude Van Damme stop to marvel at the beauty of a horse escaping the captivity of man? No. Would Bruce Willis? No. Even Tony Jaa would only do it if it was an elephant. This is the first instance of Seagal's fascination with animals. It will reappear in *On Deadly Ground, The Patriot, Out of Reach* and an interview he does for PETA.

And I'm not saying the movie's not cheesy, but it's surprisingly well put together considering the background of director Bruce Malmuth, who I'm sure you remember as the ring announcer in the first two *The Karate Kid* movies. He served in the army Special Services for 2 years and as actor, writer and director worked on 26 USO training and recruiting films. From there he went on to director over 1,000 commercials, and according to the press notes, "the Excedrin commercials in the early 1980s marked Malmuth's most recognized work." Now, this may sound like hyberbole, but in my opinion *Hard to Kill* marked a new plateau in Malmuth's career, even compared to the Excedrin commercials.

The director may have found a little bit of a personal connection to the movie too. He raised his son from the age of six as a single father, so I'm sure he had some fondness for the selflessness of Uncle O'Malley. In a way O'Malley is really the hero of the movie – saving Storm's life by pretending he's dead when he's in a coma, arranging for fake funerals for Storm and his son, raising Sonny for him, supplying the tools of revenge, and even dying in the protection of Sonny. For some reason the best human beings are not always the same ones who are hard to kill.

I suppose LeBrock's character is filling the Pam Grier role of the woman Seagal is closer to than his own wife. But she's also the love interest, and a much better one than Sharon Stone's character in *Above the Law*. She's more pro-active and she doesn't cry or whine nearly as much. But if you think about it, she's kind of a fuck-up. First of all, her nursing skills are questionable. It's just not professional for a nurse to get a crush on a patient who's in a coma. Furthermore, I don't think sexual harassment is a legitimate form of coma therapy. She asks him, "Would you like a little pussy JD?" before giving him a kitten, and then she lifts up his blanket to look at his package and says, "Puh-LEASE wake up!" Who knows, maybe this helped him wake up, but I don't think it is the kind of methodology most hospitals would condone.

Her skills as a housesitter are demonstrably poor. Housesitting in general is pretty pointless, but the poor bastard who owns this nice house (one Dr. Armstead, a friend of Andy's parents, according to the script) goes off to China and figures what the hell, let this pretty nurse lady hang out there just to be safe. She'll water the plants and burglars won't see the newspapers piling up. But what does she do, she hides a framed fugitive cop there, which leads to a huge shootout. The walls must have a hundred bullet holes in them, and many windows are broken. She is responsible for the destruction of tables, vases, plates and what I thought was a china hutch but what the script describes as "a tall T'ang Dynasty cabinet filled with priceless Oriental artifacts." The couches are all shot to shit, and whoever owns that horse that got out must be pretty pissed off. I hope the Jeep they were driving didn't come with the house. You know, the Jeep that got shot up, and then they gave it to some random Latino gentlemen on the side of the road.

One little scene that I really don't understand happens right after a car chase. There's a shot of a deliveryman crossing the street to his truck, and a looped voice yells, "Hey Ernie, you forgot my buttermilk! Shit!" As far as I can tell, the failure to deliver buttermilk was not caused by the car chase, so I can't figure out why they included this detail. And is there really such a thing as milkmen anymore?

Storm hangs up copies of articles about the attack on his family and the rise of Senator Trent to inspire him while he prepares for revenge. All the articles about Storm's alleged death have the headline "POLICEMAN, FAMILY SLAUGHTERED," but if you use the pause button to examine closely you will also notice the subheading "Advancing Ice Alters Ecology of Alaska Town." Which seems to suggest a more complicated scheme going on here than I ever realized. Also in the headlines: "Local Pupils Uninspired By Speech[14]."

Melting glaciers and uninspiring speeches aside, *Hard to Kill* is less explicitly political than *Above the Law*. There's no mention of wars or the

---

14 Sadly, local pupils will be uninspired by a speech Seagal will make years later, as you will see in the *Under Siege* chapter.

CIA, and although there are two senators involved there's not much talk of actual politics. There is one headline about the SALT II treaty which maybe implies more sinister military-industrial-complex shenanigans if Trent were to become president, but that's only if you use the pause button and then jump to conclusions. Still, we are dealing with a corrupt, murderous senator involved with the mafia and crooked cops. So it's saying something about what goes on in our government.

Is it pointing fingers in a specific direction? Maybe, maybe not. Trent's "no new taxes" line is arguably an attempt to draw a parallel with ex-CIA President of the United States George H.W. Bush and his infamous "Read my lips, no new taxes" line. *(Mason Storm: I'll read your lips, President Bush. Read 'em their last rites!)* But since the real Bush is shown on the TV, you can't really think of Trent as a Bush-substitute. So you can't really read much into the discussion of taxes except, maybe, that Trent is a Republican, since that has always been a favorite issue for Republicans.

The idea of rigging an election by sabotaging a senator's plane plays off of common suspicions and has creepy parallels to incidents before and after the creation of the movie. In 1976, rising Democratic party star Jerry Lon Litton was killed in a plane crash the same day he received his party's nomination for the Senate, and in 1978, Republican candidate for the Senate Richard D. Obenshain died in a plane crash while campaigning. In 2000, Missouri Governor Mel Carnahan died in a plane crash while running for Senate against John Ashcroft (he still won), and in 2002 Democratic Minnesota Senator Paul Wellstone died in a plane crash just 11 days before a crucial election. In the case of Wellstone, especially, the timing and circumstances of the crash (there were no flight data recorders on the plane, for one thing) caused a lot of his supporters to suspect foul play, despite what the official reports concluded. Whatever really happened in those cases, it's certainly something that could happen, and if it does I hope whichever asshole does it didn't get the idea from *Hard to Kill*. Because that would be an unethical use of Seagalogy.

Setting the opening scenes on Oscar night 1983 adds a sort of realistic texture to the movie, putting the characters into the same historical and cultural type context that we live in. Sort of like Elmore Leonard does in his stories, making Jack Foley misquote *Network* in the trunk of the getaway car in *Out of Sight* and that type of thing. But I think there's also a little subtext here – I don't think it is a stretch to guess that the writer chose Oscar night 1983 as a way of comparing Mason Storm's violent retribution to Gandhi's nonviolent protest. Mason never finds out about *Gandhi* winning the Oscars, but his friend at the police station does, and cheers for Ben Kingsley's win shortly before being shot dead. This seems to indicate that pacifism can only go so far, that we are dealing with violent people and that at some point you need to decide that enough is enough and bring violent retribution to your enemies the way Mason Storm does. You can't just let people walk all over you – you need to take them to the blood bank, it says.

The only real weakness I can find in this argument is that Gandhi is an actual historical figure who really did use non-violent protest to bring independence to India, and in turn inspired other movements across the world, including the one that ended segregation in the United States. Mason Storm, on the other hand, is a fictional character and still was only able to get revenge on a couple of people. I'm sure it made him feel better to say stuff like, "That's for my wife. Fuck you and die," but I still think Gandhi's method has the better track record, in my opinion. I mean I could be wrong. I'm not though.

Still, the movie is great.

A lot of credit for the movie has to go to the screenwriters for coming up with such a perfect vehicle for Seagal. The script is credited to Steven McKay (*Darkman II: The Return of Durant*), who wrote the original draft. But the February 17, 1989 draft, which is available online, says it was revised by Steven Pressfield[15] & Ronald Shusett[16] & Steven Seagal[17]. This version is labeled the final draft, but it has many differences from the completed film, giving you an idea what sort of things were improved by editing and improvising.

---

15 Pressfield wrote the novel *The Legend of Bagger Vance*.

16 Shusett is best known to Seagalogists for *Above the Law* and to everybody else for *Alien* and *Total Recall*.

17 You probably already know who Seagal is.

In the script they tried to give a little more character to Sonny. There are two scenes about the fact that he's rooting for *E.T.* to win at the Oscars and is upset when it loses. It is mentioned that he wears Woody Woodpecker pajamas. There's a whole section, wisely cut out of the movie, where he gets kidnapped during a soccer game. This enrages Storm of course but it serves no purpose in the plot because Sonny ends up immediately escaping to safety on his own. This I'm sure was meant to establish that he's a chip off the old block, but who cares?

They also tried to get some melodrama out of the idea of Storm shacking up with Andy when he should still be mourning his murdered wife. He tells her "I can't love you! Don't you see? It's seven years to anyone else. But it's only days for me."

This type of stuff was wisely trimmed to create a sleeker, faster paced movie. A lot of people like to give action movies shit about lack of character development, but in most movies like this it really is unnecessary to show us cute father-son bonding or the guilt of a widower starting to see other women. Okay, so I always laughed at how quickly Storm seems to get over his wife, but you know what? That's better than wasting my time trying to explain everything. Just keep it simple. I like to compare a movie like this to playing the blues. When you play the blues you don't have to be complicated or original. You play a simple, traditional song. But if you're good you play the hell out of it and you play it in your own style and it becomes your own. I'm not saying it's impossible to make a thoughtful and strikingly original action movie, but what I'm saying is that's usually not the point. *Hard to Kill* is like a good blues song because it's a story arc we've seen a million times but we love the way it unfolds in this version. Luckily they kept it simple.

I do have to say, though, that there are a few nice touches in the script that didn't make it to the screen. During the love scene with his wife, Storm throws a pillow to knock the door shut, which would've been pretty smooth. In one fight, Storm knocks a guy's tooth out, puts it in the guy's hand and makes a vague reference to the tooth fairy. Before Andy's friend Martha gets killed, she manages to throw a cat in a guy's face and then knee him in the balls. There's also the revelation that Storm was armed the whole time he was in the liquor store, but he didn't use his weapon because the bullets he uses are too expensive to waste on something like that. And a part where Sonny gets to say one of my favorite phrases, "Fuck you, Jack."

One spectacular action moment in the script that I'm sure turned out to be too *Hard to Shoot* was one where Storm runs across a row of parked cars, leaps "through the air like a night eagle – setting what looks like a new world record in the long jump" and cracks a guy's neck, killing him instantly. The best part about this awesome move is that it would've been the first time his son saw him in seven years. Quite an entrance.

It can be funny to see how familiar Seagalogical images are described in their screenplays. Mason Storm is said to look "great – a man of action, not dandified at all by the snappy attire." A shot of the other patients in the coma ward is described as "a spectral, haunting scene, full of pathos." The shot after the classic "blood bank" line is called "Storm's vengeance look." Vernon Trent is called the "Shadow Man" during his first appearance when his identity is obscured. He is never called a "Glimmer Man," though. Or "The Patriot."

I mean, there's some good lines in here. I really like the part where Storm sneaks up on three motherfuckers and it says they "don't know whether to shit or go blind."

The corniest description is of Sonny when we first see him as a 12-year old. He is described as looking "terrific, like a young colt – free and fearless – his shiny hair flying as he runs." The script contrasts this scene to "the corruption and duplicity in the world of the movie so far" and concludes that "Sonny's world seems pure and unsullied – youthful and untouched by the harsh realities of the world." I don't know, I guess maybe you can get that out of the movie, the unsullied part. Probably not the colt part though.

Some of the meaningful details that you might guess the set decorators were responsible for are actually specified in the script. For example, it makes a point of there being Nautilus equipment in the gym where he recovers from the coma, but he ignores it on account of being old school. Also it notes that Storm shoots bullet holes into a portrait of Louis XIII inside Senator Trent's mansion. This I suppose is pointing out a parallel between corrupt senators like Trent and the jealous monarch who executed people loyal to his mother in order to maintain power. You might think I'm reaching there but you'll see that throughout Seagalogy there are many instances of bullets hitting symbolic objects. Just wait.

There are two pieces of pure Seagalian dialogue that seem like Seagal could've improvised them: the bit about his past as a "white boy raised in the Orient" and the classic "superior attitude" speech. I was happy to find that neither of these were in the script, supporting my theory that Seagal makes that kind of stuff up with the cameras rolling. He could've worked with Robert Altman or Mike Leigh I bet. Maybe I shouldn't be comparing this movie to blues, maybe Seagal is really playing jazz.

The horse is mentioned in the script, but he doesn't get to escape, so that may have been some on location brainstorming. The magic of cinema. Another one of my favorite moments, Senator Trent sitting in the hot tub sipping champagne with a girl, isn't in the script either. So I'm not sure how that came about.

But you know what's the biggest difference between this "final draft" and the finished film? In the script, Storm *does* take Senator Trent to the blood bank, and he does a damn good job of it, too. Storm happens to turn his back on Trent (possibly on purpose), and Trent tries to stab him with a fireplace poker. Seagal does a *shihonage* move, flipping the bastard head first into the fireplace. His neck is impaled on the fireplace's decorative grill and as he struggles to escape his hair catches on fire.

Jesus man, I don't have a problem with how the movie ends now, but I mean... upside down neck impalement with hair on fire? *That* would've been something. Definitely an appropriate end for a murderous asshole senator. The script dryly describes it as "a fate somewhat worse than prison."

But by choosing not to impale him on a fireplace and instead to send him to the somewhat better fate of prison, *Hard to Kill* is more in line with the teachings of Gandhi and E.T. the Extra-Terrestrial. And either way, it's one of my favorites.

This chapter is dedicated in loving memory of
Lieutenant Kevin O'Malley
Adopted father
Dearest comrade
Hero

Hard to Kill (*badass working title: Seven Year Storm*), *1990*

Directed by Bruce Malmuth (*Nighthawks, The Man Who Wasn't There* [not the Coen Brothers one, the invisible man one with Steve Guttenberg]).

Written by Steven McKay (*Diggstown, Darkman II: The Return of Durant*).

Distinguished co-stars: Pretty much just William Sadler.

Seagal regulars: A guy named Tom Muzila is credited as "Muzila" in this one – he played one of the aikido fighters in the beginning of *Above the Law*. Haruo Matsuoka and Craig Dunn, two of the punks in the liquor store, played aikido students to Seagal in the opening of *Above the Law*. Nick Corello (James Valero) returns as "Nick" in *Marked For Death*. Robert LaSardo, who plays a "punk," plays Bochi in *Out For Justice*. Buddy Joe Hooker (Russ) and Gary McLarty (Shotgun Man) both did stunts in *Executive Decision*. Ernie Lively, who plays a commander, plays Todd in *Fire Down Below*.

Firsts: First appearance of ponytail, first non-ex-CIA character (unless that just wasn't revealed).

Title refers to: Seagal's character, who is hard to kill.

Just how badass is this guy? "You know they always said Storm was superhuman." "The most unstoppable son of a bitch I ever knew."

Adopted culture: Chinese herbology and acupuncture.

Languages: English, Chinese, basic Spanish. Writes and reads Chinese. Briefly dabbles in Italian-American accent.

Old friends: Just O'Malley.

Fight in bar: No, but there is one in a liquor store.

Broken glass: People thrown through shelves of bottles in liquor store, head through china cabinet, 3 guys kicked through 2 windows in hotel lobby, several windows shot out in bus station.

Innocent bystanders: assassin beats up guy who is vacuuming hospital hallway.

Terms of endearment: buddy, brother, hermano.

Words of wisdom: "First learn how to heal people to be great. To hurt people is easy." (Storm heals himself, then hurts a lot of people.)

Most awkward one-liner: "That's for my wife. Fuck you and die."

Family shit: Avenging wife's murder, protecting son. After big night of violence, goes home and wakes up son to say the Lord's Prayer with him. During a fight he pats his son on the head, goes over and breaks a guy's neck, then comes back over and hugs his son.

Political themes: Politician replaces other politician by having him killed in plane crash. Drugs planted on cop who knows the truth. Just after waking from 7 year coma, sees on TV that George Bush is president, looks as if he has just landed on the Planet of the Apes. Senator Trent vows "No new taxes, and you can take that to the bank" (reference to Bush's "Read my lips, no new taxes").

Cover accuracy: It just shows Seagal holding a gun, LeBrock clutching to his side, in front of a solid red background. The tagline accurately explains who Mason Storm is and what he's going to do. This also debuts the word "is" in his credit, as in "Steven Seagal is Hard To Kill."

CHAPTER 3:
MARKED FOR DEATH

"You fuck with my family, you die."

S eagal plays John "Hatch" Hatcher, a retired ex-military undercover DEA troubleshooter. The picture opens with Hatcher chasing the great badass Danny Trejo (*Desperado, Animal Factory*) in Columbia (I thought it was supposed to be Mexico, but IMDb says different). He catches him, beats him up and tosses him in his trunk. The idea of Trejo running from anybody is pretty silly, but hey man, suspension of disbelief, the magic of cinema, etc. Hatcher is in town for a drug deal, but his cover gets blown and in the ensuing mayhem a hooker shoots Hatcher's partner Chico (Richard Delmonte), and Hatcher shoots her about eleven times. Then he feels real bad about it so back in Chicago he goes to confession, admitting to killing the woman and various other sins, saying "I had become what I most despised."

The priest's advice is for Hatcher to "Go to [your family], and leave these things. Try to find the gentle self inside you. Allow this person to come back." He decides to take that to heart, quits his job and goes to visit his family. This prologue really has nothing to do with the rest of the movie, it's kind of like an episode of *The Simpsons* where some crazy thing happens at the beginning just to tangentially connect to whatever the episode is actually about.

The place he decides to look for the gentle self inside is in the Lincoln

Heights neighborhood where he visits his mom, sister and niece (who doesn't even recognize him). Just like *Above the Law* we get to meet his extended family at an outdoor party, and he goes around and hugs everybody. None of them are said to be in the mafia, though.

Later he attends high school football practice to say hello to the coach, his old friend Max (*They Live*'s Keith David). Max happens to notice some Jamaican gangsters in letterman's jackets sharing crack with the white kids on the bleachers. He gets real mad but Hatcher tells him to "leave it alone man, leave it alone."[18] We, as Seagalogists, know that he is most likely not gonna leave it alone. He is probably gonna get involved somehow, is my guess. But we could be wrong.

One thing Hatch and Max don't know is that right there in the suburbs a Jamaican crack kingpin named Screwface (Basil Wallace, *Rapid Fire*) is fighting over territory (the high school?) with a Columbian Noriega lookalike named Tito Barco (Al Israel, who is legit because he has parts in both *Scarface* and *Carlito's Way*). They're pretty serious about it so they're using voodoo curses on each other. A chicken gets beheaded and everything.

The magic battle is actually started by Tito when he goes to the sorceress with "the most frightening power" for help. She tells him that Screwface is "abakua, the leopard people," which is a reference to Afro-Cuban secret societies that have been around since the early 19th century. She says that he is muy malo because he is also "majadero." Since Tito speaks Spanish, he ought to know that she is calling Screwface a silly person or a fool, but instead he acts scared. She takes a sexy bath, spits out some Bacardi and cuts a chicken's head off in front of a photo of Screwface. It seems to have at least some effect, because it causes him to wake up scared in the middle of the night. Way to curse, sorceress.

As luck would have it, the shit hits the fan right in the same bar where Hatcher and Max go to pick up chicks. Imagine, you're out with an old friend having some drinks when all the sudden a Jamaican dude yells "Blood and fire!" and starts firing a machine gun. That's just not what

---

18 This is the exact opposite of David's character in John Carpenter's 1988 masterpiece *They Live*. In that one David is the guy who wants to just leave it alone, and it's not until he and Roddy Piper wrestle in an alley for five and a half minutes that he's convinced to take a look at what's going on in the world.

you want to have to deal with immediately after retiring. As soon as he hears gunshots Hatcher grabs a random woman bystander and pushes her to the ground, because he loves saving people. It's one of his passions in life. He's still looking for the gentle self inside so he uses the non-aggressive force of aikido to break up the shootout, which really pisses off the Jamaicans. That's why they mark him for death. A guy named Monkey says, "Me no know you now, but I promise you, you's a dead man walkin!"

Even so, Hatch maintains an isolationist philosophy. Having learned from years of counterproductive intervention in Columbia he tells Max that trying to stop drug gangs is like trying to plug holes in a dam with your fingers, toes and tongue. "Way I look at it, you come home, mind your own business, watch your own yard. And then, if trouble finds you, you go after it and you bite its head off before it does the same thing to you."

No more than 30 seconds later trouble *does* find Hatcher in his own yard (or his sister's yard, anyway) when Screwface's thugs drive by and shoot the fuck out of the house, hitting his niece ("They hurt my baby!") After an emotional afternoon in the hospital, where Hatcher almost cries (a showstopping exhibition of Seagal's growing acting range), he and Max get ready to go bite that head off.

There's a moment I love in movies like this called *the look*. It happens between Robert Forster and Fred Williamson in *Vigilante*, between William Devane and Tommy Lee Jones in *Rolling Thunder*, and between Seagal and David in this one. It's a moment where some horrible shit has gone down that changes attitudes about everything. And then the two guys come together and maybe they have a line or two or, in this case, they say nothing at all. They just give each other *the look* and it's like a silent agreement that righteous blood is about to be shed. In this case, Hatcher is in the hospital looking at his niece in critical condition. Then he leaves the room and finds Max sitting in the hallway. And they give each other *the look*. Immediately they start walking toward the camera and suddenly it cuts to Hatcher kicking a door down. It's like they were in the hospital, they got up and walked straight into revenge.

On the warpath, Hatcher beats down an ex-mobster in bikini underwear named Jimmy Fingers (Tony DiBenedetto, *Raw Deal*) and a bunch of stuntmen in rasta wigs, including one that looks kind of like Richard Pryor (Jeffrey Anderson-Gunter). The portrayal of the Jamaicans is very over-the-top, and they use the word "blood clot" many times. Screwface is a memorable villain because of his spooky contacts and his crazy dialogue like "Everybody want go heaven. Nobody want dead. Fraid?" and "Stop thee blood clot cryin'. Everybody must dead. It's yer turn." In the traditional show-how-evil-the-villain-is scene (think Senator Trent in the hot tub in *Hard to Kill*) Screwface interrupts a domino game by knocking over the table, tearing off one of its legs and beating a guy with it. They don't show how he was doing in the game but I betchya ten bucks he was losing, is why he did it. Fuckin Screwface, man. What a fuckin cheapskate. And it's not like he can't afford to pay up, either.

Screwface has a philosophy similar to Hatcher's "bite its head off" one. But the way he puts it is, "If a man commit a crime against you, he must be paid back a THOUSAND times." A thousand may be an exaggeration but he definitely tries more than once to punish Hatcher for the crime of interfering with a shootout. His most impressive attempt is when he sandwiches Hatcher's badass black 1970 Mustang between a truck and a bulldozer and then tosses a Molotov cocktail inside, calling it "my sister, goddess of fire." Luckily Hatcher manages to escape and introduces Screwface's sister to his cousin, lord of somersault.

Joanna Pacula (*My Giant*) provides a somewhat distant almost-love interest, and some voodoo expertise on the side. But she stays behind when Hatch and Max team up with a Jamaican cop named Charles (Tom Wright, who would later reprise the role [or at least play a character by the same name] in another voodoo-themed film, *Weekend at Bernie's II*). There's a nice touch when they go to buy weapons – Hatcher asks the arms dealer if he's still sober and tells him to stay off the Nembutal. They've built up a relationship over the years, like he's the clerk at the corner store or something.

After a big weapons-preparation montage culminating in Hatcher shooting up a side of beef (it fucking deserved it, I bet) they are suddenly sneaking up on Screwface's mansion in Jamaica. I have no idea how they got all those weapons through customs, or how they even carried all that shit. I guess the magic of cinema. Anyway Hatcher has a sword fight with Screwface where he first splits the bastard's crotch and then cuts his head off!

The three go back to the mean streets of suburban Chicago to tell Screwface's men that their boss is dead. Charles has a pretty good idea, instead of just telling them that Screwface is dead and hoping everybody'll take his word for it he makes it more definitive by holding up Screwface's severed head for everyone to see. (Wait a minute, how did he get *that* through customs? Was that his carry-on?) But even as he's holding it there Charles is impaled from behind by none other than... holy god, how is this possible... Screwface! Who still has his head on! What the shit? There's Screwface's head, cut off, and there in the same shot is Screwface's head, not cut off... that's two Screwfaces. How in the world? Something doesn't add up here.

Well, the gang interprets it as "magic power," but of course Screwface is actually twin brothers pretending to be one guy. So Hatcher fights Screwface to the death again, and we can all be thankful for this second chance because it is unquestionably one of the best climaxes in all of Seagalogy. It would've been cool if he literally bit the guy's head off, but what he chose to do instead is even better. Hatch grabs Screwface #2 by the skull, pokes out his eyeballs with his thumbs, rams him all the way through a cement wall, cracks his spine over his knee and throws him down an elevator shaft, where he is impaled on a conveniently placed metal protrusion type deal. That's four deaths just for this one twin! Then Hatch looks down at the body and quips, "I hope they weren't triplets."

Fucking classic! And it's the last line of the movie. Hatcher carries Charles' dead body out into the street, and it goes to the credits. As far as we know the Hatcher family is still marked for death, the niece is still in bad shape, and I got a strong feeling he hasn't found the gentle self inside yet. So you're left with many questions to ponder. But it's a great ending. I always respect a movie that knows to quit at a high point.

Seagal is of course a fan of reggae, so he used the Jamaican theme as an excuse to get Jimmy Cliff in the movie. Cliff is seen in a club performing and even does a song that, according to the credits, was co-written by

Seagal. (Seagal also gets a co-performing credit, so I assume he's on guitar.) Cliff acts as sort of a Greek chorus I guess because he sings a song called "John Crow" that talks about the characters in the movie, saying Screwface's time has come, adding: "So now I go take you down the road to doom / And John Crow, we're going yum your supper soon."

I'm not sure if John Crow means John Hatcher and if so, what exactly is up with his yummy supper. Also I don't know why, if Jimmy Cliff is concerned about Screwface's activities, he doesn't get involved here. I've seen *The Harder They Come*, I know what he's capable of.

But I do know that, as a clean-living, upstanding citizen, Cliff is more representative of Jamaicans than the vicious "posse members" of the movie. You see, a news reporter emphasizes that less than one percent of the Jamaican population are posse members, and this figure is also repeated in a disclaimer on the end credits.

I go back and forth on whether this is as good as *Above the Law* or *Hard to Kill*, but it definitely has a bunch of Seagal's best scenes and moments. The fights are great, with Hatcher throwing people all over the place, taking on multiple people at the same time and continuing to get more brutal. There are numerous broken limbs, a severed head and the unforgettable death of Screwface II. Hatcher stabs a guy with his own knife, hits a guy in the head with a sledge hammer and impales a guy's throat with a skewer. If you watch it with the English subtitles for the hearing impaired you will get to see the sound effect "[vertebrae crack]."

Seagal sports several different excellent fashions, including the standard Nico Toscani black sport jacket/blue jeans combo, a trenchcoat, and most notably a puffy black jacket with dragons on the front and a tiger on the back.

Keith David adds a lot to the movie. He's a really good actor who treats even a role like this with enough conviction to make the story more convincing. Seagal has never had a better or more equal partner. After Hatcher causes the death of two chumps, he has a pretty good exchange with David that you can almost imagine Clint Eastwood doing:

"One thought he was invincible, the other thought he could fly."

"So?"

"They were both wrong."

Director Little isn't exactly a master, but he really hits the mark in a scene where the Jamaicans crash a car through a Tiffany's. Hatcher and Max come in and destroy a lot of jewelry cases in a big fight, completely oblivious to all the rich people running around screaming in terror.

Little also gave roles to Danielle Harris (the actress who played the niece) in *Halloween 4* and to Screwface Basil Wallace in *Free Willy 2*.

Released a month and a half before *Predator 2*, *Marked For Death* managed to be the first to exploit the problems with Jamaican drug gangs in Los Angeles at the time. Most of Seagal's early movies were distributed by Warner Brothers, and later by Sony/Columbia/Tri-Star. This is the only one he ever did with 20th Century Fox, and it was the studio's second most profitable film in 1990, following *Home Alone*. To this day many action fans remember it fondly as "the one where he fights the Jamaicans" or "the one with Screwface."

Marked For Death (working title: *Screwface*), 1990
Directed by Dwight H. Little (*Halloween 4: The Return of Michael Meyers, Free Willy 2: The Adventure Home, Murder at 1600* [as in, "1600 Pennsylvania Avenue. An address that changes all the rules."])
Written by Michael Grais & Mark Victor (*Death Hunt, Kojak, Poltergeist, Cool World*)
Distinguished co-stars: Keith David, Danny Trejo, Jimmy Cliff, Tony Williams (The great jazz drummer is listed in the credits as part of the Jimmy Cliff Band, but I did not notice him. If he's really in there it's his only movie besides *'Round Midnight*.) Teri Weigel (Sexy Girl #2) is not exactly distinguished but has an impressive porn resume starting a Dirty Debutante the year after this came out.
Seagal regulars: Peter Jason (Pete Stone) plays Millie's father in *The Glimmer Man*. Nick Corello, who is credited as playing "Nick" in this one, was in *Hard to Kill*. The bartender, Craig Pinkard, was the chop shop foreman in *Out For Justice* and was on the submarine in *Under Siege*. Kerrie Cullen, one of the hostages in the department store assault, did stunts in *Executive Decision*.
Firsts: First time political themes have little to do with the plot. First time they don't make a big deal about him going to Asia, or explain how he knows aikido. First time working with producer Julius R. Nasso. First dick shot in a Seagal film (Screwface's, not Seagal's). First use of magic in a Seagal film. First time Seagal participated in the soundtrack. First time he had cameos by famous musicians.
Title refers to: Hatcher's family, who voodoo lady says is "marked" by African black magic.
Just how badass is this guy? "I know you. You love the killing, but you's an empty shell

inside." Also we know that he is not allergic to cats.

Adopted culture: None, unless you count the Asian themed dragon/tiger jacket. Surprisingly, Hatcher doesn't demonstrate any knowledge of Jamaican culture.

Languages: English, hand signals.

Improvised weapons: Skewer through throat, sand kicked in eyes.

Old friends: Football coach Max (the great Keith David), FBI guy Rosellini, Jamaican cop Charles, recovering alcoholic biker arms and surveillance supplier guy.

Fight in bar: Two, actually – a shootout in a bar, and later a sword fight in the bar area of a dance club.

Broken glass: Man thrown into mirror. Man jumps through window into car. 5 jewelry cases broken in fight. Shelves of bottles smashed in bar.

Innocent bystanders: Various innocents are terrorized by the car chase through the park and Tiffany's. Nobody gets punched out that doesn't deserve it, though.

Terms of endearment: Mon.

Weirdest one-liner: "God made men."

Family shit: Comes home to visit his mom, sister and niece after growing disillusioned with undercover police work. Tells doctor to treat wounded niece "like the President of the United States." Goes to confession.

Political themes: Police corruption. As an undercover cop he lied, slept with informants, took drugs and falsified evidence.

Cover accuracy: Good. There's a silhouette of Seagal with a gun, apparently wearing the same coat he wears in the movie. Also a shot of him with a knife or a sword. The tagline accurately states the facts: they attacked his family, they killed his partner, now he's "very, very angry." And it's true that "Now, Steven Seagal is Marked For Death." Although that seems more like something to be upset about than something to brag about, but oh well, that's how Seagal rolls.

CHAPTER 4:
OUT FOR JUSTICE

"You tell your brother I'm gonna cut off his head and piss down his throat."

Even among the classic films of Seagal's Golden Era, *Out For Justice* is a standout. It's a serious, gritty crime drama with better production values and classier direction than the previous three (thanks to director John Flynn, who did the great Vietnam vet revenge movie *Rolling Thunder* and the pretty good Richard Stark adaptation *The Outfit*). The music is real good – less cheesy electric guitar noodling and keyboards, more low notes to warn you when some cold shit is about to go down. Think *Jaws* meets *The Terminator*. Seagal even does a better acting job than usual, seeming tougher because he scowls all the way through and goes lighter on the smarmy smartass routines when facing opponents.

The script by David Lee Henry has a few of the usual Seagal motifs, but doesn't follow the expected formula at all. There is no opening flashback in another country, no military or CIA backstory, no explanation or mention of his interest in Asian culture. He doesn't find any corruption in the police force or the government, he doesn't get framed, he doesn't have to stop anybody from doing anything. He just wants to kill one particular guy. And the entire movie takes place over one day in one neighborhood in Brooklyn as he tracks this guy.

Of course, you still get some good laughs. For example, it opens with a quote from Arthur Miller, maybe the most balls-to-the-wall pretentious touch in any Seagal picture. Also, Seagal does a not particularly convincing Italian-American accent for the whole movie, saying "ova heeya" all the time. And check out the low-cut vest with no shirt underneath, which he sometimes tops off with a beret.

But it's easy to forgive all that, partly because the opening scene is grade-A classic fuckin Badass with a capital B. Hell, I will throw on a capital S at the end too, the opening is straight up *BadasS*. Seagal plays NYPD narcotics detective Gino Felino. He's staking out some warehouse or something with his partner Bobby Lupo (Joe Spataro), who he says has been acting funny lately. Waiting for the right moment for their "$3 million bust," Gino gets distracted by a pimp beating up a pregnant hooker. He can't just stand idly by while that happens so he moves in early, breaking up the beating but blowing the bust.

The pimp apparently knows him, and threatens to "fuck your wife and kill your—" before Gino grabs him by the neck, smashes his head through the passenger side window of a car, then swings him by his tie into some garbage cans. The pimp yells "Gino, you son of a bitch!" and makes a run at him, but Gino flips the bastard head first through the windshield. There is a shot from inside the car, through the broken window as Gino steps into the shot. Freeze frame, and bang! It says STEVEN SEAGAL in giant letters, filling the whole god damn screen. And then a clank as...

OUT
FOR
JUSTICE

...is stamped onto the screen. Truly, without a doubt, the best opening title sequence Seagal has ever had.

Next we meet our villain, the weasely, mustached "wannabe wiseguy" Richie Madano, played by William Forsythe (*Once Upon a Time in America, Stone Cold*). He locks up a whole bunch of money in a vault and tells his buddies that if they stick with him until the end of the night, it's all theirs. "How long could the night be?" one of them asks naively, and Richie just starts laughing. And keeps laughing. Because he knows what he's about to do. You know what, there's a catch. This is not one of the better freelance gigs, in my opinion.

What he's about to do is murder Bobby in cold blood and broad daylight, on a sidewalk, in front of his wife and kid and "a hundred witnesses." And then casually walk away. And then when his crew gets upset in the getaway car he has them stop in the middle of an intersection, he pulls out a crack pipe and starts smoking it, and then he flips out on a random lady who yells at him for blocking traffic. He walks over and shoots her point blank in the head. See, one thing that would've been helpful for Richie's crew to know in advance: Richie is an insane crackhead and he's really not planning to make it through the night. This is one thing that really makes *Out For Justice* unique. It's a simple premise, but an unusual one. Usually a villain in a movie is expected to have some kind of plan, some kind of ultimate goal. That is not the case with Richie. He kills his girlfriend and Bobby Lupo before the story really begins, and that's all he really had planned. After that he just wants to smoke crack and "have a party" with some hookers, maybe kill a few people if it comes up. He wants to have a fun time until he dies.

When Gino finds out that his old neighborhood acquaintance Richie killed his old friend Bobby, everybody (both on screen and viewing at home) knows that he's gonna be the one to track down Richie and kill him. In other words, he's gonna go out for justice. And the rest of the movie is about Gino trying to catch up with Richie before the other police, or the mafia (who want to kill Richie because he makes them look bad). Meanwhile Richie goes around smoking crack, saying he wants to "party," and doing more fucked up shit like shooting his disabled friend for no reason. And the dude wasn't even in his wheelchair at the time. What the fuck Richie, jesus. Crack is wack.

Gino finds Richie pretty quick and there's a really well shot car chase over bumpy roads, with both cars bouncing like hydraulics in rap videos. Richie gets away so Gino does everything he can to find out where he's hiding: meet politely with the Don (who he's on a first name basis with), go pick a fight with every single person inside a bar (including an Asian guy named "Sticks" who spins two pool cues as weapons), fight a bunch of guys in a butcher shop, visit Richie's parents, and even unjustly arrest Richie's hot sister (Gina Gershon). Along the way he makes up with his wife Vicky (Jo Champa), who he was about to divorce, and saves a puppy that he sees get thrown out of a car. Every once in a while they show Jerry Orbach as a police captain, and you start thinking maybe you're watching *Law and Order*.

This is the only Seagal movie where he goes to visit the parents of the villain and tells them he's going to kill their son. And he's an honorable guy so later he apologizes to the dad "for the way I behaved in your home." A very good Seagal moment. You always gotta get some honor in there if you can.

Out For Justice is one of the Seagal pictures where the director has left the biggest imprint on the movie (second only to *Belly of the Beast* in that category). From the very beginning it feels very different from the previous three Seagal pictures. It feels darker and more serious. The look is very gritty and realistic. The use of handheld cameras, musical montage and Jerry Orbach seems to predict the style of cop shows that would follow in the 1990s and 2000s. The music is by David Michael Frank, the same guy who did *Above the Law* and *Hard to Kill*, but the style is completely different – more of a bombastic, orchestral sounding score that heightens the drama of the situations with its low, foreboding tones.

Those memorable opening credits are written in grey, which seems appropriate for this movie. Even more than before, Seagal's character blurs the line between good guy and bad guy. Like in *Above the Law* he's a cop with connections to the mafia, but in this one he actually goes and meets with them, makes deals with them, tells nostalgic stories about them. It's repeatedly mentioned that he couldn't do the things he does without his badge, but I'm not sure I agree with that. There is no oversight from his overseers. Some may disagree with what he plans to do, but all factions see it as an inevitability, and only doomed bad guy henchmen are stupid enough to stand in his way.

Like other Seagal characters, Gino is a smartass. When a guy points a gun at him Gino says, "Don't be a bad guy. Whaddyou wanna shoot me for. Eh?" Then he takes the gun. "Don't be a bad guy like that. Be a nice guy." But the wiseass side is a little toned down from previous characters. He seems much grimmer. There's a scene where he's driving around looking for Richie, and when you see him drive by from a standing-on-the-street POV the scowl on his face is actually scary. When he's fighting he mostly keeps his mouth shut and avoids one-liners. Considering all the violence he inflicts with unusual objects such as corkscrews[19] and bar towels, it's very admirable that he avoids puns. That takes real restraint.

The violence in the movie is hardcore and very memorable. Asked in 2007 about his "favorite death scene" Seagal didn't even mention the legendary multi-death of *Marked For Death*'s Screwface, instead responding "I thought the way I killed Richard [sic] Forsythe in *Out For Justice* was pretty cool[20]."

Gino and Richie are a lot alike. They're tied to the same neighborhood, they know the same people, they both idolize the wiseguys, and most of all they're both bullies. They go around pushing people, belittling them, humiliating them. Before you have any idea Richie is going to shoot the guy in the wheelchair he's talking to him and he starts spinning him around in circles for no reason. Gino never seems nearly that mean, because all the people he bullies are steps on the path to Richie. But he sure knows how to push people and intimidate them. He puts both Richie's sister and his father in jail on bogus charges. When he goes into the sister's office he just starts tossing all her papers around and keeps pushing her down into a chair. When he goes into Richie's brother's bar he goes behind the bar, pushes the bartender over, starts throwing glasses and bottles every which way. He shoves a guy violently into a phone booth and closes the door, not once but twice.

Just like with Richie, you question Gino's sanity by the end of the movie. Gino talks to a mobster just after killing Richie, and the guy is so taken aback by the way he's acting he asks him if he's sick.

Every fight scene in this movie is a classic. Seagal is in top form and convincingly dominates his opponents, even when he's on his own against everybody in the bar. He's as fast as ever but a little beefier by now, which makes him look more menacing. Over and over again people make the same mistake of going at him with a weapon only to find that weapon used against them. A meat cleaver, a baseball bat, a rolling pin,

---

19 Schwarzenegger would never have passed up "You're screwed, Richie!"

20 *The Friday Night Project*, February 9, 2007.

a frying pan, pool sticks, a corkscrew, you name it. Don't try to use against Gino Felino what you would not like used against you. For example, if you use a meat cleaver you will find it quickly planted in your leg, or you will get some fingers chopped off. And to add insult to injury he might whack you on the head with a sausage. (That's what happens when you fight a guy like Gino in a butcher shop.)

In this movie he causes a lot of pain. One guy he knocks with a pool ball wrapped in a bar towel, causing him to yell "Motherfucker you knocked my teeth out!" Another guy he shoots his leg off with a shotgun (!), and the guy yells "You took my leg! You took my leg!" At the very end he kicks a guy in the balls causing him to cry, "My balls! My balls! Balls!" He breaks a lot of bones, shoots a guy in the throat, punches a guy in the balls, throws a guy out a window, etc. This movie has it all.

William Forsythe's Richie Madano is a great villain. He's always good in these sorts of over-the-top roles, like the crazy biker in *Stone Cold* or the almost demonic sheriff in *The Devil's Rejects*. In this role some of the intensity is internal. I love the way he interacts with his crew. They're always uncomfortable with the crazy shit he's doing, but try to hide it. They stick with him due to some combination of loyalty and the promised payday, but they look horrified by most of the things he does. When he shoots the woman in traffic they can't believe their eyes but they quickly try to get past it and strut along at his side. There's one scene where they're in the car and they get comfortable enough to start talking about one of them trying to get rid of a mouse in his house. You get to watch Richie smoldering in the front seat until he yells "Shut up about the fuckin mouse!" He knows this is his last night on earth and he is just not interested in spending any more of it on this mouse topic.

Richie has a lot of typical tough guy qualities, like arrogantly throwing his money around and trying to insult people by asking them if they have balls and that kind of thing. But I can't emphasize enough what a unique villain he is for this type of movie. He doesn't do a big speech about what he's up to (because he's not up to anything) or why he's doing it (some Polaroids of Bobby Lupo naked with Richie's girlfriend do the job). As far as action movies go, this is a pretty realistic portrait of a man who has completely lost his mind.

Seagal definitely takes a risk by trying to challenge himself as an actor, and I would argue that he is mostly successful. True, the accent causes problems, and it's one of the movie's only weaknesses. But you still have to give him credit for playing the character so different from his previous movies. He also speaks Italian, has a couple long monologues telling stories about growing up, and has to have emotional moments with a variety of people (the Don, Richie's father, his wife, his partner's widow, his son).

If you can't get past the accent, here's a trick you can try. Turn on the English subtitles and switch the audio to French. Personally it's too weird for me to see these rough characters speaking a romance language, but who knows, you might want to try it.

The only other major weakness is the two scenes dedicated to the subplot about Gino adopting a puppy named Corragio. These scenes seem cheesy and unfinished, like deleted scenes on a DVD. I wouldn't be surprised if they were added after the fact to try to lighten up the movie. I'm all for Seagal with a puppy (theory of badass juxtaposition) and it's funny that he refers to himself sarcastically as "an animal lover" since he actually is one in real life. But in this particular movie the scenes feel out of place. The first one involves Seagal seeing an asshole throw a puppy out of his car. After he figures out what happened he says, "Please God. Let me run into this guy some day." And you're thinking, "Please God, don't let them tie this loose thread up at the end." But the Lord works in mysterious ways so He lets them do an epilogue where Gino literally runs into the guy on Coney Island or somewhere and happens to recognize his car. This leads to an amazing ballkicking from behind, which is certainly enjoyable. But then the movie ends with the dog peeing on the guy's head. Not exactly the best note to end the otherwise classiest movie of Seagal's career on. That's why I admire the ending of *Marked For Death* so much. You need to know when to hold 'em and when to fold 'em. And the time to fold 'em is definitely before a dog pees on a guy's head[21].

Jerry Orbach is not the only notable in the cast. Julianna Margulies made

---

21 I can think of one exception to the peeing dog rule. The WWE horror movie *See No Evil* ends with a dog peeing in the dead killer's eye socket. This is a great ending because it so bluntly dashes your expectations of the killer coming back to life at the end. Other peeing dog endings, unfortunately, do not play off of genre conventions in the same way and are therefore not as powerful.

her screen debut as Rica, Richie's ex-junkie sometime girlfriend. Shannon Whirry also debuts as Terry Malloy – she would go on to become one of the queens of softcore thrillers, starring in such Gregory Dark films as *Animal Instincts 1 & 2*, *Body of Influence* and *Mirror Images II*. Gina Gershon has an early role as Richie's sister Patti. And John Leguizamo appears as "Boy in Alley." It took me a while to figure out where he is in the movie, but his scene is during one of the musical montages. He's standing in an alley and Richie comes up and punches him in the face for no reason. Then Richie steals a bag of coke from the boy's leather jacket and points a gun at his head.

You may also recognize Raymond Cruz, who plays a character named Hector. He plays soldiers in a lot of action movies including *Under Siege*. And Afifi, who plays "Go-Go Dancer," later reunited with Seagal to play "Female Mercenary" in *Under Siege 2*.

Like in *Marked For Death*, Seagal surreptitiously co-wrote a song that plays on the end credits, "Don't Stand In My Way," a white man's blues song performed by Gregg Allman. The song describes Gino Fellino as "This bad boy back in Brooklyn / with such a hunger in his eyes." The song also mentions that he "strikes like a rattlesnake from out in the bush," an activity he prefers to do "when push comes to shove and shove comes to push." I would guess that in this case Richie killing his partner = push coming to shove, and nobody telling him where Richie is = shove coming to push.

Seagal also co-wrote another song in the movie called "Bad Side of Town." It is not clear which side of Brooklyn is the bad side. You might need to be more familiar with Arthur Miller plays to know the answer to that one.

Various types of mafia are a motif throughout much of Seagalogy. In *Above the Law* he is related by blood to Sicilian Mafioso, in *Marked For Death* he faces the Jamaican mafia, in *Into the Sun* he fights Yakuza and Tongs. *Out For Justice* is the one that has the Italian mafia most organically worked into the story. His respect for certain gangsters and his disdain for others are presented very matter-of-factly. It's not clear whether or not the audience is supposed to be uncomfortable that a cop is taking meetings with the mafia. Gino follows his own sense of honor instead of the actual laws he's supposed to be enforcing. In a way, he's like the corrupt cops Seagal opposes in some of his other movies, except that he is, as I'm sure you've caught on by now, out for justice and not money or power.

Although I credit John Flynn with the style of the movie, it's easy to imagine that executive producer Julius Nasso had some influence on its content. Like Seagal's character in *Above the Law*, Nasso and his parents emigrated from Sicily when he was 3. He grew up in Brooklyn. His first involvement in the movie business was as a gopher and translator for the great Sergio Leone on his last film, the gangster epic *Once Upon a Time in America* (which, of course, featured William Forsythe as Cockeye). Nasso later moved to L.A. and met Seagal. Like any aspect of Seagal's life, it's hard to sort the fact from the fiction when it comes to his early days with Nasso. Some sources say Nasso was an intern on the early Seagal films, while Nasso himself claims to have been involved in the foreign distribution of *Above the Law* using his connections in the pharmaceutical industry. At any rate, his first producer credit was on *Marked For Death.*

According to a pretty cruel profile in *Vanity Fair*[22], Seagal liked Nasso because of his Italian tough guy persona and his "colorful" connections. But Seagal himself probably wouldn't agree with that statement. When *Spy Magazine* wrote about Nasso's alleged mafia connections (among other things), Seagal filed a defamation lawsuit (later dropped), denying, among other things, the implication that he would associate with criminals. Whether Seagal knew it at the time or not, Nasso really did have a connection to members of the Gambino crime family. Seagal and Nasso produced eight movies together (including 2000's *Prince of Central Park*, a Seagal-less drama starring Nasso's son Frank) but after Seagal became more involved in Buddhism in the late '90s, he allegedly said he wanted to stop making violent films to improve his karma. So, according to Seagal and federal prosecutors, in December 2000, Nasso, his brother Vincent, and members of the Gambino crime family tracked down Seagal in Toronto (where he was filming *Exit Wounds*, not exactly

---

22 Zeman, "Seagal Under Siege" in *Vanity Fair*, October 2002.

a study of pacifism in my opinion) and threatened him, demanding he pay them $150,000 for each movie he makes. They tried to shake him down again the next month in Brooklyn.

At the end of 2002, Seagal became a witness in two racketeering trials in Brooklyn Federal Court, one against Peter Gotti and six others, the other against the Nasso brothers. Some press reports seemed skeptical of Seagal's claims that he had been extorted by the mafia, and defense lawyers tried to embarrass him, claiming he led "a bizarre lifestyle" and leaking stories about an ex-CIA operative who was supposedly going to testify against his character. But Seagal was quickly vindicated when recordings of the conversations between Nasso and alleged members of the Gambino crime family were presented at the trial. After more than a year of denying the charges, Nasso finally agreed to a plea bargain in August of 2003. He served 9 1/2 months of a year and a day sentence and paid a fine. After he got out, Nasso started claiming he was innocent again, a ludicrous story considering the wiretap recordings that had effectively forced him to plead guilty. But Seagal, being less vengeful than Gino Felino, released a statement saying of his old friend, "I'm happy he's out of prison and I hope he has a fruitful and prosperous life."

Nasso soon built a new mini movie studio on his estate in Staten Island and threw a big party to celebrate. Performing in a large backyard tent was none other than Chuck Mangione, whose tape was in the car stereo in *Hard to Kill*.

In 2002, Nasso had sued Seagal for $60 million, accusing him of reneging on a deal to make four movies together. Seagal denied there had ever been such a deal, but in 2008 made an out-of-court settlement: Nasso dropped the lawsuit, while Seagal reportedly agreed to pay Nasso $500,000, and even write a letter supporting Nasso's application for a presidential pardon from his extortion offence. This time it was Nasso's turn to release a statement: "I'm glad it's behind us. I wish him the best." It's nice to see a peaceful end to the ugly fight these two were in. In life, as in *Hard to Kill*, sometimes it is best not to take anyone to the blood bank.

The story of Seagal and Nasso could be a book of its own, but I only mention the mafia trial because of its relevance to *Out For Justice*. The criminal empires depicted in most Seagal movies are more the stuff of action movie fantasy than of real life. But this story of Brooklyn wiseguys and wannabes feels pretty authentic. And I got a feeling that Nasso had a hand in that.

Out For Justice is missing the politics of the other Seagal movies of the period, but it's worth it. It feels more like a legitimately good '70s badass picture. The script doesn't seem like it was necessarily written for Seagal, and I'm positive that if it had a star more respected by the current critical establishment – like, say, Mickey Rourke, Jan Michael Vincent or, I don't know, some prick from *Three Men and a Baby* – that it would be acknowledged as some kind of a classic. Or at least have a reputation as an under-recognized revenge picture of the early '90s.

On the other hand, it probably wouldn't have ended up the same movie if someone else was starring. Producer Arnold Kopelson told GQ in 1991, "Every frame of this movie has Steven's imprimatur on it, which is not the case with most actors I've worked with. He's a filmmaker. I would expect that to some people on my production he's also a pain in the ass, but what's important is Steven's concept of perfection."

All of Seagal's movies are connected, that's the concept of Seagalogy. But at the same time, there is a wide spectrum of qualities that people look for in a Seagal picture. So *On Deadly Ground* may be the funniest, *Belly of the Beast* or *Out of Reach* may be the craziest, and *Under Siege* may be the most impressive for people who like big studio action movies. But whenever someone asks me what is the *best* Steven Seagal movie, I tell them *Out For Justice*.

Out For Justice,1991
Directed by John Flynn (*The Outfit, Rolling Thunder*)
Written by David Lee Henry (*The Evil That Men Do, 8 Million Ways to Die, Road House*)
Distinguished co-stars: Gina Gershon, Julianna Margulies (debut role), John Leguizamo (as "boy in alley"). Julie Strain is also in there somewhere, but that doesn't count.
Seagal regulars: Robert Lasardo, who plays "Bochi," was a "punk" in *Hard to Kill*. Charles Daniel, who plays a cop, plays someone named "Chic" in *On Deadly Ground*. Afifi (Go-Go Dancer) graduates to badass female mercenary in *Under Siege 2*. John Leguizamo (Boy in Alley) has a bigger role than Seagal in *Executive Decision*. Raymond Cruz (Hector) plays Ramirez in *Under Siege*. Joe Lala who plays "Vermeer" (that's the pimp's name?) plays a guard in *On Deadly Ground*. John Rottger (Commander Green) did stunts in *On Deadly Ground, Executive Decision* and *The Patriot*. He was a technical advisor for both this and *The Patriot*. Frank Ferrara and David Webster both play commandos here and did stunts in *Out For Justice*. Ousan Elam, one of the marines in the movie, did stunts in *Executive Decision*

and *The Glimmer Man*. Another marine, Richard Piemonte, did stunts in *Out For Justice*, *Under Siege 2*, *Executive Decision* and *Fire Down Below*. Conrad E. Palmisano, who plays the Strike Team Leader, plays Richter in *On Deadly Ground* and is a veteran Seagal second unit director (this, *Marked For Death*) and stunt coordinator (this, *Marked For Death*, *Out For Justice*, *On Deadly Ground*). Luis J. Silva, who plays Luigi, did stunts in *Marked For Death*, *Out For Justice*, *Under Siege 2*, *The Glimmer Man* and *The Patriot*. (Wait a minute, Ryback wasn't the only one who was on the boat *and* on the train.) Drucilla A. Carlson (Captain Spellman) was script supervisor on *Above the Law*.

Firsts: Holds accent through entire movie.

Title refers to: Seagal, I guess, is out for justice.

Just how badass is this guy? Nobody really says in so many words, but it is clear everybody knows it by how they fear him.

Adopted culture: None, though he has samurai swords in his house.

Languages: English, Italian.

Improvised weapons: sausage, bar towel, pool cues, pan, rolling pin, corkscrew.

Old friends: Everybody in the neighborhood, including his partner Bobby, his enemy Richie, Richie's parents, Don Vittorio, a bartender, and a kid named Picolino who sells seltzer on the street.

Fight in bar: Yes – big fight scene, and later a mafia shootout.

Broken glass: Pimps head through passenger side window and windshield, glasses in bar, guy smashed through glass door, another guy thrown through a window, Richie's head smashed through a window.

Terms of endearment: My man.

Most awkward one-liner: "That's for Bobby." (You spent the whole movie avenging Bobby, dude, you didn't have to point it out at the end.) The only other thing close to a one-liner is when he says to Gina Gershon, "You tell your brother I'm gonna cut off his head and piss down his throat."

Family shit: Almost brings son to play baseball (but then his partner gets shot). Reconciles with wife that he was going to divorce. Saves abandoned puppy.

Political themes: Mild police corruption theme when mobster says "You know how many cops I know that make my boys look like altar boys?" (Seagal says, "Ain't that the truth.")

Cover accuracy: No complaints. It's a posed photo of him in all black standing in some smoke machine fog holding a shotgun and looking mean. The tagline is "He's a cop. It's a dirty job... but somebody's got to take out the garbage." Corny, but it's just stating the facts. This also uses an 'is' – "STEVEN SEAGAL is OUT FOR JUSTICE."

SILVER ERA

1992-1997

CHAPTER 5:
UNDER SIEGE

"He's more than a good cook. You have no idea."

Seagal's fifth film was his biggest mainstream breakthrough, and his most palatable film for non-Seagalogists. The one that made him into a mainstream movie star for a little bit. It's his biggest picture and one of his most effective. At the same time it reunites him with his first director, Andrew Davis, and returns them to the same corrupt intelligence agency theme they explored together in *Above the Law*. So this is a big Hollywood action movie that puts some politics in there without seeming silly.

It streamlines the Seagal formula, using some of the usual classics but updating the action to a more technology-driven, *Die Hard*-based deal. But by far the biggest breakthrough for Seagal is the title, which only has two words in it instead of three. Also he doesn't have a ponytail. (I guess Andrew Davis must not like the ponytail.)

Seagal plays ex-SEAL Navy cook Casey Ryback – "Expert in martial arts, explosives, weapons and tactics. Silver Star. Navy Cross. Purple Heart with cluster. Security clearance revoked after Panama." We find out later that during the Panama invasion he lost his platoon due to bad intelligence, and came home and punched out his commanding officer. So if he wants to stay in the service his choices are to be a yeoman or a cook, and I guess he must not like to type. Now he's the personal cook for Captain Adams (Patrick O'Neal) of the USS *Missouri* and he's a cook who plays by his own rules so he refuses to wear his fancy dress uniform even when President Bush I (*Hard to Kill*) is on board to make a speech. "If I had your ribbons, I'd wear 'em to bed," the captain says. (And Ryback may have some ribbons the captain doesn't even know about – see his niece's comments in *Under Siege 2: Dark Territory*.)

It's the captain's birthday, and untrustworthy XO Commander Krill (crazy fuckin Gary Busey) is planning a surprise party. A special type of surprise party where he's in drag and Tommy Lee Jones is wearing a tie-dyed shirt and studded leather jacket, pretending to be in a white blues band called Mad Billy and the Fabulous Bail Jumpers. Ryback tries to get into the spirit and starts cooking up a bunch of pies, but Busey spits a big loogie in one of the pots. (That's when you know for sure he's evil. But I guess you already know with Gary Busey it's either evil or Buddy Holly.) Ryback punches that asshole right in front of everybody so they call it striking an officer and lock him up. And instead of climbing through the red tape to put him in the brig, they just use the meat locker.

So even if you're kind of thick, at this point you've probably figured out that this is the type of party where they take over the ship and steal the nuclear weapons on board so they can sell them or, failing that, blow up Honolulu. Tommy Lee fires the first shot, because he turns out to be William Strannix, an ex-CIA crazy fuck using his unique skills against the government that decided to cancel him along with his covert operation. Krill kills the captain while still in drag (he hides the gun in his wig). And they lock everybody else up. So Ryback has to escape the meat locker, get in contact with authority figures in the outside world, save the other crew members along with cake-jumping Missy July 1989 Erika Eleniak ("I am an actress, okay? I did a *Hunter* episode and a *Wet 'n' Wild* video") and then lead them into battle against the terrorists to retake the ship and what not. If you've seen *Die Hard, Die Hard 2, Speed, Speed 2, Sudden Death, High Risk* or *Under Siege 2*, then you know the drill.

While the USS *Missouri* was the site of the Japanese surrender at the end of World War II, there will be no surrender in this battle. Ryback gives Strannix a little bit of what Screwface got – after a long knife fight he thumbs one eye out, stabs him in the head and then bashes his head through a monitor. I have praised *Marked For Death* for ending almost immediately after the villain's spectacular death, but this being a bigger movie and the introduction to the Silver Era, they have a little more to do – namely, a deluxe military funeral for the captain, on the deck of the ship. The movie obviously had a lot of cooperation from the Navy. They didn't film on the actual USS *Missouri* – instead they used the USS *Alabama* – but they are sure to show off the authentic settings as the movie comes to a close. They even go to a majestic helicopter shot of the *Missouri* at the end of the credits. Some movies put a little joke or a surprise twist at the end of the credits, this one has a display of military hardware.

While Casey Ryback is certainly similar to Seagal's other characters, he did put a little bit of a different spin on it this time. In every previous movie he was a cop, this time he's not. He's a soldier so he's also spouting off information about weapons. While he can be unprofessional while talking to officers, he is serious about his job when the shit goes down. One nice touch is when he escapes the meat locker and sees Private Nash (the asshole guard who wouldn't listen to him) laying on the ground, he immediately goes up and checks his pulse. Let bygones be bygones.

This is also the first Seagal movie where he has another passion unrelated to fighting or Asian culture. Usually his whole life is about police work and revenge with a side of aikido. At best, playing catch with his son. Here he is a great cook[23], and his sous chefs seem to love him. There are lots of good lines about being a cook, like when Strannix finds dead bodies and says "This is not the work of a cook." Or when Miss July says to Ryback, "You're not a cook!" and he says "Yeah, well, I also cook." Seagal later described Ryback's philosophy as, "I can hurt you, but I'd rather not, so let me just cook[24]."

He uses a couple cooking knives to kill some guys and the microwave to detonate an explosive. Still, I think they missed a major opportunity to work more of a cooking theme into this movie. It goes without saying that he should be wearing an apron or chef's hat during some of the

---

23 This fits with my Theory of Badass Juxtaposition, that a badass is made more badass by having a passion for something sensitive such as an art or a small child or animal.

24 *The Friday Night Project*, February 9, 2007.

action scenes, and use measuring spoons to fill up some bullets or something. And obviously it should be called *Recipe For Disaster*. Unfortunately he missed the boat on this one, and then Jackie Chan blew it playing a TV chef in *Mr. Nice Guy*, before Stephen Chow finally picked up the fighting-chef ball in *God of Cookery*. Still, I think there's plenty of room for Seagal to work in that direction if he ever does an *Under Siege 3*. Maybe he uncovers a terrorist plot while competing in an *Iron Chef* competition or something. There are many possibilities.

To me one of Seagal's many admirable qualities is his love of inserting his somewhat progressive politics into dumb action movies. Usually if a dumb action movie has any politics in it at all they come from a jingoistic, xenophobic type point of view, especially in the '80s. Think about what happened to Rambo in *First Blood Part 2*, or the high school football team that took on invading communists in *Red Dawn* (which John Milius made as a tribute to the Mujahadeen fighting off Russian invaders in Afghanistan). Remember *Rocky 4* and its vision of the world where Russians are genetic experiments with all the money in the world at their hands while us freedom loving Americans have to run around in the snow and use logs for weight training? Bruce Willis's *Die Hard* marked a major change in action movies and was obviously the biggest influence on *Under Siege*, but it dropped the politics of the book it was based on and didn't take much of a stance on anything except to position the working class as better and more heroic people than the coke-snorting office yuppies. In fact, director John McTiernan says on the DVD that he wanted the villains to be merely thieves, not terrorists with a political cause, because when you have that it makes the movie less fun. *Die Hard* takes place in a pretty simple world, it's a world where authority figures are good unless they're lazy or dumb, and bad guys are just evil foreigners who need to be thrown out of a building. (It's a great fuckin' movie, don't get me wrong.)

1990's *Die Hard 2* had echoes of the Iran-Contra affair in its plot, but that was two years after Seagal and Davis had already worked it into *Above the Law*. Seagal was the first to consistently portray evil CIA deeds not as the work of a couple bad apples, but as a regular part of intelligence agency work. *Under Siege*'s villain, Strannix, is a guy actually trained by the CIA to do exactly what he is doing – take over military vessels. In fact, he has a North Korean submarine at his disposal because he told his boss he had sunk it (the counter-terrorism equivalent of taking home office supplies). Admiral Bates (Andy Romano) asks the CIA's Tom Breaker[25] (Nick Mancuso), "Could you explain to me how this nut could hold a top position in one of our intelligence agencies?" Before getting cut off, Breaker begins, "High level covert operatives like Mr. Strannix are under great stress. They're creative thinkers who by their very nature—"

In 2003, real life Deputy Defense Secretary Paul Wolfowitz gave a similar defense of DARPA's controversial plan for a "terror futures market," where business men could put money on what targets would be bombed and what leaders would be assassinated: "The agency that does it is brilliantly imaginative in places where we want them to be imaginative. It sounds like maybe they got too imaginative in this area."

Of course, Strannix is more than just an imaginative thinker, he's a guerilla paid to commandeer warships and submarines. After his "Project Cleopatra" is cancelled, the CIA attempts to assassinate him and fails, inspiring him to create our current troubles on the USS *Missouri*. While the real CIA probably hasn't ever had a blowback exactly like this before, there is certainly a long history of our intelligence agencies supporting unsavory assets who later bite us in the ass (those Mujahadeen being probably the most obvious example). The movie points out how crazy that approach is. "You've been financing this god damn maniac's private army, and it didn't occur to you that it might be a problem?"

While Strannix is the bad guy, Tom Breaker[26] of the CIA is portrayed broadly as a weasel, a prick and a scumbag. His program for "train[ing] everyone in the CIA who's crazy" has caused this problem in the first

---

25 Man, something creeps me out about that Tom Breaker guy. I know, he's a scumbag and everything, but there's something else about him. I can't quite put my finger on it.

26 Holy shit, I know what it is! It's that movie *Black Christmas*. Nick Mancuso is the voice of the obscene phone calls in that movie, the guy saying, "It's me, Billy!" and all that. In the movie we never really see him, and he's still at large at the end. So for all we know that was Tom Breaker. In the '70s he made obscene phone calls, hid in a sorority attic and killed a bunch of college kids. Then he became the head of the CIA specializing in training crazy people to steal submarines and shit. Hell, maybe he was *already* in the CIA when he was hiding in that attic. That's just what he did after work to blow off steam. Man, this information puts *Under Siege* in a whole different light.

place but he's willing to "just blame it on the cook" if things don't work out. And when Strannix jokingly mentions the '60s, Breaker[27] gets bitter. "Look, Bill, if this is about reliving the '60s, you can forget about it, buddy. The movement is dead." [28]

Most of the movie's politics come out through discussions between Strannix and the Pentagon, but when Ryback comes face to face with Strannix he doesn't miss the opportunity to deliver one of Seagal's trademark probably-improvised-speeches:

"All your ridiculous, pitiful antics aren't gonna change a thing. You and I... we're puppets in the same sick play. We serve the same master. And he's a lunatic and he's ungrateful, but there's nothin' we can do about it. You and I, we're the same."

In fact, Ryback may be more similar to Strannix than we're even allowed to know – when they come face to face they immediately recognize each other, but it's never explained how. All we know is that it's "been a long time."

Like many Seagal pictures, *Under Siege* today is more prescient than it ever gets credit for. Not just because of the blowback theme, but because it shows the danger posed by nuclear weapons and the need for better security of any nuclear materials. (Seagal will revisit this theme more than a decade later with a suitcase bomb in *Black Dawn*.)

As great as this picture is, it officially marks the beginning of the Silver Era of Seagal, and it is sad to say goodbye to the Golden Era, when everything was more personal. Gone are the more intimate, street-based tough guy stories of his first four films. For now on he is more likely to be taking on highly trained teams of terrorists than the guy who killed his favorite priest, or his wife, or shot his niece, or killed his partner and also some lady in traffic. The action becomes more based on explosions and military hardware, with less emphasis on stealing bats from guys or bashing a guy's head through a drink cooler or a china cabinet or something. He spends lots of time explaining what different weapons are

---

27 Wow, I'm looking at his filmography and he was in *The Matrix* too. Mancuso is all over the place.

28 Wait, never mind. He wasn't in *The* Matrix. He was on a TV show called *Matrix*, where he played "Steven Matrix." Probably the main guy.

called, what they do and how to use them – valuable time that could be used to break a guy's arm in half, stab a guy through the neck or shoot a guy's leg clean off. I enjoy the action in this picture, but all of the explosions and shootouts in the whole movie don't add up to the power of the freeze frame on Seagal after he threw the pimp through the windshield in the opening of *Out For Justice*.

Under Siege was the first box office hit to clearly be modeled after *Die Hard* – the ads even quoted a critic who called it *"Die Hard* on a boat."* Like Bruce Willis's John McClane in *Die Hard*, Ryback finds himself coincidentally stranded in a structure taken over by guerillas and must fight them off with limited means. McClane stays in contact with a sympathetic police officer on the outside, while Ryback communicates with a situation room in the Pentagon. Both movies have villains who pretend to be fighting for some political cause but who are actually just trying to get money. The most obvious lift is when Ryback jumps off the side of the boat with a rope around his waist to avoid an explosion (Bruce Willis's John McClane jumps off the building tied to a fire hose).

So it's fair to call *Under Siege* a *Die Hard* rip-off. But one major difference people don't always acknowledge is that Ryback is a very different character from McClane. McClane is a cop, Ryback is a military cook. McClane is at a party on vacation when the shit goes down, Ryback is on duty on a Naval war ship. McClane is beat to a pulp throughout the movie, having his bare feet cut up by glass, banging himself up until he's covered in blood, dirt and grease, while Ryback (like almost all Seagal characters) hardly gets scratched. McClane is a wiseass who constantly talks to himself, Ryback is not above being a smartass but mostly remains stoic. Most importantly, Ryback remains calm and confident throughout the conflict, McClane is always horrified and swearing to himself that he's fucked. However, both are cynical rebels within the system and are capable of fighting off terrorist armies single-handedly. So they'd probably get along, if not hang out[29].

---

29 I once had the opportunity to ask Bruce Willis if he had seen any of the better *Die Hard* knock-offs, and if so whether he felt like someone was walking on his grave or if he was able to enjoy them. He replied, "I have seen a few of the knock-offs. Being a movie fan, I didn't want to judge just because I chose not to make *Die Hard in a Deli* – which you must see, by the way – but no, there was no grave-rollin'." This is not the same as a definitive statement that John McClane and Casey Ryback would get along, but it's the best I can offer.

I'm sorry to say that the movie's biggest flaw is Erika Eleniak's character Miss July Jordan Tate. The only reason the villains need to bring her along is to give the officers boners so they'll be more willing to overlook protocol, and she has a similar role in the movie itself. Poor Ryback has to drag her whiny ass along with him while trying to retake the ship from terrorists with nuclear weapons. He does attempt to hide her in a locker but she won't stop banging on the door so he has to babysit her. She's stupid and annoying but he teaches her how to fire a semi-automatic. After she encounters a soldier who signed up for college money and somehow does not know how to fire a gun, she is so disgusted by his cowardice that she instantly transforms into a serious soldier and manages to kill #3 bad guy Colm Meaney. In the very last scene, the Captain's funeral, she is seen on the deck wearing a sailor uniform. Maybe she needed some clothes to change into, or maybe she chose to abandon her promising acting career to join the Navy. (Hey sailor, didn't I see you on *Hunter*?) True, she was wearing a military jacket for her stripper routine earlier, but I don't think they have strippers at most military funerals. And she is wearing pants.

There's also a part at the end where Ryback kisses her, a completely unearned moment but I don't know, I guess maybe he's been into her since he saw her boobs and has been keeping it in his pants as long as terrorists are at large.

While there is some funny dialogue between the two, there doesn't seem to be any other good reason for Ryback to have a sidekick. And if he had to have one it could've been someone more tolerable. Unfortunately he seems to be a magnet for annoying people (see Morris Chestnut as Bobby in *Under Siege 2*).

One positive thing I can say for having Eleniak in the movie: she was in *E.T.*, the movie Seagal's son was rooting for at the Oscars in the script for *Hard to Kill*.

Like Seagal, Andrew Davis was taking a step into the mainstream by doing a big studio movie like this. But like always he continues to work with some of his favorite actors from previous films. He'd already directed Tommy Lee Jones in *The Package* (and would soon direct him to a best supporting actor Oscar in *The Fugitive*). Joseph F. Kosala, the real cop who played Strozah in *Above the Law*, also has a small part as "Engine Room Watch Officer" (he's the guy who asks if this is a joke and then gets shot).

Tommy Lee Jones makes a great villain, and this was back before he became a household name with *The Fugitive*. Like Seagal he hadn't completely broken into the mainstream yet. He was the guy from *Coal Miner's Daughter* and *Rolling Thunder*.

It's somewhat miraculous to have Jones and Busey as villains in the same movie. Seagal has faced a lot of high profile villains over the years (Michael Caine, Kris Kristofferson, etc.) but rarely two of such high quality at the same time (as much as I love the team of Eric Bogosian and Everett McGill in part 2). Throw in Colm Meaney and you have the best team of villains in any Seagal film.

Once again Davis's direction is topnotch and I think he deserves a lot of credit for Seagal's breakthrough into the mainstream. But in later years, Davis would unfortunately play down Seagal's role in the movie. In a July 2005 interview with moviehole.net he said, "Bear in mind, he was really only in *Under Siege* for 41 minutes. It was Tommy Lee Jones most of the time." This seems like kind of a ridiculous quibble. Without a doubt there are scenes focusing on Tommy Lee Jones's activity, just as *Die Hard* abandons Bruce Willis at times for scenes about what Alan Rickman is up to. But whether you are an Oscar nominee or not you're not going to get around the fact that it's a Steven Seagal vehicle. And a good one, too. You should be proud. You're not going to honestly tell me your movies with Keanu Reeves or Arnold Schwarzenegger were better than this, are you? (Perhaps Davis's attitude is explained by his other comment about Seagal, that "he was a puppy dog" on *Above the Law* and "he was very open to trying things," but that by the time of *Under Siege* "he was a bit of a star.")

Credit is also due to writer J.F. Lawton, who is best known for writing *Pretty Woman* (he wrote the original script, *Three Thousand*, the one where she died of a drug overdose at the end) and for creating the TV show *V.I.P.* starring Pamela Anderson. *Under Siege* was not originally written as a Seagal vehicle, it was a spec-script called

Dreadnought. Okay, so we've already acknowledged that in some respects it's a *Die Hard* rip-off, but it's a well-written one. The way the attackers get past military protocol by throwing a surprise party for the commander is particularly inspired. (Too bad the captain's birthday happened to be right before the *Missouri* was gonna be decommissioned. If he'd been born in the winter maybe none of this would've ever happened.)

There are a couple of lessons you can learn from *Under Siege.* Ryback represents a man with great discipline, training and honor who also manages to think for himself. His insistence on being an individualist within the Navy is pure fantasy, but it's a fun one. Early in the film Ryback is somehow allowed to wear the trademark Seagal all-black, causing everyone he encounters to ask "where are your dress whites?" He refuses to call his superiors "sir" if they're dicks to him. He manages to skip the President Bush photo opportunity because "you know how I feel about ceremonies," and also skips a chance to meet the president because "I got a lot to do." But at the end of the film, for the Captain's military funeral, he wears his uniform for the first time, attends the ceremony and proudly salutes. This is not a sign that he has changed but that he has great respect for the Captain.

For further development of this theme, pay attention to what happens to Private Nash (Tom Wood), the grunt assigned to guard Ryback while he's detained in the meat locker. Ryback tries to appeal to Nash's common sense. He points out that it's unusual to be locked in a meat locker, and that he should call the Captain and ask him what he thinks. But Nash is stubbornly suspicious because of Krill's claim that Ryback "is an extreme psychopath. He hates officers. He hates America." Nash's attitude is easily recognizable to Americans. He's just trying to do his job, you can't entirely blame him, but he's also a gullible idiot. What would it hurt to call the Captain? He's stuck on the specifics of the protocol and ignoring the meaning behind the protocol. Ryback is correct that this guy is brainwashed and needs to learn to question authority. And besides, anybody that trusts Gary Busey over their own instincts has some problems.

Another lesson you can learn from the movie is to *never* hire Bad Billy and the Fabulous Bail Jumpers to play at your party. Not worth the money. I once met a young man who grew up near the Navy base where *Under Siege* was filmed. He says that during this time some of Seagal's young daughters went to the same private school as he did, and he would see Kelly LeBrock picking them up after school. One day, he claims, the school arranged to have Seagal speak at an assembly. Seagal stepped up to the microphone wearing all black and supposedly said, "I just want to tell you – mind your parents, stay in school, and don't do drugs. Thank you."

Apparently that was it. As Seagal left the stage, some of the kids booed his brevity, including my young friend, who received detention. In his next movie, *On Deadly Ground*, Seagal will do a much longer speech about pollution and alternative fuel resources and people will make fun of him for that too. The moral of the story is that you can't win. Either people will boo you for keeping it simple or they'll cut you for being long-winded. But really, both approaches have their merits. While we mourn the loss of the simpler hand-to-hand street fighting of the Golden Era, we must also welcome the big ass explosions of the Silver.

Under Siege, 1992
Directed by Andrew Davis (*Above the Law, Holes*)
Written by J.F. Lawton (*Pretty Woman, Cannibal Women in the Avocado Jungle of Death* [also director]). Revisions by Steven Seagal, Mike Gray & John Mason (all uncredited).
Distinguished co-stars: Gary Busey, Tommy Lee Jones, Bernie Casey.
Seagal regulars: Miguel Nino, who plays one of the commandos, played Chi Chi Ramone in *Above the Law.* Joseph Kosala (Engine Room Watch Officer) was also in *Above the Law,* as was Gene Barge (a member of the Bail Jumpers band). Tom Muzila (Cates) was in both *Above the Law* and *Hard to Kill,* as was commando Craig Dunn. Craig Pinkard (who plays "Submariner") was in *Marked For Death* and *Out For Justice.* Raymond Cruz (Ramirez) was in *Out For Justice.*
Firsts: First Seagal film without 3-word title, first successful *Die Hard* knock-off, first time Seagal worked with a director for a second time, first time he wasn't playing a cop.
Title refers to: The USS *Missouri,* and by extension Mr. Casey Ryback, are under siege.
Just how badass is this guy? "Ryback's a warrior. He's the best there is."
Adopted culture: None.
Languages: English, reference to hand signals (though you don't actually see them)
Improvised weapons: microwave bomb, pylon on rope, table saw.
Old friends: Everybody on the ship, especially the captain. He even apparently encountered the villain in the past some time, although it's not clear when.

Fight in bar: No, there is no bar on the aircraft carrier.

Broken glass: Not much, but Tommy Lee Jones gets his head through a monitor.

Terms of endearment: buddy, my man.

Family shit: We don't hear anything about Ryback's family until part 2.

Political themes: Another CIA blowback theme. Guy in Pentagon: "You've been financing this god damn maniac's private army? And it didn't occur to you it might become a problem?" Also Seagal tells a soldier he was brainwashed at boot camp and needs to question authority.

Cover accuracy: Fairly accurate. The poster is dominated by a photo of Seagal wearing his dress uniform, something he makes a point of only doing for a funeral at the end, but he does wear it in the movie and it visually conveys that he's in the military. The only quibble I have is that he's described as "a lone man" with "a deadly plan of attack" which is mostly true, but fails to give credit to his dumb sidekick or the soldiers who help him once he's freed them. Strangely, this is the only Seagal poster with a drawing on it – the logo includes an illustration of a Navy SEAL or ninja type rappelling.

CHAPTER 6:
ON DEADLY GROUND

"You're a macho man with a code of honor. You won't shoot me in the back."

After gaining mainstream credibility with *Under Siege*, Seagal could've been expected to do some more *Die Hard* rip-offs, maybe a sequel, some cop buddy movies. He did all those things, but first he pulled a Gus-Van-Sant-remaking-*Psycho*-after-*Good-Will-Hunting* maneuver. He cashed in what clout he had to make his directorial debut – a preachy, environmentally themed action movie taking place among the Eskimos. It's the corniest, most unintentionally hilarious movie of his career, up there with *Roadhouse* as a classic goofy action movie done with a straight face. But it's also Seagal's most sincere and his most ballsy. By the end of the picture Seagal is basically an environmental terrorist, blowing up an oil rig to protect Alaska from pollution. Then he makes a big speech about the tyranny of big business and possible solutions to the environmental crisis.

For obvious reasons this is the most important picture in all of Seagalogy. It demonstrates virtually every major theme of Seagalogy, and then some. This movie is what Seagal is about. You can't understand Seagal if you haven't seen *On Deadly Ground*.

Seagal plays Forrest Taft, an apparent ex-CIA oil rig firefighter turned mystical environmental terrorist. When we first meet him he's a self-proclaimed "whore," using his skills to put out fires for the Aegis Oil Corporation, a Halliburton-like group of assholes who blatantly bully Native Alaskans, pollute their land, lie to the press and even murder whistleblowers. Despite his questionable ethics, Taft gets a heroic introduction starting with his boots as he steps off a helicopter and panning up to show his fringed jacket as he turns around, lighting a cigar, and squints. He had to be flown in because he's the only man who knows how to adjust a chain and then push a button that causes a big ass explosion that puts out the fire. There's a great shot of Taft standing with his back to the explosion, pushing the button, and the fire completely fills the frame. When the bomb goes off, everyone hits the deck except for two men: Taft and his boss, the openly evil Aegis Oil chairman Jennings (played by Oscar winner Michael Caine, with his hair dyed black). I have no fucking clue how to explain this scene, why only Taft could push the button and why a huge explosion would put out a fire. But I'm sure it must make sense. I mean why would they put it in there if it didn't make sense. These guys are professionals.

Taft's old man buddy Hugh Palmer (Richard Hamilton) tells him that the fire was caused by faulty equipment that Aegis refused to replace. It's too late to investigate, though, since Taft just blew up the evidence. Discussing this fucked up bullshit over some drinks, Taft gives in and says, "Listen to me. I left my day pack and some weapons up at your place. I think I'm gonna pick 'em up and go into the hills." That's the kind of guy we're dealing with here. A guy who wears a fringe jacket and has enough weapons to stash them in more than one location. Later we find out he also has a shack full of explosives up on top of a mountain "just in case." And he doesn't even need weapons to take on a whole bar full of oil workers, as we'll learn early on, in the legendary Cupcake Scene.

This is the scene where an oil worker named Big Mike (the always reliable character actor Mike Starr) taunts a drunk Native American dude and calls Taft "cupcake" for looking upset about it. Taft responds by beating the holy living fuck out of 14 of Big Mike's friends, breaking lots of furniture, windows and limbs, throwing a guy through a window, causing a guy to cry "My nuts!" and even pounding an old man into the ground. Then he convinces Big Mike to settle this by playing what he calls "the hand slap game." Mike will try to slap Forrest's hands and if he is successful, he gets to hit Forrest as hard as he can. But if Mike misses, then Forrest gets to hit him instead.

Now, just a little hint for all you bullies out there, or anybody who finds themselves in a situation like Big Mike finds himself in here. Generally speaking, if you're fighting a guy and he offers to play a silly children's game of some kind, there is gonna be some kind of catch. Yes, it *sounds* like it would be easy to slap a guy's hands. But why the fuck do you think he's suggesting this, man? Because he's good at not getting his hands slapped. Unfortunately for Big Mike, he must have a big ego when it comes to his handslapping skills, so no matter how obvious it is that it's a trap, he accepts the offer. Well, maybe it's for the best, as we'll see later.

Just as I predicted, Big Mike doesn't stand a chance against a true hand slap game champion like Forrest Taft. Forrest's aikido skills, or his CIA training or something, gives him the ability to move his hands out of the way really fast, so he keeps getting to punch Mike until the asshole falls to the floor and pukes. Finally, Taft ends the game by asking Mike, "What does it take to change the essence of a man?"

Mike sobs and says, "I need time to change. Time."

"I do too," Forrest says profoundly. "I do too." Patting him on the shoulder like an old buddy.

For a bar fight, this sure is a complexly constructed scene, and not just because they had to choreograph Seagal dispatching fifteen separate characters each in a different way. Storywise, the reason for the scene is for Hugh to convince Taft to investigate the faulty preventers. But there's a lot more than that going on. We learn a little more about his past and his relationship with Hugh (Taft calls Hugh "Bubba," Hugh apologizes for what he said earlier, Taft claims he never was a "good man.") We learn that three workers died in the fire, including a friend of Taft's named "Lorenzo" who we never hear about again. We learn that there is tension between oil workers and the other locals, most of whom seem disgusted by Big Mike's racism and bully tactics, but afraid to do anything about it because (as we also see in this scene) oil workers stick together and consider themselves a team. We also see that Taft is on a first name basis with the bartender, who seems to have accepted the fact that Forrest will fight in honorable brawls but tries (unsuccessfully) to convince him not to break anything (which of course tells us that he does this sort of thing all the time). Throughout the fight we see shots of her covering her eyes in disgust to show that she disapproves of the violence but is either too powerless or too apathetic to stop it.

Then we've got this simultaneous storyline going about Big Mike and how he taunts the "little Native man" (as Taft condescendingly refers to him), calling him "Cochise," "Pocahontas" and "Geronimo," and making emasculating, homophobic remarks to Taft, trying to lure him into the conflict. He finally succeeds by knocking the Native man over and kicking him. This leads to Taft's conquest of the oil workers and his introduction of the hand-slap game. Taft defeats Big Mike mentally by getting him to accept the game, then defeats him physically by playing it. He attacks him psychologically, repeatedly making sarcastic comments about his balls and his manliness, giving him a taste of his own medicine. Once Big Mike is in physical pain from the game, Taft further emasculates him by yelling at him like a drill instructor or an asshole gym teacher. "You're a man, right? You're a man, right? Here we go 'man.' Put your hands up! *Put your hands up!*"

And then, of course, there's the surprise twist to the scene: the "I need time to change" moment, probably the greatest moment in all of Seagalogy. Who would have ever thought that Taft's fight with Big Mike would not end with Big Mike unconscious and defeated, but instead with mystical music playing as he admits that he is a flawed individual, Taft confesses that he is too, and the two separate peacefully? Is there another movie in the history of cinema with a scene like that? Not that I know of.

"What does it take to change the essence of a man?" This is the first of three profound questions Taft asks his foes. The second is "How much? How much money is enough?" and the third is "What does one say to a man with no conscience?" Well, okay, I guess the third one isn't as profound, but it's a question you need to consider once a guy has refused to take the time to change the essence of a man, and does not know how much money is enough.

After changing the course of Big Mike's life forever, Taft takes Hugh's advice and uses his security clearance to investigate the records of the "faulty preventers" that caused the oil fire. Meanwhile, the brass at Aegis have figured out that Hugh is anonymously tipping off the EPA to the problem. Since there are not adequate whistleblower protections in place, they are able to send John C. McGinley and Sven Ole Thorsen to Hugh's house to torture and kill him using a decorative bone and a pipe fitter. And Taft is next on the list. Convincing him that there's another fire to be put out, they lure him to where they can blow him up (along with Hugh's body, and the pipe fitter, but not the decorative bone) and leave him for dead.

Fortunately, Taft turns up alive in the Inuit village, and this is when the sacred journey we heard about before really kicks into gear. The village elders see in him "the spirit of the man bear[30]." He gets into the whole poetic spirit of the thing and claims to be "a mouse, hiding from the hawks in the house of the raven." They use old school Native American techniques to remove shrapnel from his back. Later he tries to sneak off in full Eskimo fur gear, but gets attacked by the sled dogs. One of them even bites his crotch.

On Deadly Ground has a lot in common with fellow preachy action star/director Tom Laughlin's *Billy Jack*. Both deal with righteous, outraged heroes who struggle with the morality of violence while fighting against corrupt fat cats. Not the least of the similarities is that both heroes are taken in by Native Americans who tell them their spirit animal (rattlesnake for Billy Jack, bear for Forrest Taft) and then give them symbolic hallucinations. In Taft's vision he explores a cave and has to choose either the company of an old hag or a writhing naked woman. He takes a while but chooses the old lady. (But what if it was a trick because you would *assume* the naked chick was a trick but she actually wasn't. Then Taft would've really missed out.) He also fights a bear[31] (played by Bart the Bear, the respected bear actor who co-starred with Anthony Hopkins and Alec Baldwin in the David Mamet-scripted *The*

---

30 I really think this would've been a good title for the movie. Steven Seagal is... *Spirit of the Man-Bear.* Only in theaters.

31 It's worth noting that the bear fight, although extremely brief, is better than the one in Sonny Chiba's otherwise topnotch *Karate Bear Fighter.* In that movie the bear is obviously a guy in a suit. Here you can tell Seagal is face-to-face with a real bear.

Edge) and falls in a river. I'm not really clear whether this is only a vision or a flashback to what happened to him between the time he got blown up and the time he was brought to the village for healing.

Unfortunately, by aiding the enemy of Aegis Oil the Native villagers put themselves on the deadly ground, and there are consequences. It's clear that nobody's playing around here. Taft takes Masu (Joan Chen), his Inuit guide and translator, and goes into survivalist mode. Not only does he have stockpiles of weapons to go to, he has a pair of pants and boots that he somehow knows will fit Masu. (Looks like Hugh Palmer must've worn women's pants.) Publicly Aegis accuses Taft of sabotage, a complete fabrication that happens to correspond with his actual plans for the near future. He's worried that the rush job is going to cause the thing to blow up, so his solution is to blow it up. Actually, he has an idea for imploding it which will prevent the oil from spilling. (This implosion idea is the part of Seagal's environmental policy that would be most difficult to implement in real life.)

Aegis gets desperate, and their security force isn't cutting it. Since corporations have used mercenaries (or, uh, "independent contractors") in the Philippines and Angola they decide they can get away with it in the untamed frontier of Alaska. So they call in Stone (R. Lee Ermey) and his team to try to hunt Taft down. They chase him through the woods and eventually to Aegis-1, where there is a big climax with explosions, etc.

Taft and Jennings both stayed on their feet for the explosion at the beginning of the movie, they have that in common. But in fact they are opposites. Jennings dedicates his life to running a huge corporation, Taft is a rugged individualist who breaks his bonds with the company. Jennings dies a greedy bastard, Taft turns his back on money. Jennings hates the smell of animals, Taft is part bear. Jennings is willing to destroy the Alaskan way of life to get Aegis-1 running, Taft warns all the workers to get off Aegis-1 before he blows it up. Jennings has no morals but doesn't get his hands dirty himself, Taft is against violence but kills or hospitalizes a few dozen people during the movie. It's a great conflict between the asshole who seems to enjoy fucking over everybody in the world and the guy who can't let an asshole like that get away with it. I'm not sure this works on a mythic level, maybe more of a cartoon level, but it's a rivalry I can enjoy.

Jennings is a unique villain because, while he does order a few murders, most of his evil is not violent. He's just a greedy bastard who is willing to screw over people and nature if it helps him to get more money. He has a profound contempt for environmentalists, tribal leaders and OSHA, because they all call him on his shit. He's also just a regular old asshole. He cruelly yells at underlings such as a makeup lady. In one unusual touch he insults the director[32] of the PSA he's filming, telling him, "Listen, if you have any great ideas, just keep em to your fuckin self, okay? And leave this shit to me." So at least in the context of this movie, Seagal is against egomaniacal primadonnas who ignore the director's vision, no matter if people want to accuse him of that himself or not.

Taft apparently gets $350,000 a year from Aegis, but it's not clear what he does when there aren't any fires to put out. He's an important part of the company and inner-circle enough to accompany Jennings at a press conference, but not as close to him as the topnotch team of miserable assholes he has working for him. You have John C. McGinley as MacGruder, some sort of security liaison who kisses Jennings's ass, hires mercenaries, and himself goes to torture and kill Hugh Palmer. This guy is a grade-A weasel with a righteous sense of entitlement. After he shoots an unarmed tribal elder he whines that it was in self defense and almost seems to believe it.

MacGruder is accompanied by Sven-Ole Thorsen as Otto, but he's more of a traditional henchman. The strong, silent, Sven-Ole Thorsen type.

Rounding out the team is Shari Shattuck as Liles, Jennings's heartless bureaucrat of doom. One of her "just how evil is she?" scenes is the one where she suggests lowering the standard compensation package for spouses of dead oil workers because she feels it's "unnecessarily generous." In the end, true to her every-man-for-himself philosophy, she abandons Jennings on the oil rig, claiming that she, uh, has to go to the

---

32 The director is played by Irvin Kershner, best known as the director of *The Empire Strikes Back*. Kershner is probably in here because he also directed the James Bond film *Never Say Never Again*, for which Seagal was Sean Connery's martial arts instructor.

bathroom. She tries to flee like a coward, but her truck crashes and blows up. And it's one of those classic action movie numbers where she is about to crash so instead of trying to turn the steering wheel she holds her hands up in front of her face.

And then there are the mercenaries. R. Lee Ermey was a real drill instructor who started acting after basically playing himself in a bunch of war movies, most famously *Full Metal Jacket*. He's got a shtick that he repeats a lot but I always find it enjoyable, even in horrible garbage like that fucking *Texas Chain Saw Massacre* remake he was in. In this one he gets some funny, tasteless lines like when he tells one of his men, "I want you to protect this entrance like it was your sister's cherry, Tonto[33]."

But maybe the most interesting appearance in the movie is Billy Bob Thornton as the mercenary Homer Carlton. It's a small role that some people might miss if they weren't looking for it. This was the early days, the same year Thornton shot the short film *Some Folks Call It a Sling Blade* but a few years before he became a household name in the feature version, *Sling Blade*. Although he had no clout at this point in his career he's the only mercenary that gets real dialogue, a funny, obviously improvised moment where he muses about whether his rifle looks cooler with the stock in or out. "When I kill the son of a bitch I wanna feel good about myself."

On Deadly Ground is daring in so many ways it's ridiculous. Obviously the in-your-face environmental preachiness (and especially the speech at the end) were a big risk, and they are the main thing people mention when making fun of the movie. But there is more than just a speech at the end that are unorthodox in this genre. The whole point of the movie is for the heroes to stop an environmental catastrophe from occurring, and their method of prevention is to blow up the oil rig. In other words, sabotage on a grand scale. Usually in a movie the good guys are trying to *prevent* something from blowing up, they're not trying to blow it up themselves. And usually the villain's big plot is to intentionally kill

---

33 "Tonto" is about the only epithet Big Mike missed earlier when he was calling that poor guy "Pocahontas." But the way this character reacts, it seems like it's really his name. I'm not joking, I think his name is supposed to be Tonto.

someone or steal something or destroy something. In this one, their scheme is to get an oil rig online fast so they can keep the drilling rights. It's their shortcuts and faulty equipment that pose a danger to the environment and therefore to the people and animals of Alaska. What other action movie uses a plot device like that? Taft's solution is probably not one that we're going to be able to use in our own communities, but at least the *problem* he's facing is closer to the real life problems people face than, say, the terrorist plot in *Under Siege*.

The depiction of "the spirit world" is also not something you expect to see in an action movie, and at that time not even in a Seagal movie. But it's such an important aspect of *On Deadly Ground* that the working title of the movie was *Spirit Warrior*.

All this with the bear and the raven and the old lady in the cave – I mean, that kind of stuff could fly in the hippie days of *Billy Jack* but it turned off some of Seagal's audience, people who grew up watching Stallone and Schwarzenegger movies. They're used to seeing him as a plain old cop or soldier and now all the sudden he's a damn half-bear spirit warrior in a fringe jacket.

Some people also think it's corny to show so many animals in an action movie. But as Seagal said in *Out For Justice*, he's "an animal lover." Animals have had key roles in *Hard to Kill* (the horse that escapes) and *Out For Justice* (the dog he adopts) and they will later figure prominently in *The Patriot* and *Out of Reach*. But nowhere are they paid more respect than in *On Deadly Ground*. The movie opens with a shot of an eagle (we will hear the classic "eagle caw" sound effect a record five times throughout the movie) closely followed by a polar bear. A raven shows up a few times and is said to represent God to the Inuit people. Taft is declared by the chief to be a bear, and also he fights a bear. He uses dog sleds to travel and is also attacked by sled dogs when he tries to sneak away. He's more down with the animals than Jennings, though, who films a commercial with caribou and then yells, "Fuck, these animals stink! Bring me a washcloth!" The movie ends with a montage of second unit or stock footage of animals – the raven, the eagle, some whales, some mountain goats, some kind of pelicans or something – and each gets to make an animal noise as they are shown. It's like the cinematic adaptation of Old McDonald.

Of course, the mainstream action fans turned off by these unorthodox touches might be placated by the fact that this has way, way, way more explosions than any other Seagal picture.

As a director I honestly think Seagal did a good job. The photography is beautiful, there is a stronger use of visual language than in a lot of his movies (like his introductory hero shot and the shot of him and Jennings standing in front of the explosion), the fights are well staged and there are many unusual, distinctive scenes (the Cupcake scene, the environmental speech) that make it stand out from the rest of his filmography and from the genre as a whole.

One stylistic aspect that's different from all of Seagal's other films is the heavy use of ADR (additional dialogue recording) to spruce up scenes. You are constantly hearing off-screen, unidentified characters commenting on the action to show how amazing it is. When Taft shows up at the fire in the opening, a guy says, "Hey, Forrest is here! That fire is as good as out!" During the Cupcake Scene there are all kinds of comments including "Oh shit!" "Leave him alone you dickhead!" "This guy doesn't have a fuckin clue!" "Oh, Jesus." "Don't hurt him, Forrest." "HOLY FUCK!" I don't think I've ever seen a movie that uses so much of this technique, and since this is the only film Seagal has directed I have no choice but to assume that it's part of his directorial style.

As I've mentioned before, the field of Seagalogy rests on the belief that in the films of badass cinema, or at least in the case of Seagal, it is the presence of the star that ties the movies together more than it is the vision of the individual directors. But that doesn't mean I don't believe in the old French auteur theory that the director is usually the "author" of a film. The fact that *On Deadly Ground* is directed by Seagal only reinforces these beliefs because, with more complete control over the content of the picture, he made the ultimate Steven Seagal film. It's not only that it contains many of the motifs shared throughout his entire filmography, but that it's the *very best version* of those motifs. The *ultimate* in Seagalogy. So you've got…

The ultimate bar fight: Especially in the earlier films, fights in bars are crucial to Seagal films. But there is no doubt that the Cupcake Scene is by far the most spectacular and memorable of any of them. Only *Out For Justice* has a bar fight that is arguably better on an action level, and none even come close for the drama or originality of the scene.

The ultimate politics: In a sense this is a departure for Seagal politically, because the politics of his previous films always stuck to the topic of dirty deeds by CIA agents or cops. But this is by far his most openly political film and, as over-the-top as it is, I think it's his most insightful. The stock footage and the speech he makes at the end might as well be a rough draft for Al Gore's Academy Award-winning documentary *An Inconvenient Truth*, made twelve years later. In those days, the public view of environmental awareness was mostly about trying to recycle paper and conserve water. Seagal went after the big fish, the corporate polluters and the policies that make it more profitable not to change, as well as discussing the suppression of technology and the media's part in covering up the problem.

Although *Fire Down Below* is his only other movie that deals with the environment, the subject is widely considered a major component of his persona and something he is often mocked for. As he says in the movie, "They have made it a crime to speak out for ourselves, and if we do so we're called conspiracy nuts and we're laughed at."

The ultimate animal lover: Seagal's appreciation for animals is important to several of his films, but none as much as this one. It opens and closes on montages of animals, he fights a bear, he metaphorically becomes a bear, etc.

The ultimate distinguished co-star: Of all the respected actors that you're surprised would be in a Steven Seagal movie, Caine has got to be the biggest and the one with the most trophies on his mantle.

The ultimate spirituality: Seagal deals with different types of religion and spirituality throughout his films. In this one he goes into detail about "the spirit world," going on this vision quest when rescued by the natives. Later he seems to turn on their religion, almost dismissing it as make believe, saying (among other things), "Maybe I should send my spirit guide over to Aegis-1 and stop it from going on-line so that Jennings can't fuck you and your people out of your land and your way of life forever." After finding Buddhism I'm sure he wouldn't appreciate this attitude towards spirituality anymore, but this is the one movie where he explicitly discusses the place for religion in his life.

The ultimate Just How Badass Is This Guy? scene: I always appreciate these moments, which are in most Seagal films, where someone (usually the bad guys) either know Seagal's character or read a file on him and they make a dramatic declaration of just how dangerous this motherfucker is. *On Deadly Ground* not only has several classics in this area, it has the very best one ever, a little soliloquy performed by R. Lee Ermey:

"My guy in DC tells me we are not dealing with a student here. We're dealing with a professor. Any time the military has an operation that can't fail they call this guy in to train the troops, okay? He's the kind of guy that would drink a gallon of gasoline so he could piss in your camp fire. You could drop this guy off at the Arctic Circle wearing a pair of bikini underwear without his toothbrush and tomorrow afternoon he's gonna show up at your poolside with a million dollar smile and fisful of pesos. This guy's a professional, you got me?"

I always thought that was a funny piece of dialogue. I never really understood what it meant until I got ahold of an undated early draft of the script and saw the ending as originally scripted:

EXT. JENNINGS ESTATE – AFTERNOON

Two GORGEOUS WOMEN IN BIKINIS, early 20s, float on inflatable mattresses in a large backyard swimming pool. They giggle and splash water at each other.

Jennings comes away from an outdoor tiki bar, wearing swimming trunks, flip-flops and a silk bathrobe. He struggles to carry three large cocktails with lemon wedges and umbrellas, sipping his to keep it from spilling.

JENNINGS
(flirtatious)
Now now, ladies, let's not fight. It's time we as Americans came

together and—

Jennings is startled to see Taft standing next to the pool, smiling. He wears bikini underwear, and is very tan. Wadded up pesos poke out from between the knuckles of one tightly clenched fist.

JENNINGS
You! Wh-what… why are you—?
TAFT
I came for my toothbrush, asshole.

FADE TO BLACK.

Nah, I'm just fucking with you, I made that up. That would be funny though if any of those weird details he mentioned paid off somewhere. The pesos I understand, he stopped by Mexico on his way to your poolside. But the bikini underwear? The toothbrush? I don't get it. Nice use of imagery though.

On Deadly Ground is to Seagalogy what *Femme Fatale* is to Brian DePalma's filmography. It takes all the classic Seagal motifs and themes and throws them into overdrive. Like the over-the-top DePalma touches in that movie, the super-charged Seagal-times-ten feel in this one is a godsend for serious scholars of his works, but it can be offputting for the uninitiated. In fact, this movie pretty clearly marks the point when the mainstream audience turned on Seagal. He was wearing his heart on his sleeve, putting himself out there, and that's not always a gamble that pays off. A lot of people laughed at the idea of putting this sort of message in a violent action movie, believing that the use of standard action movie tropes (solving the problem with explosives, for example) damages the credibility of the argument. But some would agree with me that the essential truth of the idea still comes through. In their special *On Deadly Ground* issue, *Impact: The Action Movie Magazine* quoted a Greenpeace activist named Pamela Miller who said, "I thought the violence was gratuitous and the plot oversimplified the native's way of life, but the essence of truth was represented." The comedian and harsh Seagal critic

David Cross put it less kindly during a live commentary at the 2002 Olympia Film Festival: "The sad thing is, he's basically right. But he's this idiotic, retarded clown."

I don't agree with that "retarded clown" bit, but it's true that Seagal is "basically right." The essence of truth is represented. In defending the stories Seagal tells about his life, his psychologist friend Robert Frager told an interviewer, "A part of Steven lived in Japan so long that he is Japanese, and in Japan the literal truth is not as important as the emotional truth. In Japan there is another level of reality, one where the literal facts don't matter as much as the social and the emotional facts.[34]" I believe this same "level of reality" applies to storytelling. While *On Deadly Ground* is far from a literal depiction of the real world, it does contain that "emotional truth" that is more important. And I think the fact that Seagal puts this message in the context of a lowbrow form like an action movie, as opposed to a respectable mainstream drama where an ecological message would seem more natural, makes it more subversive and certainly more entertaining. Maybe it's not as successful at that as, say, John Carpenter's *They Live*, but it's coming from the same place.

The earlier Seagal films of the Golden Era are my favorites, but it is *On Deadly Ground* and the films that follow in its wake that make Seagal such a fascinating figure. Before this movie, he was a popular action star, like so many others. Only now did he become *Steven fucking Seagal*.

On Deadly Ground, 1994
Directed by Steven Seagal
Written by Ed Horowitz (*Exit Wounds, K-9: P.I.*) & Robin U. Russin (nothing else)
Distinguished co-stars: Michael Caine, Joan Chen, R. Lee Ermey, Billy Bob Thornton, John Trudell (poet and former chairman of the American Indian Movement).
Seagal regulars: Patrick Gorman (one of the oil executives) played a CIA interrogator in *Above the Law*. Joe Lala, who plays a guard, was the pimp in the opening of *Out For Justice*. Fumiyasu Daikyu (Maktak) plays an Embassy Attache in *Ticker*.
Firsts: Seagal's directorial debut, first sign of his interest in Native American culture and the environment.
Title refers to: fuck if I know.
Just how badass is this guy? "Forrest Taft is the patron saint of the impossible."

---

34 Richman, "Black Belt, White Lies" in *GQ*, March 1991, p. 307.

"Delve down into the deepest bowels of your soul. Try to imagine the ultimate fucking nightmare. And that won't come close to this son of a bitch when he gets pissed."

Adopted culture: Eskimo/Native American.

Languages: English, Inuit (during vision quest only), hand signals.

Improvised weapons: Decorative rope (taken off the wall during bar fight), tusk, tree (used for booby trap), empty 2-liter bottle (used as some kind of silencer?), helicopter blade, pipe, cable (used as lasso).

Old friends: Hugh Palmer.

Fight in bar: hell yes – the best ever.

Broken glass: Glasses on bar tables, guy thrown through office window in bar, windows shot out in Hugh's house, head rammed through gun cabinet, door window shot out in refinery, guy thrown through office window on rig.

Innocent bystanders: MacGruder shoots and kills Masu's elderly father for no reason.

Terms of endearment: brotha, cupcake, sweetheart.

Weirdest timing for a one-liner: "This is for my father." (Masu says only after Taft has already dropped Jennings into oil.)

Best one-liner: "I wouldn't dirty my bullets."

Family shit: No mention of his family.

Political themes: Large corporations pollute the earth, endanger and destroy lives in the name of easy profits. Technologies that could save resources are suppressed for the sake of those same profits.

Cover accuracy: Well, if you take the picture literally it doesn't make any sense. In the foreground, Seagal poses with a rifle and his embroidered fringe jacket that he wears in the movie. Off in the distance is one lone burning oil well and a shed in the middle of Alaska, with some tiny firefighters (possibly including Seagal) spraying water on the flames. I don't know why Seagal would be standing in front of it posing, but if you accept that they are two separate incidents collaged together then it is perfectly in tune with the movie.

CHAPTER 7:
UNDER SIEGE 2:
DARK TERRITORY

"What the hell? This isn't the produce list. This is—oh my god!"

eagal's first sequel, and one of his most effective attempts at mainstream movie-making (not to mention one of the all time top five *Die Hard* knock-offs) opens with a god damn space shuttle taking off! There's some very artful space shots with sunbeams and everything, all done with top of the line for the time computer animation, which tells you right off the bat that 1) this is very expensive and respectable for a Seagal film and 2) it's going to have more special effects than stunts, really. But at first I was thinking, is this the wrong movie? Or are they gonna tell us that Casey Ryback is an astronaut now? Maybe the official chef of NASA. Is this gonna be *Die Hard* on a space shuttle? Speed at zero Gs? Nope[35]. Turns out it's the launching of the Grazer One satellite that the terrorists will use to, you know, terrorize everybody.

Meanwhile, in the ATAC control room down on the small planet of Earth, the intelligence agency fuckwads test out their new toy. That

---

[35] I wonder why nobody *has* done *Die Hard* on a space shuttle? I guess it would be hard to have some regular guy just happen to be on the space shuttle. But the geniuses of Hollywood would be able to come up with some phony baloney explanation, I'm sure. If they can put a leprechaun in space they can put a John McClane there too.

asshole head of the CIA Tom Breaker (Nick Mancuso) is there and mentions that, once again, Congress doesn't know about what he's up to. The satellite has a camera so powerful that they use it to look at titties on a beach, and they casually mention that it also has weapons on it. *And by the way isn't it too bad that Travis Dane isn't here? Good ol' Travis Dane, what a nut he was to invent this satellite but then get fired and drive his car into a lake leaving behind a mysterious note. It probably didn't mean anything, so we're not worried about it. Anyway, let's look at those tits again.*

Then we are re-introduced to Casey Ryback (Seagal), the non-pony-tail-wearing, ex-SEAL turned Navy cook turned USS *Missouri* rescuer (see *Under Siege*). By now he is a popular chef with his own restaurant called the Mile High Café, but his second in command is annoyed at him because he's always going off on "some kind of special op or something" (he just got back from one, a thrilling Casey Ryback adventure that only exists in that space between parts 1 and 2, a space called *our dreams*). Now Casey has to leave again because his brother who he hadn't spoken to in 5 years died in a plane crash, and now he has to take his niece Sarah (Katherine Heigl of *Grey's Anatomy* and *Bride of Chucky* fame) to California on a train which may or may not be taken over by terrorists while they are on it, who knows. I'm not gonna give it away in this paragraph, you'll have to keep reading to find out.

I mean who knows, maybe they go on this trip and there are no terrorists. Maybe *Under Siege 2* is more of a relationship drama about the awkward situation of a decorated warrior traveling with a niece he hasn't seen in years. By getting to know his niece he is able to come to terms with the problems between him and his late brother. Maybe he's under siege not by terrorists, but by unresolved issues from his childhood.

Okay you're right, it gets taken over by terrorists. But don't get a big head about it, either it did or it didn't, you had a fifty-fifty chance. It doesn't make you fuckin Nostradamus. Anyway it turns out that the aforementioned weapons genius Travis Dane (acclaimed playwright and monologuist Eric Bogosian) has decided to steal the targeting codes, take the passengers hostage and use the train as a moving headquarters while he uses the satellite to cause an earthquake in China (stock footage of Aegis Oil blowing up from *On Deadly Ground*) and then call up various world leaders to see how much they're willing to pay for some more strategically placed earthquakes. Of course there need to be some bad guys for Ryback to sneak around and kill one-by-one, so Dane has a group of mercenaries with him, led by the scary looking Penn (Everett McGill of *Twin Peaks* and *The People Under the Stairs*).

Also, for some reason Dane keeps quoting Louis Pasteur ("Chance favors the prepared mind.") He probably just likes the quote and is not necessarily obsessed with Louis Pasteur. They never show him drinking milk or talking about pasteurization or anything like that.

The shit goes down after Ryback has schmoozed his way into the train's kitchen, where the staff watch in awe as he whips up a microwave cake for his niece. He's also made buddies with the female bartender and discussed his memoirs (*Ryback's Tactics*) with her as he works on them on his Newton brand handheld computer device.

When a merc busts into the kitchen, one of the chefs grabs a cleaver. The attacker fills him full of holes and asks, "Any other heroes?" Ryback chooses to answer non-verbally, beating the dude senseless and tossing him out the door. Bitch. You kill a chef in front of Ryback, you die immediately and horribly and you deserve it just for being such an idiot. Dumb fucking mistake, man. I bet that guy was kicking himself all the way to Hell.

Soon Ryback runs into a porter named Bobby (Morris Chestnut, the kid that dies at the end of *Boyz N the Hood*, but you'll wish he'd die in the beginning of this one). Bobby is the most unfortunate aspect of the movie, a painfully unfunny comic relief sidekick whose jokes consist of 1) overconfidence while hitting on Sarah 2) overconfidence in his non-existent martial arts skills and 3) various mugging. I guess Cuba Gooding Jr. wasn't available. Ryback stays optimistic though and teaches this chump how to fire a gun just like he did Erika Eleniak in part 1. This lenient attitude toward bad comic relief was a grave error that led to a string of mediocre buddy movies for Seagal.

Then they kill some guys, save the day, etc.

The style of action is much more big and Hollywood and artificial than in earlier Seagal pictures. This is an early use of the digitally mapped green screen backgrounds that are so common today, so there's more composited special effects than any other Seagal movie (outside the train windows, behind people hanging from ropes or ladders, explosions behind people). The biggest action moments are mostly models, computer effects and stunts combined with green screen footage. At the climax, for example, Ryback runs down the aisle of the train as it crashes and flattens in on itself.

There's also an awesome scene where Ryback is off the train and has to get back on so he hotwires a truck, drives it up a higher road so he can pass the train, then jumps the truck over the train, dropping out the door, rolling down the hill and jumping onto the top of the train. That is not the work of an aikido artist (or a cook), but it sure is cool.

Don't get me wrong though, there's plenty of organic action mixed in with the showoffy technology stuff. Ryback seems to spend most of the movie climbing on the top and the side of the train. Sometimes it's obviously a stunt double, but at least it's a real guy on a real train. And there are some shots that are clearly the real Seagal on a real train. There's also plenty of quick aikido moves to disarm mercenaries and break their wrists or necks. Ryback has a great knife fight with Penn that lasts longer than his climactic fight with Tommy Lee Jones in part 1, and best of all it manages to work its way into the kitchen where Ryback can take advantage of the cooking theme a little more than before. When he knocks the knife out of Penn's hand it lands in a dish rack, which I thought was a nice touch. When Ryback wins (spoiler) he says, "Nobody beats me in the kitchen."

One thing that makes *Under Siege 2* stand out is the high-quality villainy of Eric Bogosian. This is just not a guy you would expect to play a villain in a Steven Seagal picture. In fact, it's probably more surprising that they could get him than that they could get Michael Caine. Apparently Jeff Goldblum and Julian Sands turned down the role, which is for the best. Whoever thought to cast Bogosian deserves some kind of Seagalogy top secret medal that they can't show anybody. Digging into his experience as a monologist on stage and in Oliver Stone's *Talk Radio*, Bogosian delivers arrogant, sarcastic lines in a completely different way than your typical Hollywood heavies. You really believe that he's smarter than everybody else and pissed off about it. I always thought it would be cool if they got Spalding Gray to play the villain in part 3 so they could continue the monologist tradition. But it wasn't meant to be. I really can't name any other monologists, so I don't know who it should be. Not Jay

Leno.

You also gotta hand it to Everett McGill, he's one scary looking mercenary. I already declared Tommy Lee Jones and Gary Busey the best villain team of any Seagal picture, but Bogosian and McGill run a respectable second.

Their supervillain scheme is a pretty good one too. In the grand tradition of Hans Grueber they are not true terrorists, but just some greedy pricks with a get-rich-quick scheme. The takeover of the train is somewhat incidental. It happens to be where the agents with the access code are vacationing and also serves as a handy moving base of operations to keep their signals from being traced. They use the Grazer One satellite to cause earthquakes wherever they want to, and they plan to do that under the Pentagon, where they say there is a secret nuclear power plant. So it will be a problem. If this was a James Bond movie (or any movie, really) they would probably hold Washington for ransom. If you don't pay us a hundred million dollars or whatever, there will be an earthquake at the nuclear power plant. But instead of getting paid to *not* do it, they want to get paid *to* do it. Hey there world, pay us and we'll do this to America. It's a pretty cynical and sadly half-believable scenario.

The use of secret, weaponized satellites is interesting too. The militarization of space is already in the works and seems destined for some kind of horrible consequences, with or without the help of Travis Dane. I'm afraid this might be another issue that Seagal is ahead of the curve on.

By the way, if you're wondering what the hell "dark territory" is supposed to mean, it apparently really is railroad terminology. It means a section of track that because of geography and distance is not able to use signals or transmit with radios or cell phones. I'm not sure how true that is in this movie, since Ryback is able to send a fax by hooking up his Newton to the phone line on the train. But there are references made to the train being in dark territory. Dane says that the fact that they're moving is why they can't be traced, but maybe it helps that they're in this dark territory. I don't know.

The reason there's such a term as "dark territory" is because the lack of signals creates a risk of two trains getting on the main track at the same time and colliding. Instead of worrying about this type of accident, Dane causes it to happen on purpose.

Today dark territory is not quite as dark, because many trains are fitted with GPS equipment, linked to satellites not unlike Grazer One. However, train conductors still try to use the term when possible, I bet, because it sounds cool.

Seagal fares very well in his first sequel. Somehow moving from a Naval battleship to a civilian train really manages to make it seem like a different movie, not a rehash. There are lots of little parallels between the first and second movie, but they're subtle enough that I didn't even notice them at first. Like, in part 1 the takeover happens while Ryback is making pies, so they end up getting burnt. In part 2 it happens while he's making a cake, so it never gets finished. In part 1 Ryback is imprisoned in a walk-in freezer when the shit goes down, in part 2 he intentionally hides in one. (Luckily this one opens from the inside.) The first one ends with Ryback at the Captain's funeral in full Navy dress uniform, in part 2 he puts on the same outfit to visit his brother's grave (and for the movie poster photo shoot).

The beloved characters of Admiral Bates (Andy Romano) and Captain Garza (Dale A. Dye) reprise their *Under Siege* roles of arguing and freaking out in a control room. They get to ask that CIA dickhead Tom Breaker the same type of questions about cancelled programs and why he would hire a maniac like Travis Dane to work for an intelligence agency. Looks like Breaker didn't learn a god damn thing from the time Tommy Lee Jones almost nuked Hawaii. Bates pointedly observes, "You'd think we'd learn something from that."

What they really need to learn is how to communicate with these maniacs who they train to do scary things. If they had tried to work things out with Strannix in part 1 instead of assassinating him, maybe he wouldn't have used the USS *Missouri* and a nuclear submarine to terrorize the nation. Same goes with Travis Dane. He makes this deadly satellite so what do they do, they cancel the program and fire him. All they had to do was keep him on the payroll building evil robots or something, or give him a good severance package and invite him to company picnics. Hell, they could finance his next one man show. Instead they dump his ass unceremoniously, so he has no choice but to fake his death and then take over the deadly satellite and what not.

Even Ryback could stand to learn from these events. He had some sort of unexplained falling out with his brother and didn't speak to him for five years. From the sound of it he could have talked to his brother and worked things out, but he waited too long, his brother died in a plane crash and now it's too late. But unlike Tom Breaker he admits his mistake and seems determined to make things better. Even his teenage niece, who is understandably angry about the situation, adopts a mature outlook and improves her relationship with her uncle. After he saves her from terrorists.

It's interesting to learn that in between running a restaurant, going on special ops missions, going to military funerals and saving the world, Ryback is also writing those memoirs. He works on them a little bit at the bar in the train. Later, we see on his Newton that chapter one is titled, "Don't be a hero." I wonder if that is sarcastic, since we're talking about a guy who never listens when, for example, Eric Bogosian says, "No hero shit." Clearly he believes in "being a hero." So maybe he is quoting the type of thing terrorists often say to him, in order to belittle them and their terroristic cliches. On the other hand maybe he's pulling an Evel Kneivel type deal. Maybe he really is telling his readers not to be a hero themselves since they don't have the same Navy SEAL background and top secret medals. I don't think *Ryback's Tactics* will ever be published, so we'll just have to imagine for ourselves what he would have said. Fortunately, utilizing the magic of the pause button we *are* able to see Ryback's recipe for fruit salad with crystalized [sic] ginger on his Newton. So here it is:

Fruit Salad with Crystalized Ginger

2 cups Granny Smith apples
2 cups papaya cubes
1 cup kiwi slices
1-1 1/2 cups poppy seed dressing
1/4 cup crystalized ginger

1 cup raspberries
1/4 cup seedless grapes
2 tablespoons lime juice
fresh mint leaves
Mix fruit in large bowl, add dressing. Serve in dessert cups, sprinkling generously with ginger. Add a few

[note: this is all we're able to see of the recipe, but I'm guessing he just says to add a few mint leaves and enjoy. But don't be a hero.]

Like *Under Siege*, this is one of the best Seagal movies for non-Seagal fans. Seagal is pretty much at his best, because he wears all black and stays real grim and stoic. None of the smartass banter, one-liners or even speeches. The movie has some of the same political themes as part 1, but it comes through in the control room without Ryback ever having to say anything about it. He fights fast, scowls and squints a lot, and with the help of special effects pretends to do some pretty incredible stunts. And he looks almost as skinny as he did all the way back in *Above the Law*.

Although development of an *Under Siege 3* has been rumored for years, it's never gotten off the ground. The most persistently rumored plot involves Ryback on a hijacked plane, which sounds like an uninspired scenario to me considering we've already seen it in *Passenger 57* and Seagal's own *Executive Decision*. Another long percolating rumor, sourced to an alleged radio interview with Seagal, is that the movie would involve terrorists taking over a hot air balloon. Obviously this cannot be serious but I'd like to think Seagal really made that joke.

Whatever the case, it's hard to imagine Seagal returning to the series at this point, and Andrew Davis has denied involvement. I'd like to think that the lack of a third film just means Ryback has been able to live out his years at the Mile High Café, enjoying the success of his memoirs, perhaps testifying at some hearings where Admiral Bates finally exposes what Tom Breaker's maniacs in the CIA have been up to all these years. After all if Ryback keeps getting stuck on different types of hijacked transportation, you have to wonder what the point is. When will this endless cycle of hijacking end? Well, for now it seems to end here, in dark territory.

Under Siege 2: Dark Territory, 1995

Directed by Geoff Murphy (*UTU, The Quiet Earth, Freejack*, second unit director for all three *Lord of the Rings* films [seriously], which almost makes him an Oscar winner for best director).

Written by Richard Hatem (*The Mothman Prophecies*) & Matt Reeves (co-creator of *Felicity*, directed *Cloverfield*).

Distinguished co-stars: Eric Bogosian, Everett McGill, Morris Chestnut.

Seagal regulars: Morris Chestnut later graduated from wacky sidekick to lead villain in *Half Past Dead*. Afifi Alouie, who played "go-go dancer" in *Out For Justice*, returns as "female mercenary," who is a good shot and does the most damage on Ryback. Producer/future enemy Julius Nasso plays "hostage #3" – he also plays "Actor" in *Fire Down Below*. The bartender, Warren Tabata, played somebody named Oovi in *On Deadly Ground*. Mercenary #1 is played by Peter Greene, who you may recognize as Zed from *Pulp Fiction* or Redfoot from *The Usual Suspects*. He later reteamed with Seagal for *Ticker*. Denis L. Stewart, who is credited as "Holy Mercenary," was first assistant director for both this and *Executive Decision*.

Firsts: Seagal sequel, title with subtitle, wacky sidekick.

Title refers to: a train, and Seagal, who are both under siege in dark territory.

Just how badass is this guy? "This is a Navy Cross. It's awarded for bravery. This one's my father's. Uncle Casey's got 2 of 'em. And he's got medals at home that are so secret he can never show them to anybody[36]. So he's not gonna let anything happen to us. I guess he's a hero."

"He's the best there is."

"You definitely a bad motherfucker."

Adopted culture: none.

Languages: English.

Improvised weapons: bomb made with concentrated coconut oil, lighter fluid, flare gun.

Old friends: Admiral Bates and Captain Garza are old buddies from the USS *Missouri* takeover.

Fight in bar: No, and it's a shame because there actually is a mini-bar on the train.

Broken glass: A window panel in a train door gets shot out. Unfortunately, those windows are too small to throw somebody through.

Family shit: Ryback has a photo of himself with his brother, his niece, and a teddy bear. "She's the only family I have left." So he buys her a teddy bear, not realizing that she is now too old for that shit. "I guess I'm not trained for this," he says. That's Uncle Sam for ya, he'll teach ya how to survive in a jungle eating nothing but leaves and waterbugs, but when it comes to a train ride with a teenage girl, you're on your own, chump.

Political themes: Spy agencies are militarizing space by telling NASA it's only a weather satellite. Their rationale is "What Congress don't know can't hurt 'em. Or us." The U.S. knows China has a chemical weapons plant, but they hypocritically pretend they don't know. The movie also continues the *Under Siege* theme of spy agency blowback. Admiral Bates asks about Travis Dane, "Why in hell would you hire a god damn maniac like that?"

---

36 What the hell kind of medal is so secret you can't show it to anybody? The medal for alien autopsy? Maybe they're actually just embarrassing medals, like the Outstanding Recovery From Hemorrhoids medal or something like that. You don't go showing that one off to your niece.

And the response is, "Admiral, sane people don't build weapons like this."

Cover accuracy: The DVD cover is a dynamic action shot of Ryback holding a gun, riding the side of the train as the rear cars are on fire. This doesn't happen in the movie, but it does look cool and is completely different from all the other Seagal covers. The tagline on the cover is fairly accurate except that it describes "a top secret nuclear satellite," which is not exactly what this thing is. The movie poster was a much weaker design. It showed a large picture of Ryback in his dress whites, which he only wears at the graveyard in the last scene. Overlapped with this is a picture of the Grazer One satellite firing a beam and blowing up the train on a bridge, which of course doesn't happen (and the satellite doesn't even fire a visible beam). But at least it shows you the pieces of hardware that are in play in the movie.

CHAPTER 7.5:
EXECUTIVE DECISION

"Well... who the hell else is gonna do it... you?"

Although he had just politely delivered his first sequel (and a good one, too), the wicked Hollywood overseers still had unfinished business with Seagal: he had to be punished for *On Deadly Ground*. Their sentence was *Executive Decision*, a slick cousin of the *Die Hard* type movie about soldiers and a couple consultants trying to board and recover a hijacked airplane while it's still in flight.

Seagal plays U.S. Army Special Forces Counterterrorist Strike Team Leader Lieutenant Colonel Austin Travis, a U.S. Army Special Forces Counterterrorist Strike Team leader sent to recover a stolen Soviet nerve toxin called DZ-5. During the opening credits. Travis leads his team to attack a mansion where he personally knifes a dude in the neck. They shoot some guys and blow up some windows but when they get there they can't find any of this nerve toxin. The mission is a failure, so it makes Seagal look bad.

Of course, it's unusual to see a movie that looks like it's intentionally trying to make Seagal look bad. Unlike the majority of his roles, this one was not written specifically for him. In the script, Travis is described as "leader of an elite special forces commando team, early 50s, graying hair, still hard and lean, a man of incredible drive and endurance." Seagal was 45 at the time, and does not have his hair grayed in the movie.

Next we meet Dr. David Grant (Kurt Russell, but not acting as cool as Snake Plissken) who it turns out is the asswipe who sent Travis and his boys on this wild goose chase. He's an upper class terrorism expert/intelligence type dude with a Phd., the implication being that he's some kind of sissy that sends Steven Seagal out to do a man's job while he stays safely at home and goes to rich people parties. (Actually, the implication is that this is what everyone thinks, and that he must prove his manliness through the course of the movie.) In fact he's at one of these parties, wearing a tux, and flirting with a chick by talking about hockey, when he gets called in to discuss the hijacking. He arrives at a large five-sided building in D.C. which the screen tells us is "National Military Command Center." He's still wearing his party tux, so Travis (in fatigues) takes one look at him and says, "Jesus." You see, there is some class tension going on here. Also this is the old *Die Hard* motif – McClane happened to be barefoot when the shit hit the fan, Grant happened to be wearing a tux. Same basic principle.

The brains at the pentagonally-shaped "National Military Command Center" believe the terrorists on the plane may have the missing nerve toxin, so they're thinking of shooting the plane down, killing 400 American passengers. But this is not acceptable during an election year. Travis suggests using an experimental technology invented by a wacky eccentric named Cahill (Oliver Platt) where a fancy Stealth-like fighter jet flies up below the commercial airliner, attaches a little tunnel to it and allows the Strike Team to climb on. Also, Travis suggests that Grant and Cahill should come along. (This is his character's best personality quirk – he resents these white collar workers who watch from the safety of their desks as he risks his life, so he tricks them into going along with him on dangerous lifesaving missions. Ha ha ha, suckers.)

So they use the Travis plan, but while transferring into the secluded basement area of the plane where the terrorists won't see them, Joe Morton (*Brother From Another Planet*) is knocked unconscious. Trying to help him out, Grant ends up accidentally getting onto the plane along with the soldiers, but the tunnel becomes unstable and he has to shut the hatch or they'll all get sucked out into the air and plummet to their miserable deaths. He won't do it, but Travis, still down in the tunnel, heroically shuts the hatch, saving all their lives. And getting himself sucked out into the air. *Shwhoop!* You just see a faraway special effects shot of him flopping out of that thing and disappearing. This is 43 minutes into the movie. They haven't even killed a single terrorist yet. Nobody has been thrown through a window. There hasn't been a fight in a bar at all, much less a life-changing conversation between flawed men. The party is just getting started, and Seagal gets sucked out the fucking airlock. You don't even get to see his face when it happens.

The story continues as Grant and the gang try to sneak around, rig up cameras, communicate with a flight attendant (Oscar winner Halle Berry), identify the sleeper agent among the passengers, defuse a bomb and kill the leader, a guy who looks like the Arab answer to John Saxon (actually, he's not even Arab at all, he's the guy who plays Poirot on British TV). When the secretary of defense makes the "executive decision" to send fighters to trail the jet, you see them taking off from an aircraft carrier. And I half expected Travis to climb up out of the water and say, "Take me to that plane." Or maybe something cool like "I almost missed my flight." But it doesn't happen.

Even at the end after Grant has killed the terrorists *and* crash landed the plane himself, Travis still doesn't show up at the scene. In other words, he's dead! He's in less than half of the movie. John Leguizamo, who played "boy in alley" in *Marked For Death*, this time gets way more screen time than Seagal. You would think they would at least give Travis the honor of a military funeral, like they did for the dead Captain at the end of *Under Siege*. After all, his plan and sacrifice made the whole mission possible. Without him, they either would've shot down the plane and killed 400 innocent people, or they would've fucked the whole thing up and the terrorists would've unleashed nerve toxin and killed millions. But he *was* there, so they were able to save the day and take all the credit. The movie ends with the hero hooking up with one of the women he went through so much turmoil with, like they did just before the end of *Under Siege*.

Now look, I'm not gonna sit here and criticize what Grant does in this movie. The dude is clearly a hero and has passed the Lieutenant Colonel's test, getting off his ass and doing a counterterrorist strike for his damn self. But let's be honest here. If Travis had boarded the plane first, all this other bullshit would've been unnecessary. He would've busted into that plane, shot a guy in the face with his own gun, twisted a guy's hand back unnaturally, broken another guy's leg, thrown one guy out the emergency exit, strangled another guy with an oxygen mask, etc. He would've made a big speech to Poirot about how they both were trained by the CIA and then he would've poked the guy's eyes out with his thumbs, impaled him on the flight stick and then crammed him in the overhead luggage. The movie would've been over before it was an hour long. That's the only reason why they had to get rid of Seagal so early in the movie. Otherwise, it would not be believable that they needed this many guys to save the hostages.

And as far as the studio was concerned, there was no reason for Seagal to have any more screen time. It is documented that although he was only on screen for about 15 minutes, "it was because of this cameo that the film did so well at the box office[37]."

Some people have asked me if I really consider Travis to be dead. After all, it is a common cinematic rule that if the character is not shown dying then they will return at the end. For example, everybody was upset that Tom Cruise's son turned out to be alive at the end of *War of the Worlds*, but I never considered he could be dead since it happened off screen. The filmatists don't even have to intend for the character to survive – Whistler was clearly supposed to be dead in *Blade*, but since the gunshot took place off screen they were able to say in part 2 that the vampires kept him barely alive. As Michael Caine's character Jennings says in *On Deadly Ground*, "If your god damn cleanup goons haven't found his fuckin' body then the son of a bitch is alive."

But you know what, I'm not in that kind of denial. I appreciate that he was given the opportunity to die in a movie. He's never done that in another movie unless you count *Half Past Dead* since he collapses and is medically dead for a while. Well, and *Hard To Kill*, that happens to him in that one too. But this is the only one with a permanent death, so I appreciate the novelty.

---

37 Moyer, "Steven Seagal Filmography," in *Martial Arts Legends Presents Shigemichi Take, Shihan – Steven Seagal The Spiritual Warrior Who Prospered On the Island of Budo*, June 1998, p. 106, top photo caption.

Other than being such a horrendous insult to Seagal, this is a decent terrorism-themed action movie. Some of it seems a little creepier post-911, with its talk of shooting down planes, sleeper agents, biological agents, special ops strikes against terrorists and plane attacks on Washington. There's even a part where Grant uses a glass of water as a prop to make a point about the deadliness of DZ-5, kind of like Colin Powell's infamous anthrax show and tell at the United Nations. I wouldn't really say the movie is prophetic or ahead of its time though, since it overestimates the American response to a crisis like that. Of course the part about special forces boarding a hijacked plane is a fantasy, but at least according to the official story of 9-11, we couldn't even get a plane in the area to shoot down the hijacked plane. So this movie takes on a different meaning now.

Usually a movie like this has one token Arab-American character working in a control room somewhere to prove that the movie is not racist: *whoah, why did you think it was racist? I am shocked. We have a guy in our control room who is Arab-American. But we go out for drinks with him and everything, he is totally just like a regular guy, in fact it didn't even occur to me until just now that he is even a different race or religion than me. Wait a minute, that guy's Arab-American? I didn't even know. Yeah, come to think of it, he is. But I like to think that we are all Americans, we are all in this together.*

This movie does not have a token Arab good guy – instead it takes the more bizarre step of having one of the terrorists get offended when he realizes this is a suicide attack and say, "This has nothing to do with Islam!" That's right, not all Islamic terrorists are religious extremists. Only *extreme* Islamic terrorists are religious extremists. Some of them are reasonable guys like you and me who do not take kindly to their fellow hijackers using religion as an excuse.

Anyway, there are many parallels to *Under Siege 2*. Our heroes go through the passenger luggage to find weapons and equipment, and Seagal does not have a ponytail, just to name two examples.

My biggest complaint, besides the untimely death of Lt. Col. Austin Travis, is all the god damn electronic bleeping and blooping in this movie. There are all these bombs and detonators and cockpit equipment and what not that are always making their little electronic noises. And then some location or time or something gets written on the screen and it beeps as it types out. I guess that is the type of fancy computers they have in the counterterrorism community – the ones that go bloop bloop bloop when they type out where you are and what time it is in all capital letters. They got some ridiculous computers in that business. No wonder they couldn't stop 9-11.

Executive Decision, 1996
Directed by Stuart Baird (supervising editor of *Die Hard 2*).
Written by Jim Thomas & John Thomas (*Predator*).
Distinguished co-stars: Kurt Russell, Joe Morton, John Leguizamo, Oliver Platt, B.D. Wong, J.T. Walsh, Oscar winner Halle Berry.
Seagal regulars: John Leguizamo had a walk-on as "Boy in Alley" in *Out For Justice*, so this is a big step forward for him. Robert Apisa (Jean-Paul Demou) appears uncredited in *The Glimmer Man* as Smith's bodyguard. Joe Cook, who plays a Chechen, plays William T. Bowers (uncredited) in *Half Past Dead*.
Firsts: First supporting role for Seagal. First movie where he dies.
Title refers to: The secretary of defense's executive decision to shoot down the plane.
Just how badass is this guy? They never say.
Languages: English, hand signals.
Political themes: President is out of the country during national crisis. Administration won't shoot down plane because it will hurt re-election. Poirot became a terrorist because his family was killed in the Gulf War. Military and intelligence agents don't trust each other. Sleazy senator on plane (J.T. Walsh) only tries to intervene when it's pointed out that it could help him in his presidential campaign.
Cover accuracy: The cover is honest enough to show Kurt Russell and not Seagal (Seagal might be one of the dudes in silhouette though). There are no big names listed, and Seagal gets the "and" credit at the bottom, so it is not misleading.

CHAPTER 8:
THE GLIMMER MAN

"You are one mysterious motherfucker."

With *Under Siege*, Seagal had combined his own brand of action with the popular *Die Hard* formula and brought his career as a mainstream action star to new heights. But by 1996 the Die-Hard-on-a-blank subgenre was old hat. One newer trend was the gloomy serial killer thrillers pathetically trailing in the footsteps of David Fincher's 1995 picture *Seven*. With *The Glimmer Man*, Seagal unwisely combined his usual CIA corruption themes with a serial killer plot and *Lethal Weapon* type buddy movie and ended up with what I consider one of his worst pictures. And in fact, this might be the stumble that caused Seagal to fall out of the role of traditional Hollywood movie star, forcing him to reinvent himself as a prolific creator of DTV action. If it weren't for the superior *Fire Down Below*, this movie would be the clear tipping point between Seagal's classics and the ones where fans had to lower their expectations.

Seagal plays Vietnam vet ex-CIA-assassin New York homicide detective Jack Cole, who has just arrived in LA to team up with wisecracking LAPD detective Jim Campbell (*I'm Gonna Git You Sucka* director Keenen Ivory Wayans) to track "The Family Man," a sicko who has been killing Catholic families and nailing their bodies to the wall, Jesus style. Which in my opinion is an incorrect interpretation of the scriptures. You're not supposed to do that, if you ask me. Just my two cents.

Soon Cole and Campbell notice a change in the murders, and the trail leads to a local rich guy, the Russian mafia, the CIA and – holy fucking crap – Cole himself, as Campbell begins to uncover his connections to the victims and pieces of his Mysterious Past. Who knows what will happen?

(I do. A bunch of people will get thrown through windows.)

One thing I do like is that Seagal lets it all hang out in this one. He just doesn't give a fuck what other people think of him, even when his own sidekick keeps making fun of him. From the very beginning Cole is unapologetically the later Elvis-in-the'70s Seagal that people make fun of. He's noticeably larger than in previous movies and wears a shiny Asian-themed jacket with Tibetan prayer beads. He's still able to do some fighting but some of his dialogue is hard to understand and he delivers a lot of his lines in a smarmy, sarcastic tone that I guess must be his way of riffing with his comedian co-star.

For the first time the other characters actually comment on Seagal's unique fashion sense, saying "Nice coat," calling him "Mr. Love Beads" and ridiculing his "sensitive ponytail." The fashion in this movie really is incredible, with Seagal sporting all kinds of crazy outfits except for in one conspicuous scene where he gets a polygraph test from internal affairs and wears a regular suit and tie. It's weird to see Seagal wearing what a real cop might wear. I guess you gotta be professional when you're getting a polygraph. But it would suck if he was uncomfortable in the tie and it made him fail the test.

I assumed at first that these giant shiny coats must be the reason the movie is called *The Glimmer Man*. But late in the movie they get around to explaining that Cole had that nickname as a CIA assassin because "Suffice it to say to the people he hunted for us he was known as the Glimmer Man. There'd be nothing but jungle... then a glimmer... then you'd be dead."

That brings up some questions. Mainly what in shit's name kind of a nickname is that? And why would you see a glimmer? Are we really supposed to believe this big old lump is so quick you only see a glimmer before he kills you? And what exactly is this glimmer like, anyway? Could he also be called the Dazzler? Or the Sparkler? Or the Twinkler?

The Shimmery Man? And for that matter, if these people are all dead then how does anybody know whether or not they saw a glimmer? Maybe they happened to blink right when the glimmer happened, and they only saw jungle, not glimmer. Or maybe they saw Cole clearly, with or without the glimmer, but just weren't able to defend themselves. You can't just assume they saw a glimmer unless there is some kind of evidence. Unless somebody carved "glimmer" into the jungle floor with a twig as they gasped their last breath, this glimmer man story just does not hold water.

The screenwriter, Kevin Brodbin, is an Irish former journalist and publisher, who was involved with the publication of *Empire* magazine. *The Glimmer Man* was the first script he ever wrote, he sold it on spec. Still, I wouldn't be surprised if he just wrote down "Glimmer Man" as a placeholder, assuming he would go in and put something better there later, and then he just never got around to it. I can't imagine another likely explanation. I have a hard time buying the idea of somebody writing that on purpose. Oh well, at least it's an original title. It stands out.

The action is a pretty good mix of the old school street fighting Seagal and the *Under Siege* big explosions Seagal. There are several fights, including one where 3 guys finally figure out to pile on him at the same time instead of taking turns (he uses a nutgrab to escape). Nobody yells "My nuts!" or "My balls!" but he does make one guy scream "ow ow ow ow ow ow ow!" Then there's a big car crash scene where his car flips and skids down the street upside down, and he climbs out the window before it crashes into (I bet you can't guess it) a gas truck, causing a huge explosion (ah shit, how did you guess it? Have you seen this movie already?)

But it would be wrong not to point out that this movie has a weird over-reliance on the old man-through-window trick. Seagal does this in almost every movie, but in this one he does nine different variations on it. Let's take a look:

To save the life of a suicidal teen, Cole tackles the kid, carrying him out through a window (1) and back in through another (2). Later, he goes into a restaurant for corrupt CIA fuckers, gets in a fight, and throws a guy through a window (3). On his way out he gets in another fight and throws another guy through a window (4) and then another guy (5). Later Campbell gets in a fight on his own, his TV gets knocked over and somehow that causes a huge fire (?). So he has to jump through the window (6) to escape a fiery explosion. (He lands on a car, breaking its windows by crushing it – you know the routine – but we won't count those since he doesn't actually make contact with the windows.) Soon after that he is in a hotel, gets shot, and falls through a window (7). But he hangs onto the ledge, so Cole rappels down, grabs him and swings in through another window (8). Then Cole fights the main bad guy Donald and yes, throws him through a window (9). I am convinced that this movie was sponsored by the North American Sugar Glass Workers Union.

The Glimmer Man came out only a year after *Seven*, and it must've taken Brodbin some time to sell the script, but it's still hard to believe all the similarities are a coincidence. Mismatched white/black detective duo hunt Catholic-themed serial killer in a city where it always rains (Los Angeles!), then it gets personal when someone close to the detective becomes a victim. They even do a half-assed rendition of Seven's arty opening credits montage. I guess maybe the script just happened to be similar and then they threw in the credits and the rain because of the popularity of *Seven*? Hard to say.

And obviously the script had to be somewhat rewritten to fit Seagal. I doubt Brodbin just happened to write one about a Buddhist cop. And the use of herbal remedies is something Seagal had been interested in for years.

I'm sorry to report that I don't think Seagal is cut out for serial killer movies. They're just too gloomy. He's obviously not going to pull off a seriously gritty murder drama, and it's more fun to root for him to fight off an army of thugs than one murdering pervert. The attempts at dark humor are just kind of creepy and awkward. It's not funny to see Seagal tease Wayans about his home and all his belongings being burnt to ashes. And there's a fucked up scene in the morgue where Cole slits open a dead woman to show that she has breast implants. At the very end they make a big joke where Campbell complains that Cole has ruined his life, but it's not very funny because it's too true. He should've just left that poor bastard alone. I mean look, I'm not a *Scary Movie* fan either, but that doesn't mean the guy has to get completely fucked over.

And there are some weird loose ends. Like why did the CIA killers put Cole's fingerprint on a body? They need to make up their mind whether they're trying to pin this on The Family Man or The Glimmer Man. That just didn't make any sense.

There is kind of a parallel going on between Cole and the serial killer. They both have their nicknames – The Glimmer Man and The Family Man – based on the circumstances of their murders. The killer is a weirdo who got so religious he started crucifying people for his God. Cole is sort of the other way around, a CIA killer who "ended up in Thailand, chanting in some temple or other. They say he was saved by a holy man." He is now a Buddhist and says violence is against his religion (although he makes many, many exceptions throughout the movie). When he tracks down the killer in a church he says "This is God's house, don't make me do this." Then he shoots the man and looks up to the sky as if checking for God's reaction.

With all this traveling and discovering himself and crap, it's no wonder he seems so detached from his family. He mentions early on that "the ex moved out with the kids[38]." Then the ex gets killed, and he goes to the woman the kids are staying with to tell them the bad news. And you're kind of thinking, what are the kids doing staying with this lady? And is Cole just gonna leave them there? Shouldn't the kids be with their surviving parent, even if it's this guy?

Later on in the movie he says to "tell my wife I'm okay." So my only guess is that lady must've been his wife! But why did he act like she was just the babysitter or something? What kind of a husband is this guy? He just blew one marriage and he's already blowing off this one? What a jackass. Er, uh, maybe not a jackass, per se. Did I say jackass? I don't think I said jackass. Hey, what was that glimmer just now?

And then there's the whole buddy movie aspect. Wayans tries to play it half serious and half wiseass, with most of his jokes being obvious jabs

---

38 The daughter, by the way, is Alexa Vega, one of the stars of those *Spy Kids* movies.

at Cole's necklace or his love of Chinese herbal remedies. You can tell Seagal is trying to be funny too. Director John Gray said, "I think the audience will see another side of Steven, a side that shows humor without giving up anything they might expect from him." But there just aren't good jokes in this movie. He's funnier when he's playing it straight.

The Glimmer Man, *1996*
Directed by John Gray (writer and director of TV movies including *The Day Lincoln Was Shot* and the 2001 remake of *Brian's Song*. Not the same guy who wrote *Men Are From Mars, Women Are From Venus*).
Written by Kevin Brodbin (*Mindhunters, Constantine*).
Distinguished co-stars: Brian Cox.
Seagal regulars: Tommy Lee Jones could've been a returning Seagal vet. He was set to play Mr. Smith, but dropped out shortly before filming. I'm not sure what he did instead, since he had no movies released in 1996 – his next one was *Volcano* in '97. John P. Gulino (*Task Force Lawyer*) is a serious Seagal regular, playing Joey Chips in *Fire Down Below*, Hotel Manager in *The Foreigner*, Marshall in *Today You Die*, and a jewelry store owner in *Black Dawn*. He's even in the Seagal produced *Prince of Central Park* playing the deputy mayor. George Fisher (Misha) did stunts in two of the most important pictures in Seagalogy, *Above the Law* and *On Deadly Ground*. Viktor Ivanov (one of the Russian detectives) did stunts in *Executive Decision*. Somebody named Maridean Mansfield Shepard is apparently an uncredited extra as a homeless woman in this one and as a casino patron in *Fire Down Below*.
Firsts: First Seagal buddy movie. First time bad guys make fun of his clothes and ponytail. First movie score by Yes guitarist Trevor Rabin, who would go on to become one of Jerry Bruckheimer's favorite composers for crappy action movies. First screenplay by Kevin Brodbin, who went on to write *Constantine* as well as Renny Harlin's entertainingly ridiculous *Mindhunters*.
Title refers to: Seagal, who was once nicknamed "The Glimmer Man," due to some kind of glimmeriness that he caused.
Just how badass is this guy? "He was a brilliant soldier. West Point, that sort of thing. I found him in Vietnam. Recruited him for a special projects unit. The Program, we called it. He handled a lot of, uh, odd jobs for us... He was booted out of The Program in '84. Went native on us. Made up his own assignments. Disappeared for months."
Adopted culture: Tibetan buddhism, Chinese herbology.
Languages: English, Chinese, hand signals.
Improvised weapons: credit card (for slashing throats), bulldozer blade (for impaling), telephone.
Old friends: evil CIA head (Brian Cox).
Fight in bar: No, but there are two fights in a restaurant (one on the way in, one on the way out).
Broken glass: A new record: people thrown through 9 windows. Also a head through a TV.
Terms of endearment: buddy.

Words of wisdom: "Once in a while you should cry 'cause like, it cleanses the soul, you could use a little of that."

Most awkward line: "Now get your ugly white ass out of here, and don't come back."

Family shit: Has to tell his kids their mother is dead. Also apparently has a new wife.

Political themes: More CIA corruption. The head of the CIA sells chemical weapons to terrorists while at the same time testifying before Congress, who are trying to find out where they get their covert op funds. The terrorists are euphemistically referred to as "liberation fighters" before Campbell points out that means terrorists.

Cover accuracy: The blue tint on the collage of Seagal and Wayans's faces accurately conveys the gloomy tone of the movie. Also there is a cool shot of Seagal (I think) walking casually away from an explosion.

CHAPTER 9:
FIRE DOWN BELOW

"Well ain't you slicker 'n possum shit?"

Fire *Down Below* is a huge step up after the gloomy misfire of *The Glimmer Man.* Other than the usual dumb Hollywood stereotypes about small towns and country folk, it's pretty respectable as a Kentucky fried version of the classic Seagal formula.

(Get it, Kentucky fried? Because it takes place in Kentucky. That was like clever movie critic wordplay type shit. Not to brag but that coulda been right there in *Entertainment Weekly.* That was slick.)

Seagal plays Jack Taggert, an armed Environmental Protection Agency agent who goes undercover as a carpenter for the "Appalachian Relief Mission" in a small Kentucky town to investigate reports of deadly toxic waste being dumped near the water supply. (Do EPA agents really go undercover? And do they really carry guns? Are they allowed to kill somebody if it will help the environment? Are they required to recycle their bullet shells? I don't know the answers to any of these questions.)

The thing opens with a short montage of photos of Appalachian types playing banjos, and zooms in on one kid that I guess maybe is supposed to be Seagal. So it's sort of like the bluegrass version of *Above the Law* (which opened with actual photos of young Seagal). The opening credits play over shots of Seagal flying a small plane into the Appalachians, as he flashes back to brief clips that explain everything we need to know:

his partner was sent to investigate pollution reports and is the latest in a long line of federal agents to die in the area. Now it's his turn to investigate, and he has to find witnesses this time or the charges won't stick. I liked this quick and to the point opening, which doesn't waste the first 15 minutes to establish that he appreciates the partner's friendship and that it means a lot to him. Instead they just show him saying, "I appreciate the friendship. It means a lot to me."

Seagal drives into town in a red pickup truck saying he's "Just here doin' God's work." He hangs out with the reverend (Levon Helm, drummer for The Band), visits kids with mysterious illnesses and starts fixing people's roofs, porches and steps. Meanwhile he's "asking a lot of questions" and sneaking off to take water samples. The first fight comes when a kid pees into the waterfall that he's taking samples from. He angrily chases down the kid and is led right onto a marijuana field, whose proprietors are not happy to see him. He makes some lame jokes about the movie *Deliverance* but also has a good line: "I was just out for a Sunday stroll. I guess it's not Sunday." Then he does some aikido moves, steals a guy's gun, gives the gun to the peeing kid and struts off. It would've been cool if the kid shot him in the back and he had to figure out what to do from there. I mean, that's what the *Gummo* kids would've done. But oh well. Maybe some other movie.

As the story continues Taggert starts helping out Sarah Kellogg (Marge Helgenberger), a beekeeper who has been the town misfit ever since she was wrongly accused of killing her dad when she was 16. Also she needs her steps fixed, but it turns out that is not a euphemism for anything, it is actually a literal description of a problem she has with her house. Meanwhile, most of the town works to stop Taggert from finding evidence of the dumping, because they're either paid off by or directly working for the people responsible. In on it are the sheriff (country singer Ed Bruce), the weasely son of the mogul responsible (Brad Hunt), and some redneck henchmen. Even Taggert's buddy the reverend is being careful not to give him any useful information, because he wants to keep his church open.

The guy responsible for dumping the waste is Orin Hanner, Sr. (country singer Kris Kristofferson [*Blade*, *Payback*]), who grew up in this town but for most of the movie stays at a distance in his penthouse office in the big city. He seems to spend all his time hanging out with young model types, and he even has a bed in his office. In the grand tradition of Senator Trent's poor jacuzzi etiquette in *Above the Law*, Hanner rudely throws out the brunette he's about to get it on with (Petrice Jordan) by saying, "Cover up and get the hell out of here, Natalie. I've got a meeting." Later a blonde (Lisa Coles) who runs away in the face of violence says, "Call me." There is a scene where he plays golf inside the casino he owns while drinking champagne and talking on his cell phone. If that's not an asshole, I don't know what is. Plus, he uses his son Orin Jr. as the hole and throws money on the ground for him, calling it his "allowance."

So that shows what a jerk Hanner Sr. is, and to show what a nice guy Taggert is there's a scene where he sees that Sarah hasn't sold enough honey to pay for all her groceries, so he buys the rest of her groceries and all of her honey and then gives her a ride home. (But if you watch the scene it seems that he never actually gives her the groceries. I'm sure this was not intentional. He has a lot on his mind with the investigation, he just gets forgetful is all.) Later there is a scene where she goes to get something out of his truck, finds his handgun, and gets scared. At first I thought it was weird that somebody out in the Appalachians would be surprised to find a gun, especially in a pickup truck. But I figure maybe it's because it's a handgun and not a rifle. She might think he's a little bit fruity to be carrying around such a small gun.

Hanner's son runs the cover-up operation in town and tries desperately to earn his dad's respect. His reward is constant humiliation. When he asks if he should "take out" Taggert, pops says, "You couldn't take out a cheeseburger from a drive-thru window." His dad tells him to instead have Sheriff Lloyd "get something on him" and get witnesses. "I can do that with one phone call," Junior says proudly. (Let me guess – the phone call will be to Sheriff Lloyd, and you will tell him to get something on Taggert and get witnesses. Man, you really know how to handle this shit, junior.)

Junior is not a fighter. He spends most of the movie pouting and whining. At an outdoor dance, Taggert spontaneously climbs on stage and plays guitar with the band, and Junior looks jealous. I guess he can't play guitar either. There are not any scenes where Taggert outshoots him at hoops or lifts bigger weights than him though, unless those scenes were cut. Maybe they could've had a race or a tug of war match also. But no, just the guitar scene.

When Taggert finally faces Junior down in a bar and beats up all of his minions, he gives him a speech about "doing the right thing." Like Big Mike in *On Deadly Ground*'s similar bar scene, Junior breaks down. He says, "Yes sir." This demonstrates that Taggert is a more respectable father figure than his actual father, even with his ponytail and goofy coats.

Another parallel to *On Deadly Ground* is that Seagal gets to make an undeniably correct but socially awkward speech. But this time they were clever enough to work it into the plot instead of sticking it at the very end where everybody would get up and leave. Taggert walks into the church in the middle of Sunday service, walks right up to the pulpit and says, "Excuse me reverend, do you mind if I say a few words? Thank you all. Please be seated." And then he basically says it's time to cut the shit, everybody knows what's going on here and everybody knows what needs to be changed. Rich people are taking advantage of you and you are letting it happen. "And if there's anybody out there who thinks that the $300 that they gave you to buy a new satellite or look the other way is worth selling out the legacy of your ancestors and the future of your children, please raise your hand."

(I personally could relate to this scene, because I remember this one time Bush sent me a tax cut refund check to pay me off while he tossed out every possible social program and committed atrocities across the planet. It came with a letter recommending that I buy myself a DVD player. I mean thanks for the money asshole but I'd rather not be involved in this mess. In other words, if I was in that church I would not be raising my hand.)

Most people will laugh at this scene, and I know I did. But at the same time I have to admit that it's pretty fucking cool. If somebody walked into my church and made that speech, I would enjoy it. It's better than yet another sermon trying to find wisdom in the Sunday funnies. I mean I love Jesus and I love Snoopy but let's keep them separate. You don't want to cross that line. Anyway, righteous indignation in action movies hasn't been this good since *Billy Jack*, if ever. There are so many situations in life where people are doing stupid shit for a little money. I wish you could call upon Taggert to come make that speech and make the fuckers feel guilty.

Fire Down Below is a less silly attempt at an environmentally-themed action movie than the previous effort. The politics are similar, pointing out how heartless corporations take advantage of the poor and can get away with anything because the fines for polluting are much lower than the amount of money they save by doing it. And though they show the EPA as being pro-active enough to send in armed undercover badasses to take care of business, it also turns out that Taggert's boss is a stooge for the polluters, just like in real life. The character's relationship with the people of Kentucky seems slightly less condescending than his Native American journeys in *On Deadly Ground*. He fixes their houses up and talks about all the nice people he's met all over Appalachia, but he never dresses up like them.

In addition to the environmental issues, *Fire Down Below* shows another one of Seagal's passions: music. It's the first time he plays guitar onscreen. The cast is also loaded with musicians: Kristofferson, Bruce (co-writer of "Mamas Don't Let Your Babies Grow Up To Be Cowboys"), Helm, Harry Dean Stanton, Mark Collie, Alex Harvey (songwriter for Kenny Rogers), Randy Travis, Marty Stuart and Travis Tritt. There's even an appearance by Loretta Lynn's twin daughters Patsy and Peggy.

As an actor, Seagal is on his best behavior. He gets some pretty good lines and he delivers them with more charm than usual – there's not much of the smarmy, sarcastic tone he usually uses for banter with villains. Best of all there is a legitimately good truck chase between his pickup and a Mack truck, one of the best vehicle action scenes in any of his films. In the end a bullfighting type maneuver on Taggert's part causes the death of his pickup but also causes the Mack to drop 300 feet off a cliff. So it's a tie. (This scene apparently took 2 weeks to film and the drop was shot from seven different cameras.)

It's nice to see that the town mostly accepts Taggert, despite his tastes for the usual outlandish Seagalian fashion styles. He wears a long black leather jacket with multi-colored stripes, a fancy Asian flower-themed shirt, and in one scene a fringe jacket like in *On Deadly Ground*. The worst they do to make fun of him is call him "pretty boy." He doesn't look fat, but many of his moves are noticeably sped up. The fight scenes are mostly short, but involve lots of broken noses and arms, at least 5 direct hits to the balls and a few large explosions.

There is of course a scene where toxic waste spews onto the bad guys, and it is glow-in-the dark green. Just like in cartoons. There's also a part where he grabs two snakes that somebody put in his house. The most memorable action scene besides the truck chase is a shootout at the gas station, and you could probably guess what flammable liquid ends up spraying everywhere. Seagal throws a lit flare right into a gas pond, knowing that one of Hanner's henchmen will catch it. Then he says, "Tell your boss I'm coming to get him. You know what, on second thought, I'll tell him." And he shoots the flare out of the guy's hand, so it will fall into the gas... but then shoots it again somehow knocking the fuse off and saving the day. (He does not say "Psyche" or "Just playin'.")

Once we find out that the EPA is corrupt and powerless over polluters, Taggert says that he has quit the EPA. This makes sense until later when he reveals that he was "just kidding" and is actually in the EPA. I don't get the joke, I guess. Otherwise, this is an underrated, top of the line Seagal movie in my book. (My book is called *Seagalogy*.)

Fire Down Below, 1997
Directed by Félix Enríquez Alcalá (directed episodes of *ER*, *Sliders*, *Profiler*, *L.A. Firefighters*, etc. The only TV he's done that I can vouch for are his two episodes of *Blade: The Series*, which were topnotch).
Written by Jeb Stuart (one of the writers of *Die Hard*! Also *48 Hours* and *The Fugitive*) and Philip Morton (some TV movie called *12:01*).
Distinguished co-stars: Kris Kristofferson, Marge Helgenberger, Harry Dean Stanton, various country music celebrities, photos by Shelby Lee Adams.
Seagal regulars: Dan Beene (Dilbert the Grocer) plays Richard Bach in *The Patriot*. John P. Gulino (Joey Chips) is in *The Glimmer Man*, *The Foreigner*, *Today You Die* and *Black Dawn*. There's apparently an uncredited casino patron named Maridian Mansfield Shepard who was an uncredited homeless woman in *The Glimmer Man* and an uncredited casino bouncer named Larry Reynosa did stunts in *Above the Law*, *Marked For Death* and *The Glimmer Man*. Lisa Coles, who plays the "Blonde Beauty," will return as a reporter in *Today You Die*.
Firsts: First time Seagal plays guitar on camera.
Title refers to: The fiery day-glow green toxic waste beneath the town.
Just how badass is this guy? He makes a guy scream "Ow! My nose! My nose!" and another guy yells, "I've never been hit so hard in my life!"

Adopted culture: He mostly stays true to himself, but he does show off his bluegrass guitar skills.

Languages: English.

Improvised weapons: lumber from the back of his pickup truck.

Fight in bar: Yes.

Broken glass: Various truck windows, lights in mine, diner windows, cooler in convenience store.

Terms of endearment: buddy, baby.

Most awkward one-liner: "You're a piece of shit, and I'm ashamed of you."

Family shit: He specifically states that he has no family.

Political themes: Business abusing the environment in their quest for money (this time the pollution glows in the dark, so it's easier to spot than in *On Deadly Ground*). Poor people are paid off to support causes that go against their interests.

Cover accuracy: The art is dominated by a large blue Seagal face, but it also depicts some sort of night time fire at the bottom, which is an overly literal take on the title, in my opinion.

interlude:
MY GIANT

My *Giant* is a 1998 comedy starring Billy Crystal, inspired by his friendship with wrestling legend/iconic sticker Andre the Giant. In the movie Crystal's character befriends a giant man who he finds is doomed to die of heart defects, much like Andre. (Don't feel too bad though, Crystal's relationship with Andre lasted 3-4 days while filming *The Princess Bride*). Crystal plays an obnoxious wannabe Hollywood agent who has a wacky slapstick car accident and is saved by a giant named Max, played by 7'7" Transylvanian ex-center for the Washington Wizards Gheorghe Muresan.

Part of the plot revolves around Crystal trying to get Muresan a part as the villain in a Steven Seagal film called *Double Or Nothing*. Seagal's character would be trying to stop terrorists from blowing up the Las Vegas strip. Seagal of course plays himself and you see him filming one fight scene, then being introduced to Muresan. Seagal portrays himself as kind of a dick, but not really enough to be funny. He tries to be nice and as a favor calls Crystal's son on the phone. But the kid doesn't believe it's him and makes fun of his acting and ponytail.

Although Seagal is in the movie for less than 10 minutes, Warner Brothers figured he was enough of a selling point to put his picture on the back of the DVD and mention him in the plot description. Still, the fact that he was parodying himself in a lame Billy Crystal comedy may have been damaging to his momentum. After all, he followed it up with what would accidentally become his first direct-to-video feature.

On its own and not just as a curiosity for Seagal completists, *My Giant* is a little below passable. I kind of like the premise and Muresan is a good choice for playing an Andre the Giant type. (In recent years, Matthew McGrory from *The Devil's Rejects* and *Big Fish* was supposed to star in a movie about Andre, but he died before it came together.) Unfortunately, the very best jokes are only mildly amusing, the portrayal of filmmaking doesn't seem even remotely believable and there's a plodding orchestral score trying to convince you it's a whimsical fairy tale. I'm sorry, but if it's a shot of Billy Crystal driving along a road in a convertible I don't want some orchestra trying to convince me it's fuckin *Batman*. Worst of all, Crystal spends the whole movie lying to the childlike Muresan to exploit him, and by the time he sort of straightens things out at the end we already decided he was a dickhead 90 minutes ago. Sorry bud, too little too late. I'm sure they'll still let you sing corny parody songs at the Oscars, though. They don't care about cruelty to giants over there.

To this day, Seagal has never abused a giant.

[transtional period]

1998-2002

CHAPTER 10:
THE PATRIOT

"You're the best damn immunologist we have in this country."

Seagal plays Dr. Wesley McClaren, an ex-CIA naturopathic doctor in the small town of Ennis, Montana. The picture begins with Seagal's animal motif so familiar from *On Deadly Ground*. We see an elk before we see any humans, then a herd of cattle as McClaren and his grizzled sidekick Frank (L.Q. Jones) ride in on horses and lasso a sick cow so they can give him an herbal shot (the doc says antibiotics don't work anymore). Then they follow the vultures to find a sick baby horse. Knowing that the movie is about a deadly virus, you assume the horse is the first victim – a warning shot, a canary in a mine shaft, a dramatic omen of the horrors to come. No, turns out it's not the virus, this scene has nothing to do with anything. But McClaren has a daughter named Holly (Camilla Belle) who is a girl, so she likes ponies.

After Dr. McClaren nurses the baby horse with what Frank calls "home cooked jungle juice," the doctor heads for the office. He is held off by a break in the police standoff that has been going on with Floyd Chisolm, a local militia leader who quizzes his troops on Thomas Jefferson and FDR quotes before swallowing a few drops of a deadly chemical weapon and going to give himself up. Floyd is portrayed as a very misguided patriot. The TV news refers to him as a neo-nazi, but we see no evidence of this – I'm guessing it was a postproduction decision to make sure the audience isn't tempted to side with him.

It's implied that the hero and villain may know each other personally, although it's a little more ambiguous than in *Under Siege*. Dr. McClaren refers to Floyd by his first name, but there is no acknowledgment that they met at a gun show or were in an American history book club together or whatever.

Anyway the doctor gets to the office where we see that he is real popular. What I mean by that is there's a looped line of somebody honking their horn and yelling, "Hey how you doin' Doc?" as he crosses the street. He helps the elderly townsfolk, who can't afford to pay for his services, but luckily he's willing to barter for carpentry and blackberry pies. "We'll get that kidney up 'n runnin'," he says.

But McClaren can't live the humble pie-eating life of a small town doctor forever. Before he knows it, Floyd (on trial for sawing off a shotgun on video) has spit in the face of a judge and begun the spread of the deadly man-made virus. It turns out that the reason McClaren quit the CIA is because they had used things he created "in the wrong way" and wouldn't listen to him about the danger of stockpiling chemical and biological weapons. Sure enough, there has been some NAM-37 missing, and it has indeed fallen into the wrong hands. Hands belonging to Floyd. And now the Man wants McClaren to help clean up their mess.

But McClaren don't work for the Man no more. He works for the people of Ennis, Montana. If you're thinking he's going to start kicking ass, fighting off the terrorists with his deadly CIA doctor skills – well, believe it or not you're actually thinking wrong. Because it turns out – and I'm guessing this is why the movie went straight to video – he's not so much an ass kicker as an ass healer. Sure, there is an action scene in the hospital about 42 minutes in. He kicks a guy into a vending machine and there is a hilarious shot of him punching a guy who then falls softly through a very thin wall. And there's another small bit of action, sort of, 70 minutes in when he steals a gun from a soldier trying to cuff him. But most of this movie is not about action. It's about Dr. McClaren trying to care for the sick, watching the virus spread, discovering that for some reason his half Native American daughter, his Native American sister-in-law and his Native American father-in-law are all immune to the virus. Hmmmm…what is the pattern? It's hard to imagine what kind of common denominator there could be between these three Native Americans.

At a certain point in the movie I started to wonder what the deal is with this guy Frank, anyway. I know Seagal characters often have loyal friends, but it seems like there must be something going on here that they're not telling us. Frank seems to be on call 24 hours to do favors for McClaren. He rides with him, watches his daughter, delivers messages, brings him coffee, and even blows up a car with dynamite to save him. All throughout the movie McClaren will call Frank and ask him to do some task, and Frank immediately does, like he doesn't have his own life. A doctor in a small town in Montana doesn't get a personal assistant, does he? I don't get it. I know loyalty is a virtue but Frank seems to go way too far, like he's the good doctor's manservant or something.

I started to wonder, you know, maybe these two are in love, but they are afraid to tell Holly, or maybe they don't want the town to know about it. But just when I started to wonder that, Frank pulled some stupid shit, turned his back on some guys he shot and started doing a jig. So he gets shot and dies. McClaren comes by just in time to yell, "Fraaaank!" and see the dead cowboy's hat float away in the wind (almost as if he faded away, like one of those Jedis). But the way McClaren reacts to his buddy's death... I'm pretty sure he didn't just lose the love of his life. I figure they were just real good friends. Unless he's very good at hiding his emotions. But even Heath Ledger smelled that jacket at the end of *Brokeback Mountain*. I think you'd be able to tell for sure if they were in love. Not that it's any of our business.

There is one thing that happens here that you don't see in most movies. After Frank dies, McClaren actually carries the body on horseback to where he wants to bury it. He doesn't just leave him there to rot like, say, Antonio Banderas did to Steve Buscemi in *Desperado*. I guess when you're a doctor you have the stomach for carrying around dead bodies. To be fair, Seagal's character also carried the body of Charles, the Jamaican cop in *Marked For Death*, but that was the end credits, and usually in the middle of the story filmatists find it's easier not to deal with burial.

Dr. McClaren may have a bunch of friends and a blackberry pie, but he's gonna need the resources of his former employer if he's gonna stop this virus from killing everybody. So he puts on some round glasses, cooks up a fake DARPA ID card on his computer (they should really start using a watermark or hologram or something), and brings his botanist sister-in-law to a secret underground military complex in the mountains that nobody else knew about. (I guess the ID must be good for him plus one.) After convincing the infected soldiers that he's supposed to be there, there is a climactic scientific research montage, full of thrilling beakers and intense test tubes. After hours of bubbling and mixing different colored liquids has failed to save the world, McClaren throws a fit and smashes everything in his office. Then, in the grand tradition of the invention of penicillin, they discover the cure by accident: it's Grandpa's Native American tea recipe, made out of wildflowers he calls "red medicine." Grandpa may spend too much time in the "spirit world," but it turns out his flowers are the antidote to NAM-37, so planes fly over Ennis and dump flowers on everybody. It's like a parade.

They never mention why McClaren didn't catch the virus. Maybe he is so down with Native Americans that he too is immune.

The politics of the movie are pretty unorthodox. It has the usual Seagalian disdain for the behavior of covert government agencies, but this time it adds the element of the militia movement. The militia here are killers and nazis, as you'd expect. But Seagal goes out of his way to show sympathy for their movement. A news reporter makes reference to the sieges at Waco and Ruby Ridge as "fiascos" – an accurate description, but not one we'd really see on the TV news. In one of Seagal's trademark probably-ad-libbed touches, he states at one point "I think the ideology of some of these folks is good." And Floyd's criticisms of the government are shown to have some validity. These are not sentiments you usually see in an action movie. Of course, Floyd doesn't live up to his idealistic statements. After many innocent people have suffered, one disillusioned, baby-faced follower asks Floyd, almost in tears "Is this what Thomas Jefferson would've wanted?" (So the kid has come to his senses, I guess[39], but I seem to remember hearing these guys were neo-nazis. Makes it hard to side with him.)

---

39 Kind of like the hijacker in *Executive Decision* who decides what Poirot is doing has nothing to do with Islam.

More notable is the chemical weapons theme. McClaren says, "You gotta destroy this shit. You cannot keep stockpiling this stuff." In The Post 9-11 World, where anthrax attacks are a reality and stolen chemical weapons seem like a likely scenario, Seagal seems ahead of his time yet again.

The Patriot is written by M. Sussman and John Kingswell, adapted from the 1974 novel *The Last Canadian* (also published as *The Last American* and *Death Wind*) by Canadian journalist William C. Heine. Now you gotta give these two credit because they adapted the shit out of this book. They adapted it so much that the movie has almost nothing to do with the book.

The book tells the story of Gene Arnprior, an American expatriate living in Canada who sees on the news one day that a mysterious virus is killing Americans, first in a small mountain village west of Denver and then spreading rapidly across the country. Gene has a bad feeling and immediately borrows a company plane and takes his wife and two sons out to a remote cabin. This turns out to be a good idea because in less than a week there are only a few thousand people left alive on the continent.

In *The Patriot*, the virus never leaves the small town and Steven Seagal discovers a cure for it. But the book is a little more epic. By page 50 all but a few thousand North Americans are dead, the United States government has put their military under British control, the president has been assassinated and astronauts have been stranded in space so long they decided to commit suicide. The Arnprior family stays in the cabin for three years, remodeling it for the winter, growing vegetables, learning how to hunt, prepare meat and find honey. Then a carrier of the virus happens to wander by, infecting and killing all but Gene.

At that point it turns into more of an *Omega Man/The Quiet Earth* kind of post-apocalyptic story as Gene (now a virus carrier) fixes up a motor home and travels the continent running into various survivors, having to kill some of them and falling in love with another. Like *Dawn of the Dead* he has lots of fun scavenging from society's leftovers that he finds in stores, hotels, etc. Heine puts a lot of thought into the survivalist aspects of the story, always allowing time for Gene to do maintenance on any vehicles he steals before they are operable. Even though he has the run of the continent it's not like he can just pick things up and be ready to go. He has to deal with a lack of electricity, deteriorating mechanical parts and other post-apocalyptic pains in the ass.

But the story gets pretty silly and dated when Gene starts running into problems with the Russian Army, who are watching the coast with submarines. He gets betrayed by a fellow survivor who is a Marxist and then starts getting targeted by the Russians. He manages to evade two atomic bombs (something Seagal has not tried yet, though he will throw an exploding suitcase bomb in the water in *Black Dawn*) but his girlfriend gets blown up. The Cold War theme is corny but you have to admit it gets pretty badass at this point because Gene blames the Russians for the death of his girlfriend, his wife, his sons, his country and his former country, so he decides he's going to travel there to infect them, knowing that just by setting foot there he will kill an entire continent.

In the movie the virus is unleashed by a neo-nazi militia to protest federal tyranny, here it is also man-made by a crazy Russian weapons designer who blames America for something that happened during the Vietnam War and infects them by sending a poisoned doll to a little American girl. In the end, the governments of England, Russia and China unite to nuke Asia, killing Gene and destroying the virus so that the world can start over again, and some of the debris lands on the graves of the Arnprior family and soaks into the soil so that Gene can be together with his loved ones. If Seagal had adapted the book faithfully it would've been his only death scene besides *Executive Decision*.

The only thing the movie has in common with the book is that there is a deadly virus spreading. Otherwise there is not a single character, name or incident that is the same or similar. Maybe the closest thing you could argue to a similar incident is that the carrier who comes by and causes Gene's family to die happens to be Native American, and in the movie Native Americans are immune to the virus. (But not carriers, and they don't kill the hero's family, they are his family.) So you could probably chalk this one up to coincidence.

I wonder what the deal is? Why would they pay money for the movie rights to an obscure book, and then make a different movie? At what point did this turn from an apocalyptic epic about a Canadian man travelling a dying continent to a Steven Seagal movie about a small town stopping a virus with potpourri? It's just one of those things, I guess.

The production values and acting are better than some of Seagal's subsequent movies, and for this we must credit Australian director Dean Semler. A highly acclaimed cinematographer, Semler won both the Academy Award and the American Cinematography Award for *Dances With Wolves*. But personally I'm much more impressed that he shot *Mad Max 2* and *Beyond Thunderdome*. As a director he's only done one other movie[40], the enjoyable forest fire action thriller *Firestorm* that attempted (and failed) to turn football player Howie Long into a bankable action star.

So in many ways *The Patriot* is an admirable effort, but due to its ridiculously low action quotient it is a least-favorite of many Seagal fans. In a way *The Patriot* is the virus that infected Seagal's filmography from that point on. Although it was reportedly intended for theatrical release, it broke the wall between Seagal and the DTV world. After this one skipped theaters, more and more of his movies were planned from the beginning as low budget straight to video affairs. Maybe he wanted to make less of an action movie and more of a drama, I don't know. But after this almost all of his movies were lower on action than in the old days (theatrical movies like *Exit Wounds* being happy exceptions) or relied on obvious stunt doubles.

The Patriot, 1998
Directed by Dean Semler (*Firestorm*, cinematographer for *Mad Max 2* and *Apocalypto*)
Written by M. Sussman and John Kingswell, based on the novel *The Last Canadian* by William Heine. Paul Mones (*Double Team*) was mentioned as the writer before the movie came out and was ultimately credited as co-producer.
Distinguished co-stars: Well, I wouldn't say distinguished, but Camilla Belle, who plays his daughter, has since gone on to become a well known young-hottie actress in movies like *When A Stranger Calls* (remake) and *The Quiet*. Also, Ayako Fujitani from the *Gamera: Guardian of the Universe* trilogy plays McLaren's assistant. In real life, of course, she's Seagal's daughter.
Seagal regulars: Dan Been (Richard Bach) played Dilbert the Grocer in *Fire Down Below*.

---

40 Unless you count *Super Mario Brothers*, where he was cinematographer and the Internet Movie Database lists him as one of four directors (he and Roland Joffé allegedly being uncredited directors).

Firsts: Seagal's first straight-to-video movie (but originally intended for theaters).

Title refers to: the militia nut villain, Floyd Chisholm, because he's part of the "patriot movement."

Just how badass is this guy? "Call the next man on the list." "There is no next man on the list."

Adopted culture: Native American (through marriage).

Languages: English, and a few ceremonial words in some Native American language.

Improvised weapons: Wine glass.

Old friends: "Little Richard," a guy working in contagion containment for the CIA.

Fight in bar: No.

Broken glass: 2 windows in the hospital, 1 vending machine, and Seagal jumps through a window with his daughter.

Single parenting skills: Above average. He cooks omelettes, makes a poo joke, scolds his daughter for not doing her homework on time. Lets her ride horses. Says, "I don't gamble with my little girl's heart." But he does say "asshole" in front of her.

Political themes: Unusually open-minded towards militias: "Listen, I got nothin' against playin' army. I don't mind that at all. I think the ideology of some of these folks is good. But there's assholes everywhere, and Floyd is an asshole." Against governments using chemical and biological weapons: "You gotta destroy this shit. You cannot keep stockpiling this stuff. It's what's gonna take out the human race. Now, whether it's the Russians, the Chinese or the Americans, somebody's gonna steal it and somebody's gonna let it go." There is talk of the CIA experimenting on people and Floyd even makes a reference to the CIA creating "this AIDS thing." Seagal's character shakes his head, possibly scoffing at the idea, though according to *Vanity Fair* Seagal once wrote a script about that very concept.

Cover accuracy: A giant Seagal head oversees three helicopters and a SWAT team out in a field. That works.

CHAPTER 11:
EXIT WOUNDS

"What am I, a shit magnet?"

From 2000-2003, director-of-photography turned director-of-every-thing-else Andrzej Bartkowiak created a loose trilogy of dumb action movies, all said to be based on other works. The pictures are all produced by Joel Silver and star a group I call "The Joel Silver Players": DMX, Anthony Anderson and Tom Arnold appear in all three pictures while Jet Li, Isaiah Washington and some kid named Drag-On each appear in two. The first, *Romeo Must Die*, was originally announced as an "urban" hip hop and kung fu update of Romeo and Juliet, but turned out to have very little connection to Shakespeare's play at all. The third was *Cradle 2 the Grave*, which believe it or not was described as an update of Fritz Lang's noir classic *M* when it was first announced in *The Hollywood Reporter*. It turned out to be something about a jewel heist, nuclear weapons and guys driving around doing tricks on four-wheelers. There's a part where Jet Li forces Mark Dacascos to swallow a nuclear weapon, then kicks him to make it explode. I've only seen *M* once but I feel confident in saying I would remember it if something like that happened to Peter Lorre's character.

But the subject here is #2 in the series, *Exit Wounds*, where Seagal sits in for Jet Li and the credits tell us it is based on the book by retired police officer turned author and writing professor John Westermann. Now to be fair, this movie has more to do with the book than *The Patriot* did with its alleged source material. For example, the main character has the same name and occupation, and there is one line of dialogue from the book that is also in the movie. But in my opinion, as well as in measurable scientific fact, it is not very faithful to the spirit or tone of the book.

Westermann's book is not a standard thriller. It is the story of fuckup police officer Orin Boyd, who gets transferred to the notorious Precinct 13 (15 in the movie, with respect to John Carpenter I guess) both as punishment and as an undercover mission to find proof of corruption. But you almost forget he's undercover. The story unfolds as more of a series of days in the life of lazy cops trying to avoid work, spending their shifts in bars or with their mistresses. The cops like to get in scuffles, make casually racist remarks and fart during briefings. It turns out late in the book that some of the officers were involved in beating a guy to death and covering it up, and are also working for a local reverend/crime boss. There is no fancy gimmick like manufacturing t-shirts soaked in heroin (as in the movie), just your usual street crime. Boyd only goes into action in the end when the sergeant who sent him to the precinct takes him off the case, and he decides to put on a John Travolta mask, go out and kidnap all the crack dealers and numbers runners that he's been learning about, take their money and run to Honduras.

It's a good book full of gritty detail and humorous observation, so as enjoyable as the movie is, it's kind of sad to watch this book get shamelessly retardified for the big screen. Westermann's Orin Boyd is an extremely troubled dude. He's an alcoholic, his bosses worry about him and even when he gets sent to detox he sneaks out for a drink. He's been depressed since his partner got cancer and retired. He hasn't gotten over his wife leaving him, and he follows her around spying on her having sex with her new boyfriend, even pulling out his gun and contemplating shooting either the boyfriend or himself in the head. He barely has a relationship with his young daughter, and when he tries to bring her to his ratty apartment on Christmas she's afraid to go inside.

In the movie though, he's not troubled at all. He's just another one of those cops that Plays By His Own Rules. The way he "fucks up" is to sneak off and single-handedly take on an army of militants to save the vice president of the United States (Chris Lawford) from assassination.

That part never happened in the book.

And he doesn't have a ratty apartment. His apartment is just fine, with a nice display of his commendations and medals on the wall, and a baseball in a baseball mitt to imply that he likes baseball. Which counts as characterization in a movie like this. In the book he drives a piece of shit pickup truck that breaks down on the freeway two different times. In the movie he drives a badass black El Camino that gets blown up during the assassination attempt, and the next day we see him driving a shiny black truck with the papers still attached to the window (like he went out and bought it that morning). When that one gets wrecked he forces Anthony Anderson to loan him his yellow Hummer, but he doesn't seem all that concerned about losing two cars in as many days. (Wait a minute, is he supposed to be on the take? I never picked up on this before.)

Also in the book he has a mustache. Why didn't Seagal grow a mustache for the movie? That would've been cool.

The movie Boyd does mention that his wife left him, and there is a line about Vietnam which could maybe be interpreted to imply the Vietnam vet background of the book's Boyd. But here he's a legendary hero cop who saved the vice president, who we never see drinking or contemplating suicide, who is forced to go into anger management only as comic relief (and we're supposed to laugh at the very idea of anger management classes). He's just like any other lead in a dumb action movie.

Since the type of police atmosphere depicted in the book has morphed into a ludicrous Hollywood version, it completely wipes out the substance of the story. Precinct 13 was a place where no woman had ever worked, because they were afraid to. The movie's Precinct 15 has a sexy female commander (Jill Hennessy). I wouldn't dream of giving away whether or not Boyd slips up and makes inappropriate comments to her before he realizes that she's the commander. The movie version of Boyd's partner George Clarke (Isaiah Washington) is a serious, good-hearted cop who wants to clean up the neighborhood he grew up in, and is devoted to his wife and young daughter. In the book he spends his shift standing against a brick wall until he can sneak into a bar. He tells Boyd, "Eight hours in the freakin' street, my dick gets hard and my balls start smoking. I need some pussy, and I ain't joking. Something my new bride don't quite understand yet." He has an ongoing affair with a Puerto Rican welfare mother named Gloria, who doesn't know he's married and always believes him when he says he's going to give her money to improve her situation, even though he never follows through.

The book does have a few incidents of violence. A couple police shootings, even a grenade at the end. The movie is a Steven Seagal movie though, and it's not called *The Patriot*, so it's full of epic car chases, huge fiery explosions, relentless shootouts, flips, kicks, people getting thrown through glass, etc. Okay, so the flips is something new. In order to come back to the big screen, Seagal had to give in to the popular 2000s trend of wirework. By being attached to wires later erased digitally, he was able to do moves gravity would not really allow, especially at his age. I didn't really believe he was doing some of these moves, but apparently he was. The making-of documentary on the DVD shows him on set with the wires, trying not to hurt himself. Unfortunately he did, while doing a motorcycle stunt, and limped around with a cane for the rest of shooting. (He can't complain – a stuntman named Chris Lamon apparently hit his head during the upside-down van slide and died six days later.)

Okay, so it's not the book, it's a Seagal movie. No fucking shit. So how good is it on that level, Vern. Well that's a simple question but it's a complicated answer.

On one hand, this is a movie that's gotten pretty far away from the personal touch of the early Seagal pictures. It contains none of the spiritual, ecological or CIA corruption themes that are dear to his heart. The only line that sounds like a possible Seagal improvisation is when he tells mean boss Bill Duke "You remind me of those bureaucrats in the '60s sending kids off to die in Vietnam." But later on this pays off in another exchange, so it was probably scripted.

Seagal's character has no family or close friends and doesn't even care about the safety of his vehicles, so there's not all that much at stake. There's nothing for him to get righteously indignant about. There are no speeches, no monologues.

In fact, I think Silver and the other producers made a conscious effort to make it less of a Seagal picture, thinking that would be the only way for him to have a big comeback. They made him lose weight, he cut his ponytail, he uses wires, there is no mention of the CIA, black ops or even special forces. There is one major hand-to-hand scene that is a little reminiscent of the Golden Era, but most of the action is of the post-*Under Siege*, big studio action movie variety: cars flipping and crashing, lots of guns, less martial arts. It's a less personal, less intimate type of violence.

On the other hand, the movie is well-produced and it's so silly and over-the-top that it's a hell of a lot of fun. Although it's not his last theatrical release it's better than Half Past Dead, so it's almost like his last hurrah for the big screen. While the action in general isn't as personal as I'd like, it is fun, and there's way more of it than in any of his movies since. Things get nasty, and more than one character is impaled. There are shootouts, car chases, man-to-man fights, improvised sword fights and more. If you just want to see the action scenes don't worry, you won't have to wait as long as you do in a lot of movies.

But the story is enjoyable too, because it's full of all kinds of ridiculous ideas and twists. You have to appreciate that bullshit with the vice president in the opening. And the heroin-soaked t-shirts thing has got to be the best clothing-related master plan since the exploding blue jean rivets in Van Damme's *Knock Off.* The screenwriters try to keep you guessing about who's on whose side, so more than one cop turns out to be a traitor. The one that I genuinely didn't see coming though (what I'm saying is this is a spoiler, people) was the twist with DMX. For the first half of the movie he seems to be a drug dealer villain. Then all the sudden in the middle of a fight he asks Boyd if he wants to see what's really going on, brings him inside to show an elaborate operation he has going on. Turns out he's not really a drug dealer, he's a "dot com gazillionaire" who has gone undercover with spy cams in order to tape cops committing crimes and broadcast the footage on the web. You don't get that in every movie.

Another big surprise is when the commander/possible love interest is abruptly killed in a car chase (there's an impressive shot of her head hitting the windshield). Boyd just gives a sad look, then steals a motorcycle and continues the chase! This is the difference between Orin Boyd and Casey Ryback. Ryback would've at least checked her pulse.

I've always gotten a kick out of the scene where Boyd blows up a helicopter using a handgun uzi-style. A reader named Hagen Voss informs me that Seagal's favored old school Colt 1911 did in fact have automatic models despite its 7-round magazine. But bullets that can blow up a helicopter? No wonder the VP wants to regulate handgun ownership. There's also a funny scene where Seagal and Michael Jai White yank the blades off of papercutters and use them as swords. Flipping ensues.

The supporting cast is strong. You got Isaiah Washington, who was great in *Out of Sight* but is now better known for referring to one of his co-stars as a "faggot" on the set of the TV show *Grey's Anatomy*. Then there's Michael Jai White, best known for being cut out of *Kill Bill*. He's not as good of an actor as Washington, but he's a better martial artist. He's the guy that everybody on the internet wanted to play Blade in the TV series before they cast Sticky Fingaz. Shortly thereafter he starred in *Undisputed 2*, but ironically he was playing Ving Rhames's character, not Wesley Snipes's.

Comic relief characters are never a good idea in Seagal pictures, but Anthony Anderson and Tom Arnold aren't too terrible. A lot of people thought their improvised riffing about asswiping and sex with fat women during the end credits was the best part of the movie. Anyway, they sort of have to be in there because they're kind of like the R2-D2 and C3P0 of the Bartkowiak trilogy, tying them all together. At the time, Anderson was just some dude from *Big Momma's House* and *Trippin'*, and soon he'd be doing crap like *Kangaroo Jack, Scary Movie 3, My Baby's Daddy, Agent Cody Banks 2*... but now that he's been in *Hustle & Flow* and *The Departed* maybe he gives some retroactive sheen to this movie. I don't know.

I like what they did with Bill Duke. He's only in a couple scenes, but he almost gets to play two standard Bill Duke characters. First he's the tough-lovin' commanding officer that he's played in more than 10,000 (ten thousand) movies over his career. But later he shows up ready to kick ass and it's like we have Bill Duke from *Predator* back. Congratulations Bill, you're back in the game.

But most impressive is DMX. He was already a platinum selling rapper, and he was pretty good in Hype Williams' independent movie *Belly*, but he wasn't a movie star yet. He doesn't exactly give convincing line readings, but he has such a natural charisma and movie star presence that for the first time somebody stole a movie right out from under Seagal. When *Exit Wounds* was a hit (it made about $51 million, almost three times as much as *Fire Down Below*) a lot of people gave the credit to DMX, instead of considering it a Seagal comeback. The *Vanity Fair* article incorrectly called *Exit Wounds* a "DMX vehicle" with Seagal co-starring.

In "the rap game" DMX is known for his gravelly, barking voice and his heavy emotion (on stage he sometimes gets so worked up he starts crying). In this movie he's less thug, more smooth. He looks handsome in a turtleneck sweaters and well-tailored suits. In real life his whole back is covered with the tattooed names of all the dogs he's owned, but in the movie these are mostly hidden and never showcased.

He holds his own on the action front. He even jumps through a window early on, like he's trying to prove himself to Seagal. Later he does a cool trick where he lays on the ground behind a barrier and tosses his rifle in the air, yanking on the trigger with the gun strap. He also bangs a guy's head against a ceiling sprinkler. After killing him he does a slow motion turn and closes his eyes as the sprinklers drench him – you're not sure if it's supposed to be a badass look or a *Shawshank Redemption*-style cleansing of the human spirit.

When I first saw this movie I really thought DMX had great potential as a movie star. Things looked good when he signed on to star in Ernest Dickerson's Donald Goines adaptation *Never Die Alone*, but (through no fault of DMX's) the movie just didn't work. He has only shot a few movies since, and none of them have been released yet (January 08). Meanwhile, he's had dramatic conflicts with his record label, drug problems and arrests, and these have all caused setbacks in his music career. I hope he figures things out soon because despite his troubles he's obviously a talented guy. I still think he could do some really good movies – both silly action movies like this and more serious material.

So how and why did they make a book like *Exit Wounds* into a movie like *Exit Wounds*? I don't know. It's not a particularly well known book that's going to draw in fans, like *The Da Vinci Code* or something. And it's not like any of the surface stuff they took from the book is original enough that they needed to go to the book store to find it. I guess the biggest asset they took is the name Orin, because you don't usually see movie characters named Orin. For that type of name you gotta option a book.

The whole thing doesn't make much sense, but it's overshadowed by the precedent of *The Patriot* being allegedly based on *The Last Canadian*. At least this movie and book have a few tiny, unimportant things in common. Those ones didn't have the same characters or premise or anything.

In interviews, Westermann seems happy about (or at least amused by) the casting of Seagal as Boyd. Noting that "The book is very different from the movie" he also raves about DMX, whose casting impressed his 13-year-old son.

Orin Boyd returned in another Westermann book, *Honor Farm*, where after beating up a corrupt right wing state senator he gets sent to a county jail and has to investigate the death of the police commissioner's son from inside. The rights to *Honor Farm* were included in Joel Silver's option of the *Exit Wounds* book, but despite the movie's success there has never been talk of a sequel. Besides, if there were an *Exit Wounds 2* you'd want it to have DMX's non-book character, and you wouldn't want it to seem too similar to *Half Past Dead*.

As a comeback for Seagal, *Exit Wounds* was short-lived. Seagal was shown respect in entertainment industry headlines during the opening weekend, but by the time of *Half Past Dead* they were treating him as a has-been again. But you know, que sera sera. He needed to have the attempted big screen revival before he could dive full hog into the DTV Era.

Exit Wounds, 2001
Directed by Andrzej Bartkowiak (*Romeo Must Die, Cradle 2 the Grave, Doom*. Director of photography for *Speed, U.S. Marshalls, Lethal Weapon 4, Terms of Endearment*, etc.)
Written by Ed Horowitz (*On Deadly Ground, K-9:PI*) and Richard D'Ovidio (*Thir13en Ghosts*), based on the novel by John Westermann.
Distinguished co-stars: Isaiah Washington, Bill Duke. Jill Hennessy, who plays Annette Mulcahy, later played the title character in the TV series *Crossing Jordan*. George Eads is in there uncredited as a car salesman. He went on to be one of the stars of *CSI* (he was buried alive in the episode Tarantino directed, that's the only one I've seen).

Seagal regulars: Shawn Lawrence (O'Malley) will later play Agent Shepherd in *Out of Reach.*

Firsts: First time co-starring with a rapper. First theatrical movie in four years. First time working with Joel Silver. First Seagal DVD to contain extras.

Title refers to: The title of the book that the movie is supposedly based on.

Just how badass is this guy? "Boyd's such a badass, man – he knows karate and judo, he could easily win one of those toughman contests!"

Adopted culture: None.

Languages: English, Spanish (briefly).

Improvised weapons: Pipe, scissors, fire extinguisher, paper cutter blade, chair. His opponents use a power sander, a fluorescent light and chains.

Fight in bar: Yes, a night club called Static.

Broken glass: Guy thrown into car window, DMX jumps through window, Anthony Anderson kicked into cocktail glasses, broken bottle, fluorescent light, bouncer thrown through glass wall, various car windows, commander hurled face first into windshield, phone booth run over, cops blown through windows by explosion.

Innocent bystanders: Guy headed to hot date gets motorcyle stolen by Seagal.

Family shit: Wife left him: "Same old cliché, got tired of all those sleepless nights."

Political themes: Not much. You could probably read something into the bit with the vice president in the beginning being against gun control and being saved by guns, but I don't think the makers of this movie had a political thought in their heads. They wanted to give Seagal a comeback and to them that probably meant holding him back from expressing himself.

Cover accuracy: One of the most artfully designed Seagal posters, this one has Seagal and DMX's faces inside the shape of a gun, with some guys representing "a gang of crooked cops" coming out the tip. Also a fancy sports car is involved, which is indeed accurate.

CHAPTER 12:
TICKER

"Well you know, one thing about hitting the bottom. After that, there's only one way you can go. And that's up."

Ticker is a movie about trying to stop Dennis Hopper from blowing people up. But really, it's a movie about getting beyond hope and fear and learning the nature of your own mind. I'm not actually sure what exactly it means to learn the nature of your own mind or what it has to do with stopping Dennis Hopper from blowing people up, but obviously that's because I haven't learned the nature of my own mind. And I sure as shit haven't gotten beyond hope and fear, which I'm sure doesn't help.

Okay, I just took a moment to understand the nature of my mind and now I realize I gotta apologize for making fun of the Seagalian philosophical portion of this movie, the only element that makes it interesting. In this unimaginative low budget thriller Seagal plays Glass, ex-Department of Defense leader of the San Francisco bomb squad ("Zen leader" according to the back of the DVD). He's not the actual lead here, he becomes the sidekick/guru to Detective Ray Nettles (Tom Sizemore), a burnt out ex-detective trying to track down terrorists while dealing with guilt over the unexplained car bomb death of his smiling, waving, high-fiving, saluting wife and kid.

Nettles has a partner named Fuzzy, played by Nas. Although he co-wrote the movie *Belly* and starred in it alongside Seagal's *Exit Wounds* co-star DMX, Nas is not really known as a movie star. The son of a jazz trumpeter, raised by his mother in the notorious Queensbridge housing projects of New York, Nas is a multi-platinum rap artist who *The Village Voice* once called, "easily one of the most important writers of the century." *Classic Material: The Hip-Hop Album Guide* describes Nas's legendary debut album *Illmatic* as "fearless, shocking, and literally *unbelievable.*" *The Vibe History of Hip Hop* says, "Not since Rakim first grabbed his gold microphone had a rap artist so successfully melded the relationship between the sound of words and the meanings they held."

In *Ticker*, though, he doesn't get very good words to say. He has lines like, "You feel that draft? It's cold. (cough cough) Ray, them demons inside you? Let them go, Ray. Before it's too late." Everything but "I see a light ahead…" Because this is the type of movie where the dialogue seems like it was created by a computer program. I mean, these are actual lines from the movie:

"We got a situation here."

"Looks like we got ourselves a hot little number here."

"Talk to me Glass. All hell's breaking loose up here!"

"Something's wrong. It's too easy."

"What the hell's going on? Hold your fire, damn it! Hold your fire!"

I mean, these are not lines somebody types. They're lines you get off of a wacky refrigerator magnet set. I hope they at least have shortcuts for these type of things. So they just hit SHIFT+F1 instead of typing out Tom Sizemore's "Oh no man come on. Don't die on me. God damn it, don't die Fuzzy![41]"

So Nas says a few lines with clichés about somebody's inner demons, gets billed above Seagal, then dies 16 minutes in. A reverse *Executive Decision*. This movie is *Executive Decision* except Nas is Seagal, and Seagal is either John Leguizamo or Oliver Platt, and there's no plane. Anyway, what happens is Nettles and Fuzzy happen to be walking near a warehouse in the middle of nowhere talking about letting go of the demons. When they see

---

41 It's possible that these lines were never typed at all. An early draft of the script, available online, doesn't include any of this dialogue, and instead of talking about demons just has Fuzzy (called Rice in this version) saying "Take your time… one day at a time, kid."

a truck pulling up they think it's suspiciously late for a delivery so they draw their guns and run in to "sign for it." Sure enough, Alex Swan (Dennis Hopper) and two other terrorists in leather jackets are receiving a shipment of bombs. So they have a shootout, Fuzzy dies, and all the terrorists get away except for their gal pal Claire (Jaime Pressly, Emmy nominee for *My Name Is Earl*, but I will always remember her from the cover of *Poison Ivy: The New Seduction*) who gets knocked out and taken into custody.

Before I go on I should mention one thing. When we see Seagal choppered into a mansion to defuse a bomb in the opening scene, he is wearing a black leather trenchcoat (his other attire for the movie is an official bomb squad coat). Fuzzy and Nettles both wear black leather jackets. Dennis Hopper and both of his cohorts wear black leather trenchcoats. At the end of the movie when Claire gets out of jail she puts on a leather trenchcoat, although hers is brown.

What I'm saying is the costume designer on this movie *really* likes leather jackets. Or another possibility, maybe they got a good deal on bulk leather jackets. It's a low budget movie, man, they gotta take any deals they can get.

Come to think of it, I have a third theory: maybe there are only two or three jackets, and the actors share them. So Seagal's coat is also Dennis Hopper's coat. I'm pretty sure you never see both coats in the same room at the same time. There are many possibilities.

Also, as long as I'm off on a tangent, I got a criticism for the hair stylists. I don't want to be an asshole, but didn't anybody notice that Tom Sizemore had a cowlick throughout the whole god damn movie? They make him look all slick with his black leather and close cropped hair but then he's got a fuckin Dennis the Menace weed growing out of his dome. Was this an intentional character quirk, to add vulnerability or something? To imply a childlike sense of wonder? What's the deal?

Well, anyway. When Claire is locked up, she refuses to talk to anyone except Nettles. She explains that her husband was a famous architect who blew the whistle on something or other, so he got offed. This was probably pretty disillusioning to her, and as we'll find out in the movie, different people deal with tragedy in different ways. Her way was to hook up with some leather-jacket-wearing terrorists to get revenge on the city.

Swan and his two henchmen, Vershbow (Michael Halsey) and Dugger

(Norbert Weisser), are the type of villains who repeatedly refer to their bombings in terms of art. They overuse the metaphor throughout the movie, constantly referring to their "masterpiece" and comparing it to Michelangelo and the Sistine Chapel. (They probably know more about bomb history than art history, so the reference is not gonna be very obscure.) They consider Claire their muse, so they start a series of bombings, threatening not to stop until the cops let Claire go.

Early in the movie I thought Dennis Hopper was trying to be funny by occasionally using a phoney accent. Then I realized *oh, he's supposed to be Irish*. I guess that's how he distinguishes his character from the mad bomber he played in *Speed*, but it's too bad he has to do such a half-assed, Kevin-Costner-style in-and-out accent. Within a single line of dialogue he'll forget he's supposed to be Irish, then remember and overcompensate, then just figure *fuck it* and talk like Dennis Hopper again.

Like all movie cops, Nettles is not supposed to be on this case, but you know how it is when somebody killed your partner, you gotta disobey a direct order, do a little investigating on your own, etc. When Nettles first visits the bomb squad, who are portrayed as a group of wise-talking, colorful-shirt-wearing eccentrics like the teams of scientists in movies like *Twister* and *Titanic*, it doesn't go well. The young secretary with the multi-colored hair mistakes Nettles for a pizza delivery man! I don't know about you, but I never seen a pizza boy who looks like Tom Sizemore in a slick leather jacket. This is a tight knit group who have their own lingo and use a bomb defusing robot to serve coffee. So Nettles doesn't fit in. He asks Glass why he isn't out there trying to catch the mad bomber, and Glass has to explain to him in a sarcastic tone that there are actually cops called detectives who are the ones who find the bombs, and the bomb squad are the people who then try to defuse the bombs. I mean I understand why Nettles is frustrated but Glass is obviously right in this case. You don't go yell at a taxi driver when your bus isn't on time.

Since they don't see eye-to-eye, what they gotta do of course is team up. For most of the movie, Seagal seems to be just delivering a supporting acting performance, not being an action hero. When the shit goes down in the opening scene, he is in the basement cutting wires while everybody else is getting shot and exploded. He doesn't even shoot a gun very often (there's a good shot of him strutting in empty-handed while everybody else is pointing their guns). I thought this was an attempt to try something different as an actor, actually playing a character instead of stringing together some action scenes. Maybe this character Glass isn't even a martial artist, I thought. But then at the end he gets attacked in a hallway and does some aikido.

One little touch I liked, there's a pretty random scene in the movie where Nettles's watch stops, and Seagal teaches him how to fix it (telepathically, I guess, since he doesn't actually give him any specific instruction). In the climax of the movie, Claire's watch turns out to be a part of the "masterpiece" bombing plan, which made me worry that Nettles would have to use his newfound watch repair skills to save the citizens of San Francisco. Fortunately, this did not happen, so the earlier scene was able to remain just a nice moment. I mean, that's not something you've seen before, Steven Seagal teaching Tom Sizemore how to fix a watch. That's what movies are all about is shit like that.

The climax does have Nettles defusing a bomb, though, with Seagal offering tech support via walkie talkie. It's the traditional giant fancy bomb with digital readout and colored wires. This is kind of like an Ikea bomb, dealing with it doesn't require any tools. That's good, because Nettles doesn't carry any. You'd think he'd at least need a Phillips-head screwdriver, but he lucked out.

There is a great Seagal touch to this generic scene though. Before Glass gives Nettles instructions on how to defuse the bomb, he first calms him with a philosophical pep talk:

"Now listen to me man you're just gonna hafta go beyond hope and fear, don't get attached to living or dying, or anything else, and understand that death is just another stage on the playground. You have to be able to feel it. And the way you'll be able to learn how to feel is by coming to know the nature of your mind. And even if you do go today you'll be back. So if you're not attached to living or dying, you have nothing to fear, if you have nothing to fear you're gonna calm down and just listen to me, 'cause I'm gonna guide you through this. All right?"

Normally in a Seagal movie you assume that Seagal added a speech like this to the script or improvised it on set. In this case, you know for sure it's improvised, because this is the first Seagal movie to include a DVD commentary track. Director Albert Pyun and producer Paul Rosenblum give one of those frustratingly minimalistic commentaries where they sometimes go 5 or 10 minutes without saying anything, and you forget you are listening to a commentary track and get involved in the movie, then all the sudden they start talking again and scare the shit out of you. (Same thing with Rudy Ray Moore's commentary on *Petey Wheatstraw, the Devil's Son-in-Law*.) But when they do talk they are honest and informative about the low budget circumstances of the movie, and also very complimentary towards Seagal and his dedication to the movie.

Watching the movie, I noticed something seemed a little weird. There are many low budget cheats that imply it was made for almost nothing. The Balkan terrorist in the opening scene is badly dubbed with a Triumph the Insult Comic Dog style accent. One explosion is obviously in front of a cheesy model city. Instead of showing a guy fall out a window, they show a close-up of the window crashing and then have a long, fading yell, as if he fell off a cliff. Police radio conversations take place over a black screen on the opening credits, making it feel like a radio play. And there's a scene where Dennis Hopper and Jaime Pressly are driving and the backgrounds are obviously blue screened – it's especially noticeable when Hopper "pulls over" and the moving background just jerks to a stop as if put on pause.

But then there are helicopters, SWAT teams, big shootouts with lots of screaming extras, explosions with people flying through the air on fire, etc. So I figured maybe it's not that low budget.

Well, on the commentary Pyun and Rosenblum are very upfront about how this was done, and point out a lot of interesting things. For example, the entire opening sequence, except for the shots of Seagal, is made up of footage taken from other movies. The last shot of the movie, with Seagal and Sizemore walking off into the horizon, is actually shot with doubles in silhouette. Hopper and Pressly never even met each other (which is the reason for the weird blue-screened driving scene mentioned above). It was a 12 day shoot, Seagal shot for 6 days, and Hopper, amazingly, only shot for 1 day. Even Seagal and Sizemore apparently didn't shoot much together, which is odd since it's sort of a buddy movie. This explains the weird phenomenon in the movie that whenever the police get a threatening phone call from Alex Swan, Glass is able to listen in on a speaker phone over in the bomb squad office.

They also mention that according to Seagal, his German shepard Kaos Seagal, who plays the bomb sniffing dog, cost him $100,000. Now, I have some experience with dogs and I would have to say that it is really not possible for one to be worth $100,000. Dogs can be nice animals and good pets, but they're still dogs. They sniff asses, pee on their favorite places and literally eat shit, straight out of a litter box. This better be one amazing fucking dog, one that can fly, shit diamonds, maybe drive a car or teach your kid French. What kind of a Buddhist lama spends a hundred grand on a dog? That's a luxury I do not understand.

I gotta be honest, I was sort of dreading this one. I kept putting off watching it. On one hand I was kind of excited to see Seagal do a movie with Tom Sizemore and Nas. On the other hand, I knew it was directed by Albert Pyun. His biography on the DVD makes a big deal out of the fact that he's done as many movies as he's spent years alive on the earth (over 40) and even says that he served an apprenticeship under Kurosawa. But I mean come on, Darth Vader was an apprentice to Obi Wan Kenobi, man. That doesn't make him a good guy. Pyun is the director of movies like *Cyborg* and *Nemesis*. Cheap, murky, ugly, unimaginative, and incredibly boring movies. Not the kind of thing I'm into. So I was surprised at how watchable this thing was.

This isn't one of Seagal's better movies (oh, for fuck's sake, no), but it's an important film for Seagalogists because it shows that Seagal actually can add something of his own to a generic, no budget action movie. The screenplay was written in 1989 and for some reason stuck around for more than a decade. Before Seagal came aboard it almost became a made-for-cable movie starring Chuck Norris. In this book I've been pointing out things that happen over and over again in Seagal movies, but here is an example where Seagal insisted on doing something slightly different. According to the commentary track, the scene at the "Jazz Cat" blues bar was supposed to take place at a strip club. Seagal said he had strip club scenes in a lot of his other movies so he suggested the blues bar, where we see a live performance by an all star band including Clarence Gatemouth Brown, Billy Preston, the Meters' Zigaboo Modeliste, and none other than Steven Slowhand Seagal on lead guitar and vocals. (That's the cool blues name they gave him on the credits, I'm not making a joke about deteriorating aikido speed.) Seagal wears a beard and Blues Brothers hat and sunglasses. Unfortunately, you only see him in one shot, there is no bluescreening to put Slowhand in the background while Glass sits in the crowd. Maybe some other time.

I would also argue that the "Zen leader" element of the story is the one somewhat unique aspect of the movie. It is a theme throughout the movie that the characters are dealing with tragedies in their past: Nettles with the death of his wife and kid (and now partner), Glass with the death of his "boys" from the D.O.D., Claire with the murder of her husband, and I figure Peter Greene's character is probably dealing with something too since he's such an asshole, always making fun of Nettles for having a dead family. All of them deal with the problems in different ways, but it is Glass who is calm and accepting of his tragedy, and throughout the movie he gives Nettles advice until he finally is able to visit his wife and kid's graves without blowing his brains out.

Ticker, 2001
Directed by Albert Pyun (*Cyborg*, *Captain America*, *Dollman*, the *Nemesis* series, *Omega Doom*, etc).
Written by Paul B. Margolis (*MacGyver*).
Distinguished co-stars: Nas? Dennis Hopper? Tom Sizemore? Ice-T? I don't know who counts anymore. Romany Malco, who plays T.J., later was very funny in the comedy *The 40 Year Old Virgin*. But he also played MC Hammer in a TV movie. I guess Billy Preston counts, he's playing organ in the blues band.
Seagal regulars: Peter Greene was "Mercenary #1" (actually the #2 ranking mercenary) in *Under Siege 2*. Fumiyasu Daikyu (Embassy Attache) played Maktak in *On Deadly Ground*. David Paris, who is the helicopter pilot, also flew a helicopter for *The Patriot*. Simone Levine, who plays the booking clerk, plays a DEA agent in *Today You Die*.
Firsts: First Seagal movie to feel more like a home video than a real movie. First dual role for Seagal (he still hasn't played twins).
Title refers to: Any one of the bombs they thrillingly defuse during the movie.
Adopted culture: None (unless you count Zen).
Languages: English. And according to the commentary track there was a scene they cut out where he spoke in Japanese with an ambassador in a limo. So that should count.
Fight in bar: Not with Seagal, but in the opening scene (made from stock footage from other movies) there's a part where a terrorist disguised as a bartender whips out a gun and starts shooting from behind the bar.
Broken glass: chandelier, cop car windshields, 1 guy thrown through a window. Also, Seagal's character is named Glass.
Terms of endearment: Brother, brotha.

Words of wisdom: "You got to get beyond hope and fear, learn the nature of your own mind. And then – you won't be suffering anymore."

Family shit: None.

Political themes: Not much except for this one line, which continues Seagal's career-long blowback motif: "The other one, Vershbow, he's a freelance demolition expert, just so happens he's worked for half the governments in the western hemisphere. Including ours during the Reagan administration."

Cover accuracy: The cover looks like it has a bigger budget than the movie. Sizemore, Nas and Seagal have their faces inside the letters of the logo, which is placed on top of the circuit-board for a bomb timer that's at 0. And the letters are lit from behind by an explosion. It's admirable that the movie gives Seagal the "and" credit, making it clear that he's not the lead. However, they do act like Nas is one of the stars, and that's not exactly true.

CHAPTER 13:
HALF PAST DEAD

"What kind of man signs up for that?!"

In the last Seagal movie to play theatrically in the United States, Seagal plays Sasha Petrosevitch, an FBI agent gone deep undercover as a car thief. He purposely does a bid with his partner in crime Nick Frazier ("rapper" turned "actor" Ja Rule) hoping to be trusted enough to get to Sonny Eckvall (Richard Bremmer), the elusive syndicate boss who he blames for the death of his wife.

This alone oughta be enough for a movie – a cop going so deep undercover that he goes to prison and stays in character. But this is a 2002 Hollywood action movie, man, you need more than just a hook, you need a double hook. So then, once he's undercover in prison, he also happens to be in the wrong place at the wrong time – the place being "New Alcatraz" and the time being when a group of highly skilled commandos take a Supreme Court justice hostage and try to force a lovable old death row inmate to reveal the whereabouts of his stash of gold bricks.

But shit, two hooks? That's it? No, of course not. Two hooks is not enough for modern audiences either. So Sasha also has a near-death experience (which is why he's half past dead). But I'll get to that in a minute.

When we first see Sasha, he's asleep in a dingy apartment with a gun next to him and a widescreen TV on snow. Suddenly Nick comes in with Sonny

Eckvall and some thugs. All except Nick suspect Sasha is a rat, so they administer a high-tech handheld polygraph test (the interrogation equivalent of an iPod) which Sasha passes with flying colors. Once the boss leaves, Sasha strokes his wedding ring meaningfully. I say meaningfully but all it really means is that his wife is dead, there may or may not be some revenge at some point, etc. The usual. The one thing that is truly unusual about the scene is that Seagal smokes. Otherwise it's a replay of a scene in *Ticker*, but with Seagal as Tom Sizemore ("I just can't let her go," blah blah blah) and Ja Rule as Nas (not a bad symbol for the continuous de-evolution of commercial hip hop). After trying to cheer Sasha up, Nick says, "Anyway... I got a job, man. You want it?"

And Sasha says, "Yeah."

SMASH CUT to thrilling shot of a car MID-AIR, to the tune of the DMX song "I'ma Bang."

It's the clean version of the song, though. This is a PG-13 movie, with no blood or broken bones. That's because it was made during that naïve month and a half or so after 9-11 when everybody, even me, foolishly wondered if Americans would ever enjoy big, violent, *Die Hard* style action again. So to get that rating, they actually censor the songs playing on the soundtrack, and cut out DMX saying "motherfucker." They even censored the song "Listen All You Motherfuckers," which had already been used in *Blade II*.

All you kids under 13 out there, if you were wondering what the man was saying on the soundtrack, it was 'motherfucker' was what he was saying. I'm glad I could help.

Anyway, this scene is also interesting because it is the title sequence. Which would not be interesting except that the opening scene was also the title sequence. So yeah, in case you forgot, the name of the movie is *Half Past Dead* still. I guess this is a movie designed for those assholes that come in ten minutes after the movie started and sit directly in front of you even though it's an empty god damn theater. Welcome assholes, here is the name of the movie again since you missed it before.

Well now that everybody is finally here, we can have these two get caught and go to prison. They get surrounded by an FBI team led by Sasha's old friend Williams (Claudia Christian) who I guess has seen some John Woo movies since she likes to run around with the double pistols blazing. As scrawny as he is, Ja Rule actually has a worthwhile Badass Moment during this scene. When Williams says, "I'm with the FBI. Maybe you've heard of us," Ja Rule pulls out two guns and says, "Yeah, I've heard of you." Admittedly, in real life he would've been shot down like a pitbull that just mauled a toddler, so it's hard to believe it in this movie when Williams just smiles like it's a cute joke. Still, you gotta take what you can get, and that was an okay exchange, in my opinion, at least by the low standards set by this particular motion picture.

Eventually Nick and Williams run straight at each other firing with both hands, and Sasha decides to save his partner's life by running between them and... well, you know, falling over and having a heart attack. He dies, they revive him, next thing you know he's wearing orange and lining up at Alcatraz.

(I learned from the director's audio commentary track that Sasha was supposed to have been shot, but since they don't want the children to see blood or hear the word motherfucker, I thought the first time I watched it that he was just getting old and collapsed.)

Next thing you know, Sasha and Nick are at New Alcatraz, which looks exactly like Old Alcatraz but you can tell it's futuristic by the green computer font and high tech beeping that accompanies the subtitle telling us it's New. New Alcatraz is a modern prison with TV screens everywhere, where inmates are allowed to pursue their interests such as painting murals (Kurupt's character Twitch even gets to hoist himself up with a harness for better painting) or playing golf on Playstation. Malcolm X got his education from the prison library, so if the Man wants to keep us down it's pretty good thinking to give us all Playstation.

The warden, Juan Ruiz Escarzaga (Tony Plana), is kind of like the cool, tough-lovin' high school principal who's gonna turn your life around. He wears a black leather jacket, calls himself "El Fuego" and calls inmates terms of endearment like "ese" and "homeboy." He talks tough but also bonds with the convicts, even buying a suit for Lester, the nice old train robber that's gonna be executed at midnight. He goes so far as to pat Lester on the shoulder, which in a movie like this is almost like giving a dude a big, long hug.

Lester's going down for a train heist where the train derailed and killed some federal agents. He didn't hurt anybody on purpose, so you don't have to feel bad about him being a good guy. He got away with a load of gold bars that day and he never divulged their location, which is why certain individuals are interested in stopping the execution and taking him hostage. But we don't know that yet.

As his last wish, Lester asks to have Sasha visit him, to tell him about his recent near-death experience. For maximum pre-execution comfort, El Fuego lets Lester hang out in front of a screen where he can pretend to be in his favorite relaxing places. When the background changes from a cityscape to a desert, the slide doesn't just change. It actually morphs. 'Cause it's the future. Good to see our tax dollars are going to important services like this. I mean obviously I'm not one of those guys who complains about coddling prisoners too much, but honestly, the morphing is not necessary. I don't care if the guy is gonna die, he can accept a good old fashioned slide change without inbetweening. You can't keep babying this guy.

He also gets his choice of execution method, and since he chose electrocution, the floor opens up and an electric chair rises dramatically out of the floor, or out of the earth, out of the bowels of Hell, whatever. Again, probably an unnecessary expenditure. I don't think Lester would mind walking down a hall to a chair that is permanently fixed to the floor instead of having a hidden one inside the room that rises up using hydraulics. It's all just a bunch of showoffy razzle dazzle bullshit, completely superfluous to the actual execution. Nobody needs that.

El Fuego is not the bad guy here. The bad guy turns out to be Morris Chestnut as a rogue security official only called "49er One." Having graduated from his annoying sidekick role in *Under Siege 2* to suave leading man roles in movies like *The Best Man*, he has now returned fully grown and handsome, ready to take on Seagal from the other side. And this time he really has fighting skills rather than pretending to for the sake of wackiness.

Later on he has a speech where he makes fun of the idea that he should have a "deep, dark, psychological reason" for his crimes. In my opinion, having the character say that he has no deep, dark, psychological reason for his crimes is just as corny and cliché as if he explained what the deep, dark, psychological reason for his crimes was. If not moreso. And to make matters worse, there are other scenes that imply there is one of those types of reasons for what he's doing. Pointing at a cliché is not the same as avoiding one. Stop trying to have it both ways, screenwriters.

Chestnut's character is aided by an elite team of other numbered 49ers, most notably 49er Six (Nia Peeples), a leather-clad, high-kicking hottie clearly modeled after Trinity in *The Matrix*. But with blue eye shadow, which makes her a totally new and unique character.

The judge who convicted Lester comes to witness the execution. "You want my forgiveness, that's why you come isn't it?" Lester asks, implying some sort of John Woo-ian bond between convicted and convicter. But all she will offer is a "Goodbye, Lester," like they are old friends.

Just before the execution, and while Sasha is being escorted back to his cell, the gold-digging 49ers come parachuting onto the island to the tune of "Listen All You Motherfuckers" (non-motherfucker version)[42] and take everybody hostage, including the judge. Sasha's guard escort gets shot, and Sasha plays dead. When the coast is clear he tries to use the screw's cattleprod to revive him and do CPR. Just like MacGyver would've done, I bet.

Early on there is one legitimately cool action moment when Seagal closes a set of electric doors on 49er Six's gun. Before she can fire it he flips it around to aim right back at her, then kicks it out from between the doors. At this point it could turn into a *Die Hard/Under Siege*-in-a-prison kind of thing, Seagal sneaking around on his own, killing off the 49ers one by one using different improvised weapons. Instead Seagal meets back up with the other convicts and puts together an army. Somehow they have access to the prison's armory, which is full of high powered assault rifles and missile launchers, the kind of thing you need to keep prisoners in line in the future. Again, paid for by our taxes.

Up until about this point, the movie halfway pretends that Sasha really is a criminal. But we know, man. We fuckin know. The only thing we are wrong about, he is merely an FBI agent and not some kind of ex-CIA Bosnia veteran turned FBI agent. He gets in touch with Williams on the outside to

---

42 Or maybe the title should be "Listen All You Mr. Falcons," an homage to the TV version of *Die Hard 2*.

find out more about his opponent, plans an assault, the usual. In the earlier portion of the movie, there is *Rush Hour* style cross-cultural bonding, as Nick attempts to teach Sasha how to say "a'ight." Inside, there's trouble because Nick finds out he's been lied to.

Still, they fight together against the thieves. Sasha gets to fight Morris Chestnut Thunderdome style, swinging around on chains. Nick just gets to fight Nia Peeples. It's hard to say whether this is a feminist statement (women are on an equal level with men, so it is okay to have an inter-gender duel) or just a diss of Ja Rule (it is only believable to have him fighting a woman). During one of the biggest battles Seagal and Rule don't fight much at all, they just hide inside the cockpit of a crashed helicopter, firing its weapons, while the other convicts do all the dirty work.

There is a lot of bad comic relief in this movie. You got Kurupt's character Twitch, who is "funny" because he's excited to fire weapons and gets hurled ten feet when he fires a rocket launcher. There's also a big lovable guy named Little Joe (Michael "Bear" Taliferro) who's "funny" because he's a huge black guy who's sensitive and reads romance novels. During the end credits Twitch gets a visit from his wife, the comedienne Mo'nique, so there is comic relief to relieve you from the comic relief. Two layers of relief.

Attacking the state of art and pop culture in his monologue for the 2005 Oscars, Chris Rock said that "Ja Rule is not Tupac." Which is true, and he's not DMX either. He's not a terrible actor (probably a better actor than he is a rapper) but he doesn't have the kind of badass presence you need for a movie like this. He's more of a cocky little weasel who clearly has a higher opinion of himself than anybody else does of him. Maybe he knows something we don't know about how great he is, but until he lets us in on that information maybe we should just not have him in any more action movies. I'm sure you can see where we're coming from on this Ja Rule, thank you for being so understanding about this. Later dude.

There are a few enigmatic touches to this movie that should probably be mentioned. For one, the opening scene makes a big point of Sasha being Russian. Why is this? He doesn't have a Russian accent, he doesn't have Russian mafia connections, he doesn't ever tell stories about his Russian heritage or discuss communism or the plot of *Rocky IV*. The only possible reason for saying the character is Russian is to explain why his name is Sasha Petrosevitch. But if that's the case why didn't they just call him John like every other movie?

And then there's the matter of Sasha's titanium leg. When he goes into Alcatraz, the metal detector goes off and a screw attacks him, thinking he's trying to pull something. After a big scuffle with Ja Rule in which the screw is thrown through a row of bookshelves (with no consequences), Sasha shows the warden that he has a titanium knee, the reason the alarm was set off. This is obviously setting up for something that will happen later, right? He'll have something stashed in the knee that he'll use to escape, or he'll bash somebody with the knee, or at the very least we will learn of some horrible war incident that damaged his knee and made him the man he is today. Right?

Nope. The knee is never mentioned again.

Another thing that's odd, but somewhat admirable, is that you never even see Seagal get his revenge. In an epilogue added after test screen audiences objected to the death of Ja Rule's character, Sasha explains that he put Sonny Eckvall behind bars.

Although it was nice to see Seagal on the big screen one last time, this is definitely not one of his better pictures. It's a big messy commercial vehicle, running off in ten different directions, chasing after every dumb trend in action movies and pop culture instead of looking at Seagal's strengths and building a streamlined vehicle around them. He does a little more aikido than in most of his straight to video pictures of this later period, but he doesn't seem as essential to the movie as he should. For those mainly interested in Seagal it is a little disappointing. The movie seems padded with scenes about the secondary characters, taking time away from the lead.

But it does have a little bit of the Seagal touch. In one minor subplot he is able to get a religious theme into the movie that makes it occasionally stand out from other generic '90 and 2000s action movies. He discusses God and the afterlife with Lester, saying, "I think you must've done something very bad. And now you're gonna pay for it with your life. But I think God will forgive you." 49er One, on the other hand, says, "God is dead." Which makes him a bad guy. (Lester later kills 49er One with a heroic suicide bombing. Sort of an odd choice right after 9-11, but that's

Seagalogy for you.)

I also like the part at the end where Seagal stares at the water thoughtfully, his back turned to the FBI agents digging up Lester's stash of gold bars. Perhaps he is contemplating Lester's journey to the afterlife. Thinking of the old crook standing on the shores of the River Styx, waiting for the silent boatman to ferry him across. His gold bars probably wouldn't be enough payment, but he could still have a shot. Sasha even said himself he thought God would forgive Lester. But was he right? Had Lester really done enough? Did his final sacrifice help prove his essential righteousness, or did it damage his case? Yeah he saved the day, I guess, but now he's a murderer and a suicide. Come to think of it, did Sasha's intervention even help Lester in his spiritual journey, or did it drag him back into a cycle of violence that he had spent most of his life trying to escape from? Now that Sasha's about to reach closure on his wife's death, will he be forever haunted by Lester's quest for God's forgiveness?

Or then again maybe he's not thinking about any of that, he might just not want to get his nice coat muddy. It could be either one.

The fights are choreographed by Xin Xin Xiong, a Hong Kong actor and stuntman best known for playing Kung and Clubfoot in the *Once Upon a Time In China* sequels. But I have to admit that I first noticed him in Jean-Claude Van Damme's craziest movie, *Double Team*. For that one he not only choreographed the action but appeared in an awesome fight where he holds a switchblade between his toes. Unfortunately there's nothing that memorable in this one. He brings a Hong Kong/wirework style to a lot of the fights (especially those with Nia Peeples) but thankfully leaves Seagal on the ground doing aikido. Xiong worked in conjunction with action coordinator/49er 11 Art Camacho, who is also a director of low budget action movies, having collaborated with both Don "The Dragon" Wilson and David "The Demon" DeFalco.

Half Past Dead is Seagal's second movie to feature a director's commentary track on the DVD, but it's not quite as interesting as the one on *Ticker*. Although low budget by Hollywood standards, this thing is enormous compared to *Ticker* so there aren't as many illuminating anecdotes about how they pulled it off. Writer-director Don Michael Paul doesn't come across as a jerk or anything, but it's hard not to laugh at his descriptions of what he was trying to do with the movie. By 2002, movie fans had been complaining for more than a decade about "MTV style" action movies, and here Paul is talking about this amazing new idea he came up with of a movie that is "more like a music video." He keeps referring to a "theatrical style" and "fantastical style" and editing that has "that kind of percussive feeling" like the beats of the music that he was using. In other words, those obnoxious quick cuts we hate.

Paul refers to the movie as "an action movie with a real strong hip hop vibe" and "kind of a big hip hop opera," even though the subject matter and tone of the movie have virtually no connection with the actual hip hop culture. I'm not sure why he was so excited about the idea of teaming an action star with a rapper. Seagal himself had already teamed with DMX and (sort of) with Nas, both more respected as rappers and as actors than Ja Rule.

Paul is also no Seagalogist. He is very proud of a scene where Seagal mourns his dead wife, saying that you never get to see Seagal "vulnerable" like that in his other movies. I guess he never saw *Above the Law* (where he mourns his dead partner), or *Hard to Kill* (where he mourns his dead wife), or *Marked For Death* (where he almost cries when his niece gets shot), or *Out For Justice* (where he mourns his dead partner), etc.

To be fair though, Paul does include some interesting information about the movie. The first time I saw it I thought it was a ripoff of *The Rock*, with some sad attempts at stylistic lifts of John Woo and *The Matrix*. But according to Paul the script was written ten years earlier and actually titled *The Rock* until the Michael Bay movie was made. He even reveals that his "friend Michael Bay" loaned him some unused helicopter shots of Alcatraz since they couldn't afford them for this movie. I'm not sure why you would want to brag about knowing the man most responsible for destroying the very language of action cinema that we all love, but, you know what they say, the world don't move to the beat of just one drum. (And by "they" I mean the people who wrote the *Diff'rent Strokes* theme song.) Anyway, as unimaginative as this movie is, apparently it is not a ripoff of *The Rock*. So good job on that one.

Paul talks a lot about the style he was going for in the movie, but one important element he doesn't mention is sparks. This whole movie is about sparks. There are sparks everywhere you look. Whenever there's a shootout, there are sparks. Whenever there's a machine, it sprays sparks. I'm sure if Lester had had a chance to get executed, sparks would've sprayed out of his eyes. It's like Paul figured any flaw could be covered with sparks and any scene could be made better with sparks. Sparks sparks and more sparks. As broken glass is to *The Glimmer Man*, sparks are to *Half Past Dead*. Still, on the whole, I think the movie could use more sparks. Or at least spark.

Half Past Dead, 2002

Directed by Don Michael Paul (episodes of *Silk Stalkings*; also was an actor on *Models Inc.* and the monster truck rampage movie *Rolling Vengeance*).

Written by Don Michael Paul (*Harley Davidson and the Marlboro Man*).

Distinguished co-stars: Morris Chestnut, Stephen J. Cannell (creator of *The A-Team, The Greatest American Hero*, etc.)

Seagal regulars: Morris Chestnut graduates from sidekick in *Under Siege 2* to lead villain here. Some guy named Joe Cook, who played a Chechen in *Executive Decision*, plays somebody named William T. Bowers in this one (uncredited).

Firsts: First Seagal movie with a writer-director.

Just how badass is this guy? There is no big speech about his abilities, but when it's mentioned that an agent is undercover in a prison, an FBI agent asks, "What kind of man signs up for that?!" Claudia Christian responds with a meaningful sip of coffee. Later Morris Chestnut asks, "Who's [prisoner number] 1137?" and the warden responds, "A major pain in your ass." (Which is true, though there's no way for the warden to really know that.)

Adopted culture: He does not really adopt another culture in this one, although Ja Rule tries to teach him how to say "a'ight" instead of "all right."

Languages: Just English. A disappointment since they make a point of him being Russian but do not have him speaking it. Surprisingly, he also manages to avoid dropping Spanish words on the bi-lingual warden El Fuego.

Improvised weapons: He lowers a dead body into a room with gas bombs attached to it and a note saying "BYE BYE" (an homage to *Die Hard*).

Fight in bar: Sadly, no. It would be cool though if New Alcatraz had a bar in it.

Broken glass: Seagal slams on the brakes and sends Ja Rule flying out of a car into the windshield of another, as a hilarious joke. A guy shoots, then kicks through an office window. A helicopter crashes into a big sunroof, showering glass (and sparks) below. Seagal punches through a window into a guy's face, then throws him through a windowed door. Many windows are shot out. Seagal jumps through a set of windows, then a thug shoots at him, hitting the piles of broken glass and sending them flying again. He kicks a guy into a glass medicine cabinet. Nia Peeples jumps through a window. A Rocket launcher kicks Kurupt through a window, and everyone laughs at him.

Most awkward one-liner: "Comprende this!" (said by Kurupt though, not Seagal).

Family shit: His wife was killed in a carjacking, he still wears his wedding ring and dedicates his life to busting the head of the auto-thieving empire responsible.

Political themes: Pretty low key on this one. There's one reference to the villain having Gulf

War syndrome, but when it's suggested he's getting revenge on the government he says, "Oh no, I love America. My cause is me." He also refers to his gold heist as "the American dream" at one point, which could be interpreted as an attack on capitalism. But the only blatantly political portion is a throwaway detail that most people won't even notice. During the cable news coverage of the impending execution, the scroll at the bottom of the screen says, "PRESIDENT VACATIONS IN KENNEBUNKPORT, ME. MIDDLE EAST CRISIS ESCALATES. STOCK PRICES SURGE, PESSIMISM EBBING. ECONOMY SLUGGISH, GROSS NATIONAL PRODUCTIVITY FLATLINING. .. POLAR ICE CAPS MELT, GLOBAL WARMING—"

Cover accuracy: Another artful design along the lines of *Exit Wounds*, this one emphasizing the three leads with some helicopters mixed in and Alcatraz shown off in the distance. The only misleading aspect is the tagline "The good, the bad and the deadly." Based on the layout of the poster this seems to indicate that Ja Rule is the deadly, and come on. Nobody buys that. Nice try, guys.

DTV ERA

2003-present

CHAPTER 14:
THE FOREIGNER

"I suggest you hire a professional."

The *Foreigner* begins unpromisingly in Warsaw. The cinematography is bleak and colorless, the characters are generic European villains with topcoats and furry hats. And the action is completely Seagal-less. Boring shady types spout cliches about a "client," a "close associate" and the delivery of "The Package."

Seagal gets a good introduction though, answering a phone while a hot redhead puts on clothes and leaves. Clearly a sex act has just occurred, but not one sweaty enough to require a shower. Anyway, we never see or hear about the redhead again. This is our first sign that Seagal plays a secret agent – Jonathan Cold, a former KGB double agent once caught, convicted of espionage, jailed in a Soviet prison, framed for ratting out his father, now a rogue agent for hire, or something.

Just like that backstory, the plot is more complicated than most Seagal films. It involves 1) the recent death of Cold's father, an American ambassador to Poland 2) Cold being hired to pick up "The Package" 3) Cold's relationship with his brother Sean, who's more of a team player secret agent 4) a husband and wife fighting over their daughter, using evidence of a terrorist attack on a plane as a bargaining chip (long story). Basically what it boils down to, Cold is hired to pick up "The Package," and is ambushed at the pickup spot. So he delivers a fake Package, takes off with the real one, and tries not to get killed. Late in the movie he figures out he should open The Package and find out what it is. (Duh.) With this new information he then is able to figure out what to do with it.

This is a movie with lots of the ol' shifting allegiances. When Cold first picks up The Package, his partner is a guy named Dunoir (Max Ryan). But immediately after, Dunoir starts killing people (including their boss, a guy he steals a car from, and an innocent hotel clerk) and going after The Package. Then there's a more stylish killer apparently called Mr. Mimms (Sherman Augustus) hired to kill Cold, but with no knowledge of The Package. He and Cold temporarily call a truce when Cold offers him money, and Cold and Dunoir temporarily call a truce when they are outnumbered and need to get into a particular building. (Cold ends up sniping the entire security team before they even spot him, so it's not clear why he needs Dunoir.) Also, the movie keeps trying to change your mind about whether to trust shifty industrialist Jerome Van Aken[43] (Harry Van Gorkum) or his wife Meredith (Anna-Louise Plowman).

I gotta be honest man, I gotta question Jonathan Cold's skills as a secret agent. Yes, he has the naked redhead in his apartment, that is a good secret agent skill, and he's able to trick people into blowing themselves up and crap like that. But in other ways he's pretty bad. For example, there's a scene where he asks a hotel clerk, "Have you heard of a local called Jerome Van Aken?" before realizing that he is standing right in front of a newspaper with a full front page story and photo of Jerome Van Aken. This is poor attention to detail and lazy research. Even if he was a regular guy it would be embarrassing. But this guy's a legendary secret agent.

When it comes to sniping, Cold is topnotch. But close range he's a sucker. Standing just a couple feet away from a guy he misses three times, hitting various empty bottles and vases before hitting the target. I mean honestly, it would be harder to miss the way he did than it would be to hit. But somehow he does it three damn times.

Also there's the matter of not opening up The Package until late in the

---

43 Jeroen van Aken, sometimes called Jerome van Aken, is the birth name of the 15th century painter better known as Hieronymus Bosch. I don't think this van Aken is supposed to be the same guy, though. If it is they sure didn't explain it very well.

game. Sure, when he's delivering it, I can understand why he doesn't want to know. But then when everyone is trying to kill him, you'd think it would occur to him right away that he has to open it up if he wants to understand why people are after him. I don't care if *The Transporter* says not opening the package is "rule #1." Unless there's gremlins in there you know it's gonna help to open it in this particular case.

This reminds me, the scene where Cold finally opens The Package is pretty funny for sharp eyed Seagalogists who enjoy using the pause and zoom buttons on their DVD players. Inside the box is a collection of evidence that Van Aken was involved in shooting down a commercial airliner, including the actual flight recorder. Also, so that the audience will understand what's going on, there's a stack of clippings from Russian and English newspapers about the plane crash. Cold looks confused as he reads the articles, and there's good reason: the text of one of the articles is about Charles, Philip and the Queen getting a phone call, the other is a review of a late night BBC2 show called *The Joy of Gardening*. Any article with the headline "PLANE CRASHES: Terrorist Attack In Air" probably shouldn't contain the phrase "undeniably charming," but this one does. I don't know the details of the plane crash, but I do know that *The Joy of Gardening* is, "part gentle social history, part compilation of vaguely relevant comedy clips, and part nostalgia show in the familiar 'I Love Whatever It Is' tradition." Sounds pretty good. I don't know if they get BBC2 in Paris, but if so I bet Cold watched an episode or two after straightening this whole Package thing out.

Anyway, enough about gardening. Cold is not as black-and-white heroic as many Seagal characters. I mean maybe he's supposed to be, but he gets a lot of innocent people killed or traumatized and that makes him seem like kind of an asshole. He plays a trick where he trades his rental car for the car of some German guy who looks like him from behind. First of all, this is a completely unfair deal for the German. Why the fuck you wanna trade a car you own for a car that belongs to a rental company? That's a grade-A German sucker right there, but that doesn't let Cold off the hook ethically. Just because the guy is willing to do it does not make it okay.

But more importantly, of course, Dunoir follows the German and figures out what happened, but kills the poor bastard anyway. I know I know, Dunoir is responsible for his own actions. But you also gotta blame Cold for this. You can't tell me he didn't figure out what was gonna happen. You're telling me he's so meticulous he's able to find his exact from-behind-lookalike on short notice out in the middle of nowhere, but then he doesn't think things through enough to figure out the guy could get killed? I don't buy it.

And he doesn't treat the elderly much better than he treats the Germans. In the ambush scene in the beginning when he goes to pick up The Package, the drop takes place at a little old lady's farmhouse. There's two guys there with their tongues cut out, then some dudes run in and gun everybody down and firebomb the farmhouse. Cold briefly embraces the old lady, then just mutters something about she should go to another farmhouse (I think this was looped later, to make it not quite as bad), then he and Dunoir drive away.

So yeah, he left a newly-homeless old lady at a burning farmhouse full of dead bodies. We never hear about her again so who knows what happened to her. The way bad guys in this movie come back to life and kill innocent hotel clerks and crap, I wouldn't be surprised if she got killed. Then again, she probably lost everything she had in that old farmhouse, and how's she gonna build another one? This is a woman who uses kerosene lamps, I'm betting she doesn't have a whole bunch of money stashed away in a bank account somewhere. Maybe she'd rather die.

Jesus Jon, they don't call you Cold for nothin.

And that's not even the worst of it! Some other guy captures Cold, ties him up, makes him admit that the package is in a locker at a train station and give him the key. "You better hope that package is there," the guy says. (Why would he have to *hope* the package is there? He already knows if it's there or not, doesn't he?)

Well, actually, it's not. It's a lookalike package with a bomb in it. There's no good establishing shot to show if the train station is busy at the time or not, but you can see at least 7 innocent extras passing by in the background. Then Cold jumps out a window just as the chump's knife somehow sets off a fuckin truck bomb sized explosion that literally blows fire out every single window in the station. Way to massacre innocent people again, Cold. And you wonder why you're not that close with your family.

One good thing about this scene though, Cold gets to stare his opponent down while pissing in a urinal. That's some badass shit I've never seen before. The weird thing is, I don't think he gets a chance to shake it off before he jumps through the window. And he sure as shit didn't wash his hands.

But back to how he's not that good of a secret agent, in my opinion. Cold is good in fights, but it should be pointed out that most of his action moments in the first half of the movie are unspectacular. The most laughable has him throwing a bodyguard from the down escalator onto the up escalator. It would be okay to have a small stunt like this if the movie didn't try to pass it off as a money shot. Suddenly, *Blade*-style techno music comes on and stuttery-freeze frame/jump cut editing tries to trick you into thinking you're impressed.

Later he punches a guy off a bridge, but it's an old guy, and the bridge is only a few feet high. Oh well, they can't all be winners.

The Foreigner is one of the least popular Seagal pictures, despite having more action than *The Patriot.* Casual fans have never heard of it, and most hardcores don't seem to like it. Most of the movie is dull and lifeless, and the gloomy, blue-grey cinematography doesn't help. The plot is overly complicated, Seagal is not in very good shape and it's depressingly humorless. It's definitely one of the more forgettable films in Seagalogy.

Before turning to low budget movies, director Michael Oblowitz worked in music videos. I don't remember many of the ones he did, because they were mostly for people like Corey Hart and Brooks & Dunn. But way back in 1985 he did the video for Kurtis Blow's "Basketball," where the old school rapper awkwardly lists his favorite plays and players and other reasons why "basketball is my favorite sport." The video mostly shows basketball players and singing cheerleaders but for some reason it also includes martial artists kicking and spinning nunchakas.

For his participation in that video alone I figure it's probably worth taking a closer look at Oblowitz's work on *The Foreigner.* And upon a more detailed analysis it turns out it does have some inspired touches.

Or one, anyway: a scene where Dunoir runs in slow motion away from a fiery explosion. We've seen this exact shot a hundred times, but isn't it always the hero? I can't remember ever seeing this done with the *bad guy*. So that was either stupid or clever, I'm not sure.

Actually, there's a couple good action moments in the end too. Faced with a shotgun, Cold puts his hands up, but then using patented old school Seagal fast hand movement he grabs the gun, flips it around and blows the guy away. In the same scene Cold kicks some object (a broken kerosene lamp is my guess) onto a guy, then throws a lighter and burns him up. It's the kind of thing that everybody enjoys in action movies, but the part I love is that then he kicks the guy. How often do you see a guy get kicked when *he's already on fire?* That's exactly the kind of overkill I'd like to see more of in these later Seagal pictures.

There's some funny dialogue exchanges I enjoyed. Referring to the German Jon Cold lookalike he killed, Mr. Mimms says, "My Führer sends his apologies. Hiring that sauerkraut to drive your rental and you buy his car was a nice touch. I hope you didn't go too far out of pocket on my account."

And Cold just says, "Ain't no thang."

Offering to bribe him, Cold asks, "You like the dollar bill?"

Mimms says, "Oh, dead presidents. Greenbacks." Yes, Mimms, those are two synonyms for dollars. Also you could've said clams, duckets, papers, bones, benjamins. There are many possible answers but good job on those two.

The showdown between Cold and Mimms is hilariously over-the-top and awkwardly staged. Cold leads Mimms to "an old building," promising to give him a disc with access codes to bank accounts, but Mimms pulls a gun on him. Cold says, "You know, I just somehow feel like, um, this might be the end of the road for me. But you do kind of remind me of my cousin *Delba from down on Bootalooth—*" (he slurs that last part and stops mid-gibberish to kick ass). A brilliant distraction tactic. (The subtitles translate his line as "Delbert from down around Bogalusa," whatever that means.)

You will notice that any time anybody gets tossed around in these old abandoned ruins, there is always a pile of crates and hay wherever they land. Weird. Anyway, Cold gets the jump on Mimms, but Mimms quickly comes back for more (something that happens with more than one villain character more than one time in this movie).

Mimms says, "Sweet dreams, Bruce Lee!"

Cold says, "Here's the disc!" and throws what appears to be an ordinary CD, but that we know we earlier saw him attaching explosives and a detonator to. (I know, I don't get it either.) The CD blows up, shoots *Half Past Dead* sparks everywhere, and propels Mimms through a window. He's so scared as he falls into the water that he turns white, unless that's just an unconvincing stunt double.

Cold quips, "I love a barbecue." It's really forced and poorly timed but we'll give him points since there are so few examples of attempted jokes in this movie.

Cold's final showdown with Dunoir is completely opposite of the Mimms fight. Refreshingly different. Usually the climactic fight has to be a long, drawn out battle where the villain seems to have the upper hand until the hero suddenly turns the tables. Not the case here. Dunoir has a mischievous smile and he keeps trying different tricks – pulling a gun, pulling a knife – but each one is almost immediately overwhelmed and overpowered by big ol' Seagal. He towers over the guy, pulls things out of his hands, grabs his wrists and makes him useless. The guy doesn't have a chance. It's not a very showy fight, but I would argue that it is a well choreographed one, especially compared to other movies from this stage in Seagal's career.

The Foreigner is also unique among Seagal pictures because it's a secret agent/international intrigue type of movie. It was filmed in Poland, and the story travels between Poland, Germany and France (with discussion of Russia and the United States). It is not at all in the *Die Hard* ripoff genre, although it does have a little moment directly lifted from *Die Hard* (Cold gives a gun to guy, guy pulls gun on Cold, but it's not loaded, and Cold says, "What do you think, I'm stupid?") Despite its lack of popularity, *The Foreigner* not only got a sequel (*Black Dawn*) but seems to have inspired the main drawback of Seagal's DTV era: muddled, overly complicated plots with too many double crosses and tricks. It becomes hard to follow what's going on, and most of the time it's not like you're really dying to make an effort.

So *The Foreigner* has a very different feel from all the previous Seagal pictures, but I don't think that's why the fans don't like it. The overall tone is depressing enough to dampen most of the fun in the later parts of the movie. But at least it's not a total failure.

The Foreigner, 2003

Directed by Michael Oblowitz (*This World, Then the Fireworks*, next did Seagal's *Out For a Kill*).

Written by Darren O. Campbell (writer/director of an undistributed independent film called *Second Coming*. Also played the character "Tommy" in the killer snowman movie *Jack Frost*.)

Distinguished co-stars: Gary Raymond. (I didn't know who he was either, but turns out he was in *Look Back in Anger, El Cid*, even *Jason and the Argonauts*. So that counts.)

Seagal regulars: John P. Gulino, who plays the hotel manager, returns as a jewelry store owner in the sequel *Black Dawn* – I guess he got fed up with the hotel business, moved to Los Angeles and got a job at a jewelry store just in time to get robbed by terrorists raising money to buy a suitcase bomb to avenge the CIA's assassination of their leader. Gulino also appears in *The Glimmer Man, Fire Down Below* and *Today You Die*. Jacek Samojlowicz (Assailant in Camel Coat) will play a Polish customs agent in *Out of Reach*.

Firsts: First of two back to back Oblowitz/Seagal collaborations.

Title refers to: Late in the movie, it is explained that Seagal was once "a foreigner," supposedly a term for an American deep undercover as a spy for the KGB.

Just how badass is this guy? One villain is happy that he gets to "kill a legend." But there is not a traditional Just How Badass Is He? Line.

Adopted culture: None. Although he lives in Paris, he doesn't appear to know more French than "bonjour."

Languages: See above.

Improvised weapons: Kicks some kind of kerosene lamp or something to set a guy on fire. Rigs an explosive CD. Chair legs stolen from an opponent who had already tried to use them.

Old friends: Tells a security guard that he is "an old friend" of the main villain, but he actually isn't.

Fight in bar: No.

Broken glass: Bottle dropped during shooting. Lots of empty bottles and vases shot throughout the movie. Kerosene lamp. Jumps through restroom window, subsequent explosion blows out other windows. Smashed telephone booth, shower door. A guy gets blown through a window. Angrily punches through menu-mirror in French café.

Family shit: He actually has a brother who is an important character in the movie. His brother is suspicious of him, but helps him escape from crooked CIA guys. At the end, when asked if he has an older or younger brother, he says, "Wiser."

Political themes: As usual, CIA corruption. His brother tells him, "Not everything is a fucking conspiracy, Jon." And he says, "Well that's true, just not very often in our business." The plot involves a rich businessman and CIA agents involved in biochemical warfare and terrorism. More interestingly though, a crucial part of the backstory involves proof that a commercial jet was shot down by a surface to air missile. This had to have been inspired by TWA Flight 800, the plane that mysteriously went down in July of 1996. Hundreds of witnesses saw what appeared to be a missile hitting the plane, but none of them were allowed to testify at the NTSB hearings. No one seems to agree who fired the missile or why, but the CIA and FBI definitely gave the impression they were trying to cover something up. In *The Foreigner* there's no mystery – newspaper headlines state definitively that the plane was shot down by a missile.

Cover accuracy: Seagal with a silenced pistol – fine. Eiffel Tower – sure. Two helicopters – well, I don't think that's from this movie, but they always like to get some helicopters on there. Why not? But the flipping car and the blond in the negligee talking on the phone, I don't know where those come from. And the tagline – "If they think they can stop him, they're dead wrong" – doesn't make any sense because they're not really trying to stop him from doing anything, they're trying to get the package from him. I guess "If they think they can get the package from him, they're dead wrong" doesn't have the same ring to it.

CHAPTER 15:
OUT FOR A KILL

"This gwilo professor is becoming a problem."

Near the beginning of *Out For a Kill* we are introduced to the villains: the heads of eleven Chinese Tongs, all sitting together at an Evil Table somewhere that turns out to be in Paris. Here they plot an Evil Master Plan to unite all of the Chinese crime families and wipe out every other syndicate on the planet.

Each of the villains are introduced not through action or speech, but through freeze frames and text that tell us their names, their specialties, and in some cases their hobbies (one guy likes auto racing and sky diving, another "has a penchant for French restaurants"). You're not gonna remember who's who, but don't worry, none of this information will turn out to be relevant.

"We must take special care," declares the head of the table, Wong Dai, "so that nothing and no one interferes with this historic event."

Cut to opening credits, over phoney looking model of ancient Chinese ruins. Because who better to interfere with a historic event than Robert Burns, professor of Chinese archaeology at Yale? Especially if Robert Burns is played by Mr. Steven Seagal.

I repeat. Seagal plays Robert Burns, a professor of Chinese archaeology at Yale. When we first see him, he is receiving "the prestigious and much coveted Winthrop Award for excellence in archaeology," and is introduced as "this university's most distinguished academician." Unfortunately, shortly after winning the award, Burns and his sexy female assistant (Elaine Tan) get into some shit at an archaeological dig in China.

The first sign of trouble is probably the pilot who flies them to the site (Ray Charleson). He explains that his nickname "Crash" comes from the fact that he never has. Now, wait a minute. Is this guy telling us that it is unusual for a pilot to never crash? That it is a trait so unique to him that it becomes his handle? If so, I'm never flying again. If not, shouldn't most pilots be nicknamed Crash?

Sign number two: some secret-service-looking thug walking around the archaeological site wearing a tie and shades, pretending to be an archaeologist. This guy accidentally steps square in the center of an ancient Chinese artifact, crushing it like a Dorito. Doesn't even apologize. It takes Burns a bit to observe, "Not an archaeologist, is he?" and that "somethin's up here." Instead of asking the dude what his fuckin problem is, Burns snoops around and finds a bag of heroin stashed in one of the artifacts he'd already prepared for shipping. A Jeep chase ensues and the camera follows a CGI bullet through the rear window and then through the assistant. Next thing you know Burns is trapped in his Jeep, holding a dead body and completely surrounded by armed Chinese soldiers and DEA agents. I count 30 guns pointing at him, all close range.

So the prestigious award-winning academician Robert Burns finds himself in Su-Chou Prison, China, where DEA agents Ed Grey (Corey Johnson) and Tommie Ling (Michelle Goh) disagree as to whether or not he's guilty of smuggling heroin. They don't seem to care too much about who killed the assistant, though. Out of their jurisdiction, I guess. When Burns wants to talk to his lawyer, Grey says, "That's the first smart thing you've said all day," which isn't very fair. I'm sure he said something smart about the Han Dynasty or something earlier in the day.

This is not Burns's first time in the joint, by the way. We know from a discussion at the Evil Table that Burns actually has a secret past – and not even a CIA one. It seems that "this gwilo professor was once one of the greatest thieves in Shanghai, New York and Paris. He specialized in valuable paintings and priceless Chinese artifacts. He was known as the Goei, or the Ghost." Then he disappeared, and many thought he was dead. But he turned up stateside in '85 and got busted, served seven years. Then he pulled a Malcolm X, working off his expertise in Chinese artifacts to earn a doctorate in Chinese archaeology. When he got out he was somehow able to create a new identity (meaning Robert Burns isn't his real name?) but still use his doctorate to become a distinguished professor of Chinese archaeology at some dipshit Connecticut school called Yale.

I swear on Christ's holy balls I didn't make up that stuff in the last paragraph. That is the actual plot of the movie. You know you want to watch it.

Anyway, Burns's cellmate this time around is not played by Ja Rule but some guy named Michael Junior Harvey, or MC Harvey, a UK rapper from the group So Solid Crew and winner of some game show in 2003. King starts to explain how he wound up in Su-Chou. "Truth is, I was crossing the Kazakhstan border, trafficking some weed." The screen fades to black, as if flashing back to show King's bust. We see a few frames of this as he says, "Some ragheaded motherfuckers—" but mid-sentence the movie cuts away to another scene, as if to say, 'Save it, King. We're not interested.'

This is all we see of King and Burns celling together because the DEA decides to let Burns go (thinking he's guilty and therefore will lead them to the Chinese gangs). But it seems like these two did ten years together the way they say their goodbyes:

BURNS: Once a friend, a friend for life.
KING: Take care, my man.
BURNS: You ain't goin' down a rat hole.
KING: Don't forget about me.
BURNS: Love and respect.
KING: So walk in peace, my man.
BURNS: I'll see you soon.
KING: Don't forget about me, Burns!

At this point I have some amends to make. When I first reviewed a VHS screener of this film for the popular Texas-based web sight The Ain't It Cool News, I made one serious error. In that review I claimed that after the "Don't forget about me, Burns!" the character of King was never seen or mentioned again. That would've been funny, but it's actually not true. I don't know how I missed it on that initial viewing, but there is in fact a later scene where Burns asks Tommie Ling to have King freed for "a second chance," and she agrees. We don't see him again but we do know that Burns didn't forget about him, and as long as Ling also didn't forget about him, he probably got out. That'll show those "ragheaded motherfuckers" in Kazakhstan for trying to stop the trafficking of weed. (Although maybe if King would've just stayed in he would've had time to earn a doctorate and become a distinguished professor.)

So anyway, Burns is on the loose, which you wouldn't think would be a big concern to the Evil Table in Paris. To them he's "a certain gwilo professor" who almost got blamed for their trafficking. But he's an archaeologist, and not the kind with a whip, so who the fuck cares? He's no threat to them, you would think. Or maybe just to be safe, I guess they could send some young Chinese dude to shoot him in the back of the neck and get it over with.

But the Tong heads make a major mistake: micro-managing. As evidenced by my mistake with King above, I am fallible. But unless I misunderstood something, I do believe they send two guys from the Evil Table to kill Burns at his assistant's funeral. And that's just dumb.

On the other hand, I do have to give them points for trying to kill him at a funeral. That's some cold blooded shit that I can always get behind for a villain. First time I remember seeing this was in Rudy Ray Moore's best film, *Petey Wheatstraw, the Devil's Son-in-Law*. The villain's thugs are out trying to kill Petey Wheatstraw's friends, and in the process they accidentally kill an innocent neighborhood boy. Then out of nowhere, during a depressing funeral sequence, the guys drive by, hop out of a car and machine gun everybody at the funeral! There's also a good scene in *King of New York* where Christopher Walken rides by a cemetery in a limo, rolls down the window and blows a guy's head off. But he probably did it because he loved *Petey Wheatstraw*.

Out For a Kill puts a new spin on the funeral execution motif. This is a traditional Chinese funeral ritual with a shrine, robes and incense. Suddenly there's a small explosion of sparks (way to make an entrance, fellas) and two dudes with swords jump out. Luckily the esteemed academician must have some background in the martial arts, because he grabs some wooden poles from the shrine and fights the two swordsmen. He kills them both, of course, but they get all the cool moves that get freeze-framed and slo-motioned, so in a way everybody wins. Due to his expertise in Chinese culture, Burns knows to pull down their sleeves and read tattoos on their wrists which provide clues to a riddle which he will need at the end of the movie.

Before the attack at the funeral, Burns vows to his assistant's father (also his mentor) that he will get revenge. "There is no mirror, there is no dust, there is no darkness," he says. "Only the mind is light. I think you know what I have to do."

"I will wait by the open grave for your return," the father agrees.

And then Burns fucks around for a while, staving off attacks when necessary, but not actively seeking revenge. And his wife Maya is starting to get pissed – every time they go out to a restaurant, he has to kill a bunch of motherfuckers. Like for example, they go out for dinner and he says he has to go to the bathroom. Then some Tong guys come in looking for him. He comes out of the bathroom in about ten seconds – who knows what he was doing in there or why it was important to include in the movie. But then there's a big fight with tables flipping over and everything.

Then in the middle of the night Burns thinks he hears something, and goes out with a flashlight to investigate around his Spielbergian suburban home (address: 31 Warren Str. New York, New York 10007 according to the DEA computer file). Suddenly a firebomb destroys his whole house, with his wife inside.

So he goes back to the assistant's dad, and again vows revenge. "Your daughter, my wife, both dead. I came here to make you a promise. Within one week I'll avenge their deaths, before the funeral of my wife." Good. So there's a deadline established this time, he probably should've done that in the first place. Now he knows there's a time limit, he can't be fucking around in restaurants and bathrooms and shit, there is vengeance to be wrought.

"I promise you one thing," he continues. "The souls of our enemies will be ashes and dust gone in the sky before the funeral of our loved ones. That's a promise." The rhythm is reminiscent of the classic "superior attitude, superior state of mind" speech from *Hard to Kill*. Then he gets up and walks out as the father gives his blessing in a voiceover. I don't know if this means that he gave the blessing later over the phone, or that he gave it after Burns had already left the room. Either way, it's kind of weird in my opinion. Or maybe he gave his blessing telepathically, I guess that would make sense sort of.

Okay, so now that two loved ones are dead, he finally goes into Parker mode and goes out for justice/a kill. He even tracks down the pilot Crash and pretends to want a flying lesson. Crash I guess is a very liberal and risk-taking flying teacher since he lets Burns fly that very afternoon. But he's in for an airborne version of the scene in *Point Blank* where Lee Marvin scares the shit out of a guy through the medium of bad driving. (We later find out that Crash let him do this intentionally so he could set Burns up for a trap. You see, people? You don't get good intelligence under torture.)

Next Burns ends up in Chinatown at a place called The Hidden Dragon Barber Shop. That name I guess is the filmmakers' "fuck you" to Yuen Woo Ping and Ang Lee for popularizing elaborate "wire-fu" martial arts choreography world wide with *Crouching Tiger, Hidden Dragon*. Inside the barbershop, Seagal has his first ever fight against a flying character attached to a wire. This guy I'm assuming does monkey kung fu, since he keeps crouching down and scratching himself like a monkey. He flies around and climbs up and down the walls and Burns waits in the middle of the room until the guy gets close enough for him to hit him or grab him. The scene is laughable and silly but if you think about it it fits the philosophy of aikido: do not attack, just use your enemy's energy against him. So there's no reason for Seagal to fly around or climb the walls. That's not the aikido way. The monkey guy is just a show off.

Burns continues to follow a trail of clues, battling each guy from the Evil Table and reading their wrist tattoos after he defeats them. There is one guy who speaks only in wise sayings and metaphors ("Crows everywhere are equally black!"). There's a fight in a laundromat and one in a mahjong parlor. We find out that in mahjong parlors, just like in restaurants, everybody flips over their tables when a fight is about to start. But then Burns defeats his opponent in 3 or 4 moves and leaves. I bet everybody who was playing was pretty pissed about that. They should've held off on the table flipping. In fact, I don't know why the gambling establishments in these movies don't institute some kind of ban on table flipping, or at least a mandatory table flipping fine. As it stands, any gambler can get out of a losing game just by starting a fight and flipping all the tables over.

There's also a scene where Burns and his opponent Sai-Lo (Hon Ping Tang) punch at each other and their fists collide. And a scene where Tommie Ling confronts horny sadomasochistic lesbian junkie tattoo artists. And an excellent long distance out-the-window beheading. Burns of course keeps his second vow of revenge, and takes care of business before his wife's funeral. Then for some reason he thinks it's okay to walk away in the middle of the funeral holding Tommie Ling's hand. Oh well, they've been through a lot.

The director, Michael Oblowitz, has kind of a gloomy feel to his movies, but he definitely brings more excitement and flair to this than to *The Foreigner.* That movie's saturated photography looked dull and lifeless, but this one actually has some striking, stylized uses of color at times. I think one of his weaknesses comes from the modern digital editing techniques, which make it way too easy to overlap footage and to slo-mo. He definitely overuses both, and punctuates many sequences with incomprehnsible rapid-fire montages known as "Avid farts." At least that's what I call them so that's what you should call them also, in my opinion.

On the other hand, the digital technology probably helped him to fill some scenes with very exaggerated primary colors that make the movie unique. If you watch closely, there's a shot or two of weapons in front of bright red backgrounds that could almost be out of a Seijun Suzuki movie. One surprisingly artful scene is the one where his house blows up with his wife inside. While he's outside, the whole scene is drowned in a deep sea blue. When the house explodes the blue Seagal flies away from a vivid yellow fire. Then we see him lit up in a reddish tinge in front of the unnaturally blue night sky. Even more stylized colors are used for mental flashes as he thinks about his wife's death. I didn't really appreciate them until I watched them frame by frame, but there are some nice composites of black and white and color, sort of like Robert Rodriguez and Frank Miller later did in *Sin City*. Some shots, for example, show Burns kissing his wife, with the wife in color and everything else black and white.

One stylistic choice I made fun of in my The Ain't It Cool News review of the picture was the titles telling you the time and place of the scenes. They don't think it's enough for the guy at the awards ceremony to mention they are at Yale, they actually have to write "Yale University, New Haven, Connecticut" on the screen. And worse, they have to have the letters roll out with that computer sound that computers always make when text appears on the screen. Oh wait, computers never make that sound. We only know that's a computer sound because computers always do that in movies, for no apparent reason other than to make movies less relatable to normal human beings who, by this time, have probably seen a real computer before and found out that they don't look or sound anything at all like the computers they have in movies.

The effect is even more silly on DVD than on VHS, because they decided to use the subtitle track for the titles instead of having them burned in. So when it says "Su-Chou Prison, China" it doesn't roll across, it just appears in your usual subtitle font, but accompanied by a computery "doot-doot-doot-doot-doot" sound. Worse, there are three cases where the titles happen to overlap with dialogue, so they don't show up at all whether or not you have the subtitles turned on. So right at the very beginning of the movie you have a "doot-doot-doot-doot-doot" sound effect accompanying nothing!

In my opinion, *Out For a Kill* is the tipping point where Seagalogy goes into the deep end. Maybe the earlier Seagal pictures were silly or ridiculous at times, but this is where they start to get downright crazy. They seem to be made in more of a mercenary, low budget, get it done at any cost spirit. From this point on most of the films are international co-productions filmed outside of American soil, and maybe they lose a little something in the translation. It doesn't seem possible that these movies were filmed with completed scripts. If they were, it seems like the circumstances of filmmaking didn't allow them to actually follow much of the script.

As a result, *Out For a Kill* and many of the Seagal pictures that follow are filled to the brim with weird narrative lapses, constant looped dialogue, abrupt edits and unexpected voiceover narration. For example, the DEA agent Tommie Ling narrates this movie, but you don't know that until she starts doing it out of the blue about 48 minutes in.

And I mean, who the fuck would think it was okay to combine the titles of two previous Seagal movies into one? He's not really out for justice but he is hard to kill but mostly he's out for a kill. Possible future titles: *Marked For Justice, On Deadly Justice, Under the Law, Fire Under Siege, The Ticker Man*. At this point Seagal's pictures begin to flirt with a surreal, fuck-all-common-sense lunacy similar to Jean-Claude Van Damme's surrealist collaborations with Tsui Hark (*Double Team* and *Knock Off*). So it's a sad time for serious Seagal fans but good news for those who enjoy Seagalogy as camp or with a lot of beer.

Despite, or probably because of all that, this is one of my favorites of the DTV era. It's hard to go wrong with a movie where Seagal is able to both indulge his passion for Asian culture and play a Yale professor. Plus you got swords, aikido, wire-fu, Jeep chase – a respectable variety of action. With its crazy plot, flowery dialogue and high volume of action by DTV standards, *Out For a Kill* is easily one of the most enjoyable of Seagal's DTV period.

Out For a Kill, 2003
Directed by Michael Oblowitz (*The Foreigner*)
Story by Danny Lerner (*Today You Die, Octopus 2: River of Fear*), screenplay by Dennis Dimster-Denk (*Cyborg Cop III;* also directed *Mikey*, that movie where the little brother from *Family Ties* is a killer kid). Some guy named Sam Hayes also worked on it uncredited according to the internet movie database.
Distinguished co-stars: None, but Corey Johnson (Ed Grey), Michael J. Reynolds (Dean), and Ray Charleson (Harry "Crash" Kupper, the pilot who has never crashed) were later in *United 93*. Don't ask me, I have no idea, but it's true. And Ozzie Yu, (Fang Lee, 'The Barber') played a Chinese oil executive in *Syriana*.
Seagal regulars: Tom Wu, who plays Li Bo, later played the villain General Jantapan in *Belly of the Beast*. Raicho Vasilev (Bulgarian Thug) plays Ender in *Submerged*.
Firsts: First Seagal movie to combine the titles of two previous Seagal movies. First to have

Seagal fight against "wire-fu."

Title refers to: Seagal, who has apparently stepped out for a kill. On the other hand, the villains have also stepped out for a kill. So there's kind of a double meaning there if you think about it.

Just how badass is this guy? "I don't understand how one man can walk away from certain death so many times." "We found out that this gwilo professor was once one of the greatest thieves in Shanghai, New York and Paris. He specialized in valuable paintings and priceless Chinese artifacts. He was known as the Goei, or the Ghost. Some thought he had died, but he had disappeared."

Adopted culture: He is an expert on Chinese history, culture, philosophy and archaeology, specializing in the Han Dynasty. He knows Chinese funeral traditions and when to bow to people.

Languages: He speaks and reads Chinese (I'm not sure which dialect). We can also infer that he must speak French if he was one of the greatest thieves in Paris. On the other hand, that would make him even more badass if he could steal shit there without even knowing the language.

Improvised weapons: Ceremonial wooden sticks as swords, barber's smock as whip.

Fight in bar: No bar, just a restaurant and a mahjong parlor. There is a shootout at a strip club, which would probably count, but Seagal is not involved and we mostly just see the aftermath.

Broken glass: CGI bullet goes through Jeep window and Burns's sexy assistant. At the assistant's funeral, the glass in the framed photo of her is shattered. Vases and a mirror at a restaurant. Guy thrown out window in slow motion, shown from various angles.

Words of wisdom: "There is no mirror, there is no dust, there is no darkness. Only the mind is light. I think you know what I have to do." (Yeah, you have to do JACK FUCKING SHIT until your wife gets killed, then go get revenge.)

Family shit: His wife gets blown up and he has to step out for a kill, or actually a bunch of kills, to get revenge.

Political themes: Not really any, except that the DEA willingly use an innocent man and his family as bait. "What happens to the professor and his family?" "Fuck 'em."

Cover accuracy: The DVD cover shows two helicopters, which are not in the movie. Why do they think we want helicopters in every Seagal movie? Maybe it's some superstition, they're gonna jinx it if they release one without helicopters. The VHS screener showed the helicopters in the background and Seagal holding two big guns that he doesn't use in the movie.

CHAPTER 16:
BELLY OF THE BEAST

"Nothing personal. For me, it's all about the girls. I'm just here for those girls."

Seagal plays Jake Hopper, an ex-CIA freelance operative whose loving daughter Jessica (*Nature Unleashed: Volcano*'s Sarah Malakul Lane) is kidnapped while vacationing with friends in Thailand. Not believing the official story that she was kidnapped by a Muslim terrorist group called the Abu Karaf, Hopper goes to Thailand himself to, you know, straighten things out.

Before all this, though, and before the credits even, we get the backstory of Hopper's last CIA mission. Hopper and his partner Sunti (Byron Mann) are meeting with some criminal types when suddenly gunmen storm in and it turns into a shitstorm. Taking off through an alley, Sunti shoots and accidentally kills an innocent civilian woman holding a toddler. Hopper shoots the shooters, saving Sunti's life, but the damage is done.

After the credits is a pretty spectacular black-ops scene that takes place about ten years later in Hopper's new home state of Hawaii. Hopper evades security to sneak onto the roof of a mansion and then inside, where he breaks into a safe and steals some kind of disc. Obviously most people are gonna wear all black for a job like this, including either a knit cap or a ski mask. That might even be why it's called black-ops, I'm not sure. Hopper goes halfway, wearing all black but without headgear or sleeves. Maybe he's cocky because he has the help of an obvious stunt double who is much more limber than Seagal and has very toned arms shown in one close-up.

The three best moves in the scene are definitely Seagal, though. First, he does a gratuitous somersault right after coming through the window. For all the laughs had at the expense of gratuitous somersaults, you don't really see them all that often, and you definitely don't expect them in this era of Seagalogy. But he does it and his face is clearly shown in the same shot as the somersault. Admittedly, it's a basic tumbling move that can be done by many children, but you have to appreciate what you can get these days.

Later, he does a slow motion slide across the ground so that he doesn't get spotted as he passes a window. It looks sort of like Tom Cruise in *Risky Business*, but laying down. And with clothes on. But right after doing that awesome slide, he seems pretty beat so he just kind of stumbles into the kitchen and – please trust me that I am not making this up – opens the refrigerator. For just a second there you think it's leading to a shocking moment of self-deprecation for heavier-than-he-used-to-be Seagal, but then he produces a bottle of water and starts drinking it. He acts like he just got back from a jog, but he hasn't even left the mansion yet.

So after stealing a disc and a bottle of water, Hopper returns to his fancy, window-laden home surrounded by wilderness. He literally lives in a glass house, so thankfully he doesn't talk a lot of shit about other people during the movie. Now he goes to his own refrigerator where we learn from a series of Post-it notes that his daughter insists on babysitting him, leaving him notes about not drinking coffee, getting enough sleep, etc. Some of them just say how much she loves him, illustrated by little hearts or stick figures holding hands. We also learn that Maria comes on Wednesdays and that Jorge is coming on Friday, which seems a little excessive. It doesn't seem like that messy of a house. But I guess it's gotta be a real bitch getting streaks off all those windows.

Also of note: a dentist's appointment on Tuesday at 9 am and a guy coming from the gas company Friday morning. He never mentions it but I'm pretty sure he misses both of these appointments during the course of the movie. *Hi, good morning, my name is Jake Hopper, I have an appointment with Dr. Johnson on Tuesday morning. Listen, I have to go to Thailand to rescue my daughter from kidnappers, they say it's Abu Karaf but I'm not so sure, not too many Muslims that far north. I'm not sure if I'm going to get back in time, I wonder if we could reschedule for next week some time?*

Also, Jessica has made several days' worth of meals, packed them in Tupperware and labeled what day they're for. I've seen this in other movies and it just doesn't make sense to me. Why does she give a shit if he eats the "BROCCOLI PENNE – YUMMY!!!!" on Thursday or on some other day? What if he feels like saving the lemon chicken (his favorite, she says) for Thursday, so he'll be ready for the big gas appointment in the morning? I mean if you're making him all those dinners he has no right to complain but I still don't see why you don't let him make his own decisions on what to eat when. This is America, lady. Maybe not continental United States but it's still part of the union.

When Hopper's CIA contact (Martin MacDougall) stops by to pick up the disc and tell Hopper the news about his daughter you can really see what a bad idea the glass house is for a former covert operative. Because Hopper comes down the stairs with a gun in his hand and if it was an enemy outside they would see him coming. How would he hide? Hell, what if he was in there jerking off? I don't care if he's a Buddhist, he's gonna enjoy some pornography every once in a while, I would think. But everybody in the woods would know. How are you gonna jerk off when there's squirrels and birds and shit out there, and who knows what else? You can't get a boner in front of a bear. I mean this whole set up just seems kind of risky. Anyway the agent's name is Tom Collins. He doesn't seem old enough to have invented the cocktail of the same name, so I'm guessing his parents were fond of it.

Hopper arrives in Sangkom, Thailand in what seems about the amount of time most people take to get to the grocery store. He looks like a giant, walking around in crowds where he's at least a head taller than everybody else. People always make fun of Seagal's weight, but this is one example of where his size makes him menacing. In his skinny period, like *Above the Law*, his height didn't seem that important. Now he can't move as fast but his look is way more intimidating.

Right off the plane he catches a taxi and the driver brings him to a bunch of thugs who plan to beat his ass. This leads to a market and the first big fight scene. The thugs surround Hopper with knives, but he repels their attacks one by one. This is where the direction and choreography of the legendary Ching Siu Tung first become apparent. Instead of the usual aikido, Hopper seems to do kung fu, and the chumps he kicks are launched into the air and against piles of vegetables. Seagal already encountered a wallclimbing wire-fu villain in *Out For a Kill*, but here the wires actually help him out by making his blows superhumanly effective.

In this scene you also see a creepy old bearded wizard dude watching from afar. He is clearly evil but he won't be seen again until the finale and even then nobody will explain who or what the fuck he is.

Next Hopper goes to some kind of strip/go-go bar to talk to an old CIA contact named Fitch McQuoid (Vincent Riotta). He also gets in a fight to protect one of the dancers (Monica Lo) who turns out to be named Lulu and starts following him around trying to help him.

For some reason, this is the point where Hopper decides to change into a robe and row a boat out to a Buddhist temple to get the blessing of a master. And it just so happens that his old partner Sunti is at this same temple, where he has been a monk for ten years, ever since he accidentally shot that innocent lady. As long as he's in the neighborhood, Hopper tells Sunti about the kidnapping, but doesn't ask him to help. "I'm very, very proud of you," Hopper says. "You stay a full monk for 10 years? Really, really wonderful."

So of course as soon as Hopper leaves Sunti tells the master he's turning his back on the temple to go down a path of violence. When he shows up in civilian clothes at Hopper's hotel, Hopper doesn't seem surprised at all, but he "tries" to talk him into going back to his life as a monk. That ain't gonna happen.

I don't want to psychoanalyze the guy, but this whole thing with Sunti seems pretty passive aggressive to me. Hopper acts like he didn't want Sunti to turn his back on religion and blow his ten year consecutive stretch of non-violence, but I don't buy it. He fuckin knew Sunti was gonna trade the robe for a gun as soon as he told him the situation. I mean come on Jake Hopper, who do you think you're fooling? I think what happens is he realizes that he's out here in Thailand and he doesn't have Jessica or Maria or even Jorge to pamper him, so he decides to go bag himself a Buddhist monk sidekick. And sure enough Sunti does all the legwork – in fact fresh out of the temple he already has a lead from somewhere. There's an arms deal going down with an Abu Karaf guy named Mongkol (Pongpat Wachirabunjong), if they follow this guy they can find out if the Abu Karaf really have the girls.

"Ledz doo it," Hopper slurs, and they're on their way.

The DVD chapters call the arms deal scene "Songkom Train Yard Shootout," and this scene is classic for a couple of reasons. The first reason is the person who Mongkol is meeting with. Nobody seems to notice that it's clearly a man in drag. Or maybe they are enlightened enough not to care.

The second reason is the shootout itself, one of the action highlights of the movie. Hopper sparks a huge gunfight with much more of an authentic Hong Kong flavor than Seagal's American movies. There's also a memorable move reminiscent of John Woo's silly/awesome period with Jean-Claude Van Damme and Dolph Lundgren: From inside a train car, Seagal leaps *through* the side of the car and not only shoots three guys while in mid-air, but hits each of them 4 or 5 times. Then he lands on a little cart on train tracks that he uses to roll along shooting various attackers while laying down. At last – a leisurely way of massacring gunmen.

The third and most important reason for the greatness of the Songkom Train Yard Shootout is a little moment right before the actual shootout begins. The place is swarming with rifle-toting terrorists. Spying on the arms deal between Mongkol and the female impersonator, Hopper notices a sniper about to take out Mongkol.

In order to follow Mongkol to his daughter he has to shoot the sniper, but that will reveal his presence and force him to fight off an army of a few dozen heavily armed terrorists. And poor first-day-out-of-the-temple Sunti will be in the middle of it. So instead of just jumping into action, Hopper turns to Sunti to get his consent and make sure he understands the full ramifications of the decision. "Okay. Somebody up there about to snipe Mongkol. If I let him do that, I could lose the only link to my daughter, and I can't let that happen. If I shoot him, a whole world of trouble's gonna come down on us, you know that, right?"

"Yeah."

"Here we go."

This is a distinctly Steven Seagal badass moment, combining the anticipatory thrill of an Oh-Shit-It's-On moment with a gesture of morality and camaraderie. And the shootout itself lives up to that buildup.

The battle ends with the Thai special police stepping in, and Hopper is so into killing terrorists he manages to squeeze off a couple more shots in the moments between being surrounded by cops and putting his hands up. He goes in peacefully but at the station, after calling bullshit on the general's claim that he interrupted an important "anti-terror raid," the fuckin pigs start beating him. Here he is, arrested in a foreign country, surrounded by armed cops, wearing handcuffs, what's he gonna do? Well, of course – he takes the fuckers on. It really seems like he could escape too, but FBI agent Leon Washington (Patrick Robinson) – who seems pretty nice, everybody just calls him Leon – shows up and negotiates his release.

Every once in a while we get an update on Jessica and her senator's-daughter friend, who are locked up in a dirty room guarded by three sleazy Thai thugs. One of them comes in and tries to molest "the Winthorpe girl" (as the authorities call Jessica's friend) so Jessica steals his hunting knife and stabs him repeatedly. Another guard comes in and, without even checking the off-screen body of the stabbed rapist, announces "She killed my brother!" and prepares to chop her head off with a machete. The other guard convinces him they need her alive and tells him to take care of the body, and they turn around and walk out. I only mention this scene because when they leave the room, they are clearly not carrying a dead guy. We have seen that this guy is regular sized and would not fit in his brother's pocket, even if she chopped him up, which was not the case. So although we never see it ourselves I'm pretty damn sure these poor girls spend the rest of their captivity as roommates with a bloody corpse.

This is a much more confident movie than most in Seagal's DTV era, but there is one really awkward section where Lulu, the girl Hopper stood up for at the go-go bar, suddenly becomes a main character when she shows up at her apartment and finds her roommate murdered. There must be some scenes missing here because right after she finds the body there's a weird voiceover of Sunti explaining, "They killed her roommate and the hotel is crawling with police. This place is safe." The place in question is where Lulu and Hopper sit and talk about the dead roommate, she cries, he holds her supportively, and next thing you know – there's no other way to say it – they're fuckin. Or I guess I could've said making love. Only two ways to say it.

I think we can all agree that this scene is very disturbing. One minute after the movie shows her finding her roommate dead, the movie flashes back to her finding her roommate dead. Two minutes after finding her roommate dead, she's having sex with Hopper. That's called "taking advantage."

I don't know who the fuck thought it was necessary to throw a sex scene in here, but seeing big ol' Hopper on top of a girl he barely knows who's half his age who is crying about finding her friend murdered a couple minutes ago is a little too much, in my opinion. Not to be a prude. Most people would probably assume Seagal insisted on the sex scene but I honestly don't think so because he doesn't seem into it at all. The low key acting style works for dialogue but it's kind of creepy when he's in bed.

There's another *what-the-fuck?* moment a little later on, but this one is intentional. Sunti is driving Hopper around when a woman with a scarf on her head stops them by standing in the middle of the road. Sunti asks, "Is this woman crazy?" but Hopper seems to understand what's going on. He gets out and she wordlessly leads him into a small bar and into a back room where she unwraps her scarf and drops her robe, showing off what we in America would refer to as "a nice rack." She dips a towel in a bowl of water and squeezes drops over her breasts, revealing some kind of invisible-ink tattoo. And Hopper nods that he understands. No explanation offered, but we can assume the tattoo tells him where to go in the next scene to meet up with Mongkol. In other words, terrorists sent him a tittygram.

He learns from Mongkol what he figured all along, that they had nothing to do with the kidnapping. I think what happened was Hopper's old CIA friend Fitch McQuoid, who was competing with the Abu Karaf for the arms and heroin markets, paid off the Thai special police to kidnap the girls and make it look like the Abu Karaf did it so that the CIA would take out his competition. I'm not entirely sure how it works because I've only seen the movie several times and taken pages of detailed scene-by-scene notes. You're gonna have to pay a little more attention than that to understand what the fuck is going on here. There's Fitch, there's some guy named Fernand Zadir (Kevork Malikyan), there's Mongkol, there's the transvestite who they say is named Lena (but there's nobody named that in the credits), I think there's somebody named Bridgeport and then there's General Jantapan (Tom Wu) who must be the mastermind since he's the guy Hopper fights to the death in the climax. And that's not even figuring in the evil sorcerer guy. Shit, and I thought *Syriana* was complicated.

I'll get back to the evil sorcerer guy in a minute but first I want to mention Hopper's showdown with Lena the deadly transvestite. Lena wears pumps for the whole battle and uses her feminine fingernails like tiger claws. It's a full-on kung fu fight complete with old school Shaw Brothers style sound effects, but it's a little anti-climactic. I wish Lena would've put up more of a fight.

General Jantapan *does* put up a fight. In fact, he (or somebody working with him) actually steals a t-shirt from Hopper's luggage so that he can present it to the aforementioned evil sorcerer guy in some sort of mystical ceremony in a temple full of tarantulas, scorpions and demon statues. The sorcerer uses the shirt (which we never saw Hopper wear, but I guess he packed for non-robe wearing situations) to make a voodoo doll that he keeps in a box of worms and sticks pins in during the fight. It's good to see a villain really going out of his way to prepare for a fight in advance. Good work General Jantapan, even though you're an asshole who consorts with demonic scorpion lovers.

Hopper does his homework too though, and goes to Sunti's former Buddhist master to get a magic protective medallion to wear during the fight. I never heard of magic necklaces in Buddhism but I guess a lama like Seagal would know better than I would. He gets to wear it because

"Everything you are doing is for love."

Despite the protection, Hopper knows what he's about to do (for love) is dangerous, so he tries to give some money to Lulu just in case. He tells her if he doesn't come back to call his friend Tom Collins and he'll take care of her. The first time I saw the movie I didn't realize Tom Collins was the name of the guy who showed up at his house at the beginning. I thought he was just bullshitting her and knew she probably hadn't heard of Tom Collins mix. That would've been mean.

The climactic showdown with General Jantapan (after Hopper and Sunti have found the girls) is a real showstopper. My favorite part is when the general stands directly across the room from Hopper shooting arrows at him. That's not a situation you want to get in, but Hopper knows what to do. *Out For a Kill* had a *Matrix*y CGI bullet effect that was kind of embarrassing, but this one I have to say is pretty god damn awesome. Hopper takes aim and *shoots an arrow with his gun*, breaking it in half and knocking it off its trajectory so it won't hit him. Another arrow comes at him and we see it reflected in his eye before he spins around, grabs a sword and uses it to bisect the arrow in mid-air. Fuck arrows.

As they continue the fight, we go to the evil temple where the bearded guy sticks pins in the voodoo doll, causing some serious pain for Hopper. But then the voodoo doll bursts into flames. An *Evil Dead* type camera flies from the evil temple to the Buddhist temple to show us that all the monks are praying like crazy, giving Hopper the Mystical Buddhist Ass Kicking Powers he needs to defeat the general. This is the first magic duel – hell, the first magic – in a Seagal picture. *Marked For Death* had voodoo curses but there was very little indication that they actually did anything. Here there's no doubt.

Belly of the Beast is easily one of the best and most distinctive of Seagal's DTV period. It has the strongest Asian feel and the most stylized fight scenes of any of his movies due to the unique contributions of director/choreographer Ching Siu-Tung. And the production values are nice. It feels bigger than most of his movies of this period. Lots of on-location shooting, lots of large scenes with extras, monks, guns. There's also a good amount of action of varied types (kung fu, gun fights, swords, arrows, magic).

Plot-wise it's silly and convoluted, and it doesn't make a lot of sense. The kidnappers I think leave themselves open to some criticism, because their plan is idiotic. They kill the male friends and kidnap the two girls, knowing that only one of them is related to the senator. But they should've known to let Hopper's daughter go. The whole scheme was set up by Fitch, who worked with Hopper in his CIA days. Didn't he fuckin notice? *Oh shit, that's Jake Hopper's daughter. He's gonna be pissed. He wouldn't—he wouldn't come here, would he?* You or I would've known he'd come, so you bet your ass Fitch McQuoid shoulda known. Come on, Fitch. You know better.

Of course, that's far from the most ridiculous element of the plot, and for that I'm thankful. Maybe it's not as funny as *Out For a Kill*, but it's not every day you get to see Seagal in a movie this fuckin' crazy. It's the closest he gets to Van Damme's legendary surrealist period with Tsui Hark. He gets to fight a transvestite, shoot a flying arrow with a gun, use classic kung fu sound effects, watch a guy get killed by a tomato, defeat an evil wizard – I mean, what's not to like? This is a classic.

And I think there's a little bit more to the movie than you'll notice at first, a little bit of symbolism boiling beneath the surface. Although Jake Hopper is a former CIA agent (and does freelance work), he does not trust military and intelligence agencies to save his daughter when she's kidnapped. Instead he turns to what many Seagal characters would call "the spirit world," asking for the blessing of a Buddhist master before he embarks. Before the final battle he goes to the master again and is given a magical medallion; the whole temple prays for him while he fights and that's what defeats the evil voodoo mojo that threatens to kill him. But ultimately, the guys he's fighting against are corrupt military and police officials, and their opposing philosophies are illustrated by the objects they destroy during the battle. The police fire machine guns into a shelf full of books and Buddha heads, representing their opposition to or at least their ignorance of wisdom and spirituality. For his part, Hopper throws a spear that impales a portrait of a general, showing his lack of respect for man-made authority. He also destroys what looks like a trophy case, a symbol of materialist achievements.

One motif that doesn't quite pan out, but ought to, is the fruits and vegetables motif. We learn from the Post-it notes in the refrigerator that Jessica is looking out for her dad's health, demanding "NO RED MEAT! (I'M SERIOUS!!!!)." Later, Hopper gets into a brawl in a Bangkok vegetable market. His opponents use knives and cleavers stolen from the produce stands, but Hopper just uses his hands, throwing the thugs into piles of vegetables. Meanwhile, the mysterious evil shaman (in his only appearance until the very end of the movie) looks on from the meat department, with poultry hanging all around him.

The kicker is when the last henchman standing tries to run away. He steps on a tomato that pops and causes him to trip and slide across a long table of fish and smash his face into a meat cleaver. The power of produce turns this guy into meat. Hopper's connection to fruits and vegetables is later reaffirmed when General Jantapan destroys an apple using the same bow and arrow he will later use against Hopper.

You may say I'm reading too much into this, and that's because I am. One look at the Post-it note scene shows you that although he's not eating red meat, his favorite dish is lemon chicken. So the solidarity with greens I'm describing is kind of stretching it. What, he got that belly of the beast eating tofu? Not likely. But it would be cool if there *was* a movie where Seagal got his power from vegetables, like Popeye. Vegetables are full of nutrients, so it would be a good message for the kids. And then Seagal could release his own line of organic produce.

So here we are well into Seagal's DTV era and for the first time in his career he's working with a legendary director. Sure, Andrew Davis of *Above the Law* and *Under Siege* went on to get a best director Oscar nomination for *The Fugitive*, but that was post-Seagal and he hasn't been heard from too much since. Ching Siu Tung (aka Tony Ching Siu Tung) may not be a household name in the US, but for fans of Hong Kong cinema his work is unavoidable. He directed all three of the *A Chinese Ghost Story* series, which explains the mystical voodoo vs. praying battle at the end of this one. He also did the *Swordsman* trilogy, in which a sacred scroll leads a man to castrate himself and become a woman named Asia the Invincible in order to attain the ultimate martial arts power. So that sort of explains the fight against the transvestite in the warehouse. Ching Siu Tung is even more renowned as a fight choreographer than as a director, and he performs both duties for *Belly of the Beast*. If you've seen *Hero* or *House of Flying Daggers* you know his work, and you can see echoes of it in these fights. Admittedly, they are not his best, but they are distinctly different and more fantastical than those in any other Seagal picture.

If you see only one movie from Seagal's DTV era – which would be stupid, you should watch all of them, obviously – it should probably be this one. It has the best action and production values (rivaled only by *Into the Sun* in that area) but also best exemplifies the craziness of the era, while also being the rare Seagal picture where a director manages to put his unique imprint on the proceedings.

Belly of the Beast, 2003
Directed by Ching Siu-Tung (director of *A Chinese Ghost Story* trilogy, *Swordsman* trilogy, *Heroic Trio 2* and many other Hong Kong classics; also a legendary action choreographer whose work you probably saw in *Shaolin Soccer*, *Hero* and *House of Flying Daggers*.)
Written by James Townsend (associate producer of *Wonderland*, that movie where Val Kilmer played John Holmes; writer of *Undisputed 2*). Story by Seagal (uncredited), according to the IMDB.
Distinguished co-stars: Byron Mann is about the best I can do for you. But several members of the cast, including Wannakit Siriput (Tony Taipei) were in the great muay Thai action movie *Ong Bak*.
Seagal regulars: Tom Wu, who plays General Jantapan, played a lower-ranked villain in *Out For A Kill*. Vinent Riotta (Fitch McQuoid) will return as Harry in *Shadow Man*. Martin McDougall (Tom Collins) will later play "Assistant" in *Submerged* and will also appear alongside Riotta in a 2001 non-Seagal TV movie also called *Submerged*. Riotta was also in a movie called *Ready To Kill*, which will probably be the name of a Seagal movie eventually. The two guys playing the security guards did effects on the movie. One also worked on *Into the Sun* and one on *Submerged*.
Firsts: First Seagal movie by a Hong Kong director, first to use magic.
Title refers to: Nobody really knows. It's an easy setup for Seagal fat jokes, though, which makes it ballsy.
Just how badass is this guy? "Shut up asshole, my dad's the best!"
Adopted culture: He wears the proper robes while in Thailand, and also knows kung fu.
Languages: English, Thai (I think), hand signals.
Improvised weapons: There are mostly stolen weapons – villains use cutlery stolen from a market, Seagal uses a sword stolen from his opponent.
Old friends: CIA agent Tom Collins, retired CIA agent Fitch McQuoid, possibly Leon Washington (since he knows him by his first name).
Fight in bar: Yes, in a strip club where the women wear bikinis. Later, a woman strips in a

regular bar.

Broken glass: Seagal throws a guy through a window 90 seconds into the movie, which is a record. 15 seconds later, he jumps through a window himself. In one scene, he smashes a glass table by throwing a transvestite on it. There is minimal glass breaking during the middle portion of the movie but at the end some bottles and many, many windows are shot out, and the final move is to throw the villain into some sort of trophy case.

Terms of endearment: My brother.

Most awkward one-liner: "Listen, why don't you go back to your own genetic puddle, go for a swim, BOY!"

Family shit: The whole movie is about saving his daughter from kidnappers. The beginning of the movie establishes that his daughter has an over-the-top devotion to him. His wife is dead, but there is not an explanation of how she died.

Political themes: The usual corrupt CIA themes. This one has a particularly complex world view showing an intersection between the CIA, Thai Special forces, terrorist arms dealers, heroin dealers, and some magic dude in a temple. It also shows a police force using terrorism as an excuse for unrelated activities, a very timely theme.

Cover accuracy: The cover art looks like a generic CIA thriller, it in no way conveys the strangeness or the Asian themes of the movie. Also it uses the same flipping car from the cover for *The Foreigner*, but this time going in the other direction.

interlude:
SONGS FROM
THE CRYSTAL CAVE

I n May of 2004, a pleasant surprise showed up in France: Seagal's first album, *Songs From the Crystal Cave*. And not some amateur hour karaoke sing-along album like you might expect from a movie star – Seagal is singer, songwriter, lead and rhythm guitarist, and he's better than you'd expect at all four disciplines. As the album and its single "Girl It's Alright" hit the charts in France, word spread to the States, causing confusion and laughter. To the uninitiated or the more casual Seagal fans it was a shock to see the album cover, with Seagal giving a familiar mean look while holding a guitar instead of a gun or a sword. To many, this seemed to be coming out of the blue. But in fact, Seagal has played guitar for as long as he's practiced aikido. Court TV's Crime Library, in trying to ascertain whether Seagal really ever trained in the vicinity of aikido founder Morihei Ueshiba, reports "At least one of Ueshiba's students remembers Seagal being around at the time but doesn't recall Seagal being on the mat very much. He remembers Seagal as the kid who was always playing guitar."

And while this was his first album, it was far from his first recording. Seagal had written and performed songs on his movie soundtracks for years, and in *Fire Down Below* he even played a guitar on camera.

Because of that movie, *Songs From the Crystal Cave* was widely reported as being a country album, which is way off the mark. For a movie taking place in the Appalachians he was willing to play bluegrass, but in the real world he's more interested in the blues. Normally he would never play with a pick. The album has one straight ahead blues song ("Route 23") but mostly it's an odd amalgam of Jamaican, Indian and African inspired styles. The label, Nonsolo Blues, describes the genre as "blues world."

At first glance this might seem like an odd album to come from Seagal. The songs are full of messages of peace and tolerance, but without mention of any kind of asskicking. There is no apparent Asian or Native American influence. There are no mentions of martial arts, swords or the environment. Since we're accustomed to the Seagal of movies, we expect his words of peace to be followed by acts of war. Well, that doesn't fly in the Crystal Cave.

On a closer inspection, Seagalogists can see that the album actually does have a few parallels to Seagal's films. For one thing, the music extends the movies' tendency to travel the world exploring different cultures. These aren't cultures his characters have shown an interest in in his movies, although in *Marked For Death* he went to Jamaica and saw Jimmy Cliff perform. But it's the same sort of cultural exchange – here he is recording with Indian musicians, African drummers and Jamaican DJs like Lady Saw, Tony Rebel and Lt. Stitchie. "Dance" is sort of a bellydancing song, he's got a guy playing tablas and he plays a clay pot. On "War" he sings like a long lost Marley brother.

That's another thing. Like in many of his movies, Seagal adopts various cultures and sometimes picks up their lingo and accents. On "Route 23" he's a bluesman, saying "Lord have mercy" and singing about the working man's struggles: "Black lung got from the coal mine / Cancer from the steel" On "Strut" he's dropping Jamaican slang, including multiple uses of the word "poonani." If you ever wanted to hear Seagal sing, "That would be phat / You can be my bow cat" this song might be one of your only chances.

Politically, the album is in line with some of the movies too. He's not singing about corrupt intelligence agencies, but some of the lyrics reflect the world weary views of his ex-CIA characters. In particular, "War" describes war in terms that Nico Toscani or Casey Ryback might agree with:

"... might be tobacco / Or it might be a little oil / Might be some big business / Or a little tiny piece of soil..."

And the second verse would please Austin Travis, Seagal's character from *Executive Decision:*

"Nice shirt, nice tie, nice look in your eye / So tell me why we will never see you, where the bullets fly..."

I mean, he might as well be talking to Kurt Russell there. He even addresses that Kurt's wearing a tux.

More than the politics, the album shares the sincere, heart-on-his-sleeve corniness that I love from Seagal's movies. He sings about not being for sale, about music healing the world, about different religions getting along. He's upset about "desperation, abomination, disintegration, degradation, poverty, treachery..." On "Jealousy" he attacks the tabloid media, a familiar topic for celebrities (and not exactly one the common man can relate to much), but at one point he stops singing and says, "You have turned this piece of paper into a weapon of mass destruction," and you can't help but think of Seagal's trademark political ad-libs and *Billy Jack*-style righteous indignation.

The liner notes are as open and unashamed as the speech at the end of *On Deadly Ground.* He says that "through music we can heal the world" and has a strangely humble dedication: "If there are any mistakes of any kind on this album, I am sorry. If there is any merit in this work, I would like to dedicate this to all the sentient beings and all my teachers who have given me so much love and guidance."

Hell, the album even has a distinguished co-star. Not Michael Caine, not Eric Bogosian, but the one and only Stevie Wonder playing an awesome harmonica solo at the end of "My God."

Since beginning his music career, Seagal has often said in interviews that music is his true passion in life, that he is more interested in music than in acting. And it's easy to believe him since this slick, five-years-in-the-making CD came out right in the middle of his notorious dubbed-by-another-actor period. But on the song "The Light" and on the album's dedication, Seagal speaks of "liberation through sight and sound." And can't we take that to mean through movies and music? *Songs From the Crystal Cave* proves that the music and the movies both come from the same place[44]. You can take the Steven Seagal out of the movies, but you can't take the Steven Seagal out of Steven Seagal.

Songs From the Crystal Cave, 2004
Produced by Steven Seagal, Rick Wake
Written by Steven Seagal, Greg Barnhill, Patrick George Barrett, Shaun Fisher, Marion Hall, Cleve Laing
Distinguished co-stars: Stevie fucking Wonder
Title refers to: Man, I'm not really sure. There's some book called *The Crystal Cave* which is about the early life of Merlin.
Just how badass is this guy? "Lawmakers eat my flesh and drink my blood / But I'm not for sale."
Adopted culture: Jamaican, Southern blues, Indian.
Languages: English, French.
Improvised instruments: Clay pot.
Old friends: There's a picture of him onstage with B.B. King inside the booklet.
Guitar solo in bar: I think so, on "Strut." When he talks about looking at girls' butts, it is easy to imagine this in a bar or a dance club type of setting. And then he mentions having a shot of rum. So I'm gonna say yes.
Broken glass: No, just a few broken hearts, like his girlfriend on the song "Better Man."
Innocent bystanders: See "Broken glass," above.
Terms of endearment: Girl, baby.
Words of wisdom: "Drink the music, let the melody demolish the carnage of ignorance, prejudice / Envy, greed and hate." "The true path to life is more than one / Why do you force your will with a gun?"
Family shit: Inside the booklet he writes about his late mother Patricia telling him she loved his music, and he thanks her "for this and all she has done for me."
Political themes: War for big business, war hawks who would never fight the wars themselves, class issues.
Cover accuracy: Yep, he plays a guitar. Pretty straight forward.

---

44 And the place I am referring to is not The Crystal Cave, it is the heart. Steven Seagal's heart. Unless maybe The Crystal Cave is a metaphor for Steven Seagal's heart, which is possible. Hmmm, I'll have to think about this one.

CHAPTER 16.5:
CLEMENTINE

"I'm sorry. I had no idea they kidnapped your daughter."

In this Korean production, Seagal plays ex-CIA, ex-homicide detective turned organic honey farmer Detective Jack Clementine. Nah, I'm just fucking with you. Actually Seagal has a small but important supporting role as a competitive cage fighter. The movie centers around Kim Seung Hyoun (played by Jun Lee) who is an ex-Taekwondo champion turned ex-cop turned cage fighter.

The movie opens with an emergency C-section in a hospital intercut with Kim losing his title in a Taekwondo tournament in Las Vegas. There's no dialogue to explain what's going on but you can infer that this guy is a double-chump: he missed the birth of his baby for a fight, and he still lost the fight. Great job.

Then we skip ahead to 8 years later when Kim is working as a police officer and raising his daughter by himself, because the mother apparently died during childbirth. His daughter's name is Sa Rang, not Clementine, and if you can't take movies about precocious children you better fuckin run. Even if you can stomach a plucky little girl acting the way adults think kids think adults act (at times she seems like the Korean Punky Brewster), you should be warned that she's missing all of her front teeth. At first I was impressed they could shoot a movie fast enough not to worry about her teeth growing back in, but then I noticed that which teeth are missing seems to rotate at various times in the movie. Oh well, shit happens and teeth grow.

Kim spends all day and most of the night going after gangsters, crossing the line, etc. He gets fired for illegally smashing a bunch of illegal slot machines. You know how all that red tape is. This guy's a badass with a certain kind of swagger, kind of reminds me of Chow Yun Fat in his older movies. There's a great scene where he struts into the illegal casino with his hands in his pockets, not at all afraid of taking on a whole bunch of guys by himself. He beats them up and then makes them put the handcuffs on themselves.

After he gets fired he gets called in to talk to the same gangster whose machines he smashed. "Do I know you, asshole?" he says and shoves one of the henchmen over by his face. He needs the money though so he sells out and becomes a cage fighter for this gang.

So how exactly do you raise an 8 year old when you're out all day and most of the night fighting with/for gangsters? Well, he's always available by cell phone but otherwise Sa Rang seems to be on her own. We don't see her in school much but we know she goes there because she gets busted for beating up a kid who makes fun of her for having a dead mother. So she's a chip off the old block. After school she spends most of her time shopping for her dad, like on his birthday when she prepares a fancy party for him (and of course he doesn't show up). They have to show how much she loves her dad so there's an embarrassing scene where she buys him an engagement ring thinking she wants to marry him. When an adult tries to explain to her that the law doesn't allow marrying your own father, she contemplates getting married in another country.

The adult who tries to explain marriage law to Sa Rang is a friendly female prosecutor who meets her at the grocery store and takes a liking to her. We've seen this woman on the job and she seems cool because she headbutts a pervert in two different scenes. Then she goes home with Sa Rang and is shocked to see a portrait of Kim on the wall. She didn't know he was her dad. It seems that she used to date him but he disappeared, she thought he was dead.

About halfway through the movie we discover that Sa Rang's new prosecutor friend is actually her mother. Since Kim was out of town fighting, the prosecutor's mother decided it would be best to give the baby to an orphanage, tell her daughter that the baby died, and tell Kim that she died during childbirth. So he went to the orphanage and snatched up Sa Rang before it was too late, but now they've spent 8 years thinking the mother was dead and the mother spent 8 years thinking they were dead and now they're all pissed at each other because they feel deceived and abandoned. And the mother decides she wants custody of her suddenly alive daughter.

Things get arguably worse when organized crime kidnaps Sa Rang and say they won't give her back unless Kim fights champion Jack Miller (Seagal – finally) and throws the fight in the third round. They make a big deal about how unbeatable Miller is, which is weird since they are forcing Kim to lose anyway. If the guy is so damn unbeatable then why bother fixing the fight?

But we do know for sure that Jack Miller is the shit.We learn just how popular he is when an Asian couple in the crowd says, "I can't wait to see Jack's match with that Korean guy!" The ring announcer describes him as, "The reigning 5 times heavyweight champion of the world! Standing at 6 foot 4 inches, weighing at 225 pounds. Our own king of the fighter cage champion, Jack Miller!"

Seagal's big scene is only about 5 minutes long, and the shots from the crowd are obviously a stunt double. But in the close-ups he looks good, moving fast and appearing to be in good shape. A smaller role like this might be a good chance to die (like in *Executive Decision*) or to be evil, but he does neither. He actually does a good job using facial expressions and no dialogue to convey that he is simply an athlete in a competition and not some supervillain like, to name one example, Van Damme's "Ivan the Russian" character in *No Retreat, No Surrender*. He gets beat up a little more than he does in most movies, even gets a little blood dripping from the corner of his mouth. But we don't get to see him defeated – it freezes on him after a spinkick to the cheek.

Seagal also appears in the very last scene, when he shows up at the hospital to deliver the championship belt, to apologize and to make it clear that he didn't know about the kidnapping. He acts very respectful and honorable, but there is one thing that's ambiguous: did he know that gangsters were forcing his opponents to throw the fights? He says "I had no idea they kidnapped your daughter," but that almost sounds like he's saying "Rigging a fight is one thing, but kidnapping is going too far." Even if he didn't know about the setups, is he really that good? How do we know he earned all those 5 heavyweight championships? How would the Asian couple in the crowd feel if they knew they had betrayed their countryman to support a fraud?

And as far as the gangsters are concerned, what is their angle here? If Jack Miller always wins (fair or not), shouldn't they be rigging it for him to lose so they can get better odds? Maybe it's more profitable in the long run if they keep the franchise going. But if that's the case, and if he's so good, why bother with kidnapping? It actually seems like Kim would've lost the match for real if he hadn't been inspired by the last minute arrival of his just-rescued daughter. So it seems like an unnecessary risk, a waste of resources and ultimately a counterproductive strategy.

But you know what? I don't blame Jack Miller here, and I don't even blame the gangsters. The real villain here is Sa Rang's bitch of a grandmother. What the fuck was she thinking causing all this trouble? Why would you even do that? Why would you even *think* of doing that? If I was Kim I'd go check that bitch's cabinets, because if she's got a world's greatest grandma mug in there she's got another thing coming.

Seagal's role in *Clementine* is really no more than a cameo. In fact, it's debatable whether it's bigger or smaller than what he did in *My Giant*. But I decided it deserves its own half chapter, like *Executive Decision*, because it is a genuine action movie where he gives an action movie performance, not just a comedy riff on his persona. Also, it would be a shame to write off one of his rare twenty-first century theatrical releases. And he deserves credit for trying something different. Not only is it not a Seagal vehicle, but it's not his type of movie at all. It's a balance of action movie and melodrama but with more emphasis on the latter. Seagal has done wacky sidekicks but he's never done custody battles.

The version I've seen is the region 1 DVD released by Tai Seng. In this version, Seagal's handful of lines are dubbed into Korean, but I've heard that the original Korean release has them in English. Even the American version is difficult to find; reportedly it quickly went out of print and was pulled from the shelves of video store chains.

The DVD includes some behind-the-scenes footage and some incredibly dumb interviews, but Seagal isn't shown or mentioned in any of them. There are 2 music videos, both featuring the same montage of clips from the movie, so you can see an abbreviated version of Seagal's scenes set to two different ballads. Also, the end credits show an outtake in which the little girl who plays Sa Rang giggles, "Seagal, I love you. Oh my god, I said it!"

Clementine, 2004

Directed by Du Yeong-Kim (*Live Or Die*)

Written by Hye-rim Eun

Distinguished co-stars: None are very well known in the United States, but Hye-ri Kim was in the Chen Kaige film *Together*.

Seagal regulars: Joe Halpin, the writer of *Into the Sun*, *Shadow Man*, *Attack Force* and *Prince of Pistols*, plays the bodyguard to Seagal's character at the end. He also will play Agent Thomas in *Black Dawn*.

Firsts: First Seagal appearance in a genuine foreign film. First supporting role since *Executive Decision*. His closest to being a villain (although he's really just an opponent and not a genuine bad guy).

Title refers to: The song "My Darling Clementine" and its lyrics about a father losing his daughter.

Just how badass is this guy? "He's the world champion. No one can defeat him." "Jack already kicked a bunch of asses."

Adopted culture: He is a martial artist but we only see him practicing in the US.

Languages: His handful of lines are dubbed into Korean by another actor. But whether or not his character is supposed to be speaking English is up to interpretation. All of the American characters speak in dubbed Korean – even chanting American fans in the stands at a Taekwondo competition in Las Vegas – and there's one scene where the dubbed Korean dialogue seems to indicate that it represents an English conversation.

Improvised weapons: none

Fight in bar: Only in a cage.

Words of wisdom: The hero tells him "Taekwondo is a state of mind," and he agrees.

Most awkward one-liner: "You are going down!"

Family shit: When he finds out the hero's daughter was kidnapped as a means of throwing the fight, he goes out of his way to apologize to Kim and hand-deliver the championship belt.

Political themes: He doesn't get a chance.

Cover accuracy: Well, it's kind of misleading to show him so big on the cover since he's only at the end, but oh well.

CHAPTER 17:
OUT OF REACH

"I hear you're looking for a man who writes letters."

By now we're pretty used to seeing Seagal try to foil some terrorists or save his daughter or niece or somebody. But I don't think anyone could've anticipated that we'd get to see him rescuing his pen pal from a white slavery ring. Seagal plays William Lansing, an ex-"CSA" wildlife conservationist who lives by himself in the woods and writes letters about Napoleon and secret codes to a 13-year-old European orphan named Irena Morowska (Ida Nowakowska).

The opening scene has Seagal bounding through the woods in a trenchcoat. He finds an injured bird and tries to help it. Right off the bat you can sense that this is a different kind of Seagal picture because he looks pretty crazy. (In my review on The Ain't It Cool News I described him as looking like bigfoot in a bad Dracula wig[45].) But if that didn't tip you off you'll have another clue two minutes in when you hear the first voiceover of one of Lansing's letters to Irena, and it is clearly not Steven Seagal. It sounds nothing like Steven Seagal. There are several films from the DTV era that have dialogue looped by other actors, but this is the first time I ever noticed it because it's much more frequent and flagrant

---

45 That sounds bad, but I'm not some fashion critic so I don't mean it in a judgmental way. I am a fan of both Dracula and of the sasquatch, so I consider it a pretty good look.

here than anywhere else. Even setting aside the voice actor's lack of vocal resemblance to Seagal, it's hard not to laugh at the upfront corniness of the letters combined with the earnestness of his performance. "Dear Irena, I'm glad you like the American-Indian bracelet, a true symbol of our friendship…"

With this type of ridiculousness so early in the movie you've got to accept that this is one of the ones that's going to be more enjoyable for its absurdity than for its action. When I first saw it it made me kind of sad, but on further viewings I've gotten more and more enjoyment out of it. You can't deny that it's one of Seagal's silliest premises. When Lansing receives a letter from Irena's orphanage saying that she can't write to him anymore, he immediately travels across the world to kick ass. To you or me that would probably seem like a drastic response to the letter, except we already know that he's right. Irena's been kidnapped by a white slavery ring headed up by a melodramatic cheeseball named Faisal (Matt Schulze, a veteran of both *Blade* and *Blade 2*, and therefore a true American hero despite his lackluster performance in this one).

Faisal is an unusually corny villain, and has the same almost psychic abilities that Lansing has. Somehow he figures out that this particular girl's pen pal is a threat to the operation, and that she's leaving him secret codes on mirrors and in plates of hors d'oeuvres. When he finds out that Lansing mentioned something about Napoleon, he says, "Napoleon. A soldier, an emperor, but still to some just a little corporal. Hmm?" When he sees that Irena is leaving secret messages he has an interior monologue dubbed by a different actor: "You're a very clever girl. I can see why William is so fond of you. And even more why I can't let you go. It's time to devise a killer plan for your Mr. Lansing."

He also has one of those scenes more common in the early Seagal pictures where the villain does something cruel just to show how evil he is. In this case he scares a little orphan boy for no reason, then tells the sellout head of the orphanage (Maria Maj), "The thrill of the chase, Mrs. Donata. It's always a constant source of amusement to me."

Another hobby of his is fencing, wearing an all white suit, inside an all white palace. Asshole thinks he's DMX.

I think Faisal pictures himself as a poetic John Woo type of villain, but he sure doesn't pull it off. He likes to do fancy shit like burn a rose while musing, "Pretty, isn't it? But like any rose, a company must cut its thorns." You call that a villainous speech? It doesn't even make sense. Companies don't have thorns. Roses don't cut their own thorns. And why are you burning it if the point you're making is about cutting it? You're cluttering this whole thing up. I'm sorry Faisal, you are undeniably villainous, because upstanding citizens don't kidnap orphan girls and auction them off on the internet. But you sure don't know how to talk like a villain. Just keep your fuckin mouth shut if you want people to think you know what you're doing. Or at least work on that rose-burning bit a little before the next time you say it to some lady you're about to kill. It needs a lot of polishing.

And as long as I'm criticizing Faisal I should probably point out that this punk does the wussiest thing a villain has ever done in a Seagal movie: he drugs a 13-year-old girl. I mean, we all understand why somebody might be drugged in a detective or spy story where a femme fatale or some other treacherous backstabber needs to take a powerful opponent by surprise. But for God's sake man you're telling me you're afraid of a little girl when she's conscious? Shit man, get out your fencing sword if you need that to threaten her. Anything besides drugging her.

I mean think about it. When you try to insult somebody's manhood, you compare him to a little girl. "You hit like a little girl," or "I'm gonna make you cry like a little girl" or whatever. Here is a villain who can't handle an actual, literal little girl. I can't believe I'm actually seeing this.

Even before the drugging he's playing chess with her and keeps saying those type of sinister villain lines that are supposed to sound innocuous but actually be threatening. And the shit is just embarrassing because we've seen this metaphor before. We know what chess means. It's a battle of wits. Between a grown man and a 13 year old girl. And then she gets woozy and he says, "Check mate." In my opinion this is cheating at both real chess and metaphorical chess.

Jesus, Faisal, she's 13. She can't even drive for three years. She's not even old enough for underage drinking. At her age she could be in *The Bad News Bears*. I mean, come on, dude. What the fuck?

But enough about that creep, I think we're only encouraging him by giving him so much attention. Let's talk about the hero instead. In the great Seagalogy tradition, Lansing is coy about his past. Asked how he learned some of this shit, all he says is, "I've been around a couple places." But I don't think a "CSA" background explains everything. Earlier I mentioned Lansing's almost-psychic ability to figure out what's going on based on no information at all. One character notices this but writes it off as typical Seagalian ex-CIA type skills: "I don't believe you came all this way on guesswork. You obviously have a past."

But I would argue that perhaps Lansing really has a telepathic connection with Irena. His gigantic (and always correct) logical leaps don't constitute enough data to come to a scientific conclusion. But how do you explain this voiceover in which Irena clearly states she is not writing a letter:

"I have no pen to write with, no paper. And something is very wrong with the men who have taken me. I'll try to leave you a message. Don't give up on me. I'll never give up on you."

She's not talking out loud, and she's not writing a letter, and I didn't hear no "amen" so I don't think she's praying. And when Lansing is hyper-observant enough to notice that the pattern of hors d'oeuvres on one plate is a secret code for "THIS IS A TRAP," you gotta figure something tipped him off. So you can believe what you want, but I'm going with telepathy.

Lansing does have some non-psychic help in the form of a female homicide detective named Kasia (Agnieszka Wagner) and an orphan pickpocket named Nikki (Jan Plazalksi) who saw Irena get taken away. Nikki is a strange character because he seems like he's mute, and sometimes communicates through the medium of charades. But then all the sudden he talks and nobody seems surprised. He also sneaks into the hotel mini-bar and chugs all the booze, with no consequences[46]. Lansing just says, "Oh, you think this is funny? You wanna get drunk?" End of subject.

Lansing does a lot of covert agent tricks that most Seagal characters don't bother with. For example, he makes a map on the wall in his hotel room with notations about related incidents and pieces of evidence. He also

---

46 Okay, I take it back, maybe Irena *is* old enough for underage drinking. But it's still bullshit for an adult male villain swordfighter to be afraid of a 13-year-old girl.

gets an opportunity to show off his medical knowledge when he performs impromptu bullet-removal surgery using kitchen knives heated up on a stove. Of course, we've seen this kind of thing before, but usually performed on soldiers who are stranded out in the jungle somewhere, or on criminals who can't risk going to a real hospital. This is different because he performs the surgery on Kasia, a police officer. If I were her I would've requested to see a real doctor, but I guess in the heat of the moment you don't think of those kinds of things.

But the best touch in the movie that Seagal hasn't really done before is that his character has all kinds of aliases. Every time he checks into a hotel or meets with somebody new he uses a different name. If we are to trust the credits and standard storytelling protocol, his real name is William Lansing. But the guy at the post office calls him "Mr. De la Croix." An old CSA friend turned enemy calls him "Billy Ray." At various times he's Mr. Davenport, Williams, "Bill Hale with the Global Relief Fund," Nicolai Rochenko, Dr. Gray, and "Mr. Dean Moray with the International Education Fund." I think he wants his pickpocket friend to do the same thing, because everybody calls the kid Nikki but at one point Lansing calls him Simon. All the false identities is a good touch for a covert agent, so it's surprising he hasn't done so much of it in any of his other movies.

Of course, we don't even know if Lansing is his real name. This could even be Jonathan Cold as far as we know. Or Jonathan Cold's real name could be William Lansing. Or William Lansing could coincidentally have the alias Jonathan Cold, unrelated to the Jonathan Cold of *The Foreigner* and *Black Dawn*. It would even make a good alias for Seagal himself, since he was born in Lansing, Michigan. Maybe this is an autobiographical tale of what he was really doing during those missing couple years between *The Patriot* and *Exit Wounds*. He didn't necessarily have to be on set to produce *The Prince of Central Park*. All we can do is speculate.

There is also a scene that suggests Lansing may be a master of disguise. In the scene where Seagal goes to the post office to pick up his mail as "Mr. De la Croix," he suddenly sports a five-o-clock shadow and a fur coat. He's never looked this crazy in any other movie, or any other scene in this movie, and no explanation is offered.

It's really pretty god damned sad if you think about it, this guy living out in the woods, apparently only keeping in contact with animals and his European orphan pen pal, and so private he has to put on a disguise and use an alias when he goes to the post office. It's possible that he lives such a secluded life because he is endangered by his past, but it's also implied that his experiences have made him so disgusted with himself that he'd rather hang out with birds than humans. When asked why he would go through so much trouble for a girl he's never even met, he says, "You know, some of us have done bad things in the past. And once in a while we find something that makes us feel better about ourselves. This little girl means a lot to me."

So you could draw a strong parallel with *About Schmidt*, the way Jack Nicholson's character has a breakthrough in his sorry life because of writing letters to Ndugu, the orphan he sponsors. But Jack Nicholson doesn't know shit about swords, so who cares about that asshole.

Lansing knows a lot about swords though, and the climactic duel with Faisal is a great moment in Seagalogy. Faisal isn't short, but he's shorter than Seagal. So it turns out he's the one who's gonna be channeling the spirit of Napoleon, and this is gonna be his Waterloo.

Lansing just strolls right into Faisal's palace, they point guns at each other and begin to debate who is "the predator" and who is "the prey." Irena is there and seems kind of surprised by the sight of William Lansing. She probably always pictured him looking like Brad Pitt or somebody. At least Lansing was nice enough to wear a suit for their first meeting. No tie, but it's a nice black suit, so I think it definitely counts as dressing up. If he had worn the fur coat he wore to the post office he probably would've scared the poor girl to death.

You know what would've been fucked up would be if Lansing got there and this was one of those *To Catch a Predator* setups, they think he's some kind of pervert for writing to this girl. I'm not sure how he would get out of that type of misunderstanding without breaking some bones, so in that sense it's a good thing that Irena really is a real girl kidnapped and sold into white slavery. That way we all agree that he has a legitimate reason for being there, nothing fishy.

Lansing convinces Faisal that they should "settle this like men outside without the guns" and boasts, "I despise taking human life. I'm kind of embarrassed to admit the fact that I'm gonna enjoy killing you slowly." This is a good move, because Seagal's gun battles tend to be impersonal. Hand-to-hand is always better. I mean, just look at the gun fight a little earlier in this very movie. To try to spice things up, Seagal does a gratuitous somersault, but the slo-mo makes it obvious that it's a stunt double. And somersaults should not require stunt doubles. Was it really worth getting that guy all dressed up and giving him Seagal hair just to do a damn somersault?

Faisal, like many characters in Seagal movies, has swords and axes and shit hanging everywhere in his home. He tries pulling a sword on Lansing, but it doesn't go well, then there is some aikido and wrestling in the hallway. Faisal's only impressive move is a trick he pulls when he runs away. Lansing prefers the Jason Voorhees method of confidently walking after someone instead of running after them in a panic, so Faisal is able to duck off to the side out of sight and then jump onto Lansing's neck when he walks by. It looks like that scene in the beginning of *2001: A Space Odyssey* when the cheetah jumps on the ape.

People have pointed out to me that Seagal characters are less vulnerable than most action heroes of his era, that you don't see him bleed a lot or get beaten up. That's generally true, but in this one he gets elbowed so hard in the stomach he looks like he's gonna puke and his vision gets all blurry. He recovers quickly, though, grabs a sword and follows Faisal into his extravagant all-white fencing arena for the final showdown.

Faisal holds his sword with one hand and poses like a swashbuckler, Lansing holds his with two and looks more like a samurai[47]. This is another example of when Seagal's heavier DTV era build helps him out. Skinny little Nico Toscani would not have looked cool with that sword. But Lansing looks like Ogami Itto from *Lone Wolf and Cub*. They exchange a few blows and then for the final pass, the movie suddenly turns arty. There's no music, just the sound of vibrating metal. The two opponents back away from each other and hold awesome poses as they stare each other down from opposite ends of the frame. Then they run

---

47 Note that the two-handed samurai style sword fighting also resembles Seagal's trademark two-handed pistol-holding style.

past each other and hold poses again. A trail of blood leads to Faisal, who sputters and wobbles and eventually falls over dead. The camera lingers for about a minute showing this painterly image from all different perspectives, most notably from above, a perfectly composed shot of the dead body, the red streak, and Lansing still standing there with his sword out and his back to the carnage. Partly because of its simplicity, this is the best final kill Seagal has had in a while.

And if you really pay attention you'll notice that as Lansing strikes the fatal blow, there is the sound of a predatory bird such as a hawk or an eagle. This is a sound that echoes all the way back to the end of the training sequence in *Hard to Kill*. It is the sign that Lansing is, in fact, the predator, and Faisal is the prey. It is the cry of the injured hawk from the opening scene, of the American eagle striking white slavers on foreign soil, of the United States Postal Service protecting its deliveries. Feel the talons, motherfucker.

Without saying a word, Lansing puts his arm protectively around Irena and they walk off camera, leaving the still-cool-looking dead body in the shot. This would make a perfectly succinct ending in the tradition of *Marked For Death*. But it's worth wasting that opportunity for the silly epilogue in which you learn that Irena and Nikki now live on the wildlife preserve with Lansing, who Irena says "spends most of his time by himself, wandering the forest looking for injured animals." Now Irena writes letters to Kasia (which will probably get boring fast since Kasia probably doesn't send her secret codes and American-Indian friendship bracelets).

The last shot is a keeper. The kids see a hawk (presumably the one from the opening scene, now fully recovered) and it flies away. There's a freeze frame on the hawk and then a still photo of a smiling Lansing fades in over the hawk. You'd almost think that he lost the duel and this was a tribute to his memory.

Out of Reach is one of Seagal's strangest and most inept movies, and it's just begging you to analyze the shit out of it. To say it's kind of weird for a martial arts star to make a movie about pen pals is probably an understatement, but there's a lot more going on here. There's a theme of untraditional families. The usual components of a family (or of a Steven

Seagal movie) are replaced with alternative ones. Lansing lives by himself out in the woods; instead of having a child of his own he has this deep (telepathic or not) connection with this orphan girl in Poland who he's never met. In his last movie he went to Thailand to rescue his daughter from kidnappers, now he's going to Poland to rescue his pen pal from human traffickers. In his last movie he had a cop-turned-monk partner, in others a rapper-turned-actor. Here he has a female detective for a partner, but also an almost mute orphan alcoholic pickpocket child. Before he leaves on a dangerous mission he hugs the orphan Nikki as if it's his own son. The kid then pressures him into hugging the detective and when he does, Nikki has a very satisfied smile. He probably has never seen parents before and this kind of shows that Seagal, lady cop and child pickpocket make a good family, even before bringing in a new sister for Nikki. In the end, the two kids live with Lansing and not Kasia, but they refer to themselves as "a family."

The most noticeably crazy element of the movie besides the pen pal storyline is obviously the heavy reliance on dubbing by an actor who doesn't sound even a tiny bit like Seagal. They even use it in scenes where it's completely unnecessary, like when he's writing something on a paper and they do a voiceover of him thinking the same thing he's writing. In case somebody can't read. Hell, even if they can't, he's writing down a 3-letter acronym. You don't even need to be able to read, just know part of the alphabet.

But as I mentioned earlier the villain has some bad dubbing too, both for dialogue and gratuitous internal monologue. And I'm not sure, but I think it might be the same voice. If so it shows how Seagal and Schulze are two sides of the same coin or some deep shit like that. They are sort of set up as opposites, though. Lansing is low tech because he lives by himself out in the woods helping birds and he writes letters the old fashioned way, on paper, and by the way he has nice handwriting. This other guy is high tech because he is perpetrating what Lansing calls "an online internet scam." I bet he doesn't use snail mail. In fact, he shows contempt for traditional mail by sending his thugs to Lansing's house in a US Postal Service van, with one guy dressed as a mailman. That's a nice touch for a villain who keeps fucking with people's pen pals.

To be fair though, while Lansing has a deep connection with nature, he also shows signs of technological expertise. In one scene he helps with a computer problem, saying, "This is a simple case of signal vs. digital throughput" before tapping on some keys and magically improving the resolution of a videotape. (I thought this was the single phoniest sounding techno-mumbo-jumbo I'd ever heard in a movie, but I looked it up and it turns out "throughput" is an actual computer term. So good job Lansing, you went over my head.)

I didn't know "throughput," but I do have some expertise of my own in pausing movies and zooming in to find crucial details. Careful use of the pause button reveals a few things going on in the movie that will not be spotted by the naked eye. For one thing, a newspaper article tells us that the climactic party Lansing crashes as Nikolai Rochenko is "the hottest ticket in Warsaw today" and "a virtual extravaganza, a cultural first." These quotes are not important in any way but I want to point them out because they would've been good critical acclaim quotes to put on the DVD cover.

Then there are the letters. During some of the correspondence montages you can see parts of the letters onscreen. Some of what they say matches up with the voiceovers, but not all of it. For example, the voiceovers never mention the onscreen letters' references to the book *Call of the Wild* by Jack London:

"I first read *Call of the Wild* when I was about your age. The hero is thrown into a tough situation, but manages to beat the odds."

We don't get to see the full context of Lansing's Jack London passages, but it could have at least two meanings. Obviously he mentions it as an inspirational message for Irena, telling her that like Buck, the hero dog of the book, she can overcome the tragic circumstances of her life. But the story also has parallels to the typical Seagal hero. Buck is a trained sled dog, but when his owner is killed he reverts to primitive instincts, goes off in the woods and becomes leader of a wolf pack. Lansing does the same sort of thing in reverse when he hears his call of the wild. The covert agent has settled down to live in the woods and help birds, but the tragedy of his pen pal's kidnapping forces him to revert to his old savagery and travel the globe under secret identities killing bad guys.

It's hard to say why the *Call of the Wild* references were taken out of the narration. But since someone other than Seagal did the dubbing my guess is that it was a theme he wanted in the movie that the director or other producers thought was too corny, and since he wasn't in the recording booth they took the opportunity to change it. In fact, it would be funny if the reason he didn't do the dubbing was because he didn't want to remove the Jack London references, but there's no evidence to support that.

A more obscure literary reference (at least to Americans) occurs during a shootout. Like in *Belly of the Beast* the bad guys fill a bookshelf full of holes, a potent symbol for the disregard of knowledge, wisdom and history. The specific book we see penetrated by a bullet is *Wiersze* by the 19th century Polish poet Cyprian Kamil Norwid. Norwid was an eccentric, Rasputin-looking motherfucker who lived a tragic and poverty-stricken life. He died dirt poor in Paris and was not appreciated in his lifetime, although he is now considered one of the top four Polish poets of the Romantic period. Not top five, top four. I mean think about it, if you list all your favorite Polish poets of the Romantic period and then narrow it down to the four most important, that's pretty fucking impressive. And he could be anywhere in that four, he's not necessarily number four, he could be number one and that would still technically be top four, so interpret it how you will. But some people don't even buy that, they figure he is more of a Classicist and Parnasist. Who knows how he ranks in Parnasism, could be top three in my opinion. Parnasism is of course a French style which might be why he ditched the motherland for France late in his life.

Like Irena, Norwid was a poor orphan, and of course both share a love of writing and symbols. Perhaps after her death, Irena's pen pal letters, hors d'oeuvres codes and telepathic communications will be recognized as ahead of their time, top four type works. At any rate, these bastards are shooting up Norwid's works just like they're wasting the lives of these little girls, snuffing out their potential. *Who cares?*, they figure. *They're just poverty-stricken orphans.* Well I'll tell you who cares, assholes. William fucking Lansing. Mr. De la Croix himself. Or "the American," as you knuckleheads call him. The "man who writes letters."

In case you're wondering, I'm pretty sure "Wiersze" just means

"Verse" (or "poems.") But interestingly, Norwid's first poem was titled "Mój ostatni sonnet," which literally translates to "*Above the Law.*" Isn't that weird? Oh wait, I'm sorry – no. It translates to "My Last Sonnet." I guess there isn't really a Seagalogical connection here at all. Still, a weird thing to name your first poem, in my opinion.

There seems to be another reference of some kind in the onscreen letters, but it gets cropped off in such a way that it's indecipherable to anyone but a master code breaker like William Lansing or Irena Morowska. Lansing tells Irena, "If you look up a man named Sam [the middle of the sentence is offscreen] in the library you will understand more about how I feel." There's really no way to narrow it down, it could be any Sam he's talking about there, so it's sort of a dead end. I guess I'll just take a shot in the dark and say he's talking about Sam Goody. If you look up a man named Sam Goody in the library you will understand more about how I feel.

By the way, I didn't know any of that shit about Polish poetry, I had to look it up. I could've just ended the chapter right there and tried to pass it off as a vast breadth of knowledge, but come on man who am I fooling. We Seagalogists gotta be open and honest with each other if we're gonna get anywhere.

Out of Reach, 2004
Directed by Poh-Chih Leong (*Banana Cop, The Wisdom of Crocodiles, Cabin By the Lake*)
Written by Trevor Miller (producer of something called *Pornstar Pets*). James Townsend (*Belly of the Beast*) worked on it uncredited according to the Internet Movie Database.
Distinguished co-stars: Matt Schulze doesn't seem very distinguished, but I gotta give credit to anybody who was in both *Blade* and *Blade II*.
Seagal regulars: Nick Brimble (Mr. Elgin) will play the villain, Arian Lehder, in *Submerged*. Shawn Lawrence (Agent Shephard) was in *Exit Wounds*. Jacek Samojlowicz (Polish Customs) was in *The Foreigner*.
Firsts: First Seagal movie with the word "Out" in the title but not the word "For."
Title refers to: Seagal's pen pal, who is out of reach because she is a pen pal, and not an actual pal.
Just how badass is this guy? "You saved my ass a few times, as I recall." "You have enriched my life and for doing this I am eternally grateful. Hope all is going well on the wild life refuge."
Adopted culture: Samurai swords.
Languages: Reader Hagen Voss tells me that he says "thank you" in Polish once.
Improvised weapons: I wish I could say he uses a letter opener on a guy, but no such luck.

Fight in bar: No.

Broken glass: Hotel shower door and various windows shot out. In one rare incident, a guy is thrown out a window that is already open, so no glass breaks. He does land on a parked car, though, cracking the windshield. So it's not a complete loss.

Words of wisdom: "Pave your own path, do not wait for others to lead you. You'll benefit more in the end."

Family shit: At the end of the movie he has adopted Irena and Simon/Nikki and they form a family together out in the woods.

Political themes: The movie has a cynical outlook on the world, because you can't get much worse than a corrupt orphanage that sells its kids into white slavery on the internet. But it's not a particularly political movie.

Cover accuracy: It should probably show the little girl he's trying to save, and the tagline "It's a split second between hit or miss" has no meaning, as far as I can tell. But otherwise it depicts actually images from the film, which is pretty unusual.

CHAPTER 18:
INTO THE SUN

"I couldn't sleep well knowing I hadn't chopped off your balls yet."

After the unprecedented shoddiness of *Out of Reach*, Seagal could've easily given up. He could've gone on a VH-1 reality show to cash in his chips, become an ironic pop culture icon, maybe sell some t-shirts and talking keychains. Instead he went to Japan and made a very unique and surprisingly strong Yakuza thriller, a movie with the familiar over-complicatedness of the DTV Era but with more of his interests and personal experiences invested in it.

Providing a much needed breath of fresh air in the middle of the DTV Era, *Into the Sun* brings Seagal away from Europe and into Tokyo, where he fights heroin-dealing Yakuza. Seagal plays Travis Hunter[48], a sword salesman who sometimes begrudgingly freelances for the CIA, even though he doesn't have much respect for what they do and they all think he's an asshole. Travis is a man of many names. Some people call him Master or Travis-San, and he sometimes refers to himself as Dai Ryu. But Block (William Atherton, that prick from *Die Hard* 1&2), his liaison at the CIA, calls him "Big Poppa," which is obviously the best nickname of the bunch, so that's what I'll refer to him as.

---

48 Travis is an interesting first name for a Seagal character, because in *Executive Decision* it was his last name, and in *Under Siege 2* it was his enemy's name.

Like a lot of these things, the movie starts out in an unrelated battle in the Golden Triangle, where Big Poppa and his partner codenamed Reindeer (former NFL running back Eddie George) are hiding in some bushes staking out a major heroin operation. It's a very impressive scene, because there are five elephants there. There's also a computer-generated shot of a CIA spy satellite[49] to show Big Poppa's in touch with headquarters about when to make a move. You may have flashbacks of the the pimp-through-the-window opening of *Out For Justice* as Big Poppa refuses to stand idly by when some drug smugglers rough up an innocent woman just minding her own business trying to pee. He shoots the woman-beaters, revealing his location and blowing the whole bust. It turns into a big shootout, and Big Poppa and his now wounded partner flee in a helicopter as a guy with a big scar on his face watches in disgust. (This scar will help us to make the connection later when the Yakuza and Tongs are in Thailand taking a meeting about heroin opportunities.)

After the Golden Triangle battle there's a somber credits sequence with letters floating over traditional Asian tattoos and footage of Seagal making solemn vows and cool shit like that. The score is by Stanley Clarke, the famous jazz fusion bassist and composer for most of John Singleton's movies and a lot of crap like *Romeo Must Die* and *The Transporter*. Most of this doesn't sound like Stanley Clarke though, it sounds like he saw *House of Flying Daggers* and wanted to do a serious Asian score. So the opening credits are pretty weighty.

In the next sequence we learn about a group of young hipster Yakuza who have decided to work with the Chinese Tongs, and we see them assassinate the governor (Mac Yasuda[50]). The governor's daughter is played by Chiaki Kuriyama, who you might know from *Battle Royale*, *Ju-On* or of course *Kill Bill Volume 1* where she plays Go-Go Yubari. Her role

---

49 Of course last time we saw something like this was in *Under Siege 2*, where the satellite was the big threat throughout the movie, and was invented and controlled by fellow Travis Travis Dane (Eric Bogosian). This time the satellite is not a threat or important to the plot at all, it's just an excuse to throw fancy computer shit onto helicopter shots of Tokyo. The same CGI satellite shot shows up later in the movie on the monitor in the CIA headquarters. So in addition to having a spy satellite, they apparently have another satellite or space ship or something that sends them a live feed of the satellite itself. The Tokyo bureau of the CIA is nothing if not thorough.

50 Yasuda was the associate producer of *Half Past Dead*, Seagal's last theatrical film. So in case you weren't already convinced, here's a symbolic death for the days of theatrical Steven Seagal pictures.

in this movie is 23 seconds long and consists of her standing on a balcony next to the governor while he makes a speech. Good job, Chiaki. As far as I can tell, the assassination doesn't have much to do with the plot of the movie except that it gets Big Poppa involved (re-involved, I guess, since he was already chasing the Bangkok heroin operation that teams with the Yakuza and Tongs in Tokyo). For some reason the FBI thinks the assassination is terrorist related, so they call Block at the Tokyo CIA headquarters to see if they have a Yakuza expert there. Block calls Big Poppa, because he grew up in a neighborhood plagued by Yakuza and knows all about them. He teams with a wacky FBI agent named Agent Mack (Matthew Davis, who was apparently in *Legally Blonde*) to go back to the hood and investigate. Once again, they are able to pause and zoom in on a security video to find a clue and start investigating. (The tapes clearly show the faces of the culprits, so it's not clear why the Japanese authorities never seem to be after these guys. Maybe this governor guy wasn't very popular.)

Seagal's detective work involves hooking up with various assets and getting small pieces of information. He talks to Master Cheung, an old friend in Chinatown who confirms that there are rumors that Yakuza and Tongs are teaming up. He also talks to "a leader in the banking world" (Akira Terao) who agrees to act as his liaison to the Tongs. And of course there's Nayako (Kanako Yamaguchi), who runs a night club called Fusion, and she sends him to a tattoo artist named Fudomyo-o (Kosuke Toyohara) who wants to help because his family were killed by Yakuza. He talks to an older Yakuza named Kojima (Masatoh Eve) who opposes the younger guys who killed the governor. Big Poppa and Kojima seem to be on the same page and have sort of a friendly competition to see who will kill this guy Kuroda (Takao Osawa) first.

Kuroda is the leader of the young Yakuza faction, and his guys are very different from the traditional Yakuza. They have punk hair dos and bright colored leather jackets and know how to smoke cigarettes in numerous show offy ways. You know these guys are too modern because they hang around in an apartment playing video games and listening to music. They even have one of those toy robot dogs. Kojima says "the younger Yakuza completely ignore our rules and tradition of 'Jingi.'" And it's true. For example there's a young guy who gets beat up by Big Poppa, so he comes to Kuroda and cuts off his own pinky finger "as a token of my regret," but Kuroda still kills him. How bout a little fucking jingi there, eh pal? Come on dude.

Kuroda's boys don't give two fucks about honor, they're all about being flashy and terrorizing everybody, they don't care about the old traditions that mean so much to old guys like Kojima. Kojima actually ought to be happy that Kuroda's working with the Tongs, because those guys are big fans of rituals. In the beginning they do a whole thing with religious statues where they say "today we stand in front of Quan Quong, the God of War" and they cut their hands and burn candles and shit. They actually oughta be a good influence on Kuroda, but the old guys worry that by going international these brats are becoming too powerful.

Big Poppa subscribes to the old ways too, we know this because he uses swords. This is good, because we as viewers know that swords are much cooler than guns. Guns are too easy and too impersonal. A gun is a long distance technology, a modern convenience like cell phones and iPods and yogurt in a tube. A sword goes back pretty much to the invention of tools. A sword is classic. A sword is an extension of your fist. Swords are an ancient tradition, but they still work. If you can still fight with a sword after the invention of so many more powerful weapons then clearly you deserve extra credit. Swords are beautiful for their simplicity, like the early Seagal films. A sword is just a thin piece of metal that slices through flesh and bone. A gun is a machine, you have to insert an explosive capsule and trigger a mechanism that pulls back a hammer and pounds the capsule, launching it through a tube, then it flies through the air before it punctures the flesh and perhaps splinters into the muscle. Too complicated, fuck that shit. Use a sword. Big Poppa knows.

Not only does he know the beauty of swords, Big Poppa is actually referred to as a "sword master." Early in the movie we see him at his place of business, Japan Sword,, and a conversation he has with a customer gives us a good idea of his prowess. Although Big Poppa humbly denies it all, the customer says in subtitled Japanese that he "heard a legend that you cut off a man's arm in a duel" and that Big Poppa has "the skills of the old masters."

"There is no one else as good as you."

"That's isn't true at all," says Big Poppa. "I just sell swords."

The customer wants to learn from Big Poppa, but he says he's not a teacher. We know for sure that's a lie when he goes to Master Cheung and is presented with a young girl named Mai Ling (Pace Wu) who apparently was once his student. "Her skills are much improved. She's been my shield. Now she's yours." Unfortunately he doesn't really use his shield for much until near the end of the movie, but I guess that gives us something to look forward to.

There is one major way that Big Poppa disrespects the old ways, though. When he goes to talk with his banker friend the meeting takes place at some kind of geisha performance with traditional Japanese string instruments and everything. And Big Poppa is obviously a cultured guy, he knows how to roll with all this, but then his fucking cell phone rings right in the middle of the performance! So he has to go outside. What an asshole. I hate cell phones. At least he doesn't have one of those stupid headsets, I guess. But the other guests only seem a little offended, and the situation is used as an opportunity for wacky comedy where Agent Mack pretends to be Big Poppa's martial arts student, but doesn't know how to answer any questions about it. I guess it's refreshing for the lame comic relief character to be a white guy for once. That way we can start to spread the shame and indignity across all cultures.

Big Poppa pretends to know what he's doing, but as I see it he mostly gets lucky. It just so happens that one of Kuroda's boys[51] bumps into him on the street in the old neighborhood and turns it into a big thing. He gathers up some other guys to go jump Big Poppa at a market. It's five against Seagal, but I'm pretty sure you can guess who wins and who ends up in critical condition. After that Kuroda knows about "the American" and it's only a matter of time before the two get to have a big duel. Old vs. young. Sword master vs. gun user. Asianized-westerner vs. westernized Asian.

But first a couple things have to be set in motion. Number one, swords. Kuroda tells his boys about Big Poppa, calling him, "an

---

51 The most ironic part of this whole tragic fiasco is that this guy who starts the fight is actually a Steven Seagal fan. We know this because when the incident begins he's wearing headphones, listening to "War," Seagal's anti-war reggae song off of *Songs From the Crystal Cave*. Didn't he read the booklet? "No matter how diverse or far apart our philosophies or cultures may be, through music we can heal the world."

American who grew up in Japan. Apparently he is a sword master."

One of the boys[52] laughs at the idea of swords, saying, "there are no sword fights in this day and age," and joking that it would still be cool to learn how. Kuroda gets pissed off because he doesn't think "learning how" has anything to do with it. He says, "A fight is won not by technique, but by the most furious mind." This philosophy wins out and for the rest of the movie, people do have sword fights in this day and age. And these guys must have reasonably furious minds, because they do okay for completely untrained first-time swordsmen. But not good enough. Did they really think their minds were more furious than Big Poppa's?

Well, they're not even close, as you learn in a short, awesome scene where Seagal just knocks on the door at the apartment, bursts in and slaughters everybody with his sword. A home invasion. He literally kills four guys in ten seconds. After that, almost as an afterthought, he knocks over two tables. I'm not sure why he does that, but my guess is maybe he was disappointed because the fight was so easy there was no damage done to the apartment. By making a mess of the place he makes the scene a little more horrifying for the other Yakuza when they find it[53].

Whatever he was trying to do, the Yakuza who find this bloodbath note that it was done with a sword and then still assume it was Kojima that did it. Maybe they figure a sword master would've killed those amateurs in ten seconds, no need to struggle and knock over furniture.

The second thing that has to be set in motion though is a motive for revenge. This has the weirdest romance subplot in all of Seagalogy. It turns out that Big Poppa is in love with Nayako, the club owner he gets a small amount of information from. At first you don't even pick up on it. It doesn't seem like they know each other that well, and she looks young enough to be his daughter[54]. Also, he usually talks to her in English and she responds in Japanese, so it's kind of like the way Ghost

---

52 Who, by the way, is another *Songs From the Crystal Cave* fan, because he is also listening to "War" on headphones before this conversation.

53 The scene is probably meant as a reference to *Yojimbo*, where Toshiro Mifune kills six men and then destroys their place to create the appearance of a huge battle. *Yojimbo* also made famous the type of fast swordfighting Seagal uses here – in fact there's a scene where Mifune kills ten people in ten seconds.

54 For visual comparison, look no further than Seagal's real life daughter Ayako Fujitani. She's one of the stars of *Gamera: Guardian of the Universe*, which you see Kuroda's boys watching on TV. She doesn't look much younger than Nayako, and the movie is ten years old.

Dog and the ice cream man (or Han Solo and Chewbacca if you prefer) talk to each other in different languages but understand each other. But these two are not just buddies, they're in love. The first sign is when he's talking to her and he says, "So, I love you, you be good. Okay." That threw me off the first time, but I figured it wasn't that kind of love he was talking about. I thought maybe he was a mentor to her like he was to Mai Ling, it was a teacher-student kind of love, or a family friend kind of love or something. Or maybe hippie love. Big Poppa loves everybody, he wants them to be safe. He sounds like a big cornball when he says it, but he's just being honest about his emotions.

At least that's what I figured. But you start to get more suspicious in another scene where Big Poppa calls Nayako "darling." This could easily be meaningless old man condescension, like a guy who calls a waitress "honey" or "sugar" or something. But the problem is, Nayako had already said to him "Good morning my darling" in Japanese. Clearly something's going on here, but it's still a shock when Big Poppa brings Nayako to the park and proposes to her under the cherry blossoms. He doesn't give her a ring or anything, but they confess their secret desires for each other and agree that after this one last mission he's gonna quit the CIA and they're gonna run off somewhere together and be in love forever, etc. "Together we'll find some place really beautiful, live quiet, and lead a great life together."

Then comes one of the most awkward sex scenes to date. Basically, she takes her shirt off and they hug. Then it fades out. There's one other shot where you see part of a booby and they kiss. It seems like even Seagal is kind of creeped out by this whole thing, or maybe he just wants to emphasize the romance and not come across like a dirty old man. It's an amazingly chaste and unenthusiastic love scene.

Later they have a romantic talk where Big Poppa gives her some kind of antique hairpin. It's a funny scene because it takes place sitting in a booth at Fusion, so the entire time they're having this sweet conversation there are two hot chicks swimming around in a fish tank just behind them. You don't even see that on *Cribs*. Anyway, the hairpin is a dead give away that Nayako is gonna bite it. Kuroda's henchman who was most amused by hearing about the "master swordsman" kills her with a sword and, yes, steals the hairpin.

And then it's on.

Like every Seagal picture in the DTV Era, the most legitimate criticism of *Into the Sun* is that there's not enough action. But in this one, when it comes, it's pretty satisfying. First Big Poppa and Mai Ling walk through a pachinko parlor into a back room to have a word with some of Kuroda's guys. Gary Panton of movie-gazette.com hilariously described the hand-to-hand in this scene as "a game of extreme patty-cake," but I think it's a pretty good fight in the tradition of old school Seagal. It looks like they used stunt doubles for kicking (they don't show his face when he kicks) but otherwise it's all Seagal with lots of fancy handwork and it's always nice to see one head bashed through multiple pachinko machines. Also, for the sake of tradition, a guy gets thrown through a high window.

For the climax, Big Poppa brings along his new friend the tattoo artist, who suddenly reveals that Kuroda killed his family. Seems like something he could've brought up earlier, but oh well. Poppa also specifically forbids Mai Ling from coming along, but of course, she's his shield, so she shows up anyway. You know how shields are.

They go straight to the temple where Kuroda has an office. Fudomyo-o suggests sneaking in through the back, but Big Poppa says, "I'm not in the mood for surprises. I'm goin right in the god damn front door."

On the way in he casually chops a guy's arm off, making it clear that if he really cut off a dude's arm in a duel once it wasn't that big of a deal. He can do that shit in his sleep. Basically the whole place erupts into sword fights, and then gets even better when Mai Ling shows up and does a cartwheel. On the way to Kuroda, Big Poppa kills seven guys with his sword, including Nayako's killer. He doesn't even save his fiancee's killer for last, that's how routine this shit is to him. He kills one guy with a gun and one guy with a pair of chopsticks. Fudomyo-o gets to Kuroda first, and gets shot. First, though, he gets the unforgettable subtitled Japanese line, "I couldn't sleep well knowing I hadn't chopped off your balls yet."

In fact, all the best lines in the movie are in Japanese, a lot of them spoken by Seagal. Before attacking the temple he chooses the sword he wants to use and says, "This one is so sharp. I'll use it tonight. This kills very well." And then throughout the temple scene he gets good fight dialogue with translations like "Yo, punk!" and "I shall beat you to death!"

When Big Poppa faces off with Kuroda he gets an earful. Kuroda asks, "What the fuck is an American doing swinging around a sword?" and says, "You're living in the fucking past. Times have changed!" Despite this, he succumbs to a sword duel against the sword master, and finds that his "furious mind" idea doesn't necessarily hold water. Or at least was overpowered by Big Poppa's similar theory, "No one is more fierce than someone who has nothing to live for."

The wrap-up at the end of the movie is a little weird. We see Big Poppa and Nayako holding pinky fingers in the park, but then Nayako fades away like a ghost. It seems like it's about to end with Big Poppa brooding on a bridge looking at ducks, which would be fitting since *Out of Reach* ended with a shot of a hawk. But then we see how Jewel (Juliette Marquis), a lollipop-sucking CIA operative I never mentioned before that has been following Big Poppa for the whole movie (long story) brings in a team called "Fast Beatiful Incorporated" (a CIA front made to look like an FBI front – take that, suckers) to paint all the dead bodies and weapons in the temple blue, which apparently destroys DNA evidence. I don't get it but more of these DTV movies oughta end with a bunch of swords and dead bodies painted blue.

Then we see Big Poppa driving around Tokyo at some unspecified date, and he happily takes a call from his CIA handler Block. So without his fiancée he decides to keep going with this dirty life he doesn't believe in. As if sword dealing isn't a sufficient occupation for a dude like this. It seems like a tragic way for things to turn out, but the movie plays it more like it's cool. The song "Don't Cry" played over the end credits seems to be trying to cheer us up, because Nayako will be with Big Poppa wherever he goes: "I'll be in the ocean, I'll live in the sky / I'll be here forever and don't you cry." The song is sung by Seagal himself (it's from that favorite CD of young Yakuza, *Songs From the Crystal Cave*) but I think it's reasonable to assume that the lyrics are written in the point of view of Nayako. I mean, why would Big Poppa be in the sky and the ocean, that makes no sense.

There's one thing I feel I need to point out about this character Big

Poppa. As great as he is in a sword fight, I don't think he's necessarily the best friend or ally to have. Consider the case of wacky FBI agent Sean Mack. Big Poppa brings him along, but mostly just to humor him. He (correctly) tells him to pretend to be his student and basically let Big Poppa take care of everything. When Mack goes off on his own and starts doing his job, Big Poppa says, "If you get yourself killed on my watch, I'll kill you again."

Well, the trouble is that Big Poppa isn't on the watch at all. Mack does get himself killed, and Big Poppa doesn't kill him again as promised. He doesn't do much of anything. First he won't let him help, then he blows him off by sending him on a spying assignment, and that's how he gets killed, without accomplishing anything. There's one weirdly uncomfortable scene right after Mack has been killed. Block tells Big Poppa that Mack is missing, that he's worried about him and that he's Big Poppa's responsibility. This doesn't phase Poppa at all and he says, "He'll be fine." But of course the audience knows that he's already dead.

And that forces you to go back and reconsider the opening scene in the Golden Triangle. His partner was shot and thought he was dying, but Big Poppa just laughed and told him he would be fine. We never see if he dies or not, but according to the behind-the-scenes featurette on the Japanese DVD, ol' Reindeer was "fine" in the same way that the dead FBI agent was "fine." It's like George W. Bush foreign policy: you say it's fine, that doesn't make it fun. But as long as you pretend not to be phased you win.

Maybe this is low to bring this up, but what about his fiancée? He puts these people in danger and then leaves them alone to get killed. What about that poor wounded tattoo artist, did he manage to make it to a hospital? I'm starting to think maybe he didn't.

Mai Ling does manage to live though, despite ignoring his direct orders. And for that he calls her an "idiot." But at least she's alive.

I don't want to be too hard on Big Poppa. I like the guy, and if I needed Yakuza expertise or wanted to buy a sword from somebody you know exactly who I would go to. I would be proud to consider him a friend but I would not count on him to protect me or to transport me to a medical facility. It sucks, but that's just the way it is.

Into the Sun is refreshing coming at this point in the DTV Era. We've gotten used to the gloomy European thrillers, so it's a nice change to have a colorful movie set in Japan with playful young Yakuza characters as the villains. And with all the exterior scenes shot in Tokyo (where you see the flashy electronic signs and even that beautiful pachinko parlor) it seems to have better production values than the European ones. I was getting sick of looking at those same types of buildings over and over again, and a temple is always nicer to look at than a warehouse. Also, Seagal seems a little cooler with a little warrior girl in tow. There's something appealing about a hulking, pouty American dude storming through a pachinko parlor with a mini-Lady Snowblood behind him. He should've kept Mai Ling around for the whole movie. And for future movies. When I watch the scene in the car outside the pachinko parlor where Big Poppa commands his troops it makes me want a sequel.

Even the DVD cover is a breath of fresh air. After so many interchangeable, blue-tinted collage covers, it's nice to see so much yellow. The image is Seagal in a black leather trenchcoat arrogantly strutting away from an exploding car. The emits a ridiculously huge ball of fire and Seagal also has a comically oversized gun strapped to his back like a quiver of arrows. There's an even better poster for the Japanese release, a collage in the style of old Yakuza movie posters, emphasizing the Asian cast as much as Seagal. Director mink says he prefers that poster.

Most importantly, Seagal seems into it again. He clearly enjoys returning to his stomping grounds in Tokyo (at least one scene was even filmed in the neighborhood where he used to live) and sharing his love of Japanese culture. On the making-of featurette he says he was embarrassed how much trouble he had speaking Japanese again, nevertheless he speaks far more of it than in any of his other movies. It's funny because he'll walk around with his goofball partner, and both are white Americans, but only the partner is a fish out of water.

In the making of documentary (only available on the Japanese DVD), mink says "I wanted to make sure that there was a truth to it so that I wasn't an American coming to Japan and making a movie that was American in Japan, I was making a Japanese experience with American elements through it." And I think he did a good job of that. Seagal and mink have created an elaborate visual tribute to multiple aspects of Asian cultures. You see traditional imagery like Buddhist temples, zen gardens, geishas, kimonos, bountiful Japanese feasts, an authentic Yakuza ceremony (overseen by a real Yakuza), intricate tattoos, the Chinese Tong ceremony, the swords and of course the martial arts. And this is all woven through threads of more modern Japanese living like the pachinko parlor, the neon signs, all the Japanese beers and soft drinks that you see on screen, the cameos by famous Japanese comedians and TV personalities. The European DTV entries seem so boring by comparison. Even when you can't figure out what's going on, *Into the Sun* always has interesting things to look at.

But that's where it does meet up with the other DTV pictures – the rushed shooting and rewrites lead to a story that takes a lot of effort to decode. One thing I miss about the old days – the movies were much easier to follow. They were simpler and therefore more elegant. You always understood what the bad guy was trying to do, and what Seagal was trying to do. He was trying to kill the guy who killed his wife or partner, or he was trying to stop the guy from blowing shit up with the satellite, or whatever. This one I've watched over and over again, studying it for this book, and still certain things are hard to be sure of. It took me multiple viewings to pick up some of the basic things going on, like I didn't originally understand that Big Poppa's partner really had died in the opening scene, or that time had passed and that's why he's a sword salesman now. The more I watch it the more I appreciate all the detail, but I still have problems with basic questions like "what the hell is this character's name?" and "why isn't Master Cheung listed in the credits?"

I mean, what does the assassination of the governor have to do with the rest of the Yakuza's plan? I know there's a scene where Big Poppa theorizes it was "to take attention off of" something or other, but I don't comprende. Why does Big Poppa meet personally with Kojima, then later call him anonymously saying he's "a friend?" How and when does Big Poppa go from a cynical outsider bregudgingly going to get "intel" for an agency he doesn't believe in, to a fully dedicated soldier massacring Yakuza with swords? (Note that he first does this before his fiancée is killed.) Even at the end I'm not sure why Big Poppa seems happy to do more jobs for the CIA right after his work caused the tragic murders of his fiancée and his FBI partner. What has the CIA done for him lately?

The story jumps around a lot, it could be more economical, more sword-like. They could skip over the assassination of the governor, just have him follow the Scarface guy to the Yakuza and the Tongs, show some sign of recognition when he faces the guy who was there when his first partner died.

There are some basic similarities between *Into the Sun* and the last one, *Out of Reach*. That one of course had the climactic sword duel, something he hadn't done in a long time. For this one he takes his personal interest in samurai swords to the next level by having his character be a sword salesman who accidentally reintroduces the majesty of sword fighting to a new generation of gangsters. So it's not just a one-on-one duel, but a whole house full of men and women fighting with swords. And again it has some standout overhead swordfighting shots.

Like William Lansing in *Out of Reach*, Travis is known by many names, although they seem to be nicknames rather than aliases. Like in *Out of Reach*, the bad guys mostly refer to him as "the American," but they also like to call him "my American bitch." Also like *Out of Reach*, the bad guys are a little quick to jump to the conclusion that he's a major threat. At first all they know is he beat up some Yakuza who attacked him. They have no way of knowing that he's after them. But somehow they know.

Unlike William Lansing, Big Poppa doesn't send pen pal letters to European orphans (as far as we know). But he does send a threatening letter to Kuroda, which is pretty cool. He still likes using the mail.

Other than those things though, this is a very different movie that sort of combines the overly complicated plotlines of the DTV Era with action a little closer to the Golden Era. In other words, it's half gun and half sword. I'm not saying Seagal is in his prime, and there definitely ought to be more action scenes. But when they happen, they are an undeniable improvement over recent films. Lots of fast, vicious handwork and brutal manhandling, in addition to the always welcome swordplay.

The most classically styled scene is the one at the market, where he gets attacked by five young street punks (three Yakuza and two Tongs) and quickly beats the holy hell out of them. Wrists are broken, knives are turned against their masters, motherfuckers are flipped and smashed and rammed into nearby carts and vending machines. Not only does he get to fight, he gets to boast too, because right before the fight he asks his partner, "Will you excuse me for just one second?" and afterwards tells the guy who started this sorry brawl, "You aren't ready for a fight yet. You want a fight, come back in ten years."

Seagal's heart seems more into this movie than it was in at least the previous two or three. He dubs all his own lines, he has six of his own songs in the movie, he worked his love for antique Japanese swords into the plot and he even gets a story credit for the first time since *Above the Law*.

Trevor Miller, who had written *Out of Reach*, wrote an early draft of *Into the Sun*. However, that version was judged so similar to the Sydney Pollack/Robert Mitchum picture *The Yakuza* that they would have to purchase the remake rights, which wasn't gonna happen. Seagal, who was in Thailand filming *Belly of the Beast* at the time, had read a spec script by a writer named Joe Halpin and had wanted to write a script with him. He flew Halpin into Thailand and pitched him his story for a yakuza movie. Halpin went off and wrote the script, later rewriting it based on Seagal's suggestions, all the while maintaining his day job as an undercover cop for the Los Angeles Sheriff's Department. (That actually sounds like a good idea for a movie right there. I hope he writes that some day.)

Despite his legitimate law enforcement background, Halpin seems to know how to write a goofy Seagalian scenario. If he was writing based on his experiences, I doubt he would have the FBI sending an agent who doesn't speak Japanese or know anything about Japanese culture to investigate the death of a Japanese governor. The Japanese authorities are awfully lenient in this movie, letting this guy just say "FBI" and walk right onto the crime scene. The movie actually has a strong sense of reality in its attention to the details of Japanese culture, but the story seems more based on other movies than on reality. A lot of things – the Chiaki Kuriyama cameo, the emphasis on quality swords, the young hipster Yakuza, the sword execution in a board room, the destruction of rice paper walls in the temple fight – make you wonder if Seagal was paying tribute to *Kill Bill Volume 1*.

There are even a couple odd ways that *Into the Sun* reminds me of the great Wesley Snipes picture *Blade*. For one thing, the movie's brash young yakuza scaring the old guard with their undisciplined methods is just like the way Stephen Dorff's faction of young, techno-music-listening vampires challenges the pure blood vampires led by Udo Kier. There is also the same sort of nationality issues, because the *Blade* vampires disagree with the inclusion of infected vampires into their order of people who were born as vampires, and the *Into the Sun* elders are angry that the young gangsters are working with Chinese gangs. Both movies have weirdo heroes who wear black leather trenchcoats and plow through their enemies with swords. Blade is half-vampire, Big Poppa looks like a vampire between that crazy Nosferatu coat and the impossibly pronounced widow's peak hairline. All of this is coincidental, I'm sure, but the one part that might be a deliberate homage to Blade is a cool sequence where Big Poppa drives through the city in time lapse to show how intent he is on getting to this place and swording up some motherfuckers.

Since the director is called mink, obviously you're gonna assume he's either a rapper or a music video director. In this case it's the latter. He's a protégé of Hype Williams and Paul Hunter who directed music videos for Master P, C-Murder and some others. Some of these he directed for Quentin Tarantino's production company A Band Apart, which it turns out produces music videos and commercials. mink's bio on the A Band Apart web sight says he was also a post production and visual effects supervisor on movies including *Starship Troopers* and *Die Hard With a Vengeance*, which I assume he did under a regular name[55].

Previously, mink directed a much lower budget DTV effort called *Full Clip* starring Busta Rhymes. That one has a more basic blaxploitation

---

55 By the way, I know a lot of movie fans have an automatic bias against one-named filmatists like McG or Pitof. And poor mink adds a new hurdle by the fact that he was born without capitalization. Maybe I'm not in a position to be objective since I'm a one-namer myself, but I say give people a chance. You can't judge a book by its cover unless it's a book about how to design book covers. I mean, what if Prince had come out with his first album and you never listened to him again because he called himself Prince instead of Prince Rogers Nelson? You would've missed out on a lot of Prince, that's what would've happened. I'm not saying mink is Prince. He's mink. But if you're gonna hate him choose a better reason than his name.

type of plot, which I would prefer to these type of overly complicated things where nobody can reasonably be expected to entirely follow what's going on. But stylistically *Into the Sun* is far more restrained, and therefore improved. *Full Clip* is riddled with what I call whooshy filmatism – the kind of style where the camera is constantly flying around trying to get attention, and in case the movement itself isn't enough, they add a WHOOOSHHH sound effect to accompany it. I'm sick of that kind of gratuitously flashy crap by directors trying to cover up for a lack of basic cinematic skills. Fortunately it turns out mink is not really a whooshy director – he had made more of a retro blaxploitation throwback, but it was recut by the studio. So *Into the Sun* is free of those type of stylistic distractions other than in the forgivably annoying establishing shots every once in a while that are supposed to represent the CIA satellite view of the city.

For this book I was actually able to correspond with mink, who it turns out is a Seagalogist in his own right. He described Seagal as "a John Wayne amongst WB tv actors" and pointed me toward many details he'd thrown in like the huge photo of the jet from *Executive Decision* hanging in Block's office in the beginning. He also made a convincing case for *Into the Sun* being the best of the DTV Era. In fact, he considers the DTV label somewhat inaccurate since it was funded by Sony Japan and played theatrically in Japan with a better poster and lots of promotion, ranging from TV spots to *Into the Sun* boxer shorts. In other words, it's Seagal's first Japanese film, which explains why the American DVD is bare-bones but the Japanese one is an 8-minute longer director's cut with extras.

In contrast to my theory of Seagalogical Eras, mink divides the films into only two categories: "a Seagal movie or a movie with him in it. " While a lot of people consider *Belly of the Beast* the best of the DTV Era, he doesn't think it's a fair comparison to *Into the Sun*. He considers that one "a Chinese action picture with him in it (directed by a talented guy). A very good one, and I like it, but it's not a Seagal film in structure or tone."

mink's objective was to make a film more in line with the classic Warner Brothers Seagal pictures of the Golden and Silver Eras. Did he succeed? I think the storyline would have to be more streamlined to completely fit that description, but as far as the production value, the great supporting cast, some of the action and the badass Seagal persona, he's definitely getting there. In truth, what mink has created stands on its own, far more stylish and textured than its DTV brothers, with many unique qualities not seen in its WB forefathers.

From film #1 on, Seagal's background in Japan has been a part of the Seagalogical DNA. But even in those early films he never went back there and dove in head first like he does here. It's like a homecoming, a trip to the motherland. So, while it may not be the miraculous return to the *Out For Justice* days that some of us would like to see, it is a crucial new chapter in Seagalogy. And if you're looking for a more competent and colorful straight to video Seagal picture, this is the one.

Into the Sun, 2005
Directed by mink
Written by Steven Seagal & Joe Halpin (the guy who played Bodyguard #1 in *Clementine*) and Trevor Miller (*Out of Reach*). Story by Seagal & Halpin.
Distinguished co-stars: Kenneth Low, better known as Ken Lo (*Police Story, Drunken Master II, My Father is a Hero,* etc.) Akira Terao (Matsuda) was in *Ran, Dreams* and *Madadayo,* Shoji Oki (Kojima's boss) was in *Yojimbo.* Also you might count William Atherton (*Die Hard, Die Hard 2*). And there's the tiny cameo by Chiaki Kuriyama (*Battle Royale, Kill Bill Volume 1*).
Seagal regulars: none
Firsts: First Seagal picture with a one-named director.
Title refers to: I would guess the sun represents Japan, since it is the land of the rising sun and all (and there are lots of shots of the sun rising in the movie). But he already lived there, so it's not like he's just now going into the sun during the course of this story. Going into the sun could also be a reference to going straight at something dangerous, in this case walking right into the middle of a fracas between young Yakuzas and Tongs and the older Yakuzas. Or perhaps it is a metaphor for what happens to the spirit of his dead fiancée, since Seagal sings on the end credits song that he will be in the ocean and in the sky. It only stands to reason that if you're in the ocean and in the sky you are also in the sun. Finally, Into the Sun could be some kind of Icarus reference. Who the fuck knows. In conclusion, maybe this title is a little too vague. But that's better than the generic working title, *Yakuza.*
Just how badass is this guy? "You should've seen him. God, he's fast." "An American who grew up in Japan... apparently he is a sword master."
Adopted culture: He grew up in Japan, speaks the language, is knowledgeable about the culture, sells and teaches Japanese swords.
Languages: English, Japanese, Chinese.
Improvised weapons: vending machine, chopsticks to the throat.
Old friends: Master Cheung, Mai Ling.
Fight in bar: No, not even the night club that is one of the main locations.
Broken glass: Four pachinko machines, sword cabinet, window.
Terms of endearment: Darling.

Family shit: He gets engaged and his fiancée gets killed.

Political themes: Seagal works in a little bit of dialogue about how the CIA works. "80% of the CIA's activity goes to disinformation. They pay close attention to the situation and in the end they'll decide what happened in order to fit their agenda." The movie also shows how any crime can be connected to terrorism as an excuse for US agencies to get involved if they want to.

Cover accuracy: He never walks away from an exploding car and doesn't have a giant novelty-sized gun strapped to his back. In fact he mostly uses swords in this movie. The tagline "Only one man can stop the Yakuza" is not all that fitting either since he teams with another man and a woman for the big fight at the end. He also relies on the aid of the older Yakuza, who are still thriving at the end. So he only stopped certain out of line Yakuza.

CHAPTER 19:
SUBMERGED

"There's some sick shit up in heah, alligata."

gotta be honest. I mean, not to bum you out right at the beginning of the chapter, but *Submerged* is one of my least favorite Seagal movies. It has some funny moments, but nothing that is legitimately cool or badass. It's low on action, especially hand-to-hand. The story is as muddled as everything in the DTV Era, to the point where I had to watch it three times to feel like I had pieced together most of what's supposed to be going on. But if I wasn't writing a book I sure as hell wouldn't have made the effort, because this is not a very compelling story. Any extra effort invested in *Into the Sun* must've been taken out of this one.

It seems to have promise at the beginning, though. The opening is weird and not very reminiscent of other Seagal movies. First there's a montage of show-offy music video imagery like a lady standing on a cliff in front of a red sky and phony looking windmill, scary doctors wearing Halloween masks, and a computer-animated naked lady. These are the random bullshit images that represent a mind control program that is at the center of the plot. The opening scene involves the US Ambassador to Uruguay (Leigh Zimmerman) discussing recent spy drone footage of a warlord meeting with some mystery man at a secret lab underneath a dam. She has stumbled on something she shouldn't have, so the four secret service agents on hand suddenly become mind-controlled assassins and the five of them end up dead on the floor like the end of *Reservoir Dogs*.

Seagal plays incaracerated mercenary Chris Cody. Last time he was free, the military hired him to stop terrorists who had loaded the *Damascus* with explosives. Cody was on a sub and was supposed to lead "his crew" onto the *Damascus* Casey Ryback style to save the day. He knew it wouldn't work so he forced the sub to torpedo the *Damascus*, thus preventing what his commanding officer describes as "another 9-11, except at sea." Unfortunately, the U.N. was upset and because of "political bullshit" had them all locked up. And here they are, apparently in a brig on the U.S.S. *Clinton*.

Cody isn't introduced until 12 minutes into the movie, and they try to make his entrance count. He's led in on shackles with rockin guitars playing to show he's a badass. They convince him to do another mission for them. He will get to bring his crew[56] with him and if they succeed they will get $100,000 each and their freedom. All they gotta do is rescue these five prisoners and deal with the mystery man whose face wasn't shown on the spy drone footage earlier. I'm not sure how they figured it out, but now they know he's Adrian Lehder (Nick Brimble, *Out of Reach*), and they want him terminated on sight.

"Oh, thass just terrible, I don't do things like that," Cody jokes.

Cody has a crew of seven British and American veterans, whose names and specialties are written on the screen while they are freeze-framed, and you won't remember any of those things later so don't bother reading them. (I liked it better when they did it in *Out For a Kill*, because they included hobbies and favorite foods.) None of these characters are memorable except ex-football/soccer star Vinnie Jones, who basically plays the same thug character he plays in everything before he had super powers in *X-Men 3*. Even Susan Chappell (Christine Adams), the nice doctor lady they have to bring along, turns out to be ex-Marine Corps. But they only find one excuse to ever make her fight, and that excuse is to reveal that she is ex-Marine Corps.

They also have to bring along an asshole agent named Fletcher

---

56 "The most notorious black ops unit in the world" according to the narrator of the trailer.

(William Hope, *Aliens*, *Hellraiser II*, *xXx*) who Cody immediately ditches. They pretend to be landing the helicopter and let him get off first, then they take off again. Ha ha, sucker. Well it's a good thing they did that because Fletcher is actually a double agent and the bushes were full of commandos ready to ambush Cody's team like they were leaving the house on *To Catch a Predator*.

Cody stops to pick up an old friend (girlfriend?) who is introduced in the middle of a strip arm-wrestling tournament, a direct lift from that drinking-under-the-table scene from *Raiders of the Lost Ark*. This character turns out to have almost no significance. But the detour does allow Fletcher to beat them to the dam/laboratory and conspire with the evil scientist Lehder, who he turns out to be in cahoots with. In cahoots on what, I cannot be certain. It involves selling mind control for private use by corporations, I believe. Something like that.

In the lab they have the five prisoners in hanging cages. They were the last team that went after Lehder, but they were captured and brainwashed. Lehder leaves them as a "Trojan horse" – Cody's team will rescue them and then the mind control will kick in and the prisoners will fight back. But that plan alone wouldn't allow for enough explosions so Fletcher also arranges to "give them a welcome South American style" with an army of mercenaries.

The movie's biggest action set piece is an uninvolving battle where some tanks drive down a tunnel and the good guy mercenaries fire machine guns. There are fireballs and sparks and some flaming barrels. After this goes on for a while Cody runs through and bops a bunch of guys on the head with the end of his rifle.

They manage to get all the prisoners onto the submarine. What submarine, you ask? I don't know, I'm not clear when this became part of the plan but for some reason there is a submarine there that they always planned to escape on. This is the submarine you'll see on the cover and for just over 15 minutes in the movie. They're in the sub with the rescued prisoners chained up, but the prisoners turn into assassin drones, escape their chains, and blow up the submarine.

Some of the crew escapes, but three of them die. "Oh, man," is Cody's devastated reaction to the carnage.

Once it's no longer about being submerged in a submarine, the plot gets more complicated. There is a company called Kelin Dyle involved somehow. They have kidnapped the president's wife as part of a plan to assassinate the president himself, because he's "no friend to big business." But also they kidnap Dr. Chappell to brainwash her. And they're going to kill the new ambassador to Uruguay when he goes to the opera with his wife. But also he's in the same balcony as the owner of Kelin Dyle. Cody goes to the opera in the ambassador's place. He doesn't bother with a tux, just normal Seagal gear. And the ambassador's wife doesn't seem to care that she has a new date.

Also there is some action, but not the kind of stuff you want in a Seagal picture. There's a helicopter crash, a couple car crashes (one with watermelons) and that kind of thing. The opera erupts into a big shootout, and Cody's old girlfriend swings across the opera house on a banner, so that's kind of cool. But there's very little martial arts. The aikido scenes are uninspired. Vinnie Jones gets to beat a guy pretty good but it's a short fight. About the only inspired action moment is when in the middle of a shootout Cody runs through a metal detector holding a shotgun. This is just not a very good action movie.

So the only thing that keeps you interested are the weird bits, the incompetent bits, the things where you can't figure out what they were going for. The main one you gotta wonder about is this Cody character. He sometimes talks with a goofy accent that I'm guessing is supposed to be Cajun, but they never mention anything about where he's from or his ethnic background. He's constantly referring to Jones's character Henry as "alligata." It's not clear whether that's a nickname for Henry or a term of endearment like "homey." There's one line where he says "I'll tell you one thing, if you wanna catch some catfish you're gonna hafta have some bait." So that seems to support my Cajun theory.

But there's one bit that makes it seem like he's not even supposed to be white. He tells Henry/alligata, "You got ten minutes to get yo white ass outta here, ya hear me?" He has had an interest in white asses ever since *The Glimmer Man*, I guess.

He does have a couple lines that made me laugh. In one scene he just yells "COCKSUCKER MOTHERFUCKER!" for some reason. Also I think it's funny when the ambassador is at gunpoint, giving Lehder important bank account access codes over the phone, and Cody just takes the phone and says, "Lehder, why is it that, uh, everything has to be about money?" (I'm not sure why they didn't shoot the ambassador and Cody at that point, but it was nice that he was able to get a little smartass line in.)

By the way, this rude behavior during public performances is starting to get out of control. In *Into the Sun* Seagal's cell phone rang during a geisha performance, in this one he talks and takes phone calls during an opera. Whatever happened to fucking courtesy? If we ever get to see a Seagal picture on the big screen again we're gonna have all these *Into the Sun* and *Submerged* fans thinking it's okay to take a phone call right in the middle.

Another thing that makes the character weird is that he's dubbed more than half of the time. The voice is better than in *Out of Reach* but there's way more dubbing than any other Seagal picture. So sometimes it's Seagal and sometimes it's some other guy doing a Clint Eastwood impersonation. There's even a scene where a tough guy one-liner is split between the two voices.

SEAGAL: "You've now become poison. That's why I've been hired…"
CLINT EASTWOOD IMPERSONATOR: "…I'm the antidote."

They must've thought this multi-actor oneliner was acceptable because they even put it in the trailer.

There are a couple funny touches here and there that have nothing to do with Seagal. There's a couple obvious model shots (the spy drone and the exploding dam). You don't see those too often during these digital days, so it's kind of nice. Early on, there's a scene where a mind-controlled suicide bomber blows up her own herd of goats. Also there's a crucial mini-disc (access codes or whatever) that is hidden inside a jewel-case for Julio Iglesias's 1996 album *Tango*.

I'm not sure what to make of the politics of the movie. Of course we have the usual corruption in the military and intelligence agencies. There's a little swipe at the U.N., not usually a target for Seagal. There's a part where he talks about mind control and it seems to be one of those improvised moments where he tries to include what he really thinks:

"I too have been impressed with the mind control program, but what's much worse than that is when private enterprise gets involved and, uh, uses this kind of thing for their own agenda."

Since he contradicts himself within one sentence it's hard to decipher what he's really saying. There have been rumors of secret government mind control experiments for decades, the most famous one being MK-Ultra. This might really be something Seagal believes in, but is he really saying he's "impressed" by it or is he saying it's bad and that it's even worse if it's in the hands of corporations? Is he saying that turning people into drones for a military agenda is okay but for a business one it's not? I wouldn't think he would say that but it sort of sounds that way.

Another possible political statement is in a scene where Cody hilariously hides behind a newspaper while standing in the middle of what he calls "a full scale riot." A close study of the newspaper reveals the two top headlines: "England Wins World Cup" and "US Discovers WMD In Iraq." It's possible that these were just fake headlines based on a possible future, but since it was filmed a good year or two after the Iraq war started I'm guessing it was meant as a joke about the phony WMD intelligence that helped start the war. England hasn't won a World Cup since 1966. So they're literally saying that the day they find WMD in Iraq is the day England wins another World Cup.

The style of the movie is distinct from other Seagal pictures, but not necessarily in a good way. Many of the outdoor scenes are digitally tinted yellow, which I like better than a lot of the colorless European settings of the DTV Era. On the other hand, everything inside the laboratory is tinted blue, which gives it a cheap Sci-Fi Channel look. Every time Hickox goes to a different setting he throws in a bunch of Avid farts – quick flashes of different angles accompanied by meaningless BANGS and WHOOSHES and POPS. I'm sure he figured that it tied in with the subliminal imagery of the mind control project, but I don't care. It's corny and annoying.

The score by Guy Farley (*Wake of Death*) is as schizophrenic as most of the DTV Era scores. Some scenes have a genuinely majestic theme reminiscent of *Under Siege* or even the *Rambo* films. Others have annoying techno beats and rock guitars, trying too hard to be cool. Some of the score on these things is like your grandpa wearing baggy jeans.

To me this is one of the least interesting movies in all of Seagalogy, but ironically it could've been a real standout. The screenplay for *Submerged* was heavily reworked to the point where the basic premise of the movie was completely changed. Scott Coulter, visual effects producer for

Submerged, Today You Die and *Mercenary For Justice*, told the *Fangoria* horror magazine that *Submerged* had "started out as a monster film, but became an action movie during the development process." (He also said that the title had changed to *The Enemy Within*.) Even the final, non-mutant-involving film was advertised by Movies Unlimited with an outdated description:

"Action and horror mix in this undersea thriller about a submarine crew who must battle horrendous mutants when a canister containing a dangerous chemical agent is broken. Making matters worse are the destroyer sent to blow them out of the water and the presence of treacherous mutineers."

The tagline on teaser posters was, "At 20,000 fathoms the only creature more dangerous than a biological mutant is… man." Maybe this explains why horror director Hickox got involved in the first place.

If Seagal had indeed fought "biological mutants" on a submarine, that would've been all new territory for him, and judging by the effects work Coulter has done on such films as *Mansquito* and *Komodo vs. King Cobra* it might have involved some pretty funny rubber suits and CGI monsters.

But according to Joe Halpin, who was not credited but was involved in the production, "Steven didn't like the mutant spiders that were in the original script and the studio agreed. It was changed into a straight action flick. Why the title remained *Submerged* is beyond me since they were only under water for a few minutes."

The movie may have gone through other drastic changes even after the disappearance of the mutants. The German DVD has the tagline "Under water, under cover," though of course he's not undercover and only underwater for 15 minutes. Some early advertisements and plot summaries had Cody having to wrestle a nuclear submarine from terrorists – this movie has no nukes or terrorists and he leaves the sub behind. And judging from the title, the cover, all of the advertisements and plot summaries, and common sense, it is easy to assume that the movie was originally supposed to center around a submarine. On the other hand, maybe it never did. The studio marketing department is going to have an easier time selling "terrorists on a submarine" than "mind control in a laboratory under a dam as well as on a submarine for a while and then at the opera and not very much action, sorry."

I have talked to some Seagalogists who enjoy *Submerged*, but I was not the only one disappointed. "Definitively bad" is how it was described by Martin Papich, head of the Uruguayan Audiovisual Institute. Papich was quoted in an article posted on falkand-malvinas.com where he claimed that the Ministry of Education and Culture was considering legal action against the producers for depicting Uruguay as "an exotic banana country." Myself, I never considered legal action, but I do think Seagal can do better.

Submerged, 2005
Directed by Anthony Hickox (*Waxwork I&II, Hellraiser III: Hell On Earth, Warlock: Armageddon, Storm Catcher* starring Dolph Lundgren, *Blast!* starring Eddie Griffin).
Written by Anthony Hickox and Paul de Souza (producer of *Lone Hero* starring Lou Diamond Phillips).
Distinguished co-stars: Vinnie Jones is as close as this one gets. Leigh Zimmerman (US Ambassador), like three members of the *Out For A Kill* cast, was in *United 93*.
Seagal regulars: Nick Brimble (Lehder) was also in *Out of Reach*. Raicho Vasilev (Ender) played a Bulgarian thug in *Out For A Kill*.
Firsts: First movie where more than half of his dialogue is performed by somebody else.
Title refers to: In one part, there is a submarine and it is submerged in water.
Just how badass is this guy? "He leads the most notorious black ops unit in the world," according to the trailer. But they don't say much else about him.
Adopted culture: Cajun?
Languages: English.
Fight in bar: No.
Broken glass: Head into medical supply cabinet, bottles, cabinet window, car crashes through windows, window shot out.
Terms of endearment: Alligata.
Words of wisdom: "I too have always been impressed with the mind control program, but what's much worse than that is when private enterprise gets involved and, uh, uses this kind of thing for their own agenda."
Most awkward one-liner: "Cocksucker motherfucker!"
Family shit: "They're gone," he says.
Political themes: Government using criminals for covert operations in other countries, crooked government agents working with warlords, mad scientists and big business, government mind control experiments.
Cover accuracy: While the submarine is not very important to the movie, it is in fact in the movie, and so are Seagal and a gun. The tagline "He found the enemy... on the wrong side" I guess means that one of the agents supposedly on his side is the enemy.

interlude:
STEVEN SEAGAL'S LIGHTNING BOLT ENERGY DRINK

Steven Seagal Enterprises was founded with a mission of sharing Seagal's "wisdom and experience of energy with the world," according to the official web site at lightningdrink.com. And they chose to express that wisdom and experience of energy through the medium of beverages. In July 2005 the world awoke to a cold, wet splash of Steven Seagal's Lightning Bolt Energy Drink, available in Cherry Charge or Asian Experience flavors.

Lightning Bolt is packaged in a tall 16 oz. can like many energy drinks, but that's pretty much where the similarities end. It's a different kind of beverage altogether. The concept is to provide "TRUE ENERGY" rather than just punch you up with a bunch of sugar and caffeine. This TRUE ENERGY is supposed to come from providing B-vitamins to improve your metabolism and a Seagal-formulated cocktail of Asian and South American herbs to make you more mentally alert.

The B-vitamins are definitely there, if that's really what it takes to give you energy. One serving contains 100% of your daily reccommended allowance of vitamins B3, B5, B6 and B12. That's a lotta fuckin B. And one serving is about half a can, each can is considered to contain 1.9 servings. So just drink about half of it and save that other .9 for later. Maybe keep the .9 serving in a container to drink on a day shortened by daylight savings.

The web site claims that Seagal "traveled to Asia searching for the ingredients" and that "each component was carefully chosen by Steven Seagal to incorporate the greatest treasures of Asian medicine into an all natural energy boost." After the travels and careful choosing what he came up with was goji berries, ginkgo biloba, cordyceps, ginseng, guarana, yerba mate, and green tea. The guarana works as caffeine, and the drink is sweetened with some sort of patented sugarcane juice concentrate called Polisweet rather than sucrose or corn syrup.

By comparison the most popular energy drink, Red Bull, is sweetened with sucrose and glucose, and powered by taurine, glucuronolactone and inositol. The only common ingredients between Lightning Bolt and Red Bull are carbonated water, niacin and pyridoxine hydrochloride. So it's a very different approach. Lightning Bolt has a little more in common with Rockstar Energy Drink. Like Red Bull, Rockstar uses taurine, inositol and caffeine. But it does share Seagal's preference for ginkgo biloba and ginseng (Siberian ginseng root extract as opposed to Seagal's American ginseng).

Lightning Bolt is the first energy drink to use goji berries (also known as wolfberries), but goji berries are a popular health food ingredient. More unusual are Asian cordyceps, also an energy drink first. The web site says that "Seagal discovered the benefits of cordyceps while researching immune builders in Asia." They are a rare and expensive Chinese medicine that will only grow in certain regions of Asia above 3,000 meters. The taste is said to be sweet and warm, but there is one catch: they aren't a berry or a leaf, they are a parasitic fungi that grows on caterpillar larvae and moths while they hibernate. That's why the literal translation of their Chinese name is "winter worm summer grass." If you ever saw the BBC nature documentary series *Planet Earth*, cordyceps are that weird fungus that grew out of the ant's head. Oh well, at least that's not as disgusting as the powdered deer penis in *The Glimmer Man*.

The cans and web site do not specify the source of the cordyceps.

Hopefully Steven Seagal Enterprises is conscientious enough to use cordyceps grown on an organic farm, because the excessive collection of wild cordyceps from the Tibetan plateau is believed to be an environmental threat, one that Forrest Taft would not abide by. Also, because it must be a pain in the ass to go around scraping fungi off of moths and caterpillars on a mountain somewhere.

Ginkgo biloba is a more common energy drink ingredient, but it's a fitting ingredient for Seagal to use in his formulation because ginkgo trees are in many ways the Steven Seagal of trees. They grow in both the U.S. and Asia. They have ties to Buddhism (some ginkgos planted at temples are believed to be more than 1,500 years old). They have existed for millions of years without much change, having been believed to be extinct in the wild for centuries and then turning out to have survived. They are also extremely badass trees that can grow in places where other more sissy trees couldn't even dream of growing. Ginkgo trees give shade to streets in neighborhoods that would make a maple tree sap all over itself. Only the Tree-of-heaven is said to be as urban tolerant as the ginkgo. Ginkgos rarely get diseases or are attacked by insects, because everybody knows not to fuck with a ginkgo. You're gonna get thrown out a window, metaphorically. Whatever the equivalent of a window is to a tree and an insect, that is what the insect would get thrown through if it fucked with a ginkgo.

In fact, you wanna know what a bad motherfucker the ginkgo is? I will tell you, and I am not making this up. When the atom bomb was dropped on Hiroshima in 1945, obviously most of the plant and animal life in the area was destroyed. But there were four ginkgos near the blast center that survived. They were charred and fucked up but they grew back. All four of them are still healthy and alive today. One of them has a temple built around it. Because of this courageous act of survival the ginkgo is regarded as "the bearer of hope" or "the baddest motherfucking tree ever."

Medicinally, ginkgo is supposed to help memory and increase blood circulation, among other things, but the amount used in energy drinks is not enough to have an effect. Or is it? Considering what a badass tree we are dealing with here, it might not be wise to put very much in there, somebody might get a broken wrist.

While the soul of Lightning Bolt may be pure Seagal, the same can't be said for the surface. There is a small picture of his face and his signature at the bottom of the can, but I have found that you can easily walk around drinking it without anybody noticing anything unusual. The center of the can shows a Chi symbol shooting lightning in every direction. Okay, that's pretty Seagal, but wouldn't it be even more awesome if it looked like one of his DVD covers? At least put a couple helicopters on there.

The web site is even less Seagal. Clearly it ought to include lots of shots of Seagal in action poses using his energy, but instead it has generic male and female models that could be used to advertise any fitness product (and probably have been). One thing that's cool is that the Chi symbol in the top center has animated energy shooting out of it. The models also have electrical beams emanating from their flesh. There are some cool looking panels showing Seagal, the drink itself, and a handful of goji berries, all with colorful action lines behind them to show how full of energy they are. They are about ready to explode with energy. Don't fuck with them.

The packaging and promotion are designed by a guy named Scott Macaluso, so I looked him up to see if he was just a guy who does corporate branding for fitness products. Actually he has a much more interesting collection of clients, the best known one being *The Vagina Monologues*. The weirdest one I found was his connection to a guy named Daniel Imperato, who he did two web sites for. One was for Imperato's 2008 presidential campaign, the other for some low budget movie Imperato executive produced called *The Red Worm*. The movie somehow involves the Pope and has a soundtrack by Frank Stallone. There is fire behind the logo but no lightning bolts or goji berries.

I gotta be honest, I'm not a fan of energy drinks. To me most of them taste like soda mixed with crunched up Flinstones vitamins, and caffeine doesn't do much for me. Even if it did, you can get a lot more in a cup of coffee (not that I'm into that either). But I enjoy a Lightning Bolt every once in a while, which to me proves that Seagal is a competent formulator. I started with the "Cherry Charge" flavor, worried that "The

Asian Experience" might need to be eased into a little. I was surprised at how good this one tasted – like black cherry soda sweetened with sugar cane. I don't detect any medicine taste. The flavor doesn't sustain itself, though. It starts to get old before you're done with the can. It definitely tastes better cold.

Now perhaps it's my ethnic background, having descended from the peoples of the Caucusus Mountains over there in Whiteville. But I did not like the Asian Experience as much as I liked the Cherry Charge. It's not disgusting by any means, but it has an odd flavor, a bit of a tangerine-like bitter aftertaste that I didn't care for much. The sugar-in-the-raw flavor is still there but not as dominant as in Cherry Charge. Perhaps it needs to grow on you, or perhaps you have to move to Japan and run your own dojo in order to enjoy this flavor as a white man. But I'll stick to cherry. (There is also a flavor called Root Beer Rush listed on the web site, but since it's not available online and has never been photographed I assume it hasn't really been released.)

Lightning Bolt is sold in more than 60 countries, but hopefully Zambia and some of those places have better distribution than here. If I could find this in a store instead of over the internet, and if it cost less than two bucks a can, I would definitely pick me up some more. Apparently it's 89 cents a can if you can find a 7-11 or Wal-Mart that stocks it, but I had to get mine from Amazon.com.

The big question I guess is *does it work?* But the answer is *I don't know.* I don't believe anyone's mounted any scientific studies yet. It seemed to give me a slight buzz the first time, but I didn't notice any Popeye-spinach type effects. I do know for sure that if you stay up all night and then drink it, you will still keep dozing off on the bus. So truckers, don't count solely on Lightning Bolt. You still gotta take a nap.

But I don't know, I might be able to be convinced. To be fair, I have never noticed a canned beverage giving me much of a boost, and I didn't test my endurance by breaking a motherfucker's wrist or tossing some scumbag through a window. But it's a tasty enough beverage.

If all natural energy drinks will ever replace chemical ones, they'll need time. Even Seagal's band Thunderbox were slow to convert, at one point listing 36 cans of Red Bull as the very first dressing room item on their tour rider. But since then they've made the switch to Lightning Bolt (now the third item on the list). We'll have to watch to see if they continue to play with the same amount of energy or not.

CHAPTER 20:
TODAY YOU DIE

"And I thought I was ignorant. This one crazy motherfucker."

Behind *Today You Die*'s opening titles is a sound we haven't heard in a while: the wailing white man's bluesy rock guitar familiar from TV shows and action movies of the '80s and early '90s. Between the subconscious *Above the Law* thoughts caused by the guitars and the undeniably awesome title, you might get your hopes up for some kind of throwback. A Golden Era style Seagal picture, just with a rounder face. After all, this was his first movie released after the formulation of Steven Seagal's Lightning Bolt. So it was bound to have more gusto than his previous films, you might think.

Well, don't get your hopes up. But at least it has a little different feel from the majority of the pictures in the DTV Era. The main plotline, while not exactly streamlined, is not as convoluted and indecipherable as movies like *Submerged* or *Into the Sun*. While painted as a good guy, Seagal's character is a thief, with no mention of military or CIA background. The template of the movie for once is not the murky international intrigue thriller, but the old fashioned interracial buddy movie like *48 Hours*, *Rush Hour* or Seagal's own *The Glimmer Man*.

But the most distinguishing feature of the movie is the subplot that doesn't seem to fit with the main storyline at all: something about prophetic dreams, ghosts and black magic. It's hard to explain. Because how do you explain something you don't understand?

Seagal plays Harlan Banks, a Las Vegas-based Robin Hood-like big-score thief who steals from "scumbag drug dealers" so he can "give to the poor." The movie opens with Jada (Mari Morrow), his beautiful young African-American wife (or girlfriend, it's not clear) getting a Tarot card reading. The reader tells Jada that someone close to her is "a reader of dreams, compatible with your gift of sight." She describes him as "a man of power in both the physical and the spiritual world."

We know because this is a movie that the tarot reading has to really mean something. It is a message. But then we discover that it's not a real tarot card reading, it's a dream – which itself is a message. Director Don E. FauntLeRoy assaults the viewer with an Avid fart, not just as an annoying attempt at modern style, but for its original purpose of subliminally conveying corny psychic premonitions or some crap like that. So we are treated with a digirhea blast that requires the pause button to study its series of images:

1. Harlan Banks sleeping
2. A gargoyle with a red candle next to it
3. A framed photo of a little blond girl
4. A skeleton shackled to a wall
5. Two identical framed photos of the little girl, this time with a classical painting and an hourglass in the background, and three white candles in the foreground
6. Repeat of #3 that flashes and fades out
7. A hand reaching for an amulet on a woman's neck
8. Harlan staring blankly while a balding man points a gun at his head
9. A gun firing

At this point Jada wakes from the dream, and Harlan is already sitting up wide awake in bed next to her. She tells him about the dream, but only the gun part, not the tarot cards, candles, gargoyle, skeleton, photos, painting or hourglass. But these aren't to be taken literally, as Harlan explains. "Listen to me. Dreams are symbolic. They don't often mean what you see. Later on maybe you'll tell me what you saw, I'll tell you what I think it meant. In the mean time go back to bed. I'll be back soon.

You hear me?"

He's about to leave for a daring cat burglary, but first he notices a new painting on the wall and asks her where she got it. She explains that she saw it in a dream and then found it in an antique store and "felt like karma meant for [her] to have it." So we know this "gift of sight" is for real, because it helps decorate the house.

Harlan goes to rob a mansion owned by a drug dealer who apparently works at night and has no family, staff, house guests or dogs. Harlan wears a very professional all black getup (that seems to change once he gets inside) and even rapells across a wire to an upper floor (although it's an obvious stunt double that doesn't look like Seagal's body type at all). Inside he electronically bypasses the alarm system and somehow knows the combination to the safe. He doesn't bother to wear gloves. Because he just don't give a fuck.

But before he can leave he's interrupted by a group of thugs – not the owners of the loot, but a rival group of drug dealers who have been robbed by Harlan in the past and feel that gives them the right to intercept his score. This is the best fight in the movie. It's not exactly a classic, but it involves a lot of good old fashioned furniture damage and broken wrists. To no one's surprise, the homeowner happens to have various antique swords on display as decorations, and they end up being returned to their original purpose. In contrast to the sword-on-sword contact we saw in *Out of Reach* and *Into the Sun*, Harlan dodges all the swings and then does a badass samurai style kill-in-one-blow maneuver. It goes by quick, but I approve.

Later on, Jada is still worried about him, not just because of her dream but now because of an incident she talks about as if we already knew about it, involving writing on a mirror. If I understand correctly, she was visited by a ghost who wrote something on the mirror in a mixture of English and French. "A warning, something about killing me in the past as an innocent and taking a blood oath. Repentance. Just faded before I could get it all."

This incident is never shown and, as far as I can tell, has nothing to do with anything else that happens in the movie. We definitely don't find out what the hell is going on with her being killed in the past. I have no clue what is up with this scene. But Harlan, unless I'm misunderstanding something here, thinks it's a ghost trying to help her out. "Well I believe you, you know that. I, uh, I just think that not all spirits are malicious." (There's no other mention of spirits in the movie.)

Harlan decides to take the advice of Jada, the dream and the non-malicious spirit, and get a legit job. It's a hard decision for him to make, because he loves helping people. You can see that he's pretty sad when he drives past a children's hospital with "GOING OUT OF BUSINESS" plastered over its sign. He knows that his new straight job isn't going to make the kind of cash to help out a, uh, business like that. I have always wanted to see a movie where Seagal plays an ex-black ops badass who applies his unique skills to a low wage working class type of job, but this is not that movie. Instead, his so-called legit job is a setup.

He thinks he's a driver for an armored car company. But on his very first pickup, his partner Bruno (Robert Miano) picks up $2 million from a warehouse, then instead of signing for it he kills the security guards at the place and turns the gun on Harlan telling him to drive. This is not the act of a lone wolf bad apple employee – I believe it's a fake armored car company using fake credentials to pick up money that doesn't really belong to them. But I have no idea why he would give himself away by killing the security guards right as he's about to get away clean. That is pretty much the worst plan you could come up with. If he had done nothing at all, he would've gotten away with it. Instead he killed a bunch of guys for no reason, and doomed the whole crime. Worst crook ever. He would probably be on one of those wacky "Stupid Criminal" type TV shows if he didn't have such a high body count.

In retrospect, it should've been obvious to Harlan that the job wasn't legit. Why would a real armored car company hire him not through an application and background check, but by just meeting him at a guy's house? The boss, Max Stevens (Kevin Tighe), talks in an openly evil type manner. And if that's not enough of a hint, Harlan should've wondered why he wasn't required to wear a uniform. I don't think it was casual Friday.

But there's no point in hashing that out at this point. People make mistakes. Now here Harlan is having to be a getaway driver at gunpoint, and plus, like *Reservoir Dogs*, the cops are on their ass as soon as they leave the joint. So it turns into a big police chase which is definitely the best "big action" in the movie and better than most similar scenes in this particular Seagalogical era. These types of scenes don't require much from Seagal, but the DTV movies still generally skimp on the big action. This one has a good amount of destruction and the Las Vegas strip scenery is much more interesting and cinematic than the generic streets of other DTV films. Harlan ends up crashing the armored car to knock Bruno out, and this is followed by some nicely photographed burning police cars flipping through the air.

Harlan manages to limp out of the truck. He gets out the money and a little bit of time is skipped so that we don't see what he does with it. Then he calls Jada and passes out. The cops find him and arrest him.

Under interrogation by the DEA (they say this robbery was actually "a drug deal gone south" – not sure how that description could possibly fit the crime, but they're the experts I guess) Harlan is a smartass and claims not to remember what happened to the money. He tries to tell them about Max, the bastard who set him up, but the feds claim Max is dead. They also mention that Max was a "low life freak who dabbled in black magic," which comes as a surprise to the audience, who were introduced to the guy as if he was just any regular non-magical criminal who would be played by Kevin Tighe. Then they put Harlan in the joint with the general population.

Coincidentally, Bruno ends up in the same prison. He asks Harlan where the money is and also mentions that he plans to cut out his heart. I kind of doubt Harlan believes that this guy will actually cut out his heart, but it's better safe than sorry so he does some move that causes screaming and a horrible crunching sound. In a separate incident, some bigger, scarier guys try to shiv Harlan on behalf of Max, but he beats their asses and impresses the leader of the black gang, Ice Kool (Anthony "Treach" Criss). Later he helps Ice in a dispute with the Hispanic gang.

Harlan politely lets Ice know he would be "happy to share" his $20 million stash if Ice could help him escape. This is real good timing on Harlan's part because it just so happens that a fake sheriff's helicopter is about to fly in and pick up Ice. So Harlan goes along as his "lottery ticket."

Ice wisely doesn't want to split up, because he wants his share of the money. But Harlan tells him sincerely, "You did me right, I'ma do you right," and that's enough for Ice. Seagal's character is now in the same position as the old man in *Half Past Dead*, the convict who knew where the gold from a train robbery was hidden, and he and Ice have a similar sort of honor-among-thieves thing going between them. Then Harlan meets Jada at a converted farmhouse hideout, at which point Avid Fart Dream #2 takes place.

In this dream Jada envisions water and rain, a blond woman dressed in white, lightning, a mausoleum, and some leaves. Harlan asks if it was the same dream as before, with Max, even though he had no way of knowing that the gunman in the earlier dream was Max. And she says no but that it does have the same mausoleum, even though the other dream didn't have a mausoleum. She points out that the mausoleum has a French name on it, which is the kind of detail you don't throw into a movie unless it means something. You would think. But this is *Today You Die*, so it doesn't mean anything.

Jada insists that Max is "evil" and "something beyond this earth" which I guess is how those with a gift of sight say "the fucker set you up." Suddenly Harlan and Jada are surprised to see an elaborate painting on the floor which Harlan examines and declares is "a protection diagram." Apparently another contribution from the non-malicious spirit who has something to do with Jada dying in the past as an innocent and a blood oath of repentance and what not, whatever the fuck that could possibly mean.

Then Harlan meets up with Ice, who, by the way, is never aware that he is in a magical movie, because he never witnesses or hears about any of that shit. In a scene straight out of *Money Talks*, they go to a bar to meet a blind arms dealer who declares that Harlan "walks like a black man, breathes like a killer" before giving them their choice of guns and explosives. And with those handy tools Ice helps Harlan hunt down Max's various partners as part of their agreement to refresh his memory as to where he hid the money. (Apparently prison escape via helicopter is not worth as much as it used to be if he still owes Harlan more after that one.)

Harlan and Ice drive around together making wacky improvised cultural exchange quips. Harlan interrogates one guy and gets the information he needs out of him. He says because he cooperated he'll let him go, then suddenly turns and shoots him. What a fucking sadist! He jokes about it to Ice and you have to wonder if Jada knows he does this kind of shit when he goes out.

They also do a little playing-one-side-against-the-other business where they get some Italians and Tongs to kill each other. This scene is mostly notable for the strangely culturally sensitive insult, "Fuck you, you Asian-American motherfucker!"

Before long he goes right to Max's house and, as he always does these days, walks right in the front door. Actually, he knocks first and when the doorman asks who he is he says, "Uh… Girl Scouts of America." Then there is some punching and some swinging on a chandelier. There's a little bit of martial arts in the climax here, but not as much as you'd like. In fact, Harlan is sort of disrespectful toward the martial arts. When an opponent comes in and does a bunch of show-offy moves, Harlan just shoots him *Raiders of the Lost Ark* style.

At this point in the movie there's no reason to believe that the title *Today You Die* actually means anything. The tarot card reader in the opening scene had a perfect opportunity to explain the title when she flipped over the Death card. She could've predicted that Harlan would die, but instead she was refreshingly honest and pointed out that the Death card doesn't mean death necessarily, it often just signifies change. The Avid fart vision, obviously, seems to predict that Harlan will get shot, but since Harlan never takes it seriously and since Kurt Russell is not in the movie, the audience never actually considers that Harlan could die.

Never fear. Ice Kool explains all. "Oh, you ran out of gas?" says Ice to an opponent who's run out of ammo. "Ah, hell no, today you die motherfucker! Little bitch!" So this is one of only a handful of Seagal pictures where the title is spoken out loud by one of the characters.

When Harlan comes face to face with Max Stevens the movie gets back into that weird magic subplot. Although up to this point Max has just been portrayed as a generic kingpin, the feds did call him a "low life freak who dabbles in black magic" and Jada said he was "something beyond this earth," so it's not too much of a surprise when he's found playing piano in a room with a coffin and a bunch of candles and makes a ridiculous speech that begins, "I was born with the devil inside me."

I don't think there's any way to really know what the hell this character is supposed to be up to. He talks about "mystical power between innocence and evil" and fondles the framed photo of the little girl that we saw in Avid Fart Dream #1. I don't understand what magic he is using or what he's using it for or who this girl is or why he has a photo of her, or especially what any of this has to do with stealing suitcases of money in a "drug deal gone sour." I have only seen the movie a couple of times but I think it's safe to say that it really makes no god damn sense.

But as soon as Max is disposed of, the magic subplot seems to disappear again. There is another plotline about a crooked fed (who looks like the guy with glasses from *Queer Eye For the Straight Guy* but is supposed to be tough) and the good girl fed (Sarah Buxton) who believes Harlan's story and Disobeys Direct Orders and what not.

In the end, Ice takes the money to a Swiss bank (the bank manager is played by Lesley-Anne Down, the actress wife of director FauntLeRoy) and has it donated to the going-out-of-business children's hospital Harlan drove past much earlier in the film. Next we see some nuns throwing a birthday party in front of the hospital. And in front of the hospital, for reasons that cannot be explained by science or man's logic, is the little blond girl from the photograph that Max had and that was in Jada's dream. Harlan comes up and gives her a medallion that you don't get a good look at but that you can assume is the one Jada had in her dream and around her neck. It seems like Harlan knows this girl, because he calls her "baby doll" and gives her a kiss. Then he leaves.

Next, the nice lady from the DEA comes up and hugs the little girl. She asks her where she got the medallion, and the girl says "a nice man gave it to me[57]."

This ending leaves a number of unanswered questions, the most obvious being *what the fuck?* You gotta assume that Ice Kool remains a fugitive, because he is some kind of criminal who has escaped from prison. But Harlan stands in plain sight of an agent of the law. How does he get away with that? Sure, he may have convinced them he was set up, but he still

---

57 To me it sounds like "a business man gave it to me," which is a lot funnier, but I'll take the word of the subtitles on the region 4 DVD.

escaped from prison, killed a bunch of people and clearly took the $20 million of stolen loot. And by the way, I don't see any new skylights or anything on that children's hospital, I'm pretty sure he didn't give away all of the money.

You also don't know where the money was hidden in the first place. The way the movie skips over that earlier it kind of seems like you ought to later find out what clever trick he pulled to keep it safe while he was in the joint, but no. I guess we can leave a few things up to the imagination.

You also gotta wonder about this whole dream thing. Harlan is mostly wrong about the dreams. Sure, the second dream is symbolic of something (I have no idea what), because there's no lady in white and lightning anywhere in the movie. But the rest of them actually are literal – the coffin, the candles, the painting, the hourglass, the photos of the little girl, the gargoyle – these may seem like obvious symbols but all that shit is in Max's pad. It's literal. Well, I'm not sure about the skeleton shackled to the wall, but maybe that was in there too. And the guy holding a gun to Harlan's head – the part he specifically told her was only symbolic – actually happens.

Harlan also said that he might help her interpret her dreams later, and the dream itself called him "a reader of dreams." But he never did try to read the dreams, which is probably a good thing. That way he gets to avoid the embarrassment of being wrong about what the candles and the gun and shit symbolize. I can only imagine what kind of crazy nonsense he would've come up with and then Jada would have to tell him "You know what the candle symbolized? That there was a candle."

And what about this ghost? The French name and writing? The mausoleum? The protection diagram? The past life talk? Is it related to the little girl who was in the dream and also at the hospital? What the hell is going on? I am not all that literal-minded of a person, but Jesus man, this thing makes no god damn sense. If it was a David Lynch movie people would come up with some horse shit that the movie supposedly means, but for a DTV movie starring Steven Seagal and Treach most people will just shrug and forget about it.

There's some weird continuity in the movie too. Not just the typical shot-to-shot continuity screwups (like the scene in the farm house where

Jada is suddenly wearing no pants) but even basic story stuff. Like, right after Harlan gets arrested, Max's people say that the cops found the truck abandoned with no money. But in the next scene, the feds repeatedly ask Harlan where the truck is. Like maybe he hid it in a sewer or some bushes or something.

There's not really any aspect of the supernatural side to this movie that seems to make much sense. Obviously there are some movies where you're not really supposed to understand everything that's going on, but I never get a feeling that Seagal pictures are meant to be that way. It seems like you're supposed to understand why Max is magic and what he's trying to do with the little girl, and who the little girl is. The dreams and magic side of the movie is so incomplete and so separate from the rest that it's easy to assume that, like *Submerged*, the script was heavily rewritten from whatever it was originally supposed to be.

Sure enough, Seagal was accused of making unauthorized changes to the script ("including dialogue") in a lawsuit filed by Kill Master, one of the production companies, and sales agent Nu Image. Seagal was also accused of losing the production millions of dollars in reshoots by showing up late and leaving early from shooting. The suit also involves another movie, *Mercenary For Justice*, which he allegedly only showed up for under threat of lawsuit, and brought a rowdy entourage who "continually harassed, intimidated and threatened the production and members of the production team with requests and demands that were inappropriate, outrageous or not contractually required." (Like what, a case of Cherry Lightning Bolt in every trailer?)

Of course, these Kill Master guys could be full of shit. The movie is obviously better than *Submerged*, so how out of line could Seagal have been? At least he dubbed his own dialogue. Seagal denied all the charges and claimed the lawsuit was a pre-emptive attack on him because he wasn't fully paid for *Mercenary For Justice*, and had accused the production of fraud, allegedly spending $5-$7 million less than the budget on the books. His lawyer also disputed the claims of the interfering entourage.

One of Kill Master's claims was that they had pre-sold the movies based on certain plot elements that were now in jeopardy due to Seagal's unauthorized script changes. A plot description on All Movie Guide mentions a casino heist, but changing a casino to a warehouse sounds more like a budgetary issue than a rewrite (backing up Seagal's side of the story). The summary also says that Harlan "has powerful psychic abilities and can punish a man simply with the powers of his mind," something that I sure as fuck didn't pick up on if it was supposed to be going on in the movie. Movies Unlimited's synopsis mentions that "when Seagal has a supernatural experience while incarcerated, his life is forever changed." That doesn't happen in the movie either.

If you can ignore all the dreams and magic, though, it's at least more competent and watchable than fucking *Submerged*. If not for the supernatural it would be more in the *Into the Sun* category – not good enough to be great, not bad enough to be funny. Seagal does seem like he's drinking the Lightning Bolt and trying a little harder.

Or is he? I was impressed by the car chase through Vegas, but a little less impressed after I found out it was stock footage taken from another movie: 1997's *Top of the World* starring Peter Weller and Dennis Hopper. It turns out *Today You Die* is full of lifts from other movies in the Millennium Films library. I mentioned earlier the scene where Seagal rappels into a drug dealer's home to rob his safe, and how the stunt double didn't look like Seagal's body type at all. You know why? Because it's actually Jean Claude-Van Damme's stunt double, breaking into a museum to steal a Faberge egg in 2001's *The Order*. Van Damme co-wrote *The Order* with Les Weldon, who also was one of the writers on *Today You Die*, and apparently remembered he had that footage. The whole scene of Harlan preparing the equipment and firing the grappling hook is from the other movie, they just took out the shots that showed Van Damme's face. People always ask me why Seagal and Van Damme haven't ever been in a movie together. Well, technically they have. But they were playing the same character.

I've also heard that the exterior shots of the prison are from the disappointing Walter Hill/Wesley Snipes picture *Undisputed*. It is from the same production company and looks like the same prison, but I didn't notice any identical shots. Maybe they just like that location. This use of stock footage might support Seagal's allegations if he had made them toward this movie rather than the next one. It's easy to imagine them scripting a car chase and including it in the budget, then just using the old one from the Peter Weller movie and keeping the extra cash. Anyway, it was a good chase, too bad it was leftovers.

And yet you still have to give Seagal some credit for effort. He mixes up his character a little bit. It's rare that he plays a character who has a good relationship with a woman, but he's actually very close with Jada. He sleeps in the same bed with her, tries to comfort her when she's scared, and calls her constantly to let her know he's okay (or not okay that time when he's been set up and shot). Mari Morrow's performance as Jada is also stronger than almost any previous Seagal love interest. She's not an interesting character but she has a strong presence, comparatively.

One thing Seagal tries again that I'm not a fan of is faking some kind of black dialect whenever he's trying to impress Ice Kool. You know how some white people start picking up an unconvincing drawl when they're trying to fit in with black people? It makes me squirm. Seagal can always get away with saying "Ain't no thang," but there are other lines that almost fall into Vanilla Ice territory. When Ice tells him "You's a cold motherfucker," he either says "Ice cool, y'all" or "I's cool, ya'll" (see, that's why they need to put English subtitles on these things). He also has the line, "Let's put it like dis. Let those who should be liberated get goin where they got to go." But I suppose this sort of thing is explained in the movie. White people can say those kind of things if they're the kind of white people who walk like a black man but breathe like a killer.

Ice Kool is semi-charismatic, even though he's not nearly as funny as he's obviously trying to be. In the rapper-turned-actor-sidekick rankings I put him second, above Ja Rule but below DMX. (Nas in *Ticker* doesn't count because he was Tom Sizemore's sidekick, not Seagal's.) Treach was from the group Naughty By Nature, most famous for their song "O.P.P." Unlike those other guys he's many, many years past his success as a rapper, so some people would probably assume he's a has-been cashing in on his name by tossing out quickie roles in the DTV market. But personally I give Treach a lot more credit than that, just because he was the star of *Love and a Bullet*, one of the best DTV movies I've seen. It's a hitman movie from the writers of that Mark Wahlberg movie *The Big Hit*.

The Wahlberg movie is a bigger budget theatrical movie, and it has better action. But I think the comedy angle is more successful in *Love and a Bullet*, and Treach deserves some credit for pulling that off. All in all, *Today You Die* is an okay effort. It's not the revival that the badass title had me hoping for, but it's not one of the worst either. Somewhere in the middle ranking for the DTV Era as far as quality and absurdity go.

Today You Die, 2005
Directed by Don E. FauntLeRoy (*Raging Bull**)
Written by Danny Lerner (*Out For a Kill, Shark Zone*), Kevin Moore (*Larva*) and Les Weldon (*Replicant, In Hell, Raging Sharks*). Also an uncredited Joe Halpin (*Into the Sun*).
Distinguished co-stars: I don't know if he's distinguished, but I like Kevin Tighe.
Seagal regulars: Nick Mancuso (Agent Saunders) was of course Tom Breaker, the head of the CIA in both *Under Siege* films. John P. Gulino (Marshall) also appears in *The Glimmer Man, Fire Down Below, The Foreigner* and *Black Dawn*. Simone Levin (DEA Agent #3) played a booking clerk in *Ticker*. J. Anthony Pena ("Hispanic") will return as Guard #1 in *Black Dawn*. Lisa Guerrero (Reporter) played "Blonde Beauty" in *Fire Down Below* (then known as Lisa Coles). Erik Betts (Max's bodyguard) will play Henchman #3 in *Black Dawn*. Dennis Keiffer (Garret Gang #2) will play an uncredited henchman in *Black Dawn*. Tim Gilbert (Garret Gang #4) did stunts in *Above the Law* and *The Patriot*. Troy Gilbert (Casino Guard #2) did stunts in *Above the Law, Fire Down Below* and *The Patriot*. J.J. Perry (Thug) did stunts in *The Glimmer Man* and *Black Dawn*. Joseph Ojomoh (uncredited inmate "Tiny") will earn his credit as Guard #2 in *Black Dawn*. Jerry Trimble, who plays Teabag, has not been in a Seagal movie before, but he was in two movies with titles similar to Seagal movies: *Executive Power* and *In the Name of Justice*. Same goes for Robert Miano, who plays Bruno; he was in *Executive Target* and *Out For Blood*.
Firsts: Surprisingly, Seagal's first reference to dream interpretation outside of a vision quest type of scenario.
Title refers to: In a rare case, it is actually a line of dialogue. When Treach's character is in a gun fight and his opponent runs out of bullets he yells, "Oh, you ran out of gas? Ah, hell no, today you die motherfucker! Little bitch!"
Just how badass is this guy? "A man of power in both the physical and the spiritual world." "Walks like a black man, breathes like a killer." "I see your handwork is handsome."
Adopted culture: Definitely enjoys black culture, trying to speak ebonics and giving people a pound when appropriate.
Languages: English, ebonics, dream interpretation.
Improvised weapons: A small table.
Fight in bar: No.
Broken glass: Windows shot out, dishes, mirror, guy thrown through window, shattering reflective windows on exploding building.
Words of wisdom: "I just think not all spirits are malicious."

Most awkward one-liner: "You know what Bruno, I got some advice for you. I think you should, uh, be my motherfuckin' guest."

Family shit: Close relationship with his wife.

Political themes: Little or none. You could argue that the children's hospital "going out of business" is a statement about our country's backwards economic priorities, but I doubt it.

Cover accuracy: Not too bad. I don't know about the fiery sky, but a prison and a helicopter are involved in the movie, as pictured. However the tagline "What Seagal does in Vegas, nearly destroys it" is pretty exaggerated. He flips a couple cop cars I guess, and blows up a building. But I don't see how that counts as nearly destroying Vegas.

*first assistant cameraman (uncredited)

CHAPTER 21:
BLACK DAWN

"Open the door and throw that bitch out!"

In his first sequel since *Under Siege 2*, Seagal reprises the character of Jonathan Cold from the secret agent saga *The Foreigner*. Cold this time is described as "Ex-CIA, current freelance operative specializing in covert operations and nuclear weapons intelligence." They never mentioned that last part in *The Foreigner*, but I guess everybody has their hidden talents. According to CIA files, Cold went rogue and killed six agents back in the first movie, and then was killed in Prague a year ago. But according to Cold (whose story is more believable since he's clearly still alive) he's still working for the CIA in a "top secret column" for doing things "probably considered by most people to be immoral or illegal" but "that we have to do in the interest of United States security around the world."

In this case the immoral and/or illegal activity is disguising himself as a doctor to bust notorious weapons dealer Michael Donovan (Julian Stone) out of prison. Imagine that – not only busting a guy out of prison but going as far as impersonating a doctor. That *is* immoral. What if he had to give somebody CPR or something? Fortunately, he seems to know what he's doing, and as far as we see he doesn't use his disguise to look at a patient's boobs or anything creepy like that.

By busting him out he gains Donovan's trust, but Donovan's crazy long-haired brother James (John Pyper-Ferguson, a guy who had a small role in *Unforgiven*) seems jealous and suspicious. Despite James's objections, Cold accepts a $100,000 offer to come into the fold as their nuclear arms expert. They're in the middle of a deal to buy a suitcase bomb from a Russian physicist named Myshkin (Matt Salinger[58]), and they need Cold's expertise to make sure it's the real deal. Then they have to meet up with a scientist named Macabe (David St. James) who has been using his coffee mug to smuggle plutonium out of the nuclear test facility where he works. And then they'll sell the whole deal to a group of young Chechen terrorists who want to set the bomb off in Los Angeles as revenge for the CIA assassination of their leader, Aslan. Meanwhile, the Chechens keep doing diamond heists trying desperately to save up enough for that nice bomb they want so badly.

So it's a complicated story, but the direction is competent enough that it's much easier to follow than most of the recent Seagal pictures. To add another layer of complication, a former student of Cold's named Agent Stuart (Tamara Davies, the DTV Nicole Kidman) is doing surveillance on Donovan and finds out Cold is alive and apparently working with weapons dealers. Meanwhile, she doesn't know it, but her section chief Greer (Timothy Carhart) really is involved in the plot. Jesus man, all this intrigue over a silly suitcase.

The opening scene is the assassination of Aslan, interspersed with cheap looking, melodramatic opening titles like a Mexican action movie. The dialogue "Spare no one Julia" and "or we die slaves" is worked into the techno score and repeated endlessly, emphasizing that these Chechen terrorists are serious about becoming martyrs. But the accents, washed out cinematography and setting had me worrying it would be another gloomy, colorless Euro-thriller. Fortunately the setting moves quickly to Los Angeles and this is actually one of the more involving and entertaining Seagal screen stories of the era.

This one really kicks in when Agent Stuart is captured by Donovan's men and is about to be killed. Cold turns out to have a conscience, so he puts up a fight, revealing his true colors. Donovan's response is a

---

58 Believe it or not, Matt Salinger is the son of J.D. Salinger. Yes, *the* J.D. Salinger. But if you recognize him it's probably from *Revenge of the Nerds*.

sarcastic, "I'm disappointed, Jonathan. I thought we had an agreement." I don't know why villains are always such smartasses. Why can't they be sincere every once in a while? If he already knew he couldn't trust Cold then why the fuck did he get involved with him in the first place? You'd think these people would be more careful about this type of shit. You think you're gonna nuke Los Angeles and nobody's gonna come after you? You might want to think these things through a little more in the future. But you can't, because you're dead.

Anyway, Cold's response is, "Shit happens, y'know." He grabs Stuart and jumps through a window with her, leading to the obvious choice for action highlight of the movie: a ridiculous truck chase. They land in the back of a passing dump truck. The driver doesn't seem to notice, he just smiles dumbly until a bullet meant for Cold and Stuart goes through the roof and wounds him. So what he does, he keeps driving, swerving and plowing through other cars. Eventually he gets hit by another bullet, this time in the head, just before Cold grabs him and tosses his corpse on the front of one of the cars in pursuit, then hops in and takes over the wheel. The chase continues for a while until – of course – they are headed straight for a truckload of flammable materials and also, by the way, it turns out the brakes aren't working. Fuckin brakes, man. You think they work, but wait until you're headed toward a truckload of flammable materials at top speed. Then we'll see how good they really work.

Then there's another great moment where Cold tells Stuart to jump and she does. Laying on the ground, she watches the truck crash and explode, thinking that her teacher has just been turned to ashes right in front of her eyes. Suddenly, Cold is just standing nearby. You see that? That's how fuckin cool he is. He can jump out of a truck without even being seen and then just be standing there on his feet. Out of nowhere. Like some sort of glimmer man.

There's a lot I don't understand about the truck chase. Number one, how did they get so lucky that a dump truck happened to be driving by at the exact moment they jumped through the window? Especially since this previously was an abandoned warehouse in a deserted area, the kind of place where you know you can make deals and kidnap CIA agents, because you know some dump truck isn't gonna drive by and witness something. Number two, why did the driver of the dump truck go on such a high speed rampage after being wounded? Was that just something he always wanted to do and the bullet wound inspired him to follow his dreams? Number three, why was Cold so cavalier about tossing an innocent working man out of a truck? It wasn't even 100% sure he was dead, and I didn't see Cold checking no pulse. And even if he knew for sure the guy was dead, was it really appropriate to toss his fuckin corpse on the front of a car as a distraction? That's no way to treat a body. But I guess that's what we should expect from a guy who blows up a non-abandoned train station to get one guy and leaves an old lady alone after her house gets blown up. Jonathan Cold is not as conscientious as your usual Seagal character. Maybe that's just the difference between a CIA agent and a Navy SEAL. Jonathan Cold would never check the pulse of the guy who locked him up like Casey Ryback did.

By DTV standards, this one works pretty well for a lot of reasons. Almost all of the supporting characters have a little more oomph than a lot of the no names in most of these DTV movies. James Donovan (who takes over after his brother dies) is a crazy guy sort of in the mold of William Forsythe. The leader of the Chechens, Nicholi (Nicholas Davidoff) looks like a pretty boy version of Wolverine from X-Men, and has lots of corny lines like, "Finally we have reached our target: the great city of Los Angeles" and "We are days away from realizing Aslan's dream," which in this case means a nuclear attack on Los Angeles and probably not whatever that magic Jesus lion in *Chronicles of Narnia* dreamed about. Myshkin, the Russian physicist, is funny too, because he describes his bomb as "small but powerful. Like the heart, if you will," and always refers to it as a "she." Even Julia (Noa Hegesh), a Chechen henchwoman, is kind of cute because when she runs away from an exploding car she turns and looks at the explosion instead of pretending not to notice it like you're supposed to do in these movies.

One of the big questions about the characters is what exactly would motivate each of them to be involved in this suitcase bomb scheme. Sure, the Chechens have this whole Narnia revenge thing. And the Russian probably doesn't give a shit about Americans. But then you got an American scientist and American criminals and a CIA section chief all willing to help out.

The criminals are just crazy bastards, but even they start to have qualms. Late in the game James asks a henchman, "Are you ready to give up your home to a bunch of lunatics?" and then decides that after they get the key to the diamonds they're going to kill the Chechens. (It would be more honorable if that had been the plan all along instead of a last minute change.)

This scientist Macabe, as far as I can tell, is just a sleazy Benedict Arnold motherfucker willing to kill hundreds of thousands of people in exchange for an equal amount of dollars. And the worst part is he has a big house, he seems to make a lot of money already. What a bastard. The best detail, if you pay enough attention, is that he has a full-sized flagpole in his front yard. Ain't that the truth? The guy that tries to shove his supposed patriotism down your throat is the same guy who steals plutonium from the government and sells it to terrorists to use on his own city. Come to think of it, maybe this guy really hates living in Los Angeles. All that traffic and shit. The dudes with ponytails talking too loud on their phones about who's representing who. Maybe he hates all that shit, and that's why he did it. Understandable, maybe, but not ethical.

And the CIA guy Greer, well, his motive is left a mystery. We find out in the end that he "created" Aslan, and told him where to set off the bomb. It's apparently part of some plan but he dies before he can make a big speech explaining it. Was he trying to allow a terrorist attack as an excuse for a power grab, like the burning of the Reichstag? Your guess is as good as mine. But I like how it's left to the imagination.

I also like the teacher-student relationship between Cold and Stuart. She claims he taught her everything she knows, but at first it seems like all she knows is how to take surveillance photos. She doesn't seem to be a go-getter agent like Jonathan Cold. It kind of seems like a mistake on the movie's part but then when he rescues her and they're on top of the high speed dump truck he berates her for getting captured and says "you haven't learned a god damn thing." Later on, there are a couple little things you notice that maybe she learned from him. For example, in a shootout Cold does a technique Seagal likes to use every once in a while where he hides behind something, then holds the gun up in the air and busts off a bunch of shots in different directions without being able to aim. He also uses a similar method to shoot around corners. Later, we see Stuart use the same type of technique, like in one scene where she's being chased down stairs so she points the gun up behind her and fires at random.

Stuart doesn't know much about computers, she has to have a computer expert with her at her secret mannequin factory hideout to look up files on his laptop. And maybe she got this from Cold because when he needs to break into some CIA files to figure out which scientist is smuggling plutonium, he goes to a young nerdy guy named Billy (Ryan Bollman, *Children of the Corn II: The Final Sacrifice*).

Stuart's computer expert figures out who Macabe is first. Also he uses a good search engine because he types in "McCabe" but brings up a listing of "Macabe." This type of thing might be needed because apparently the CIA keeps pretty shoddy records. I noticed when they show Jonathan Cold's file that they spell his name "Johnathan." And he's their own employee. I wonder if they spell it wrong on his paychecks?

Cold's computer expert Billy manages to break into the CIA's email, which is impressive. Please note that one of CIA section chief Greer's emails has the subject line "birthday." Sorry Greer, you might not be making that party. Also he has no spam in his inbox, which fucking figures. Of course the CIA has better spam filtering technology than the public. Hell, those fuckers are probably the ones behind all that "greatOnline –Pharmacy-" and "qSEXUALLYjEXPLICITe: Hello !.!" type shit I get every day.

Cold's computer expert is a little luckier than Stuart's. Stuart's gets killed, Cold's not only lives but happens to live ten blocks away from the scientist he ends up tracking down.

Another thing Stuart learned from Cold is faking credentials. In the opening scene Cold and his team[59] make a fake doctor's ID to get him into the prison. Much later on, Stuart gets into the nuclear facility with a fake ID from the EPA. This actually brings up a pretty crazy possibility for revisionist Seagalogists. I'm sure I'm not the only one who thought it was a little suspicious that an EPA official was allowed to carry a

---

59 By the way, Agent Thomas (the bald guy) is played by Joe Halpin, former undercover narcotics officer and writer of *Into the Sun*, *Shadow Man*, *Attack Force* and *Flight of Fury*.

sidearm, as Jack Taggert did in *Fire Down Below*. You heard me right, and I think you know what I'm trying to ask here. I'm asking what if Jack Taggert is not Jack Taggert, EPA agent. I'm asking what if he's Jonathan Cold with fake EPA credentials, the same things he later taught his student Agent Stuart to make? Of course, in *Fire Down Below* he is shown dealing with his EPA superiors. But maybe he tricked them too. This is Jonathan Cold we're talking about here, after all. "One of the best operatives in the field."

In the next to last scene we learn that Cold and Stuart used to screw. He refers to it as a "3 night stand" but she seems to think it was longer. It should be pointed out that this is highly unethical, it violates the code of conduct for teacher-student relationships. But anyway I'm glad they kept it in the past so we don't have to watch another awkward sex scene like in *Into the Sun*.

There are two things that happen over and over in this movie. The first is people quibble about whether or not people are allowed to have guns at a meeting. The Donovans have to meet with Cold, with the terrorists and with two different scientists, and every time there has to be a discussion about "you said no guns" or "give me your gun" or whatever. Every time, people get all offended but they end up coming to an agreement. The other thing that keeps happening is people keep being watched. Stuart and her partner spy on the Donovans from a warehouse across the street or from a parked car. Other CIA people spy on her just sitting in a parked car. Most of the time it seems like there is no one in this area at all except for 1) criminals and terrorists and 2) people in parked cars spying on them. It seems like everybody, including Cold, should be paying more attention to the parked cars. But they act like they're invisible.

There are a couple instances though when there are innocent bystanders nearby, always in the construction business. There was the dump truck driver mentioned earlier, but there's also a great moment where Cold comes out of a warehouse after a big shootout and a random construction worker asks him, "You all right man?" Which is a good thing to ask. It would be cool if there was always a nice dude asking Seagal if he's all right after a big fight.

The action is decent, even though it's almost all guns and stunts. There's not much martial arts involved. Even in the flashback to *The Foreigner* they show some of the shootout in the old lady's cabin, but they leave out the awesome part where Cold lights a guy on fire and *then* kicks him.

The climax is not a real stunt, but a fakey green screen affair where Cold and Stuart take the suitcase bomb (set to go off in less than five minutes) onto a helicopter. They try to find the deepest part of the ocean and toss it in. As the case sinks to the bottom a school of fish scatters – the poor scaly bastards. At least they died defending their country. Their brave, aquatic sacrifice makes it possible for you and I to live our lives every day, loving our families, breathing the air and walking on solid land. Anyway there's a mushroom cloud and a glow and the helicopter gets knocked around but then everything seems peachy. When Stuart asks if they're going to be okay, Cold quips, "Looks like we might be, but uh, we could be glowin in the dark for a while." And then they laugh. Ha ha.

So if you're curious, it turns out rock beats scissors and water beats 5-kiloton nuclear bomb. In my opinion, *Black Dawn* is not a very realistic movie. In the featurette included on the DVD, director Gruszynski says that "obviously it's a genre picture so it is a story that is taking some, you know, poetic license." As an example he points out that a real suitcase bomb, using today's technology, would have to be much bigger and too heavy to carry around. That's the least of the unrealistic details in this story, but still, I think *Black Dawn* makes a good point about dangers facing western countries in the post 9-11 era. While the security measures in nuclear testing facilities are no doubt different from what's depicted in the movie, numerous reports have concluded that our facilities are not secure and present a potential for catastrophic terrorism.

On May 3, 2004 at the German Marshall Fund's Transatlantic Center in Brussels, the Strengthening the Global Partnership Project by the Center For Strategic and International Studies and the Nuclear Threat Initiative held a "scenario-based exercise on catastrophic terrorism" which, like Seagal's film, was called Black Dawn. 55 current and former senior officials and experts from the European Council, the European Commission, NATO, 15 member states and various international organizations gathered to discuss the prevention of nuclear terrorism.

The exercise revolved around the hypothetical scenario of al Qaeda acquiring a 10-kiloton nuclear device and detonating it in Brussels. The movie involves Chechen terrorists detonating a 5-kiloton bomb in Los Angeles, which is different. But the final report from Black Dawn emphasizes the importance of securing nuclear sites and employing former nuclear scientists, two security measures that would've helped out in the movie.

According to the report, "Whereas other exercises have focused on consequence management, Black Dawn emphasized prevention, specifically asking what European governments and institutions can do to prevent terrorists from acquiring and using nuclear, biological or chemical weapons and materials." The report does not mention the use of Jonathan Cold in this prevention, or Jonathan Cold-like agents. In fact, it concludes that "The best, maybe the only, effective means of preventing a nuclear terrorist attack is to secure all weapons-usable nuclear materials. Once these materials go missing, only luck on the part of [Jonathan Cold] or mistakes on the part of terrorists are likely to stop an attack."

Also, maybe it didn't occur to the participants, but the final report doesn't give any indication that Black Dawn discussed the possibility of taking the nuclear weapon in a helicopter and tossing it in some water just before it blew up. It is possible that this aspect of the movie is not 100% scientifically accurate. The final report discusses some grim consequences in the Brussels scenario, including 40,000 initial casualties, 300,000 injuries, structural and infrastructure damage, economic and social impact and substantial radiation damage throughout Belgium, the Netherlands and Germany. In the movie, the water seems to have done the trick. It's not even clear whether the fish died. (Either way they are heroes, though.)

I sure never would've guessed they'd make a sequel to *The Foreigner*. Normal people have never heard of it, and most Seagal fans consider it one of his weakest. I myself didn't appreciate it at all until I started studying it for this book. Of course, they don't market this as a sequel. The box makes no mention of it. Only Seagalologists or people who see it on the USA network (where it is mysteriously retitled *Foreigner II: Black*

Dawn) will notice a connection. But in retrospect, Jonathan Cold is the perfect Seagal character for continuing adventures. We all know that Seagal characters are usually ex-CIA, but these two movies really do operate more in the world of secret agent trickery than in his others. This one even has a slight *Mission: Impossible* feel with his team of specialists helping him to disguise himself as a doctor and fake a medical emergency in order to steal the prisoner during an emergency transfer.

One nice secret agent touch Seagal adds this time around is that he wears a suit and tie for almost the entire movie. At the very end, having lunch with Stuart after saving the world, he still has a suit on but doesn't have a tie. Because now it's time to relax.

The only other continuing Seagal character we've seen so far is Casey Ryback in the *Under Siege* pictures. In part 2, we find out that Ryback has opened a restaurant. But Cold would never do that. He says, "I think you know me well enough to know I couldn't've opened up a coffee shop or something." It's not his style. He's in this for life.

I would definitely like to see more Jonathan Cold adventures, and I'd even like to see them bring back some of his colleagues, like Agent Stuart. I'm not sure if they'll be glowing in the dark or not, though. Maybe they have to come back to fight mutant fish. Not on a submarine, though. That would be stupid.

I should mention that early in this movie you see Cold driving, and there is a McDonalds french fry box on the dashboard. It seems kind of crazy that Seagal would leave that in the shot when so many people take potshots at him for his weight, but I guess he really doesn't give a fuck, like a good Buddhist. As far as the movie though, I think he may actually give a fuck. I have to congratulate Seagal for the decent quality of this picture. I didn't notice any dubbing or stock footage, and that's what I call effort. The DVD producers also deserve credit for including a couple minor extras and the all important English subtitles. On the making of featurette, Tamara Davies mentions doing "6, 7, 8 takes" of the helicopter scene. You hear that America? Seagal does multiple takes. He's trying to get it right.

The best extra is an interview with Seagal. Unrelated to this particular movie, he talks about his love for Asia and claims "I'm a lot more Asian than I am American." He also describes what he's trying to do with his movies (he mentions laughter, inspiration and "leading people into contemplation" more than once). He encourages people to try to be successful while respecting ethics. He even seems a little bit humble, admitting that "I've, like any other actor, been in and out of the top of my game." He comes across as a very nice and likable guy, although you can't help but notice he's wearing a shiny blue gown and sitting outside on an ornate throne.

Black Dawn is by no means the top of his game, but it's a decent game for this late in the career. I guess it's easy to say that after sitting through *Submerged* a couple times, but I really mean it. I don't know about contemplation, but it definitely made me laugh and be happy.

Black Dawn, 2005
aka *Foreigner II: Black Dawn* (title used when it airs on the USA network)
Directed by Alexander Gruszynski (first time director; cinematographer of the Brian Bosworth classic *Stone Cold* as well as Ringo Lam's first Jean-Claude Van Damme picture, *Maximum Risk*).
Written by Martin Wheeler (he wrote two DTV Wesley Snipes vehicles: *7 Seconds* and *Razor's Edge*).
Distinguished co-stars: None.
Seagal regulars: John P. Gulino (jewelry store manager) played a hotel clerk in *The Foreigner*. Not sure if they are the same guy, twin cousins or what. He was also in *The Glimmer Man, Fire Down Below* and *Today You Die*. J. Anthony Pena (Guard #1) and Joseph Ojomoh (Guard #2) both had bits in *Today You Die*. Veteran Seagal screenwriter Joe Halpin, who played a bodyguard in *Clementine*, returns as Agent Thomas. Dennis Keiffer (a henchman) was also in *Today You Die*.
Firsts: Seagal's first straight to video sequel, first flashback to another movie, first one where he's wearing a suit and tie for the entire movie, first nuclear explosion.
Title refers to: Nuclear terrorism.
Just how badass is this guy? "One of the best operatives in the field." "Dead or alive, Cold is a dangerous man."
Adopted culture: None, unless you count that he taught his student how to use chopsticks as a weapon.
Languages: English only.
Improvised weapons: Throws a dead body onto a car. Hotel bystander (hooker?) throws glass lamp at Agent Amanda.
Old friends: Agent Amanda was his student long ago.
Fight in bar: No.
Broken glass: Slo-mo two-person jump through window, windshield hit by truck, truck windshield shot out, breaks door glass with flashlight, glass lamp thrown and shattered on wall.

Innocent bystanders: The dump truck driver is killed by gunshots during the truck chase. A homeless person's encampment under the overpass also gets run over during the chase. A hooker (or mistress?) throws a lamp at Stuart when she hides in their hotel room, a rare instance of a bystander fighting back.

Family shit: No mention of his family this time (although we know about his brother and father from *The Foreigner*).

Political themes: Continues with the old CIA dirty tricks theme. Makes the eerily timely point that our nuclear facilities are not secure enough and could lead to disaster. Traitorous scientist has full-sized flagpole in his front yard, the son of a bitch.

Cover accuracy: The one weird thing is the silhouette of a dude doing a flying kick on another guy, which has nothing to do with the movie. It's also weird because the flying guy is in almost the exact same pose as Jason Scott Lee on the cover of *Dragon: The Bruce Lee Story*.

CHAPTER 22:
MERCENARY FOR JUSTICE

"Tiger, this is Mouse. What's happening at the beehive?"

Mercenary For Justice is a watchable if forgettable chapter in the saga of Seagal's DTV Era. It opens unpromisingly with all of the worst qualities of the period: overly confusing conflicts, characters introduced through annoying freeze frames and titles, almost complete lack of Seagal for the first 13 minutes, and when he finally does show up his very first line of dialogue is obviously dubbed by someone else. Seagal plays John Seeger, decorated Gulf War hero turned mercenary. I would say hero turned mercenary for justice, but I get the feeling that at first he's supposed to be a regular mercenary who then learns to instead be a mercenary for justice. At least that's what his maybe-ex-girlfriend Maxine (Jacqueline Lord) seems to think. She's working for the same guy and betrays Seeger to punish him for what she says is his creed: "care for no one, fight for everyone." Don't worry, he'll show he's really for justice and she'll come to appreciate it. It's not clear exactly when or why these changes take place, but it doesn't take long.

Seeger and a team of mercenaries are surrounded by French troops on a resort island called Galmoral. They're apparently staging a coup to reclaim this small piece of African land from the French and make it a democracy. Whatever exactly is going on they got screwed and are having a hard time escaping. They were hired by some asshole named Anthony Chapel (Roger

Guenveur Smith) who is subtitled as "Black Opps Producer," which I guess must mean "Black Opportunities" or something. Chapel is making conference calls to "CIA Dirty Deeds Man" John Dresham (Luke Goss). Dresham demands "plausible deniability" and Chapel openly says that he told his "independent contractors" they were liberating Africans when actually the fight is so they can "get rich off of diamonds and oil."

In these scenes Seeger is a mercenary who may be at least somewhat for justice, because he's clearly uncomfortable with the other half of their team. Kruger (Langley Jack Kirkwood) and Dekerk (Vivian Bieldt) are a couple of racist South Africans who, while Seeger and his guys are holed up by the "Frenchies," are busy kidnapping the French Ambassador and his family to use as a get out of jail free card. The ploy works, but Seeger doesn't like it, saying "I oughta fuckin kill you right now, boy." (When a gun is pointed at him he quickly backs down and says, "Yeah, maybe not right now.")

We don't see Seeger do much besides fire a machine gun, but he was apparently crucial in this Special Opportunity. Chapel hired Seeger's best friend Radio Jones (Zaa Nikweta) because he was the only one who could convince Seeger to come along. We don't find out much about Radio, especially considering that the movie ends up sort of revolving around him. He has the line "I shouldn't've dragged you into this, John. They used me to get ahold of you, man! (AHHHGHH!!!)" as he's shot to death. He does manage to ask Seeger to take care of Eddie and Shondra, which turns out to be sort of what the movie is about.

Seeger escapes to the safety of Dade County, Florida, where he shows up at Radio's house. His wife Shondra (Faye Peters) and son Eddie (Tumi Mogoje) already know Radio is dead. Seeger gives Shondra a comforting hug and a roll of hundreds, saying "I'm gonna look after you and the baby now." (Eddie has got to be at least 10, probably older, so I'm glad he didn't hear that.) Looking out the window Seeger notices two CIA guys parked in a car planning to kill him, so he sneaks out and kills them instead. Then he is surrounded by mercenaries including Kruger and Dekerk, and for the second time in the movie he surrenders to them ("Now there's two ways we can do this, John. We can all end up looking like Swiss cheese, or we can go have a nice cup of coffee. What's it gonna be?" "Let's uh, let's go have a cup of coffee.")

See, Chapel already needs Seeger for another Black Opportunity. There's this Greek arms dealer named Ahmet Dasan (Peter Butler) who needs his son busted out of prison. The guy is pretty rich, he describes himself as "a billionaire many times over," although Chapel demotes him to "millionaire extraordinaire." Chapel still has the South African mercenaries for racism in his stable, as well as Maxine and the team's computer expert for justice Samuel (Michael Kenneth Williams), but he needs Seeger. So while Seeger is busy with his nice cup of coffee they also kidnap Eddie and Shondra. Those two will be playing the part of the French ambassador and his family in this scenario.

Once Seeger accepts the mission the movie gets much more interesting. He gives the team a *Mission: Impossible* style briefing on how the prison break is going to go down. What he doesn't tell them (or the audience) is that he, Samuel and Maxine have a different plan in mind. As the story unfolds so does their actual plan, which uses trickery, computer hacking and some violence to save Eddie and Shondra, kill Chapel, Kruger and Dekerk, and bust both Dresham and Dasan.

The kind of tricks they use are typical heist movie or secret agent stuff, a little different from normal Seagalogy techniques. I like that they're cocky about it, they have what would be described as a bold plan, playing around with the authorities. Maxine leaks to the CIA that Seeger plans to rob the "black vault" at a bank in Capetown, putting all the local police and CIA agents at the bank while his guys are breaking into the prison. Then, once things are wrapped up at the prison she tells them that the bank was just a diversion from the prison, so the cops all head for the prison, at which point Seeger really does rob the bank!

A lot of the plan is implausible, obviously. For example, it's kind of a stretch that a dumb security guy at the bank would believe Seagal was a Lieutenant with the Capetown police right after the real CPD hotshots just left. But in these later Seagal movies the plots are always this complicated but rarely come together neatly like this in the end. So it's admirable.

The movie ends with a solemn military funeral for Radio, another Seagalogy motif dating back to *Under Siege*. It's such a serious ending it feels like it's really supposed to work as melodrama. You could see an old John Woo movie ending this way and the audience would get emotional about it. But come on man, we hardly even saw Radio. Apparently he was a communications specialist, which may be why his parents named him

Radio. But we don't know that guy at all. Sorry for your loss though.

I don't know, it's an okay ending, but it could've used an eagle or some other animal.

The action of course is an entrée of gunplay with a side order of explosions. I really didn't get much enjoyment out of the opening battle. Director FauntLeRoy says on the making-of featurette that they watched *Saving Private Ryan* and *Black Hawk Down* 20 times as research for this scene. They even have a part where sad violin sounds play over the battle as if to ask "what madness hath man wrought?" instead of the "isn't this awesome?" you generally want from a Steven Seagal picture. They're doing a low budget action movie but they're going for this big studio horrors-of-war style so it's all chaos without much momentum or context, you don't really attach yourselves to what the characters are doing or have any "oh shit, you gotta get out of there" kinda moments.

But when Seeger does get to do hand-to-hand there is a little hint of the Golden Era in there. He twists and breaks a lot of arms. There's a funny part where a guy lunges at him and he does the aikido wrist twist thing while still sitting down in a chair. Definitely my favorite scene is when he's at a fancy restaurant eating lobster with Maxine and he goes to the bathroom. A hitman hired by the CIA tries to attack him in the shitter, but Seeger just beats the holy hell out of the poor chump, breaking a faucet off on his head, using him to knock urinals off the wall, dunking his head in the toilet. At one point he just slaps him hard five times in a row, like he's hammering a nail into him, or maybe trying to fix the reception on an ornery TV. (We used to do that before cable, kids.)

This is the best fight in the movie, but the scene is more memorable for the one line that the hitman speaks. When Seeger steps out of the stall to confront him his attacker yells, "That's it for you, poophole!" I don't know how, but somehow I neglected to mention this line when I reviewed the movie for The Ain't It Cool News. A reader named Duncan O'Sullivan kindly e-mailed to tell me he couldn't friggin' believe I had failed to mention it.

I explained to Duncan that the line is not quite what it seems. If you check the English subtitles, the thug actually doesn't call Seeger "poophole," he calls him "poepol." I looked it up and it turns out it's from

South Africa, it's an Afrikaans slang word for "asshole." So, I guess literally he is calling Seeger a poophole, but presumably the word doesn't sound as ridiculous in Afrikaans as it does in English. He's just calling him a prick, he's not calling him a weiner face or a big doody head.

But that doesn't change the fact that it sounds like he's calling him "poophole," and obviously Seagal, FauntLeRoy and the other Americans involved in the production were willing to let that happen. So it's noteworthy. Good call, Duncan.

Before we move on, a note about bathrooms. Bathrooms are turning out to be a minor motif in DTV Seagalogy. In *The Foreigner* there was a confrontation and bombing while he was taking a piss in the train station restroom. In *Out For a Kill* he got up to go to the bathroom but got attacked before he got there. In the next one, *Shadow Man*, he will have reason to enter a women's restroom. Here you can only assume he really had to take a shit, unless he could somehow sense that a guy was in the next room and if he pretended to have to take a shit the guy would follow him and try to kill him. Even then, why not just go into the room and get the guy? I guess the bathroom was the best place to fight considering the use of urinals, but I don't know, I'm thinking he really had to take a shit. Whatever was going on, he never did get a chance to take a shit, and not surprisingly he doesn't wash his hands. After beating the guy down and destroying the bathroom he has a funny bonding moment with Maxine's bodyguard Bulldog (Adrian Galley) and they walk out as buddies. It's a good ending to the scene but I think it would've been pretty great if he stopped to wash his hands after beating the guy up. Plus it's a good example for the kids. I don't care how fancy the restaurant is, there's still gonna be germs on the toilets.

There are some weird continuity issues. After Seeger kills the two CIA guys in Florida we hear that he also killed one of the South African mercenaries. Even though there was no scene where this happened Seeger seems to agree with the claim, saying "three people died today." There were only two that we ever saw, unless the third was some sort of metaphor for the day the innocence died or something like that. Another more subtle goof is when the security stooge at the Capetown bank refers to Seeger and Maxine as "the Americans" even though he is supposed to believe their story that they are Capetown police. But the funniest is not so much an error as just an unacceptably shoddy editing job. Seeger is in the backseat of Dresham's car holding a gun to his head when a cop happens to walk up. Dresham takes the opportunity to drop out of the car but when he turns around Seeger has magically teleported himself to a moving van about ten or fifteen feet away. The cop doesn't even see it happen, he opens up the back door and is surprised that Seeger is gone. This is a move that not even a skinny little ninja could pull off, let alone big ol' hulking John Seeger.

But overall the quality of the production is slightly more professional than we've come to expect at this point. There's that first Seagal line that's obviously dubbed, and another one later where he says "Asshole alert!" Roger Guenver Smith also has some looped dialogue in one scene. It sounds like some British guy speed-reading off of a cue card, but the voice is close enough that I'm only 90% sure it's not him. Other than that Seagal and friends seem to be there when needed, not as often replaced by obvious doubles as in some of the other movies, and the main plot pretty much makes sense, it doesn't seem like they rewrote the entire story in the editing room.

There are a few little touches that might be notable to detail-conscious Seagalogists. One, this is the first time Seagal has had a character name that sounds like his real name. This is not Joe Halpin writing, this is a new guy, so he might have just written "Seagal" in the script and they had to change it to "Seeger." A more interesting touch is a reversal of a cliché seen in many action movies and Seagal pictures. When Chapel finally violates his own rule and pulls a gun on Seeger, a familiar conversation ensues – the old "you could never shoot me" routine. Seeger says, "Go ahead. Come on, shoot me down. I didn't think so. You know why? Yeah, because I'm the only son of a bitch who could do the things that you always want gettin' done."

This is weird because of course it's usually the hero who pulls a gun on the villain, and the villain who makes a speech about how the hero could never live with himself if he shot him, or it's against his code of ethics, or that type of shit. But then the hero shoots anyway and it's supposed to be ironic. (See *On Deadly Ground* for this type of scene as performed by Oscar winner Michael Caine.)

Instead of shooting Chapel as he walks away, Seeger actually allows him to drive away, but produces a detonator and blows up his car while it's still in sight. They make it a funny death for Chapel because he has a goofy smile and he's grooving in his car to a recording of the piano music we saw him play earlier in the movie. A good way for an egomaniac like that to kick it, I guess.

The supporting cast is pretty good. I like Luke Goss, who plays Dresham. In England apparently he's known for some pop group called Bros, but I have to respect him as an actor because he played Nomak in *Blade II*. Jacqueline Lord is also solid as Maxine. She's beautiful, she looks a lot like Catherine Zeta Jones, but without the cell phone commercial/Michael Douglas baggage. Somehow Lord pulls off being completely feminine but not laughable when firing a gun or slitting a guy's throat, yelling "This just ain't your motherfuckin day!" I also liked Adrian Galley, the big bald guy who played Bulldog, despite (or more likely because of) his dubbed voice that sounds like the bad guys in the English versions of Jackie Chan movies.

Ironically, the worst actor in the movie is also the best actor in the cast, Roger Guenveur Smith. I admire this guy going back all the way to playing Smiley in *Do the Right Thing*. He was great in *Get On the Bus* and *He Got Game*, and he's been in plenty of good non-Spike-Lee-directed roles like *King of New York*, *Deep Cover* and the TV series *K Street*. But man, he's terrible in this one. I think he's supposed to be British because he has some sort of aristocratic accent and he complains about "Yanks." He makes some amusing choices to show what a priss his character is (I think he might've improvised the part where he says "Excuse my language" immediately after using the fuck word) but it doesn't make up for the ridiculousness of his shifting accent. He somehow talks in a gentle voice and goes way over the top at the same time. I'm not complaining – he's actually kind of an enjoyably hammy villain like John Lithgow in *Cliffhanger*. But the guy is definitely capable of better.

Kind of funny that they got American Guenveur Smith to play British and British Luke Goss to play American. Goss pulls off the accent better, though.

At this point in his life and career, perhaps it's inevitable that Seagal does these murky spy capers full of double crosses, shifting allegiances and dirty tricks. He can't trust his "Black Opps Producer," he can't trust the CIA, it turns out he can trust a woman, but at first she was against him. Having been betrayed by his old friend and producer, extorted by the mafia, teased by the media, being reportedly somehow connected to the convoluted Hollywood private eye scandal, perhaps these movies are subconsciously reflecting Seagal's grey view of the world. But *Mercenary For Justice* shows that he wants to do the right thing, and that he's still capable of making a somewhat-sensible story out of all this intrigue.

Mercenary For Justice, 2006
Directed by Don E. FauntLeRoy (*Today You Die*, cinematographer for *Into the Sun*).
Written by Steve Collins (wrote some independent movie called *Gretchen* and a bunch of shorts you never heard of, because they are shorts).
Distinguished co-stars: Roger Guenveur Smith (Smiley from *Do the Right Thing*).
Seagal regulars: none.
Firsts: First Seagal picture since *Out For Justice* to have the words "For Justice" in the title, first one where Seagal plays a character whose name sounds like "Seagal".
Title refers to: Seagal is a soldier for hire, but he also tries to fight for justice here and there when possible.
Just how badass is this guy? "John Seeger. The most decorated soldier in the first Gulf War. He's a wild card, Chapel." "Yes. The best at what he does." "The man's a fucking ghost."
Adopted culture: n/a
Languages: English only.
Improvised weapons: Throws a guy against a faucet and urinals (unfortunately does not wield the urinals).
Old friends: Maxine is an old girlfriend.
Fight in bar: No. Bathroom.
Broken glass: Head into bathroom mirror, glass doors shot out in bank, car windows break when a guy falls onto the car, Dresham thrown into window.
Family shit: No mention of his own family, but he looks after the wife and daughter of his fallen comrade.
Political themes: More CIA corruption. This time the CIA is involved in conflicts over diamonds and oil, but telling the soldiers that it's about "liberating" Africans. There are direct references to the concept of "plausible deniability." The movie also deals heavily with the idea of private contractors fighting wars for the US, a trend that has caused some controversy during the second Iraq war. Although it is not a serious or in-depth treatment of the mercenary issue, it does reflect some of the concerns. At the beginning, Seagal's character discusses "the creed" which he says is "Care for no one, fight for everyone." Although he quickly abandons this amoral philosophy, his South African colleagues don't.
Cover accuracy: Fine. And looks a little different from other recent covers, since it has a giant Seagal body with no head.

interlude:
MOJO PRIEST

If *Mojo Priest* were a Seagal movie, I think it would be *Out For Justice*. While *Songs From the Crystal Cave* traveled all around the world sampling different cultures and styles, *Mojo Priest* is focused, setting its sights square on the American art form of the blues. You might say it's got that *Out For Justice* grittiness too, because while it starts off with a slightly overproduced "modern blues" style to lure in the squares, most of the album is straight ahead, stripped down, authentic old fashioned blues. And, again like *Out For Justice*, the only thing that gives Seagal away is that he has to fake an accent to play the character.

Then again, maybe it's *Above the Law*. Nico traveled to the Far East where he learned martial arts from the masters; Seagal claims to have grown up in an all-black neighborhood in Detroit where he learned blues from a different set of old masters. I don't know how he could have really known any blues legends when he was growing up, but he knows them now. You don't get Bo Diddley on your album by accident. And wherever he learned it from, he sure learned it. In his movies he shows off his martial arts skills, on this album he shows off his guitar. If you figure every Seagal guitar solo counts as an action scene, this album is more action-packed than a lot of his movies.

The parallel is undeniable. The guitar is the sword. Seagal is the proprietor of two world class collections: one of ancient Japanese swords (as seen on The History Channel), the other of rare guitars (as seen in *Vintage Guitar Magazine*). And he's highly skilled in both weapons. There are a few lyrical parallels to some of his movies. Like in *Ticker*, he explores the idea of facing mortality. On the song "Dark Angel" he sings, "Well there ain't no good in fearing death, we all got to die some day."

On "Gunfire In A Juke Joint" he has to clear his name for some crime he did not commit: "Somebody done me wrong / And it gonna have to be corrected." Which is not entirely unlike his situation in *Hard To Kill* or *The Glimmer Man*.

On "My Time Is Numbered," which Seagal has called his favorite song on the album, he faces his mortality again. Note that the title is basically a paraphrase of the classic movie title *Marked For Death*.

This is a blues album, though, so the kinds of things he talks about are mostly different from his movies. There's a lot of talk about women leaving him or disappearing (including the alcoholic girlfriend he can't find in "Dust My Broom"). There's quite a bit of admiration of women's beauty and/or booty. There's a little bit of working class woe, and a couple of songs about trying to find kindness in the world.

He's got some pretty good lines here and there. How he describes the end of a relationship in "Slow Boat to China" could be described as poetic: "Sometimes a tree gets struck by lightning / Sometimes it gets old and falls apart."

But of course the most memorable line is the one about the raw deal he gets in a restaurant at the end of "Alligator Ass": "I ordered me some chicken, they gave me alligator ass." I don't think I'd be going back to that restaurant, if I were Seagal.

Since the music is not quite as layered and heavily produced as *Songs From the Crystal Cave* it makes a better showcase for Seagal's guitar playing. Judging from the credits he never plays the slide guitar, but there are plenty of songs where he plays both lead and rhythm guitar, and there are lots of good solos for him, including but not limited to "My Time Is Numbered" and "BBQ." He even plays a little drums.

There are three different releases of *Mojo Priest*. It was first released in Europe. When it came out in the U.S. it had a new cover and song order. Now there is a second American release, which has the same song order but an improved cover. This version also credits the album to Steven Seagal rather than "Steven Seagal and Thunderbox" like on the earlier releases. Since the lineup varies from song to song it probably is more of a Seagal solo album than a group effort, but still it seems kind of wrong to retro-actively take away their credit for the album.

Of the two Seagal albums I know some people prefer *Songs From the Crystal Cave*. It's definitely weirder, more original. The lyrics may be more personal and heartfelt, sounding emotional at times, getting into the politics of war and his anger at the press. But remember, I'm an *Out For Justice* guy. I think *Mojo Priest* is a better listen. It's more pure and solid. And I suppose since I first heard the songs live, then bought the CD at the show, it has more sentimental value for me. I think this band sounds a lot better in person, but the album is good enough to show that Seagal isn't joking around with this blues thing.

Mojo Priest, *2006*
Produced by Steven Seagal
Written by ? (There are no writing credits.)
Distinguished co-stars: Bo Diddley, Koko Taylor, James Cotton, Willie "Pine Top" Perkins, Ruth Brown, Hubert Sumlin.
Seagal regulars: Hubert Sumlin, who is supposed to play Seagal's adoptive father in *Prince of Pistols*, plays rhythm guitar on "Hoochie Koochie Man."
Firsts: Seagal's first blues album.
Title refers to: ""In the end it had nothing to do with magic," says Seagal. "It actually signifies power and protection. People used to call me Mojo Priest because of my martial arts and my love of meditation[60]."
Just how badass is this guy? "And he gonna be a son of a gun / He gonna make pretty women jump and shout." (From "Hoochie Koochie Man.")
Adopted culture: The blues, maybe a little voodoo on "Hoochie Koochie Man."
Languages: English and the blues
Old friends: The gypsy woman who talked to his mom before he was born in "Hoochie Koochie Man."
Fight in bar: Actually, yes. There's a song called "Gunfire In a Juke Joint."
Broken glass: "Blues in this here juke joint / Gunfire blow out the lights." (From "Gunfire In a Juke Joint.")
Terms of endearment: Baby.
Words of wisdom: "Ain't no black and there ain't no white / Ain't no darkness and there

---

60 Hopkins, "The Seagal Has Landed" in *The Richmond News*, May 2006.

ain't no light." (From "Somewhere In Between.")

Funniest lyric: "When you see my new girlfriend / You gonna have to change your underwear." (From "BBQ.")

Family shit: He is in love but his women keep breaking his heart. He either can't find them or he decides to leave them or kick them out. Also his rooster leaves him.

Political themes: None on this one.

Cover accuracy: There are three different covers, each one better than the last. The original European cover is just a headshot. The first U.S. release is Seagal on the porch of a beat up old house playing a guitar. The second U.S. release is a better photo of the same sort of thing, this time in sepia tones. All three are accurate representations of the music, the only inaccuracy being on the first U.S. version where Seagal seems to be playing an electric guitar that is not plugged in.

CHAPTER 23:
SHADOW MAN

"It ain't over 'til the wolf howls."

Imelda Staunton is a respected English actress. She has won the British theater's highest honor, the Olivier Award, three times beginning in 1985. On film she was noted for her work with Kenneth Branagh in *Much Ado About Nothing*, but it was her title role as an abortionist in Mike Leigh's *Vera Drake* in 2004 that cemented her as a great talent internationally. In 2005 she was nominated for the best actress Oscar and Golden Globe for *Vera Drake*. She won the BAFTA Award, the British Independent Film Award and prizes from critics groups all around the world. The next year, she was in *Shadow Man* with Steven Seagal.

Seagal plays Jack Foster (referred to just as "Jack," even by authority figures who don't know him), an ex-CIA aikido teacher and owner of a Fortune 500 company (not explained) out to save his kidnapped daughter and stop a deadly virus from falling into the wrong hands. But he doesn't really do much to save his daughter and I'm not entirely clear how he stops the deadly virus (toward the end he explains that he "passed it around a little bit, disseminated it, it's no good anymore.").

The movie opens, like many from the DTV Era, on some dude who is not Steven Seagal, nor as cool as Steven Seagal. In this case it's an old guy in a suit and tie sneaking away from the "MK Ultra Project[61]" laboratory where CIA scientists are doing nefarious experiments on innocent lab mice. He is being followed by a strangely familiar guy in a car. But he gets away and sticks something in his sock.

Seagal's Jack Foster is introduced promisingly with a nod to *Above the Law* (and education in general) as he teaches an aikido class. He demonstrates both the internal and external forms of a dim mak (death touch) fighting technique – the internal version causes a watermelon to explode, the external shoots a student through a wall. I like both ways. He mentions that this sort of chi should be used to heal people, not to kill them. In the movie though, he doesn't use it for healing.

Jack is about to leave on a trip to Bucharest with his daughter Amanda (Skye Bennett) on the occasion of the fifth anniversary of his wife's death. Like his daughter in *The Patriot*, this daughter likes horses, and he promises she can see one. He also meets with Grandpa George (Michael Elwyn), his father-in-law, who will be taking Amanda to Bucharest a day ahead of him and meeting up later. But, wait a minute – are you fucking kidding me? Grandpa is that same dude from the opening scene who stole secrets from the CIA. He takes the secrets out of his sock and switches them with the stylus of Jack's Palm Pilot.

Endangering Jack by planting national secrets on him is not very grandfatherly, but it's hard for us to feel too sorry for Jack because he's not being the best father himself. He disappoints his daughter by not traveling with her – he says he needs to finish a business deal. But instead he uses the extra day to hug a young naked woman with a round ass. There's no explanation of who she is and we never see or hear of her (or her ass) again.

After the hugging Jack meets Amanda and Grandpa in Bucharest. Something is not right, because an old CIA asshole named Harry just happens to be there at the airport. Jack clearly doesn't trust Harry, perhaps because of something in their agency past, or perhaps because he recognizes him as the actor Vincent Riotta, who played an old CIA

---

61 In real life MKULTRA was (is?) a notorious CIA program that started in the 1950s, exploring mind control and brainwashing through the administration of drugs such as LSD and possibly other techniques. In this movie, for some reason, it is a deadly virus that gives people cancer or influenza and kills them in 6-12 months.

friend who betrayed him in *Belly of the Beast*. While he perhaps reminisces about the awesome train yard shootout in that movie, Grandpa George gets blown up in his car and a female cabbie (Eva Pope) snatches Amanda.

So despite all this complication with MK-Ultra and car bombings and what not we have a nice simple goal for the movie: save Amanda. In his quest to retrieve his daughter Jack first forms an uneasy team with Harry and later with Anya, the very cabbie that kidnapped Amanda in the first place. He can relate to Anya because she's an ex-British secret agent turned Romanian cabbie. It turns out everybody knows that Grandpa had the formula for the deadly cancer exposing virus from the MK-Ultra program and was planning on selling it to the highest bidder, a new branch of the KGB called the FSB (Fearsome Super Badasses, maybe). It would be funny if they were always saying things like "Tell me who has the formula for the deadly cancer exposing virus from the MK-Ultra program!," but they figured out that would be cumbersome so they slangily call it "the item." Everybody wants the item so Anya kidnapped the daughter so that, I don't know, the FSB wouldn't kidnap her because then Jack might give them the item? I'm not sure.

Anyway she has his daughter, now staying with a disabled friend of hers, and Jack is willing to work with her on figuring out where the item is. This really troubled me while watching the movie for the first time because I couldn't figure out why he would be friendly to this woman who took his daughter, who still has his daughter, who doesn't even have the common kidnapper courtesy to offer "proof of life" by allowing him to speak to his daughter on the phone so he knows she's safe and then snatch the phone away suddenly and threaten him or whatever. But later we find out why that wasn't necessary. Jack explains: "You know, it seems to me you'd like everybody to think that you piss ice. Cold, hard, tough woman. But I know you. I see your heart. You're soft, you're sensitive, you're loving, you're caring, and I thank you. Come here, babe," and he hugs her.

You see? He knew he could trust her abducting his daughter because he could see her heart. He only hugs people with soft hearts. That's probably why he hugged that naked girl earlier. I thought at the time it was because she looked good naked but here he is hugging Anya, and she's not naked. She has a bra on. But even with her shirt on – I'd be willing to bet even with a coat or sweater over the shirt – he could see through to her soft heart. It should maybe be called *The Heart See-er*, because that's what he is more than a shadow man.

But Jack is not the only Heart See-er in the movie. Imelda Staunton, that one actress I mentioned in the first paragraph, has a small part as Ambassador Cochran, one of the authority figures who stand around in a room talking about Jack by his first name and getting troubling briefs about this whole "the item" fiasco as it goes down. (Think of Admiral Bates and those guys in *Under Siege*, but without giant computer screens.) In my opinion Ambassador Cochran is a Heart See-er. She doesn't ever hug Jack, but she believes in him before she's even met him. She stands up for him, supports him. She gets it. (At first, since most of Staunton's scenes have her standing around with other minor characters discussing what's going on, I wondered if they even told her this was a Steven Seagal movie she was in. But sure enough she has two scenes with Seagal. One is a conversation that could have been shot separately, but the other scene has them in the same shot. This is Seagal's most distinguished co-star since Michael Caine ten years ago.)

Eventually Jack figures out where the item is and discovers that Grandpa actually isn't dead, he faked his death in order to – I don't know – not have to ride horses with his granddaughter or something, and he really did plant the formula on Jack in order to safely and over-complicatedly transport it to Bucharest where he was going to sell it to the FSB guys. If that's not enough to prove this guy is World's Worst Grandpa, please note how as soon as he reveals himself as a bad guy he stops calling Amanda "my granddaughter" and starts calling her "the girl."

Then Jack fights some guys. In one part everybody points guns at each other and an item-wanting bad guy says, "I believe in your country they call this... a Mexican standoff? No matter how good you are with the pistol you can't get us both." And I really wanted Jack to say, "In my country we also have something called *Reservoir Dogs*." But he finds another way out, then he gets his daughter back so he gives her a horse.

When I reviewed *Shadow Man* online I said that it was Seagal's most boring movie to date and complained that the overly complicated plot distracts from the things we need to see in a great Seagal picture. I stand by that criticism, but luckily on further viewing the movie is a little more compelling and offers some interesting touches worthy of Seagalogical analysis.

Of course the movie elaborates on many Seagalogy themes and motifs. You have aikido, you have CIA corruption, you have the dangers of biochemical warfare, you have MKULTRA (also mentioned in *Submerged*). There is a family theme similar to *Out of Reach* – Anya lost her husband and daughter, Amanda lost her mother, Jack lost his wife, and they all sort of bond with each other as if forming a new family. (The only guy who doesn't get any bonding is Grandpa George, but fuck that guy.)

As usual the bad guys destroy symbols of knowledge and culture during gunfights. There's a library shootout where various books get capped and a bust of George Dinca (a professor at the University of Bucharest, according to my research) takes a JFK-style headshot.

Seagal meanwhile continues to escalate his war on testicles. He kicks a guy in the crotch two times in a row. Another guy he kicks in the nuts just before shooting him five times. The only thing that could've been better would be if he kicked the guy in the nuts after shooting him five times. Maybe next time. He also snaps a couple wrists like in the old days, and escapes from a foreign police station like in *Belly of the Beast*. Like in *Exit Wounds* he takes down a helicopter using only a handgun (he actually makes it explode). Like in *The Foreigner*, the bad guys see a big dude with a ponytail from behind and think it's him for a second. You have to figure it would be a pain in the ass to be a big dude with a ponytail, you'd have to deal with this all the time. If I had a ponytail like that I would never wear a leather jacket. It just wouldn't be worth the hassle.

There are a couple little tweaks on old Seagalogy favorites. For example, Jack is aided by an Old Agency Friend named Rogers (Vincent Leigh) who knows how to hack into government databases. This is a Seagal motif from day one – remember Watanabe in *Above the Law*? – but in this one they actually establish his existence before Jack needs him for something. He just calls up out of the blue and offers to erase Jack's tax debt from the IRS computers. If that's not a good old agency friend I don't know what is.

More significantly, there's a new wrinkle in the exploration of CIA dirty deeds. Discussing the MKULTRA problem with Jack, the Ambassador says, "You're talking about black ops. I've never liked em. It makes me sick to think our government still operates this way." And Jack says reassuringly, "Once in a while. Only once in a while." I guess he could be joking, but I don't think he is. While Seagal movies obviously leave room for the possibility of heroic CIA agents (after all, most of his characters used to be in the CIA) this is the first time he's gone out of his way to emphasize that the black ops assholes he's always trying to stop only cause trouble on occasion. (So why did the occasion have to be the fifth anniversary of his wife's death? That sucks.)

To me, one thing that makes some of Seagal's DTV pictures less enjoyable is that the plots are overly convoluted. *Shadow Man* is a good example of this type of story where there are too many factions of villains, none of them very interesting, their motives and plans overly complicated and vaguely explained. It becomes hard to follow exactly what's going on and not in a way where you're on the edge of your seat trying to figure it out. You just give up after a while, unless you are writing a book called *Seagalogy* and need to write up a plot summary.

There are too many iffy elements of the plot to just go along with it. You can't help but find yourself wondering *is it really easier for George to plant the formula on Jack than to bring it himself?* and *how exactly does Anya kidnapping Amanda help things?* and *why did George fake his death again?* and *what is this Fortune 500 company he runs?* and things like that. In my review I compared Seagal's movies to playing the blues. It doesn't have to be complicated, it doesn't have to be new, you just have to play the hell out of it and put your own flavor on it. Maybe this type of murky cloak and dagger shit is the flavor Seagal wants these days, I'm not sure. And like I said in regards to *Mercenary For Justice*, those stories do sort of reflect his experiences in Hollywood. But it seems to me that a lot of the murkiness comes from the way they make the movies, rewriting them as they go along and deciding what they're about in editing.

Co-writer Joe Halpin was kind enough to contact me after my review, and he confirmed that it is a complicated process that leads to the complicated plots (which he agreed could use streamlining). He is given a "game plan" from Seagal and the studio and incorporates it into what he described as an "ever growing script." It sounds like different elements get added in at the request of various parties, and he has to please all of them. In the end the movies get chopped until Seagal and the studio can agree on a version, and during that process a lot of the explanation (like Jack's background with the Fortune 500 company) gets cut out.

So the writing and rewriting is a complicated process that inevitably leads to a complicated storyline. Halpin humbly described himself as "as guilty as everyone" for all this, but I don't blame him, and I'm not sure I should even be passing judgment on this process of moviemaking. I'm sure the on-the-fly nature of making these later Seagal pictures is part of what makes them so weird and enjoyable. A lot of the mistakes and strange decisions are what I love about *Belly of the Beast*, *Out For a Kill* and *Out of Reach*, so I shouldn't complain if they don't hit a home run every time they come up to bat. Even in the blues your guitar isn't necessarily going to smoke every single time. Seagal says in the movie that "It ain't over 'til the wolf howls," and I don't know what that means exactly but I'm sure, even if *Shadow Man* was a little disappointing to me, that the wolf hasn't howled yet on Seagalogy.

And like *The Foreigner, Shadow Man* improves a little bit when you watch it again. In many ways it's generic enough to blend in with other Seagal pictures of its time and be quickly forgotten. The bad guys, for example, are more interchangeable euro-trash with guns, instantly forgettable. But on further study you can see that they're at least making an effort to have some memorable villains in here. Having a grandpa as the main villain is, obviously, a nice touch. There is also a henchman character whose face was badly burned in a freebase accident, and he wears a plastic mask so as not to scare the prostitutes who party at his boss's mansion. This has great potential, I love this type of shit. Unfortunately the guy takes no pride in his mask. It's a generic transparent male face, probably cost him $3.99 at the party store, and then he drew peace signs and hearts on it in Sharpie. He's no Phantom of the Opera. And he's only in one scene, introduced and then dispatched before he can either do something or create suspense in the audience wondering if he's going to do something.

Another nice try but wasted opportunity is the prick in the suit and tie who shit talks Jack to Harry. "I hear he's some kind of expert fighter. Grand Master or something? I went through some of that stuff when I was in the military. Yeah, martial arts stuff looks pretty. Looks great in the movies. But real life? I don't know."

Of course, any audience is going to enjoy seeing this dipshit face off with the "grand master" and find out just how pretty the martial arts are. Seagal's onscreen fighting style has always been quick and efficient, not as showy as a lot of martial arts cinema. So the fact that you don't even really see what Jack does to this guy gives it an extra layer of irony – these martial arts aren't that pretty, and in this scene they don't look that great in movies. A nice touch if you think about it, but it doesn't change the fact that the comeuppance happens too suddenly and confusingly to fully enjoy. Jack flips him over a ledge and then he has blood on his chest, like a bullet wound. Maybe he got shot, maybe he got Jack's trademark Exploding Watermelon Fist. I'm not really sure.

Speaking of the Exploding Watermelon Fist, that is one thing that stands out. Not just because any move that either a) explodes the insides or b) propels somebody through a wall is by definition worth including in any movie, but because it's reoccurring. Demonstrating a move early in a movie and bringing it back for the climax is a cliché in martial arts films, but it's not one that Seagal generally uses. So it's fun to see it here.

And on further analysis, there are other goofy little touches that give the movie its own feel. I like how Jack pretends to be some kind of decadent cokehead to infiltrate a mansion, asking "Do you know where I can get some of that? 'Cause I wanna party." When his cabdriver asks him if those were gunshots he heard inside he says, "No no no, that was just loud music."

Jack is also a man unafraid to face the secrets contained within the women's bathroom. Anya tries ducking inside one, in case his honor and civility will keep him off her tail. But he walks inside. I was surprised to find out that there are women making out with each other in there, I didn't know that's what went on in there, I thought it was mostly for peeing.

Women peeing actually becomes important to the plot later, believe it or not, when a female cop staking out Anya's apartment decides she has to go in and use the bathroom. Of course Jack and Anya show up while she's still there, she comes out and gets shot, just like Vincent Vega in *Pulp Fiction*.

Later on her apartment gets ransacked by bad guys looking for the item, and that is not unique to this movie. I've seen scenes like that in a lot of movies, personally, and this one doesn't have much of a spin on it as far as I noticed. I only bring it up to mention one thing that occurred to me about these commanding officer types who use hyperbole in their commands. This guy yells, "I want to know everything about her. Names, numbers... what kind of tampons she uses!"

You hear this kind of thing all the time in movies, most famously Tommy Lee Jones's Oscar-winning "every outhouse, henhouse, crackhouse, houseboat or International House of Pancakes" speech in Andrew Davis's *The Fugitive*. My question is, how confident are these henchmen about their understanding of their boss's dry sense of humor? This guy is obviously a huge asshole. He is dangerous. We know, not from this movie but from other Seagal pictures, that a guy like this might suddenly beat or kill one of his own men to make a point. So you don't want to do the wrong thing.

What I'm asking is, do you find out what kind of tampons she uses, just in case? I'm sure it would be pretty easy to find that information. Do they check the drawers and closets just to be safe? Find out the brand name, don't bring it up but just know it in case it turns out he meant that literally? Then you say "Oh yeah, Tampax, she uses Tampax" or whatever? Or maybe they got a grip on this guy, they understand that he does not literally want to know what brand or style of tampons she uses. But what if there's a new guy who's kind of slow, or even just really thorough, this guy does tell him what kind of tampons. Does this guy get beaten, fired, killed? Does the boss appreciate his attention to detail, or does he humiliate him? This should probably be explored at some point.

The final scene is a little reminiscent of *Out of Reach* because it's a happy ending involving kids, animals and a freeze frame closeup of Seagal's character smiling. But if you think about it it's totally different. In *Out of Reach* Seagal's character was a loner, so while the kids enjoyed the company of a hawk, he was off stalking the woods by himself, united with the children only through the magic of montage. In *Shadow Man*,

Jack surprises Amanda with a horse. Amanda says that the horse is beautiful, Jack smiles, and it freezes and zooms in on him, the end. So in this story Seagal's character is not alone. He is with his daughter and his daughter's horse, smiling at the joy that a horse's beauty brings to an 8-year-old girl.

The quality of the production is similar to others of the era. There is some obvious dubbing while the opening credits are still rolling. There is also some of the most obvious use of doubles of any Seagal movie, not in action scenes but just in regular every day shots. The worst one is at 1:15:21 as "Jack" and "Anya" exit a building. Freeze and zoom on that guy, it's hilarious. Come on man, that's not Steven Seagal, it's one of those guys with the ponytails that gets turned around by bad guys and is the wrong guy. What's Anya doing walking around with that guy? (Or is that even Anya?)

And the first big action sequence is a car chase that you never believe Seagal is really involved in because the backgrounds of the driving shots are so obviously green screened. But to be fair, there is more martial arts action in this than in many of the DTV pictures, and there are some good moments. For example, he pokes a guy in both eyes, leaving him yelling "My eyes!" and feeling around on the floor. (At first I thought he had his eyes plucked out and he was feeling around for them on the floor, but he probably just got poked and he's trying to find his gun.)

On first viewing, *Shadow Man* was one of the least impressive Seagal movies for me. But like all of them, it seems to grow on me. And I have heard from quite a few Seagalogists who appreciated it more than I did. For the Exploding Watermelon Fist alone it must be respected.

Shadow Man, 2006
Directed by Michael Keusch (*Samurai Cowboy*, various German and American TV shows, *Attack Force*, *Flight of Fury*).
Written by Steven Collins (*Mercenary For Justice*), Joe Halpin (*Into the Sun*) and Steven Seagal (director of *On Deadly Ground*).
Distinguished co-stars: Academy Award nominee Imelda Staunton.
Seagal regulars: Vincent Riotta (Fitch McQuoid from *Belly of the Beast*).
Firsts: First duel between Seagal and a melon.

Title refers to: Seagal? Nobody really knows.

Just how badass is this guy? "He did shit that's still classified." "He's not someone to fuck with, ma'am." "I hear he's some kind of expert fighter. Grand Master or something?"

Adopted culture: He's teaching aikido again, being called "Sifu," and when he does his trademark move there's a stereotypical Asian flute sound that appears on the soundtrack.

Languages: English.

Improvised weapons: He builds a *McGyver* style bomb connected to a phonograph

Old friends: Rogers, CIA hacker who offers to erase his tax debt and later shuts down the MK-Ultra project via computer.

Fight in bar: No, just discussions in a strip club.

Broken glass: Car window shot out, glass tables, glass blocks in the walls, cabinets

Family shit: He's taking his daughter on a trip on the fifth anniversary of her mother's death. He talks to her sweetly about being "good" and "brave" and gets her a horse at the end.

Political themes: Once again CIA corruption and the dangers of biochemical warfare, using the historic name MK-Ultra to refer to a completely different dangerous CIA scheme. This time though he says that our government only does this sort of thing "once in a while."

Cover accuracy: Well, I don't think that head belongs to that body, but otherwise it's not that bad.

CHAPTER 24:
ATTACK FORCE

"Those fucking guys have no idea what we're up against."

Attack *Force* is the second Seagal-Halpin-Keusch collaboration of 2006. Because why stop at *Shadow Man*? Seagal plays Commander Marshall Lawson, head of some kind of elite military unit. He and his partner Chief Dwayne Dixon (David Kennedy) are deployed in Paris when three of their trainees get murdered by an evil super-powered hooker (Evelyne Armela O'Bami). Dwayne (he just goes by Dwayne, it's a pretty laid back elite military unit) connects the murders to Aroon (Adam Croasdell), the pimp and club owner who it turns out is also the military's "head of the biochemical research program in Western Europe" who has gone rogue and introduced an experimental super-soldier drug to his club patrons. The stuff is called CTX, it gets you real high but it's "instantly addictive." It also alters your DNA to give you "almost super-human strength and reflexes" and can make you into a "killing machine" and a "mindless killer" with no morals or humanity.

That's all fine and good if club kids want to do that to themselves, but Aroon also plans to dump CTX into the water supply, which would apparently turn 15,000 unsuspecting non-clubgoers into CTX-heads within 12 hours. Which would suck.

Lawson trains his team to recognize CTX addicts, but it's not that hard. The main thing is they get evil looking flashes of CGI eye-enhancement. They also act a lot like vampires. They're all very attractive (mostly hot women) and wear fashionable clothes with fur collars or exposed shoulders. They also like to sit perched on high places and drop down dramatically. They are very good at throwing people through walls, and there are white flashes whenever they fight. I don't want to be a dick about it, but I really think if somebody has a problem spotting these CTX heads then that person really doesn't belong in an elite military unit.

There's a little bit of intrigue going on within the team. First of all, Lawson's old trainee and love interest Tia (Lisa Lovbrand) shows up and starts helping. Lawson says "She has a lot of special abilities. She has a lot of special techniques." This asshole named Werner (Danny Webb) who's higher up in the agency describes her as "a young, vibrant biochemist." That's not a coincidence – it turns out she helped Aroon to develop CTX in the first place. The other thing is that Werner, who by the way says he taught Lawson everything he knows, keeps interfering with their efforts to go after Aroon because he doesn't want to bring public attention to the CTX program. A couple times they also have to contend with a French cop who's been bribed by Aroon.

Aside from that traditional DTV era convolution though this is a relatively straightforward, even minimalistic story. Once Lawson tracks the CTX people to an old cathedral he puts together an "Attack Force" or "A-Team," invades, there are lots of fights with little dialogue, and then the movie ends.

Obviously many of the Seagalogy trademarks are here, but there are some new touches. Seagal has never fought opponents like these guys. Because the CTX has altered their DNA they are able to throw their foes through the air (similar to the external Exploding Watermelon Fist from *Shadow Man*), and their favorite moves involve breaking walls. They do it so much that I suspect it's important to their culture. *Attack Force* is a pretty good generic title, but I would've called this one *Wallbreakers*, because people are constantly getting thrown through walls, even brick walls. Reina, the killer hooker who kicks off this whole mess, does the trademark Jason Voorhees move of reaching both hands through a wall to grab her victim. Later she throws Tia through two walls in one toss. It's not a good idea to do a move like that in front of Lawson, though, because you only give him ideas. He throws Reina against a column. Her head dents the column, then the column falls over, causing a staircase to come down on top of her. Lawson finally masters wallbreaking in his climactic fight against the alien queen, er, Russian financer or whatever, when he pushes her through a brick wall, which is impressive for a guy who has never used CTX. Especially since he does it with one hand. And it's his left hand. Hopefully once he's done that he's gained their respect.

Lawson also gets some weaponry that's unusual for Seagal. He tells Tia at one point "I need access to an armory. You know what weapons I like." The weapons she chooses for him are called "Nanographite blades" – a couple of scythes that attach to his wrists. They're "made of the strongest substance known" and are "assimilated to his body" to even the score against the super junkies. But of course Aroon doesn't want a level playing field so he uses some kind of CD-like disc with fingerholes in it. Not sure what it does but it is probably powerful and illegal.

During the siege on the cathedral, when Aroon drops down from a column to fight Lawson, there is some kind of unspoken honor deal that happens. So instead of blowing the fucker's hopped-up head off, Lawson hands his shotgun to Dwayne and gets out the nanographite blades. Their fight is surprisingly short. Lawson stabs Aroon twice in the top of the skull with the nanographite, but offscreen. That doesn't kill him so he throws him down about three or four stairs and I guess that's all the extra nudging he needed.

The best thing about the movie is the subtle fuck-you ending. All of the CTX guys have been killed. All but one of Lawson's guys (including Tia and Dwayne) have been killed. He helps his last soldier up and they walk out of the cathedral as some ominous music plays. Then there is a shot of a car driving away. Then the credits come up.

That's it – no dialogue, no epilogue, nothing. Earlier we were told that the CTX had been released into the water. Lawson never did anything about it. Are we supposed to forget that happened? Or is this meant as a pessimistic, George A. Romero-type the-status-quo-has-not-been-restored ending? Are we supposed to think there are 15,000 of these funny-eyed CTX heads out there now?

I'm sure most people hate the resolution-less ending, and to add insult to their injury that last shot of the car driving off was already used earlier in the movie. It's funny because the first time I saw it I thought huh, that seems like what would be the last shot of the movie, the sort of driving into the sunset shot. It didn't occur to me that it actually would end up being the last shot.

But by this point you're already used to some shortcuts and cheats. In fact, this one may have even more obviously dubbed lines than *Submerged*. The first couple scenes are done entirely with somebody else's voice, except for one part where he sighs. Here and in the buildup to the cathedral attack there are long sequences that just show exteriors of cars with the-voice-who-is-clearly-not-Seagal delivering Lawson's dialogue supposedly from inside. There's also a scene where Lawson talks to the Admiral over the phone and says that he's flattered the Admiral recognizes his voice. And then he proceeds to switch back and forth between two voices throughout the conversation.

Probably the biggest laugh in the movie is not a shortcut but a good old-fashioned insult to the audience's intelligence. Now, it's not uncommon for a movie to show an establishing shot of the Eiffel Tower and still feel that it's necessary to put a title on the screen to tell you this is Paris. That's dumb, but I'm used to that. *Attack Force* takes it to the next level, using a title that says, "FRANCE, EUROPE." So this is a movie that not only assumes we can't recognize the Eiffel Tower, it assumes we don't know what continent France is in. I don't know, I guess there is more than one city called Paris. So maybe there is another France somewhere too, and it has a similar landmark. They just wanted to make sure we knew this was the Europe one.

I can't lie. This is in the lower rung of Seagalogical works. In fact, before I even saw it I was deluged with emails telling me it was Seagal's very worst to date. But I believe to the astute Seagalogist there are a number of promising developments. For one thing, Seagal is in the heat of the opening battle (well, his voice double at least) rather than one of these dull as hell TV-style some-dudes-running-around-or-getting-assassinated-in-Europe-somewhere openings. And while there's not enough action and most of it's not very good, I do appreciate the use of wallbreaking and nanographite blades to mix things up. There is also an old school knife-to-the-head and some unusually bloody squib hits (which, upon further analysis, turn out to be digital).

Stylistically the movie is also an improvement. The editing is restrained, at times deliberately paced, and there are no avid farts whatsoever. I am not a fan of white flashes, which are used quite liberally, but at least there is a logic to them (they represent the "almost super human strength and reflexes" of CTX users). The cinematography is pretty good, lots of dark shadows and night scenes, nicely composed. There's a very consistent look, with most of the characters wearing black. The music is also less hyper-active then usual, allowing itself to be ominous and orchestral at times.

There are some funny moments here and there. I'm not sure what to make of the scene where Tia explains the nanographite blades to Lawson. He says, "They'll come in handy," with no trace of pun-intended in his voice. And then shortly after he also says "I still got a few tricks up my sleeve," again not appearing to realize that he has some high tech weapons literally up his sleeve and therefore this might be construed as a joke.

Another good line is when one of the trainees says that Lawson "walks with an air of confidence rarely seen in this day and age." His buddies immediately make fun of him for saying it, but it is an unusually straightforward way of answering that age old question *Just How Badass Is This Guy?*

But what's missing is Seagal himself. I like the minimalism, but it leaves you without much Seagal. He's got to get his personality (and his air of confidence) into the movie more. Here he doesn't make any big speeches, he doesn't have many relationship moments with the other characters, he doesn't fight enough. And then he doesn't even use his own voice half the time.

Like *Submerged*, *Attack Force* began life as an entirely different genre of movie, but was changed in post-production. Even upon its release, the Internet Movie Database still listed actress Ileana Lazariuc as "Alien Queen." Contacted by co-screenwriter Joe Halpin regarding my *Shadow Man* review I didn't want to bury the poor guy in questions, but I couldn't resist asking if *Harvester* (as it was then titled) would really end up having aliens in it, or if they would disappear like the "biological mutants" of *Submerged*. He wasn't sure.

"Who knows," he wrote. "We shot it a couple ways – and now it's up to the studio and Seagal to agree on a version. Aliens are in one and

European mobsters are in another. Maybe it could be European Aliens."
To nobody's surprise they went with the European mobsters. But the result is less of a disaster than I expected, since they seem to have left all the alien abilities in the movie, just offering a different explanation for them.

Still, Halpin's answer goes a long way toward explaining the state of Seagalogy at this point in the DTV Era. Who shoots a movie first, then decides what the premise is? It's almost experimental. This sort of seat-of-the-pants movie-making, combined with whatever disagreements and compromises Seagal may have with the studio in post-production, explain the heavy use of the voice double. I had originally figured that Seagal was the one who didn't want to stretch out and fight aliens, that he was resisting taking those sorts of risks. But the fact that someone else's voice bridges what's left of the narrative together now that the movies are not about mutants or aliens might indicate that he wanted no part in it. So I asked Halpin.

"*Attack Force* was written with a sci-fi element," Halpin said, "and then the studio changed it in post by sending a second unit director to do re-shoots." That would seem to explain all those shots of cars driving around where you can't see who's driving and the voice inside doesn't belong to Seagal.

"Steven and I were unaware of this until it was about to be released. Both of us are very disappointed with how it turned out. Judging by the reviews we aren't the only ones."

Attack Force, 2006
Directed by Michael Keusch (*Shadow Man*).
Written by Steven Seagal & Joe Halpin (*Into the Sun, Shadow Man*), story by Halpin.
Distinguished co-stars: Nobody you ever heard of, unless you've heard of Danny Webb. (Turns out he was the lone survivor of *Alien 3*.)
Seagal regulars: Gabi Burlacu, who plays "Tia's agent," will return in *Flight of Fury*. Vlad Coada, another one of Tia's agents, went uncredited as "Hero Lab Worker" in *Shadow Man*.
Firsts: First time Seagal has used super hero type weapons (specially designed wrist blades).
Title refers to: The A-Team that Seagal's character brings to attack the drug addicts at the cathedral. He even says the title out loud ("I will lead the attack force") which is a rarity.
Just how badass is this guy? "The man walks with an air of confidence that's rarely seen in this day and age." "There's just two things you need to know about Lawson. One is, he's

a bad motherfucker. And two, he's a bad motherfucker." "He's a headcase. Does what he wants. We had to transfer him out."

Adopted culture: None, unless you count the CTX addicts adopting the culture of the aliens that the movie was originally going to be about.

Languages: Just English.

Improvised weapons: None.

Old friends: Tia, old trainee/girlfriend.

Fight in bar: No, just discussions in a "titty bar."

Broken glass: Seagal is pushed through a window, a soldier purposely jumps through a window, and a smoke bomb is thrown through a window.

Words of wisdom: "I ain't got no love and I'm too old for love."

Family shit: None.

Political themes: The military was using soldiers as guinea pigs for drug testing, a timely theme. The government is trying to turn soldiers into "mindless killers" with no morals or humanity.

Cover accuracy: That's not his body, and he doesn't use many guns in this movie (let alone two at a time), and he would never wear those pants, and the cover should have a dark background since the movie takes place almost entirely at night.

CHAPTER 25:
FLIGHT OF FURY

**"I wish I had the time to whoop your ass and then shoot you,
but I got to go."**

The 25th Seagal picture is actually a remake of a 1998 Michael Dudikoff movie called *Black Thunder*. Seagal plays John[62], a rogue government agent and the world's best Stealth pilot who is given a *Dirty Dozen* or *Submerged* style get-out-of-jail-free-card in exchange for flying into Afghanistan and retrieving an experimental invisible jet that has been stolen by a traitor and given to terrorists.

When we first meet John he's in the custody of government scientists who are about to give him a "mind wipe" because he knows too much after the last mission they sent him on. With the help of sympathetic operatives disguised as a nurse and a janitor, he mounts a daring escape and steals a car. After a long night behind the wheel he stops at a gas station mini-mart where he foils a robbery but violently murders everyone involved.

It's a minor scene, but one of the most interesting for Seagalogists because of its obvious parallels to *Hard to Kill*. Early in both films, Seagal's character and the plot take a detour to pick something up at a mini-

---

62 Yeah, his name really is just John. One name, like Prince, Vern or mink. Even on the end credits he's just listed as John. I would think it would be hard to get guys in the military to just call you by your first name, but we've seen it in other Seagal movies, so it must be something they allow for. Unless John is his last name, in which case it isn't even an issue, that's what they would normally call him anyway.

mart/liquor store just as it's about to be robbed. In both, the clerk is shot and Seagal brutalizes (in this case kills) all of the robbers. So we are able to compare how the older Seagal differs from the younger Seagal. Older Seagal is much more interested in getting the job done quickly, less in showing off. Instead of conversing with the thieves to psyche them out he intervenes immediately, punching through a window to grab a guy's gun. Instead of dominating them, breaking their bones and leaving them alive to think about what they've done he decides on some quickie executions. He shoots before they do and performs a Woo-style floor-slide-while-shooting. When the last guy pulls out a large hunting knife John drops his gun. That probably means he's out of bullets, but for the sake of awesomeness I'm going to stick with my better interpretation that he is *not* out of bullets, but is interested in the challenge of a knife fight.

This is probably the funniest and coolest moment in the movie. John waves his hand theatrically. At first you're not sure what the fuck he's doing, but then from his sleeve he reveals a knife of his own. As he waves it around at first it looks like he wants to fence with the guy, then you realize that in fact it is simply acknowledging that he is not just a dude with a knife, he is a highly trained and dangerously skilled knife fighter. But before the chump has time to piss his pants in fear, John tosses the knife into his neck.

At this time I think it is important to point out that these criminals were fucking terrible at their job. Not because they were killed by John – anybody would've made that mistake. But their crime was stupid from conception. First of all, a gang that large robbing a mini-mart is ridiculous. Don't they teach math anymore? This is clearly not a place that gets a lot of business, at least not on this particular day. There's only one register. Whatever business this place has done in a day, they're not even gonna be getting all of it since it's not all gonna be cash, a lot of it was probably done on debit cards. By the time these guys split up the loot they'd be real lucky to get $300 a piece. And that's if they can get into the safe.

That they would mount this robbery in the first place is bad enough, but then consider that these morons end up in a big shootout trying to get this small amount of money. Plenty of people have robbed hundreds of thousands of dollars from banks without ever firing guns. It's only common sense that it's better for everybody if no shots are fired. As soon as they start firing they have to realize they are headed toward a murder rap instead of just armed robbery. Even if they didn't all get killed they'd still be fuckin up because they probably had to pay for those bullets, and they'll have to ditch the guns. That's just a stupid waste of money, money that is coming out of a pathetic score. And since they killed the guy running the shop, they're definitely not getting into the safe.

I hate to do this guys, but you get an F. In your next life, remember that mini-mart stickups should be strictly a one or two-man crackhead or meth addict deal.

Anyway despite the great attentiveness of these brilliant master criminals a silent alarm was triggered, so the cops show up and find only John alive. Rather than hanging out with them laughing in the parking lot like in *Hard to Kill* he has to give himself up, knowing that the surveillance tape will show that it was self defense. (Well, sort of.) So the cops take him in and can't get him to talk or find his fingerprints in any database.

By this point, the $75 million experimental X-77 jet has been stolen by a test pilot named Ratcher (Steve Toussaint) during an off-the-books flight. Because the jet has "active stealth mode" (it can turn *Predator*-style invisible for short periods – *The Glimmer Plane*, if you will), he doesn't have much trouble going AWOL. Whoops. Probably should've done a better background check on that guy. Geez, who do they have training these assholes anyway, they're doing a shitty job of instilling the sort of integrity and moral fiber we need in—oh wait, actually, it turns out that Ratcher was trained by John. So this is kind of like a Darth Vader betraying Ben Kenobi type deal.

Ratcher flies the X-77 into a terrorist camp in Afghanistan, where he meets up with Stone (Vincenzo Nicoli), the terrorist who hired him, and his second in command Eliana (Katie Jones). It turns out they also have some biological weapons, so they pay Ratcher to fly up and drop two bombs that will infect the entire world within a couple days. This, in my opinion, is not only unethical, but short-sighted. If the virus spreads as planned, the entire world will go to shit in less than a week. What good is this money going to be to him in the world of tomorrow? Even if people are still using that currency by the end of the month it'll be easy to come by for people looting abandoned banks and safes. So he won't even be that rich. And eventually his beloved jets will need maintenance or repairs that he won't be trained to provide, and he'll have to give up his number one passion. I take it back, the mini-mart robbers weren't that bad, this guy is worse. Come on Ratcher, you need to think these things through. You're not even good at being selfish.

John, meanwhile, is teamed with a younger hotshot pilot who he doesn't like named Jannick (Mark Bazeley, *The Queen*). They fly in and try to hide the plane, but Jannick is captured. John goes to meet his asset-on-the-ground/lover Jessica (Ciera Payton) and with the help of her cousin Rojar (Alki David) they mount an attempt to steal the X-77 and rescue Jannick.

Since Seagal has, for the first time, made a movie that somebody else already made, this allows for a unique Seagalogical opportunity. By comparing *Flight of Fury* to *Black Thunder* we can see what Seagal (with the help of Joe Halpin) added or changed from the original story. Seagal puts his stamp on it, and we are able to clearly see which part is the stamp.

For the most part Seagal's version stays fairly close to the original. Both have a character named Ratcher who betrays his country to steal a test plane that uses an electromagnetic field to create an "active stealth" mode. Both have a pilot hero who must, against his wishes, team up with an asshole pilot named Jannick to fly into a terrorist camp, hide their plane, and (with the help of a local woman and her cousin Rojar) sneak in and steal the plane from Ratcher and a terrorist named Stone. In both versions, Jannick is captured and tortured and dies heroically while the hero steals back the plane, gets chased by Ratcher and has to defeat him in a dogfight. There are even some identical lines of dialogue ("Why fly against each other when we can fly together?" "I don't have to see you, John/Vincent. I just have to predict where you are.") And since they're from the same producer and they don't really expect you to know this is a remake, they even re-use some of the same aerial footage and establishing shots (now looking suspiciously grainy and faded compared to the rest of the movie).

Some of the story changes are obviously updates, not significant to our purpose here. For example, the design of the jet is changed to a more modern Stealth design and the hostile territory changes from Libya to Afghanistan.

The most significant change in the script is the background of the hero.

Dudikoff's character Vince Connors is a normal good guy pilot. Before he is called on the mission he's seen teaching a young man (his son? his student?) how to fly a small plane. Seagal's character John is given more of an anti-hero introduction, being on the run from the government, having a stolen car, refusing to cooperate once they recapture him. I like the way the movie leaves it mysterious what exactly his background is until it turns out that he's the world's best Stealth pilot. Which doesn't exactly explain the rest of that secret agent shit, but oh well. Anyway the guy is mysterious and dark.

In the original, Ratcher is an older white man who was Connors' mentor. In the remake John is the mentor, and Ratcher is a younger black man[63]. In both versions Ratcher is just a greedy sellout, there's no other motivation offered. But in Seagal's version Ratcher tries to justify it a little more, claiming "Makin' money is the American way." Seagal's version also gives more of a motivation to the terrorist Stone. In the original they start to mention his skinhead ties (!?) before they stop talking about his background and say that it's not important. Seagal's version of Stone has a complete bio including Oxford education and parents killed in Desert Storm, the source of his anti-American feelings.

Both versions have topless women in them. In *Black Thunder* there are two scenes with boobs. Before being assassinated by Ratcher, the guy originally set to be the test pilot is about to get it on with his wife. There is some humorously majestic music (think of the cue when the horse escapes in *Hard to Kill*) as the wife takes off her bra and the camera lingers. Later there's a scene where a woman helps hide Dudikoff from the terrorist's #1 henchman by letting the scumbag kiss her boobs. *Flight of Fury* has the same scene except the henchman has become a woman. But the old "you are threatening me, but by the way did I mention I am sexually attracted to you" trick still works on her, and she ends up being the one who exposes her breasts. So the bad guys degrade themselves, not the good guys. As they make out they cut to a closeup of John watching from the shadows, and you really don't know if he's supposed to look like a pervert or if he's just waiting patiently.

---

63 Although Ratcher is a one-dimensional villain I wouldn't read any racism into it, since Seagal has not shown any kind of an anti-black pattern previously.

By the way, while I strongly disagree with everything these terrorists are doing, I must applaud them for having a woman – a lesbian, no less – in such a high ranking position. This must be an extremely progressive area of Afghanistan. Not only do the women not have to wear burqas, but the neighborhood is enlightened and sex-positive enough that Jessica feels comfortable walking around in her silk bathrobe and negligee. Also, she keeps her gun hidden under a copy of *Surface*, a San Francisco-based design magazine that shows glamorous women on the cover, their faces showing. I'm not sure if she brought this with her or if she is able to get a subscription there. Anyway I guess those reports of the Taliban still being a threat must've been a false alarm.

Black Thunder has the better production values of the two. The flying scenes are much easier to follow (having been shot specifically for this movie, not re-edited from other sources). The cockpit footage looks more convincing. The score also sounds better, more like a full orchestra instead of obvious keyboard sounds. The incidental characters in *Black Thunder* tend to be better actors than those in *Flight of Fury* and their voices aren't dubbed.

However, I still think Seagal's version is better, because even Seagal's abortive fights of this period are way better than what Michael Dudikoff was trying to pull. I got nothing against that ninja but the fights in his movie are terrible. There is a car chase that turns into a fight in the back of a fruit truck, which is good in concept, but the moves are not impressive at all. Sure enough, I looked him up and he's not a martial artist turned actor like most of these guys – he started as a model. If he spent more time on training and less on maintaining his blond streaks it could probably be a better movie. It's mildly amusing, though, and if you know your horror icons you might be able to spot Kane Hodder (Jason in many of the *Friday the 13th* sequels), who is a stuntman but also has a bit part where you can see his face.

Not surprisingly considering the direction Seagal has been going with his last few pictures, *Flight of Fury* is one of his worst ever. But it also has its moments. While you do have to wait around forever to get to the fights, when they do happen they are pretty good. I'm happy to see Seagal getting back into knife fights like in the *Under Siege* days. There is a good metal-pole-vs.-tripod fight. And he does his trademark gunfight style where he holds a rifle out on a fully extended arm and doesn't even seem to be aiming.

The characters of General Barnes and Admiral Pembleton are pretty funny. They are constantly given stock lines like "I think it's time we let some hellfire loose on these bastards!" and "Okay, I want everything the agency's got on these *bastards!*" and "I've never known you to back out of a good fight, Budd. Let's throw the damn rulebook away!" But Pembleton is dubbed like a character in a *Godzilla* movie, and both of them delivers all his lines really different from how you expect from this sort of character. For example, when he says "Try Morse code, send out smoke signals. I don't care, do something!" he says it whiny instead of angry, so it sounds like he's not being sarcastic, he just doesn't know what to do so he is suggesting to try smoke signals.

There are some little bits of Seagal's personality in here. He sarcastically tells his interrogators that he's "just a country boy." He says "Lord have mercy" at one point. His code name is "Bad Mojo." But mostly he doesn't seem like he's trying very hard. One of the few scenes where he seems like he's into it is a really good Badass Orientation scene, the scene where he sits with his accomplices and lays out the whole plan of the type of badass shit they are about to do.

Sitting in a warehouse, John gets the bad news that the SEAL team has been defeated and Jannick has been captured. His response: "Holy shit."

He rubs his chin as he thinks about it. He looks over various satellite photos of the area and a couple weapons that are laid out for him: a gun, a few detonators, a knife. And then slowly, thoughtfully, like he's still piecing it together as he says it, he lays out the plan:

"Okay, well I see you got my tools here. If we get into the hangar we won't be able to use any guns. Perimeter looks like about 250 feet out right here with these outbuildings. This is definitely the point of least resistance... If we get inside *this* hangar where she is, can't use any guns. Only knives. We all know how to use knives. Take everybody out there. Jump in the bitch and fly 'er out, man. It's possible.

"If we can't do that, we blow her up and get out."

This is actually my favorite scene in the movie and it's not an action scene, it's an acting scene. It has a badass momentum, building from the heroes being seemingly backed into a corner to Rojar pulling out a huge knife and saying "We cut off their testicles!" (No testicles end up being harmed, I'm afraid.) But the real key to the scene is the way you can see Seagal thinking it through. It doesn't take him long to figure out what their options are. In most of this movie there is no trace of that old Seagal who used to say he wanted to be seen as a real actor and not just a martial artist. But here he does seem to be taking the character seriously, and he makes the scene work.

For most of the movie, though, Seagal doesn't seem to want to be there. John is of course a reluctant hero, he really would rather not have to go on this mission, and Seagal shows this by expending the least amount of energy possible.

And it turns out that Seagal himself may have been reluctant to be in the movie. According to Joe Halpin, both he and Seagal wanted to pass on the script, but Sony insisted on making it. Worse, Seagal and Halpin were not told that this script the studio was so fond of had already been made into a movie. "I was unaware of the *Black Thunder* movie until after *Flight of Fury* was wrapped and in post," Halpin told me. "One of the Seagal fans from the unofficial board sent me an email. I was upset about it for two reasons. Number one, they told us it was an unproduced script and failed to mention the prior movie. Number two, it was written by a writer that received no credit except a side payment and a 'thank you' in the end credits."

That writer is William C. Martell, who seemed to have a good sense of humor about the whole thing. Before *Flight of Fury* was released, fans on the IMDb message boards pointed out that the plot description and character names were the same as the Dudikoff movie and that it was too exact to be a coincidence. Martell himself posted to say that he didn't understand what was going on either, that he had not been told of a remake and that it was surreal because many of the characters were named after friends of his. Later he posted that he sure it was a misunderstanding that would be straightened out, and finally the messages were redacted.

So this was not exactly Seagal's dream project. Interestingly, his version has a subtle theme that is not taken from the original: no matter how hard John tries to get away, he is basically government property. He follows their orders and goes on their mission, and they reward him by trying to erase his memory. He escapes but is only brought in again, and despite a blatant lack of enthusiasm he obeys their orders without question. When he tries to say what he thinks about flying with Jannick he is immediately shot down by General Barnes: "I don't give a *damn* what you *think*. Jannick's *my* choice for backup. He's on the mission. Understood?"

"Yes sir."

It's something we haven't seen too many times in Seagal's films. He's saying "Yes sir," and he seems to mean it. He's being told not to think, and he seems to accept it. Throughout much of the movie he receives orders over his radio and he doesn't question them. We hear the phrase "Roger that" a lot. He's obviously doing the right thing by saving the world from a biological attack, but he doesn't have that same fire, he seems to be operating not as a hero but as a mindless tool of the government.

As far as I can tell there is not an obvious watershed moment that causes John to break the chains of mental slavery. But it must have something to do with his realization that Jannick, despite being an asshole, is his friend, and he can't leave him behind. This is the first time that the mission seems to take backseat to his own code. Later, Jannick is dying, and he radios to warn John and to ask him to go kill Ratcher. To orders from his superiors John says "Roger that," to a request from his friend he says "Roger that, brother."

Interestingly, Ratcher was trained by John, but doesn't have the same blind allegiance to authority. But he's worse, he doesn't live by a code at all, he's willing to fuck everybody over (literally *everybody on earth*) for some money. John taunts him about being a whore. "What's this about money? Uncle Sam didn't give you enough money? Your mama didn't give you enough money?"

John isn't in it for the money, but he doesn't seem to be exactly following his heart either. He's following his orders. Luckily, when the mission is completed his debt is settled. He is no longer under military authority, and hopefully he worked in a clause about them not being able to come kidnap him and mindwipe him. His last line in the movie is to tell General Barnes, "Now that I'm not in the military anymore I don't have to salute you." And you might think that would be setup for him to salute anyway, to show his respect. But no, he doesn't salute. He is a free man.

It makes you realize that for Seagalogy to take a turn in the right direction we might need Seagal to do exactly what John just did to free himself. If Seagal does a crappy movie he can't console himself with his salary. He has to ask himself, "Your mama didn't give you enough money?" He has long been under contract with Sony, so he might not have much of a choice, and obviously didn't get his way with this one. But we must look forward to the day when he no longer says "Roger that" to a studio, no longer has to salute.

Flight of Fury, 2007
Directed by Michael Keusch (*Shadow Man, Attack Force*).
Written by Steven Seagal & Joe Halpin, story by Joe Halpin. (Uncredited original **screenplay by** William C. Martell).
Distinguished co-stars: No.
Seagal regulars: Vasile Albinet, one of the rebel forces, is seen in a number of Seagal films – he is a stunt performer or coordinator for *Attack Force, Shadow Man* and *Black Dawn*.
Firsts: First remake for Seagal.
Title refers to: Either the test flight where the guy stole the plane, or the other flight when Seagal stole the plane back. Or both.
Just how badass is this guy? "This guy's extraordinary. He's unlike anything I've ever seen." "Next to you, Ratcher is probably the best Stealth pilot in the world."
Adopted culture: None.
Languages: He says the word "Sayonara."
Improvised weapons: Metal pole vs. tripod.
Old friends: He mentored Ratcher (the bad guy), knows various military bigshots.
Fight in bar: No bars in this one at all.
Broken glass: Punches through window to grab gun from gas station robber.
Most awkward one-liner: "You know, I would be ashamed of you, but, uh... I don't think you deserve my shame."
Family shit: No mention of family at all.
Political themes: Terrorists having free reign in Afghanistan might be vaguely political, otherwise it's just a light take on the "dangerous weapons will fall into the wrong hands" theme.
Cover accuracy: Another head that doesn't match the body, and another depiction of an explosion that only happens in our fears, not in the actual movie.

CHAPTER 26:
URBAN JUSTICE

"Y'know, I look at you, I see a man like me. A bad man with good intentions. I believe you."

In a movie that could turn out to be a major turning point in the DTV Era, Cory Hart plays Max Ballister, a happily married L.A. cop working to take out all the "bookie joints" in town. And I hope you understand that when I say he is happily married I mean *very* happily married. I mean hugging and kissing and taking lovey-dovey photographs as he's leaving the house happily married. I mean Goose in *Top Gun* happily married. Last day before retirement happily married. This guy is gonna fucking die.

And I'm not complaining, because who the fuck is Cory Hart? This is not the same Corey Hart who did that song "Sunglasses At Night," but he has a similar level of screen credibility. He played Chubby D'Acosta in *Road House 2* (yes, of course I saw that movie, but no, I do not remember who Chubby D'Acosta was). Before that he was the host of a TV show called *Teen Talk*, where teens, I'm guessing, talked. In this movie he's supposed to be Seagal's son, but he must be rebelling against his dad because he seems more like a soap opera star than an action star. He wears all black but in no other way resembles Seagal. Not in his attitude, not in his voice, they didn't even give him a ponytail.

Max happens to be driving in an alley when an unmarked cop car stops a yellow Ferrari. He doesn't even seem to notice what's going on and is more occupied with spilling his coffee. Then he slowly picks up on the fact that the cops are stealing money and drugs from the sports car enthusiasts. He takes some pictures, brings them home and examines them.

So he knows too much, he gets a mysterious call to meet somebody, he gets killed by an unseen drive-by shooter. Cut to his hero's funeral, where his dad Simon Ballister is introduced in extreme closeup, standing away from the crowd, behind a tree, wearing shades. Seagal plays Simon, an ex-unspecified-something-or-other father, visiting from an unspecified place, in town for

The funeral and
the revenge.

Or, as he puts it, "some personal stuff going on that makes me have to be here." We don't even know how he makes his living. Does he not have to work? Or is he using up his vacation hours for this personal stuff? What I love about this character and this story is the simplicity. At the funeral he approaches his ex-wife, she tells him that the cops won't do anything, and she won't stand for it. If he stops by the house she will give him the police files, which seems to be a request for vengeance[64]. Or at least an assumption. I suppose she was married to him long enough to know how he gets.

So he goes into a liquor store, rents a cheap apartment attached to the liquor store, then begins his investigation. When he leaves and comes back to the apartment he finds Gary (Jade Yorker), a young numbers runner who was an informant for his son. (I guess Cory Hart must've used those *Teen Talk* skills to get information out of young people.) Gary gives him advice, some of it misleading, because he's connected to the murder and afraid of his older brother Isaiah (T.J. Jones), who's kind of dangerous at this age because he's trying to prove his gangster stripes.

Even before Simon gets a bum tip to check out the East Side Gangsters

---

64 *Request For Vengeance* might not be a bad title for one of his movies, actually.

he is confronted by some of their members in the parking lot. They say he's on their turf and pull guns on him. So he beats the shit out of them. Once he's knocked them down, kicked their guns away and told them to spread the word about his search for the killer he casually gets a bag out of the trunk of his car and goes back inside the apartment. See, this is what you have to go through just because you forgot something in your car and had to go back out there. Bad neighborhood.

Later Gary gets jumped by four big racist skinheads (one of them an ugly Michael Berryman-looking motherfucker) which presents a nice opportunity for Simon to beat up more than just gangsters. But mostly it is gangsters he fights when his son's death seems to be connected to the gang Gary and Isaiah are involved with, Hyde Park, which is led by the cold-blooded Armand Tucker (the comedian Eddie Griffin, believe it or not). And Hyde Park are wrapped up in a scheme with corrupt cops, so there is some cop killing too.

Of the previous Seagal movies with 'justice' in the title, this one is most like the legendary *Out For Justice*, even though it's by Don E. FauntLeRoy, the same director as *Mercenary For Justice*. The setting is not as detailed, the situations are not as classic, but it's that same type of story about a single-minded brute storming through a neighborhood looking for a killer, and either murdering or beating the tar, crap, shit and holy living fuck out of anybody who interferes with his quest. In many ways this is a return to form for Seagal. FauntLeRoy wrote on the steven-seagal.net unofficial message boards that "We pushed as much as we could to make this the best Seagal film in years," and the effort shows. The proof is partly in Seagal's screentime, the fact that he provides his own voice for the entire movie, and the consistency of his performance. But most important for most fans this is that rare film from the DTV era that truly is action-packed.

There are seven fights. He battles two gangs, two doormen, and four racist skinheads. In hand-to-hand he beats down more than a dozen people, snapping wrists, throwing people through tables and walls, grabbing nuts, making people cry "Ow!" He beats up a doorman with one hand while holding a sandwich and a bottle of Tequila that he then gives to a homeless man the doorman had been picking on. He does a fatal wrestling move on a huge fat guy where he sits on top of him and pulls his head back until he hears a crunch. In one scene he kicks a guy six times in the balls, then turns him around, bounces him off a wall, kicks him five more times in the balls[65], kicks him in the face, and throws him down a flight of stairs. And that's just some dude, he didn't save that for a big shot like a Screwface. In one of the best scenes he doesn't get the information he wants so he suddenly shoots a guy's ear off. Then there's a shot looking up at him, towering over the guy scowling, and it's like Gino all over again, a total menace, a monster. But bigger, older, with more interesting wear and tear on his face. And without the beret.

There's also an extensive car chase/shootout and two long gun battles. By my count he kills 23 people just between the two gun fights. And many of those scenes are bloody (although the gangsters seem to have more powerful guns – sometimes when they shoot people the blood sprays about ten feet). Simon is clearly good with a gun, but he also does fine without them, constantly disarming people with his aikido moves. When Armand says "Now I know you ain't dumb enough to bring a fist to a gun fight," Simon says, "I am."

That's another thing that's improved in this movie: Seagal has some good badass lines, and he delivers them so bitterly they become even more badass. When a guy tells him "Fuck you" he roars "I'ma be doin the fuckin now!" He even makes it sound cold when he yells, "I did not come to this town to get played. I want to come here and take care of *one thing*." He really sounds pained. There's more emotion than you usually get in this type of dialogue.

But the all time classic one is when his daughter-in-law finds him preparing a bunch of guns to fight the gangsters and she says, "You're as bad as they are!"

"No," he says. "I'm a *lot* fuckin worse."

I mean, I don't care how silly you think Seagal is now, how much you think he's fat, how much you make fun of his movies and his guitars and his politics. "I'm a *lot* fuckin worse" he says, his eyes looking like they're

---

65 Admittedly, that last set of kicks is out of frame, so it's possible he's kicking him in the leg or something. But I think we can fairly assume they are all directed at the more obvious target in the groin area. I hope so, because that makes it a record-breaking eleven consecutive ball kicks.

gonna stab her. That moment is certified TFB (Totally Fuckin Badass). It instantly becomes one of Seagal's best lines ever.

Urban Justice was shot under the slightly less generic title *Once Upon a Time in the Hood*. It was probably a good idea that they dropped the *Once Upon A Time*, because that would either bring to mind epics like *Once Upon A Time in the West*, *Once Upon A Time in America* and *Once Upon A Time in China*, or some sort of fairy tale. And neither of those fit this story. The word "Urban" of course is marketing code for "Black," so even without "Hood" in the title this could be described as Seagal's first "hood movie."

"Urban" Americans have long been a crucial segment of the action movie audience going back at least to the rise of Bruce Lee and kung fu in inner city theaters of the '70s. Meanwhile, many white youths have shown a fascination with "urban" culture, especially since the advent of hip hop. So not surprisingly Hollywood has found ways to exploit these twin phenomena. The most prominent example in Seagalogy is *Exit Wounds*, with its co-starring role and soundtrack appearance by rapper DMX. Next is *Half Past Dead*, with more DMX music and co-starring rappers Ja Rule and Kurupt. And to a lesser extent there's *Ticker*, where Nas has a small role not interacting with Seagal, but was just as prominently featured on the cover.

Urban Justice has no famous rappers in the cast, and the only role hip hop plays is on the end credits, in passing vehicles and in inspiring some of the cheesy beats on the score. But this is Seagal's first film to plunge him into an American neighborhood where whites are in the minority. Instead of "the American" or "the gwailo" he is "the white boy," but he is able to navigate this landscape as deftly as he did Tokyo or Sangkom. It's surprising that it took him this long to get here – even *Leprechaun* had already come to the hood twice at this point.

It's to Seagal's credit that the racial politics are not as divisive as many films of this type. Other than being called "white boy" and using the word "motherfucker" more than usual[66], the movie doesn't really address

---

66 Seagal uses "motherfucker" or "motherfuckin" 7 times in this movie. Certainly not a cinematic record, but it's high for him.

racial or cultural differences. There is not the usual racial scare tactics since, after all, nobody scares Seagal. Obviously there are a few stereotypes promoted, and the 'n' word is liberally tossed around by the black characters, which hasn't happened in a Seagal movie before. But Seagal's character never condescends to or baits the other races. In fact, he bonds and makes peace with the leaders of both the black and Hispanic gangs, an amoral pact like he made with the Italian mob bosses of *Out For Justice* and the earlier scripted version of *Above the Law*. And Griffin's surprisingly serious character, while not exactly begging for an NAACP Image Award, is not the minstrelsy type of buffoon he often plays in movies (or that Morris Chestnut played in *Under Siege 2*, or that Kurupt played in *Half Past Dead*). This may be "urban" but don't worry, it's not *Soul Plane*.

When we began this study all those years and pages ago with *Above the Law*, the specifics of background were important to a Seagal character. We heard Nico Toscani's story from birth on, looked at his photo album, watched him teach aikido, saw what he did in 'Nam. We met his co-workers, his family (at least three generations), his priest – we knew all about this guy. But by the time of *Urban Justice* and Simon Ballister Seagal has evolved to a minimalistic, even impressionistic approach to character background. Ballister's past is left deliberately enigmatic, implied but not explained. We know he had a son who was a cop. We know he was divorced. His ex will speak to him but without emotion. If she left because he was too consumed in his work, the standard action movie divorce reason (see *Exit Wounds*), then she is still willing to take advantage of his skills now that their son is dead. But we don't know where those skills come from – CIA, special ops, organized crime? When asked if he's a cop he says "not exactly." He denies ever being in the military, but you can't necessarily take his word on that since he jokes "All the fightin stuff, I got that offa home videos."

Whatever he is, he's not cop enough to really care about crime. He has a disdain for "snitches." He doesn't mind gangs either, he just wants to kill whoever killed his son. If his son were alive he wouldn't give them a thought in the world. That's what's most interesting about the character: his code. He's kind of like Parker in the Richard Stark novels, he has only one thing he cares about (although he does have a heart of some kind, since he helps out the homeless guy). About the gangs he says, "I don't really care what their business is. I just want the motherfucker who killed my son." Later he seems to even be saying that he just needs the specific killer and not anyone else involved: "I don't care who ordered the hit. I don't care who's business is what. I just want to know who killed my son." He's not exactly a hero. He calls himself "a bad man with good intentions."

In the end he even lets Armand go. We know that Armand is an evil guy – he cruelly executes one of his men who disappoints him, he threatens an unborn baby, he may have shot his sex partners for no reason and if not he at least implies that he did something similar a week ago. Simon doesn't know any of this, but he does know that Armand shot at him, trying to kill him. Still, Simon's code does not require him to kill Armand. "You prob'ly think I'ma kill you," he says. "But you know what, I came here for one thing, and I did what I came here to do. I got no beef with you." Then he actually hands a gun to Armand, turns his back to him and walks away.

Villains like Jennings in *On Deadly Ground* like to tell the heroes that they wouldn't shoot them in the back. This is a much tougher version of that – instead of saying it, you put it to the test. *Here is a gun. Here is my back. Do what you will, chump. I'm leavin'.* Even Armand is impressed by this badass act: "That's a cool mothafucka. Now that shit was *gangsta*." And this is the last line of the movie. Simon walks in slow motion through the gathered police cars, his cold face contemplating what he's been through, coming toward the camera until he freeze-frames and fades to black, a reverse walk into the sunset.

This is the type of Seagal movie I've been begging for in my reviews: stripped down. A simple, straight forward revenge plot. No convoluted intrigue, not too many factions, more time spent on asskicking. Occasionally the fights use a herky jerky skip-frame effect and there are lots of inserts. It usually doesn't seem like he's doing all those moves in a row, and the kicks especially could be a double. But if those are the sacrifices we must make in order to get this level of asskicking then tell me where to sign. It's definitely DTV. The score gets really cheesy, and there's a painful moment where "Taps" is played at the funeral but it's clearly a keyboard trumpet. This is not going to win over the people who only like *Under Siege*. But for those with an open mind to DTV and a special place in their hearts for *Out For Justice*, this is the one you've been waiting for. It has that *Out For Justice* feel. Seagal is this giant, this "Paul Bunyan motherfucker," storming onto foreign turf, overpowering anyone in his way.

I've talked a lot about Seagal looking more menacing as he gets older and bigger. His face is getting more lines on it, more character, and his eyes are looking meaner. Combine that with a grim character like this and you get magic. He's really good in this one. I like that he avoids the type of smartass comments a lot of his characters make. This is a guy who stares you down until you cry, not a guy who jokes around with you. The one exception is a very funny moment where a doorman won't let him into the East Side Gangsters' private club so he tries to bribe him with five bucks.

You know who else doesn't joke around as much as usual? Eddie Griffin. I like some of his standup, and his movie *Undercover Brother* was pretty funny, but I don't generally expect him to be good in movies. I think it was fair for me to assume that his character would be played as a joke, or would be laughable. Instead, Griffin is very believable as a cold-hearted bastard with just the right amount of charisma and brutality to rule over other people. Yes, he's small, but he compensates. He's a mean little fucker in the tradition of Napoleon, Little Caesar or Eazy-E[67]. Griffin does seem to improvise some of his lines, and he makes his character a little too fascinated with Scarface to be a real guy living a Scarface lifestyle. But even his funny lines don't come across as punchlines or comic relief – there's too much of a threatening undercurrent. He seems like one of those guys who would only make you laugh as a way to lower your defenses so he can cut open your belly. And he has a way of rolling terms of endearment like "cuz" or "nee-UUUUUGck-uh" like he's tying them tight around your neck.

As a villainous performance it's a little more realistic than the over-

---

[67] To be fair, Griffin is 5'6 1/2", a good inch and a half taller than Eazy-E and Edward G. Robinson, and probably 4 1/2" taller than Napoleon.

the-top style we love from previous Seagal villains. But he does have a variation on the classic Senator Trent "just how evil is he" move of throwing a blond out of his hot tub so he can deal with action movie business. In Armand's version he has two girls and he invites them to go into the other room and use sex toys on each other so he can take care of some business before joining them. But then his mood shifts so instead of his threesome he decides to pull out a gun and yell at them from the other room. He mutters that he hasn't "killed a bitch in a week" and as it cuts to another scene there's a gunshot (I assume this means he shot them, or shot at them, but it could be read many ways.)

So we've got the streamlined story, the action, the dialogue, the performance by Seagal, the villain. It's all the main things you want in a Seagal movie. But what about the personality? What about the Seagalogy? I think Seagal does make it personal. In the scenes when he talks about his son in terms of mourning rather than vengeance he speaks of regret that he didn't spend more time with him when he was young, but is happy that they were able to be close in more recent years. Who knows if Seagal is thinking of his own kids, I'm not going to make assumptions about his personal life, but obviously a lot of movie stars would be able to relate to those sentiments.

But, you know, "be careful what you wish for," and it's true – there is one thing missing in this monkey's paw bargain. You wish for solid DTV action, you get it, but you don't get much of that weirdness that gave the more questionable ones their charm and uniqueness. Those weird touches – improvised political statements, crazy fashions, spiritual tangents, goofy editing mistakes, charmingly corny plot elements – that you watch and you know that *only* Steven Seagal would ever have that in a movie. Van Damme or Thomas Jane or even Stallone would never play a secluded animal rescuer who has to save his European pen pal from white slavery. But they would all play a mysterious guy avenging the death of his cop son. So that's my one complaint: *Urban Justice* is a type of movie we wanted to see from Seagal, it's a type of movie he excels at, but it's not a type of movie exclusive to Seagalogy.

But we're getting there. It's a big step in the right direction. The filmography has gone off the tracks in the last few movies and many fans have lost faith. *Urban Justice* will give them more than enough reason for hope. Now if Seagal can combine that *Out For Justice* fierceness with a little more of the *On Deadly Ground* madness then we'll *really* be in business.

Urban Justice (UK title: *Renegade Justice*), 2007
Directed by Don E. FauntLeRoy (*Today You Die, Mercenary For Justice*).
Written by Gilmar Fortis II (assistant to the co-producer of *Lethal Weapon 4*).
Distinguished co-stars: I was surprised he got Eddie Griffin at this point, but that guy was in *Norbit*, I can't call him distinguished.
Seagal regulars: Danny Trejo returns to Seagalogy for the first time since being put in a trunk in *Marked For Death*. Binh Dang, who plays a deliveryman, is a longtime co-producer for Seagal's Steamroller Productions. He was also Seagal's assistant for three films starting with *The Patriot* and did stunts for *Marked For Death, Out For Justice, Under Siege* and *On Deadly Ground.* Larnell Stovall ("Gang Member #1") has not worked with Seagal before, but he did do stunts on *Half Past Dead 2.*
Firsts: First time Seagal's character has had an adult child. First Seagal "hood movie."
Title refers to: The location and style of the justice that will be dispensed. (Also it has the same amount of syllables as *Out For Justice.*)
Just how badass is this guy? "Look, some big ass white boy – as in Paul Bunyan motherfucker – came out of nowhere up in the spot, did some kung fu shit on my little homey and me, grabbed that nigga's gun and shot his ear off." "He's a cool mothafucka. Now that shit was gangsta." "Badass white boy, huh?"
Adopted culture: Other than slightly changing his speech to mimic ebonics he pretty much remains himself.
Languages: Only English.
Improvised weapons: Unlike in *Out For Justice* he keeps his weaponry simple, pretty much only using his fists, his feet and various guns.
Old friends: None, he's a total loner.
Fight in bar: No, and not even in the liquor store that's one of the main locations.
Broken glass: Back car window, pieces of windows in car crash, shots fired through glass door, windshield.
Family shit: His son is dead and he wants revenge. His ex-wife gives him info to help him get revenge, but their exchange is cold and business-like.
Political themes: Just some more of the ol' police corruption.
Cover accuracy: This is one of the funniest covers Seagal has had due to the unnaturally attached headshot on someone else's body. Otherwise it is just a collage of the various actors' heads in front of Los Angeles. There are some bulletholes in the picture too, which is fair because there are in fact many shots fired during in the movie.

CHAPTER 27:
PISTOL WHIPPED

"At the time you were probably fuckin' drunk. Better straighten your ass out, man. You got a job to do."

Pistol *Whipped* starts where many people incorrectly believe Seagal's career resides: in the graveyard. The style is uncharacteristically operatic and John Woo-inspired. Black and white, slow motion, Seagal wearing a black suit and firing off bullets in all directions, sometimes not even looking where he's firing, like a kid showing off shooting hoops or a gunman who just doesn't give a fuck who or what he hits. Color slowly soaks in and out of the picture as Seagal floats over the tombs of our ancestors, their grave markers exploding all around him. (Man, that's cold – these guys are already dead and now you gotta murder their graves!) This is a rare flash forward, a peek at the apocalyptic battle Seagal's character will eventually find himself engaged in. He will return to this land of death, and he will rise from it.

But first we go back to the beginning, in another sacred place, The Good Shepherd Catholic Church. Seagal plays Matt[68], an ex-black ops, ex-police officer alcoholic gambler. Matt sits in the pews of the empty

---

68 Lance Henriksen's character twice addresses him as what sounds like "Mr. Connor," but everyone else – including the end credits – just calls him Matt.

church being dressed down by Father Joe (Bernie McInerney): "You're not a good guy. You sit around all day, you do nothing with your life, living off God knows what, you gamble, you're divorced, a dark past before I met you, then you were a cop and they kicked you out. I bet you don't see your daughter one day out of twenty..." He mentions that there was some drug money stolen from an evidence locker and Matt managed to avoid prosecution, but everyone (even the Father) "knew" he had stolen it. Lazy, washed up, corrupt – it's an angsty new variation on the traditional *just how badass is he?* speech. This time it's the *just how fucked up is he?* speech. Starting out with a big chunk of dialogue explaining what a loser the hero is would usually be an awkward start, but McInerney (a veteran character actor who plays a judge on *Law & Order*) really pulls it off, sounding genuinely disappointed in Matt, not scolding him. He hasn't given up on Matt. Not just because he's a man of God, but because "deep inside you you've got this, I don't know, this... this spark. This seed of decency." And you can see that spark on Matt's face as he sits listening to the father, nodding in agreement. But then the spark fades as Matt decides to leave, makes a joke and struts off to join a high stakes poker game at the Big Eastern Casino.

In some of Seagal's lesser DTV works he seems kind of tired and out of it. Here it's genuinely part of the character. He's played fuck ups before, but never like this. This is by far the most washed up character he's played. He blew it with his ex-wife Liz (Blanchard Ryan), with his job, with his gambling, he continues to blow it with his daughter Becky (Lydia Grace Jordan). He repeatedly disappoints his friend Steve (Mark Elliot Wilson), the cop who kept him out of jail and is now married to Liz. When Steve brings Becky over for father-daughter time, more often than not Matt is asleep, hungover, not ready (only once with the legitimate excuse that he's being held at gunpoint). When he goes to Liz's house he doesn't call ahead, and she lets out an exasperated sigh. Most people seem to still like him, but only because they feel sorry for him. Even his daughter, who looks after him and makes him an "I (heart) Daddy" mug, eventually gives up on him. He's always tired, he mumbles, he coughs and clears his throat, he's often sitting somewhere moping or asleep on a couch or a La-Z-Boy, his daughter has to tuck him in and pour out his booze. He's in debt, so he's selling his house, and he just lost everything in a poker game. Again.

Then all the sudden some guys pull some guns on him behind the casino. The one who doesn't get his ass kicked is called Blue (Paul Calderón), who looks like Matt's opposite: wiry, energetic, prone to dramatic poses, not very good at martial arts. He forcibly brings Matt to a big empty auditorium for a word with the mysterious "Old Man" (Lance Henriksen). The Old Man knows what Matt was capable of "back in the day, across the pond, before you took on this cop... identity thing." So he's purchased $1,235,000.65 of Matt's gambling markers from three different bookies to force him to become a hitman for a shadowy off-the-books government agency. Blue acts as the Old Man's messenger and enforcer, spying on Matt, sneaking into his house, harassing him and delivering him packages filled with cash and photos of his targets. He tells Matt that his targets are bad people, but then reminds him "They all have kids, just like you," seemingly as an act of cruelty, to torture him psychologically. *You have to do this, but don't forget to feel bad about it.*

The first target is some guy named Bruno (Arthur Nascarella), an arrogant mafia slob involved in some kind of counterfeiting arrangement with a Korean gang. Matt follows him around, maybe to see the best way to kill him, maybe to prove to himself that it's a bad guy he's gonna kill. And this guy definitely fits the bill. He stops at a produce stand and makes racist comments to the Asian woman who runs it (Nikki Takei). He's incredibly rude in restaurants, yelling at a guy and banging his head against a table, sexually harassing his waitress (Rue DeBona) and trying to embarrass her for the entertainment of his buddies. Not only that but he has himself driven around in a white Hummer. What an asshole.

When Matt finally does the deed he makes a big scene in the middle of a crowded restaurant and takes his time for dramatic effect. In a classic badass-smartass combo he abruptly sits down at Bruno's table right in the middle of a counterfeiting discussion and scolds him for his treatment of the waitress. "I just was a little bit offended and I wondered if you could apologize to her." And before long he's poking a guy's eye out with a fork and blowing Bruno's head off.

In their first meeting The Old Man described Matt's talent for assassination and how he could "walk out in one piece like a fuckin' ghost." Usually "like a ghost" means you leave no trace, or can't be proven to exist (for example, Steve later describes Blue as "a kind of ghost" because of how hard it is to find information about him). But Matt is more of a bulldozer. He follows his target all over the place and makes little attempt to blend in. He blatantly stares at him in a crowded bar, and openly asks questions about him, and then he pulls that stunt in the restaurant. In later hits he doesn't wear gloves and leaves fingerprints all over the place. So it's the other kind of ghost, the traceable but comes-out-in-one-piece kind[69].

So the movie is about Matt being forced to kill these criminals, but as long as he's up off his ass he decides to use the opportunity to straighten his life out. So a lot of the movie is about him recognizing his problems and trying to deal with them. After that first hit we see him sitting on his bed, smelling a drink and brooding while wearing a yin-yang track jacket. Clearly Matt is uncomfortable with this balance-of-good-and-evil-shit. Or maybe he's thinking he leans a little too far to the yin. The movie takes Matt's shortcomings more seriously than any previous Seagal film, and spends a surprising amount of screen time on his quest to better himself, *to change the essence of a man.* He brings his daughter to the aquarium and at first seems disinterested, but quickly reveals a natural rapport with the little girl, joking around with her and apologizing for failing her earlier, making a vow to "try to live up to my responsibility to always be there for you."

And he does try. He tries to control his drinking, though he keeps the booze around and tempts himself. He smells a bottle but then looks at his daughter asleep across the room and puts it away. He keeps pouring those drinks just to smell them. Scotch seems to be his drink of choice, and at the bar he orders Johnnie Walker[70] on the rocks. He doesn't end up drinking it, and you're not sure if he was planning to or not.

Just showing him struggle with drink is not the only thing that makes the character different for Seagal. We're not used to seeing him play a guy who's this down on himself. When his daughter jokes "You're not *that* dumb, are you?" he says, "Sometimes. I think I've proven that in the

---

69 On the other hand there's an extra at a neighboring table who doesn't seem too concerned about this violence. Maybe he really is invisible. *Like a fuckin' ghost.*

70 Being over 150 years old, Johnnie Walker is another symbol of Seagal's old school sensibilities.

past, haven't I?" He also calls himself a "dumb, unlucky sonofabitch." That seems to be the light-hearted side of a genuine self-loathing. When his shoulder is wounded he doesn't take a shot for it because "I like the pain. Keeps me feelin' weak and alive, you know." He doesn't care too much about living, so he's willing to walk away from someone and tell them to shoot him in the back. He doesn't want to be confused with "somebody who give a shit." In the graveyard shootout he's told "You're not getting out of this alive" and he says, "You know somethin' – I'm not planning on it."

He's even shown as emotionally vulnerable. When Blue taunts him about Bruno being a bastard but spending more time with his daughter than Matt does with his own, Matt says "That makes me feel terrible." And usually that would be a sarcastic line from a Seagal character, but here I think it's sincere. He can't completely hide the disappointments in his love life, either. In the bar he picks up a woman named Drea (Renée Elise Goldsberry), sleeps with her and fries eggs for her in the morning. When she turns out to be a spy for Blue and the Old Man he's genuinely hurt. You expect him to just be mad and get over it, but late in the movie he has to ask her if sleeping with him was part of the mission or whether it was her own decision. When she says she wanted to do it he asks if it was because she felt sorry for him.

People make a big deal about Seagal's physical imperviousness as an action hero. You don't expect to see him covered in his own blood like Bruce Willis and Sylvester Stallone often are. But this emotional vulnerability is even more unexpected. In the DTV Era it's pretty standard for his characters to have a quick love scene with a young beautiful woman. Why they would want to be with him has never been a question, but here it really nags at him. Seagal's biggest emotional scenes usually stem from the vengeful rage for the murder of a loved one. He gets to do that here too, but mostly he's dealing with relationship failures that are more relatable to those of us who live outside of action movies.

But just so Matt's self-esteem doesn't get too low this is the first Seagal movie to indicate that his character has a large penis. After sex Matt jokes about what would happen if Drea had a larger one than his (long story) and she says, "I don't think that's possible." This is somewhat reminiscent of Vincent Gallo in *Buffalo 66* going into a restroom and being bothered by a guy's awed reaction to the size of his junk. Hopefully Seagal won't take this boasting to the next level like Gallo did in *Brown Bunny*.

Late in the movie Matt returns to the church and gives confession to Father Joe. It's basically an exposition monologue that fills in some of the holes in the backstory we've already heard. Despite what Father Joe thought, Matt really hadn't stolen the evidence money. He was "a dirty cop," a drunk, had been cheating on his wife and was close to being thrown out of the house. But he wasn't a thief. He had saved Steve's life before, so he begged him for help. Steve lied to give him an alibi, cashing in his squeaky-clean reputation to keep Matt out of jail. So it's a complex relationship between these two. Most step-dad/ex-husband pairings haven't saved each other's asses like this. Matt feels indebted to Steve, just like he is to the bookies, and he has to work that off. Steve seems like a nice guy, and he's patient with Matt's failures as a father. Steve didn't *steal* Matt's wife and daughter, Matt clearly lost them. Finders keepers. Matt knows that he and only he dug this hole that he's in, so he can't bring himself to be angry at Steve. But still, it's gotta hurt. You know there's some resentment in there somewhere. You see the look on his face when he notices Becky's photo on Steve's desk at the police station. I mean, shit.

To me there's a moment that's genuinely heartbreaking. Once again Matt has to back out of his father-daughter-day so he can spy on a guy he has to kill. Earlier his daughter forgave him, but here he is blowing it once more, doing exactly what he promised not to do again. He goes to the car to try to talk to her but she won't even look at him. That's a pretty obvious drama moment, but what makes it work for me is the way Matt knocks on the window to try to get her attention, and keeps knocking in different goofy ways, trying to be funny. A pathetic attempt to make a joke out of the situation, to get a smile out of her. And it totally fails. He can't charm his way out of this one. You don't usually get that kind of sadness in this type of movie.

Now is where the major spoilers come in, because this is the rare Seagal movie with a big plot twist. Somewhat predictably, Steve is Matt's next target. This puts Matt in a pretty strange position. He needs to kill this guy. This guy who *sort of* took his wife and daughter. This guy who got to stay on the force. Who doesn't have a drinking problem, doesn't owe money, doesn't have to sell his house. The guy he probably wishes he was. That dark side of Matt might get a little bit of satisfaction out of killing Steve. But his initial reaction is to refuse. This guy is innocent, and he owes him. So he tries to warn Steve that someone wants him dead. Steve tells him to leave town and he refuses because he owes him, he wants to stay and protect him. Remember, he has that seed of decency.

But while Matt is a bad guy with a seed of decency, it turns out Steve is the other way around. He seems like such a nice guy, and it even turns out that it was him that anonymously paid Matt's gambling debts to get him back on his feet. But where'd he get the money to do that? It was *him* that stole the evidence money. And he killed Matt's partner. And he worked for Matt's other targets, tipping them off to police activities. But what really gets him in trouble with Matt is when he kills Father Joe. He thinks Matt might've said too much during confession, so he slits the father's throat. There's your *just how evil is he?* moment. And to make matters worse he instructs his fellow dirty cop Wheeler (Wass Stevens) to use Becky as a hostage. His own stepdaughter. This prompts Matt to say "You mother*fuck*er!"

But even then Steve doesn't really turn into a maniacal villain. He tries to justify his actions. I don't think he knows he's evil. He's just another dirty cop who hides it better than Matt did. Once Matt has fatally wounded him he tries to bond, making a grim joke about his impending death. But Matt rejects the gesture with one of the more cold-blooded badass moves of Seagal's career: he asks him whether he wants to be buried or cremated, and then does not respect his wishes! Serves you right for damaging all those tombstones, fucker.

When The Old Man first discusses the targets with Matt he says, "These scumbags have managed to get not above the law, but beyond it[71]. The law for them has no meaning, that's where we come in, in what I prefer to call our enterprise: extracurricular justice[72]." The Old Man's phrasing

---

71 I'm surprised that wasn't the title: *Beyond the Law.*

72 Ooh, that's another good one. Steven Seagal is… *Extracurricular Justice.*

is not the only thing in the movie that recalls *Above the Law*. *Pistol Whipped* harkens back to that debut by making the family important again, by making him Catholic again, by making the church a major location, and the murder of a priest a crucial plot point. It also brings back the quick, brutal aikido style that made Seagal such a revelation in the Golden Era. The fight scenes are short but man, they look painful.

The fight in the home bowling alley is my favorite. The hits look powerful and real. One guy kicks Matt and he absorbs it like a brick wall would. It looks like he hurts the guy just by standing there. Another attacker who tries to kick him is rewarded with a blow to the balls and ends up on the ground clutching his crotch. (Sadly, he does not scream "My balls!") There's also a satisfying "stick it to the man" moment in this scene because a grey-haired servant, who has the shit job of manually setting up the bowling pins and returning the balls (what is he, one of those dinosaur appliances on *The Flinstones*?) gives Matt a thumbs-up, and then they bow to each other.

Incidentally there's also a line that could be seen as a callback to *Hard To Kill*. It might be stretching it, but as a Seagalogist when I hear Steve tell Matt that he's "outmanned, outgunned," I can't help but think of the classic "outgunned and undermanned" speech. Of course Matt ends up winning, so by the logic of that speech that means he had "superior attitude, superior state of mind." And if that's the case then he must really be getting his life back together.

It's unusual to see one of the action icons seriously dealing with substance abuse in a movie, but to be fair I should acknowledge that Jean-Claude Van Damme beat Seagal to the punch on that one. In 2007 Van Damme released *Until Death*, a DTV movie with many parallels to *Pistol Whipped*. In that one Van Damme also plays a dirty cop trying to reform. His is still on the force, and not only drinks Scotch but shoots a lot of heroin. His daughter is not born until the end, and his wife hasn't divorced him yet, but they are separated. He does lie lazily around the house, and his ex-partner is the villain, and there's also a seemingly clean cop on the force who turns out to be a traitor. Van Damme's movie is darker and more serious, and to many people is probably a better movie. But then again it's a movie that other actors could have done better.

Seagal's movie is one that other actors just wouldn't do. It wouldn't have all the same goofy touches and wouldn't be as enjoyable.

Both *Pistol Whipped* and *Until Death* might owe a slight debt to a 1992 film, Abel Ferrara's *Bad Lieutenant* starring Harvey Keitel. It's not an action movie by any stretch of the imagination, but it's the dirtiest of dirty cop movies. Keitel's unnamed cop character spends the whole movie drinking, shooting up, stealing, lying, even jerking off in front of teens. Like Matt he's addicted to gambling (in his case sports gambling) and keeps getting himself further into debt. And like in *Pistol Whipped*, the Catholic church is a central theme and location. Instead of a murdered priest there is a raped nun, and instead of redeeming himself by killing the bad guys he does it by trying to forgive them and putting them on a bus out of town. At least one person involved in *Pistol Whipped* knows about *Bad Lieutenant*, because Paul Calderón (credited as Paul Calderone) appears in it as another cop. In fact, the Internet Movie Database credits him as a co-writer, but he does not receive credit on the movie.

Whether or not he really co-wrote *Bad Lieutenant*[73], Calderón is one of many people who deserve some of the credit for *Pistol Whipped* being a classic of the DTV Era. The first thing that strikes you about the movie is the better than usual cast. Calderón has had many roles in movies, TV shows and on stage, but in the world of movie trivia he will always be *the-man-who-would-not-be-Jules*, because of how close he came to getting that role in *Pulp Fiction*. When Quentin Tarantino ultimately gave the part to Samuel L. Jackson, Calderón got the consolation prize of playing the bartender. You may remember his line, "Hey, my name's Paul, and this is between y'all." He's also in *Out of Sight, Clockers, King of New York*, even Michael Jackson's "Bad" video (which means he's been directed by Scorsese). So although your average joe has never even heard of the guy I really like him as an actor and I was excited to see him in a Seagal movie, especially in such a significant part. He adds some authenticity and credibility, an unexpected treat this late in the Era.

---

73 I'm not sure he'd want credit if he wrote the jerking-off-in-front-of-teens scene. But if he wrote the part where he's high and thinks he sees Jesus and yells, "What? You got something to say to me, you rat fucker!?" that would definitely be worth bragging about.

Also not necessarily a household name, but much more recognizable, is Lance Henriksen. And while he may not have been nominated for an Oscar like Imelda Staunton,[74] he is probably the most recognizable DTV Seagal co-star since Dennis Hopper in *Ticker*. Henriksen is a legend. He's been directed by Steven Spielberg, James Cameron, Sidney Lumet, Walter Hill, David Fincher, John Woo, Sam Raimi and Jim Jarmusch. He'll forever be remembered as Bishop, the empathetic android who gets ripped in half in *Aliens*. There are also those who remember him as the ruthless vampire Jesse in *Near Dark*. In TV movies he's portrayed two of history's greatest Americans, Abraham Lincoln (*The Day Lincoln Was Shot*) and Charles Bronson (*Reason For Living: The Jill Ireland Story*). In the world of action movies he's a great over-the-top villain, memorably antagonizing Jean-Claude Van Damme in *Hard Target* and especially Brian Bosworth in *Stone Cold* (as the shirtless motorcycle gang leader Chains). His characters have encountered Damien, Pumpkinhead, the A-Team, Cagney & Lacey, The Terminator, Hardcastle and McCormick, Aliens *and* Predators, the Super Mario Brothers, Leonardo DiCaprio, Tarzan, whoever the killer ended up being in *Scream 3*, the Mangler, the giant bugs from *Mimic*, Evel Knievel, Pinhead, Bigfoot, Superman, and now, finally, Steven Seagal.

That long and varied history as a character actor can be heard in Henriksen's deep, distinctive voice, and seen in every interesting line on his face. He rarely gets shots at leading man roles, but when he does he's really good at those too. He had a good run as the psychic serial killer hunter on the TV series *Millennium*, and I honestly think he's great in James Cameron's much-derided directorial debut *Piranha II*. He's the Roy Scheider of that particular *Jaws* rip off and he's up to the task. Despite everything he's accomplished I think he's still an actor who really hasn't been given his proper due.

He also must have a hell of a work ethic because he's extremely prolific. He's what I call a "Paypal actor," a guy who's in so many movies (sometimes of questionable quality) that it seems like he just has a web

---

74 He did get nominated for a Golden Globe three times though. Imelda Staunton was only nominated once. And Henriksen won a Saturn Award for best supporting actor in *Hard Target*. Does Imelda have a Saturn Award? Fuck no! She's never even been nominated.

site where you can order him via Paypal and he'll have to show up and be in your movie, no matter what it is. That would explain how such a reliable actor ended up in *The Mangler 2, Hellraiser: Hellworld, Alone in the Dark II, Sasquatch Mountain*, etc. He's even in *The Da Vinci Treasure* and *Pirates of Treasure Island*, two of Asylum Entertainment's "mockbuster" knockoffs of studio movies. But I've never seen a movie where it seemed like he was phoning it in.

That makes him one of the rarest gems of DTV: a talented actor who's affordable, yet not washed up, and somehow with dignity intact. To do two sasquatch movies in one year and not seem like a schmuck, that's like being bullet proof. So how the hell has Henriksen *not* crossed paths with Seagal before this? It's something I'd asked myself more than once over the years, and I even heard a rumor that Henriksen had refused to work with Seagal. But either that was phony or things have changed, because here he is. Maybe it was the participation of director Roel Reiné that lured him in, because they'd just worked together in *Deadwater* (released as *Black Ops* in the States). Seeing Seagal, Henriksen and Calderón all in the same scene together I thought *that's right, I forgot – Seagal movies used to have good casts sometimes.*

Henriksen's role is small, though. He appears in three scenes, all filmed in the same location, plus one scene with just his voice coming through a cell phone. It's easy to imagine this as an ongoing series with Henriksen playing a disembodied phone voice, *Charlie's Angels* style, giving Matt his missions.

Reiné, the director, does not have a particularly distinctive style, but he's more than competent. No avid farts, just the occasional unnecessary mid-shot speed-up. There are some unique touches here and there like a point-of-view from inside the holy water at the church as Matt dips his finger into it and a scene where he practices his aim by shooting bullets at matches, grazing them and causing them to light. The style of the shootouts themselves is not as original, but they get pretty heavy and seem different from those in other Seagal movies. The fights are well done and the car chases have some pretty good crashes in them, although the green-screening on all the interior car shots is phony and destroys the illusion that these guys are really driving (one of the few overly shoddy aspects of the movie).

By the way, there's one unusual touch during the big car chase scene that you might not notice on a first viewing. At one point an SUV runs over a small fruit cart. You see fruit cart destruction in so many action movies that it hardly even registers, so you'll be forgiven if you don't notice that this is the same fruit cart where in the beginning of the movie Bruno made racist comments and Matt said that he spoke Korean and Japanese. It truly is every day that you see a car hit a fruit cart in a movie, but it's not every day that that fruit cart was a previously established location. Luckily the nice lady who runs it seems to have abandoned her post, so she doesn't have to jump out of the way. Still, a devastating blow to a hardworking entrepreneur, and a shameful waste of perfectly good fruits and vegetables.

Reiné is a Dutch director who started out in television. He did a show called *Legend of the Goat Riders*. His first feature, a Hollywood style action thriller called *The Delivery*, won him a Golden Calf for best director and was nominated for best picture. His web site rebelfilm.com claims it also "started a new era in Dutch film by making mainstream English language movies[75]." But surprisingly what makes his Seagal film stand out from others is not so much the action movie stuff as the character work. Maybe he just lucked out with this cast but he gets better than usual performances for DTV including some subtle acting moments from Seagal.

After watching the movie a couple times though I realize that the real MVP here is screenwriter J.D. Zeik. He's a playwright and a screenwriting teacher at the theater school SUNY Purchase in Westchester County, New York. His biggest success to date is the John Frankenheimer movie *Ronin*. Zeik wrote that original script, which was revised by David Mamet under the pseudonym Richard Weisz. Many say Mamet rewrote the script from the ground up, but he at least used Zeik's original theme of updating the concept of the ronin, the masterless samurai.

Pistol Whipped (Zeik's script was called *Marker*, by the way) may be a silly movie to non-DTV aficionados, but it's well constructed. It doesn't

---

75 This view is not supported by any of the Netherlanders I have polled on the subject.

have as many of the goofy plotholes and ridiculous turns that many of these movies have, it's not as clunky. When it ends it feels like it's the ending it's always been building toward, not something that was pieced together in postproduction. You can tell there were never supposed to be aliens or mutants in this movie. And most of the plot was probably on paper before they started filming.

I must admit that there's one piece of the story I really don't understand. While spying on one of his targets Matt gets jumped by two thugs in a parking garage. He forces one of them to tell who sent them, and the guy describes a 6' clean shaven arrogant prick, which Matt takes to mean Blue. But Blue later swears it wasn't him, and it's believable because he doesn't have a motive. So who *did* send those guys? I really don't know. Steve doesn't have a reason to go after him yet, and neither the arrogance or the blue suits seem to fit him. So whatever was going on there was an unclear piece of storytelling, as far as I'm concerned.

Other than that though it's very clear, easy to follow, while still being pretty complex and rolling out the backstory a little bit at a time. And there are subtle layers to the characters that you won't really notice until you see where the story ends up. For example, Steve is written as a good guy for 90% of the film, and not all of that is an act. If his crimes had gone undiscovered I'm sure he would've stayed in nice guy mode, driving Becky over to see Matt, covering for him when he's hung over, trying to cheer her up when he won't see her. Steve did lie to help Matt, and anonymously paid off those gambling debts. And Matt is probably correct that he only did those things out of guilt over what he had done, but at least guilt is a genuine human emotion. He's a villain but he's not the devil.

Matt's rivalry with Blue and The Old Man is even more nuanced. For most of the movie they seem like bad guys. Matt works for them against his will, and what they're doing seems wrong. Blue taunts him, interferes with his life, even stands outside the window creepily spying on him while he has sex. But in the end you realize Blue really is a good guy. The people he's killing really are bad, and his point about the contradictions in good and bad people does have some truth to it. He even dies backing up Matt. He can be kind of an asshole, but that's just his way of buddying up with somebody, he likes to give them a hard time. In retrospect, his comment about remembering these people have children might not have been meant to be cruel. Maybe he was just trying to keep Matt grounded. And take note that when Matt refuses his order and does not kill an asset who helped with their operation Blue does not threaten or punish him. Instead he has a philosophical talk with him.

Once you've seen the end you can go back and watch The Old Man's scenes, and you realize that he never actually threatens Matt. You thought it was just left unsaid, but it turns out that might have been a misunderstanding. When Matt asks if they'll kill him for refusing to work for them The Old Man says, "Not at all." He tells him "you can refuse." Matt takes these comments as facetious and so do you as the viewer. But by the end of the movie The Old Man has not tried to harm Matt, even when he tried to quit. Looking back you realize that The Old Man probably meant what he said. Matt really could have refused. But as The Old Man points out, "You took your life back. A week ago you were wandering aimlessly." Becoming a hitman is a therapeutic experience for Matt. It gives him the time to change.

In the end Matt and his daughter seem to be happy together. Becky says "It's good to have you back, dad." You can interpret this to mean it's good to have the old Matt back, the one who's not a lazy drunk laying around the house doing nothing. But combined with Matt's reference to "Mommy" it could also imply that he's back with the family, reunited with Liz now that the whole Steve-letting-me-get-blamed-for-the-money-he-took episode is over. And he goes into the church and gets down on his knees, maybe to thank the Lord for giving him his life back. But then Drea strolls in and gives him a photo of his next target. So we know he's still killing people.

My gut reaction on a first viewing was that this was a dark, cynical, somewhat depressing ending. Drea's demeanor has completely changed, she's moved up the ladder to replace Blue – has she become a cold-hearted bitch? She had become close to Matt, had been more loyal to him than to the extracurricular justice enterprise, not to mention sharing her "good lovin'" with him and complimenting the size of his penis. You kind of expected them to get together, not for him to return to his ex-wife. So he might've broken Drea's heart and maybe that's why she's acting this way. Or maybe it's the natural result of success. She becomes more powerful so she becomes more distant from him. She told him earlier about her resentment of the people above her, but now she seems to have become one of them.

The most upsetting part, of course, is that this guy who seems to be a happy family man again is still committing assassinations, and maybe willingly, because doesn't his house not being for sale mean he cleared up his debts? So he still has this wicked side, and has to be keeping secrets from his wife and daughter. (I mean, you would hope he doesn't tell the daughter he's doing that. She's not old enough.)

But the more I thought about it the more I understood where it was coming from as a happy ending. We've heard that Matt enjoys the rush of these missions like they're a form of gambling. The Old Man said, "He's a sick compulsive gambler. Y'know he thrives on the action, that's it." I think the fact that he's still an assassin means he's no longer drinking or gambling. He has an addictive personality, he's not gonna kick these things instantly, but I think we're supposed to understand that these killings are taking the place of his former vices. They are his nicotine gum. And we've learned that the guys he's killing really are bad guys. Not that it's justified, still, but you can see how he justifies it to himself.

I think with this Seagal has finally made the definitive version of that type of movie he's been messing with since *The Foreigner*. The ones with the nuanced world view, full of grey area and contradictions, ambiguous ethics, intrigue and double-crosses, people who aren't what they appear to be, people who can't be trusted (or in this case actually should be). This time the character relationships and loyalties are complex, but the plot isn't overly complicated. The storytelling is not muddled or convoluted, and it doesn't feel too light on the action, even after spending whole sections dealing with parenting issues instead of breaking a guy's wrist. Zeik's script has taken that plot and made it more human, more personal, more Seagal.

But after really analyzing it I'll do you one better. This is not just the culmination of Seagal's exploration of grey areas, it could even turn out to be the beginning of a new period of maturity and awareness for Seagal. People have asked me before if Seagal could ever make his equivalent of Clint Eastwood's *Unforgiven* – a sort of revisionist movie that looks back at his past as a film icon and questions or comments on the ideas in his previous work. *Pistol Whipped* isn't that movie, exactly, but it's the closest Seagal has come to that later-Eastwood approach. He has sort of turned the standard Seagal character on his head, giving him more troubles, forcing him to open up his emotions more, and to face more human challenges like being there for his daughter. In movies like *In the Line of Fire* and *Blood Work* Eastwood acknowledges his age by giving himself ailments: he needs a heart transplant, or he's out of breath, he can't run alongside the President's motorcade like he's required to. Seagal doesn't acknowledge his age physically, but by giving himself a long history. He's not just living down one past life, but two (one in black ops, the other as a cop, both ancient history).

No, *Pistol Whipped* is not on that same fierce warpath as *Urban Justice*, so in my book[76] it's not quite as badass. But from a Seagalogical standpoint it's a more interesting movie. And it's more solid, more complex, but without being any more muddled. It has Seagal stretching his persona and exploring new territory without abandoning his classic themes.

In fact, I like to read Matt's recovery from alcohol and gambling as a symbol for Seagal's recovery from sloppy, compromised DTV movies he doesn't really believe in like *Flight of Fury*. Drea says, "That whole speech I made about who I am and what I do – it was true. Only – not the details of it, but the feelings I was talking about? Those were true."

The same can be said for *Pistol Whipped*. The details aren't true, but the feelings are. Seagal has a troubled past (*Attack Force*). He's addicted to gambling (movies shot so they could either be sci-fi or not be sci-fi) and booze (other actors dubbing his lines) but now he's made an effort to leave that in the past. He's still killing people though (making four DTV movies a year). But that's part of the process. The first step is admitting you have a problem. The second step is *Urban Justice* and the third is *Pistol Whipped*.

Pistol Whipped, 2008
Directed by Roel Reiné (*Adrenaline, Drifter, Deadwater*)
Written by J.D. Zeik (*Ronin* [yes, the John Frankenheimer one with Robert De Niro and the amazing car chase], *The Touch* starring Michelle Yeoh, the TV movie *Witchblade*)

---

76 Vern, *Seagalogy*, 2008.

Distinguished co-stars: I consider Paul Calderón and Lance Henriksen to be distinguished, and I don't really care what anybody else thinks about it.

Seagal regulars: The dealer at the poker game is Matt (son of J.D.) Salinger, who played Myshkin in *Black Dawn*. Nikki Takei, the woman at the fruit cart, was the translator for Seagal's aikido documentary *The Path Beyond Thought* (that may be why he talks to her about languages).

Firsts: First time Seagal has played an alcoholic. First time trying to be a better father has been a major plot point. First time he's been in a movie with prolific action movie/DTV staple Lance Henriksen.

Title refers to: Matt is enslaved by the pistol. Henpecked. Cuckolded. P-whipped. Nobody is literally pistol whipped in the movie.

Just how badass is this guy? "A guy who can walk into an urban territory, a 5-star hotel, full of bodyguards, and take care of business, with extreme prejudice. And walk out in one piece like a fuckin' ghost."

Adopted culture: He has some samurai swords on his wall and other Asian decorations, but never talks about them.

Languages: He mentions that he speaks Japanese and Korean.

Improvised weapons: Restaurant silverware.

Old friends: He doesn't have any old friends, they all thought he stole the money.

Fight in bar: No. Although alcohol has caused Matt a lot of problems in life, the bar is portrayed not as a place of hate but a place of love. In two separate scenes he meets Drea there, then goes back to his house for "good lovin'."

Broken glass: Headlights and car windows are shot out, including on a hearse. There is also a scene where he hits a thug's head against a car window and it *doesn't* break, that's kind of unusual.

Family shit: This is arguably the most family-centric movie he's done so far. His failure as a father is a major story thread, his ex-wife's new husband is one of the central characters, his ultimate goal is to straighten things out with his daughter and in the end he seems to have even reunited with his wife.

Political themes: The character Blue, and ultimately the movie itself, make a cynical but perhaps realistic argument for grey area and contradiction in the fight against criminals. Blue feels that the people they kill "deserve it" even if in some ways they are good people, his example being that Bruno might be a better father than Matt. The Old Man argues that their "extracurricular justice" is necessary because to these people "the law has no meaning." So it's sort of an ends justifies the means, fight fire with fire kind of world view.

Cover accuracy: Once again Seagal's head is badly Photoshopped into the picture. Otherwise the images are mostly accurate – those characters are in the movie, and gambling does figure into the story. He even uses a gun with a silencer similar to the one that forms both 'I's in the title. However, the cover shows a roulette table, and Matt is only ever seen playing poker and betting on horses in the movie.

CONCLUSION

Several years ago, when I lived somewhere else and didn't know as much about Seagal, I came up with the idea for this book. I'd been writing reviews of movies (many of them straight-to-video) on The Ain't It Cool News, and judging by the "talkbacks" (little boxes where readers write their responses to your reviews, often comparing your hard work to something that could be done to the orifice of an animal) I was not very popular. In fact, I was considered illiterate, not even functionally illiterate, and anything I wrote provoked cries of "why did you post this shit Harry?" and "my [number lower than 7] year old brother writes better than that."

The one exception was whenever I reviewed a Seagal picture. I was enjoying his movies like *Belly of the Beast* and *Out For a Kill*, and started to notice all the unique ties between them, a study I realized had to be called Seagalogy. The talkbackers were surprisingly positive towards these reviews. I think it may be partly because they thought I was making fun of Seagal, and people like negativity. But if that's the case then I wasn't really getting myself across very well. I loved watching these movies. I always liked the Seagal movies I'd seen, but when I saw *On Deadly Ground* I just couldn't believe it. This guy was something else. And those crazy DTV movies cemented it. I became a Seagalogist.

Or so I said. But if I was really going to be a leading expert in the field of Seagalogy, I had to expand my knowledge. That's when I thought of writing a book. If I was gonna write a book, it would be the perfect excuse to watch every Seagal movie in chronological order. More than once. And really study them. I drew up a big chart with all his movies in order of release on the top and on the left side it had categories like *family shit, political themes, broken glass, just how badass is he?* It seemed to me like the whole of Seagalogy was one giant mathematical formula, and if I put all the data in the correct spots the answer would reveal itself. Some people said that Seagal's movies were all the same, but I knew instinctively that he was like any auteur, he was pursuing his personal vision, with variations on the same themes. As *Out For Justice* producer Arnold Kopelson told GQ in 1991, "Every frame of this movie has Steven's imprimatur on it, which is not the case with most actors I've worked with. He's a filmmaker. I would expect that to some people on my production he's also a pain in the ass, but what's important is Steven's concept of perfection."

That's what I was seeing, was that imprimatur[77]. It's not just the presence of Seagal that makes it a Seagal movie. If it was possible to make, say, *Fire Down Below* – exactly the same movie, but with Wesley Snipes or somebody instead of Seagal – you would think "Holy shit, what is Wesley doing in a Seagal movie?" Because it's unmistakable. I knew they all fit together, all pieces of one big puzzle, and I knew that only if I watched all of them, picked apart all of them, considered them as one gigantic work, I would see what it was all about.

So I started writing. If there had been no meat in there I could've never finished. Nothing against the other guys, but if I'd been trying to study, say, the films of Jean-Claude Van Damme, I don't think I would've gotten to the end. They've got some good ones, they've got some bad ones, a lot of them have nothing to do with each other. But Seagal's fit together as one consistent body of work. My hunch about Seagalogy was right. The early movies that I hadn't seen turned out to be way better than I expected. The new ones were continually getting stranger. I kept noticing more and more Seagalogical motifs, and the movies began to seem more and more awesome. So I watched, and I analyzed, and I wrote. And Seagal kept making movies. So the project grew – he filmed

---

77 Nice word, Kopelson.

more than ten movies during the writing of this book, not to mention recording two albums, going on a tour and formulating an energy drink. Well, now I have finally drawn an arbitrary line in the sand, I cut him off. This is not the neverending story. A book has to end somewhere, and unfortunately this has to be it for now. So here I sit with a library of Seagalogical analysis, and the footprints of a great journey behind me. I think back to what I wondered in the beginning, what I expected from all this. And I find myself asking a question that probably hasn't been asked too often about the films of Steven Seagal: *what does it all mean?*

In trying to find an answer to this question, the first and most obvious level to examine the films on is a political level. Most critics may not take the politics of a Seagal film seriously, but they are undeniably a major component of the films.

More than anything, Seagal films illustrate the idea that "absolute power corrupts absolutely[78]." We see this demonstrated by the behavior of politicians (*Hard to Kill*), police (*Hard to Kill, Exit Wounds, Urban Justice, Pistol Whipped*), corporations (*On Deadly Ground, Fire Down Below, Submerged*) and most of all by spy agencies (*Above the Law, Under Siege, Under Siege 2, The Glimmer Man, The Foreigner, Submerged, Mercenary For Justice, Shadow Man*). Even Seagal's characters are occasionally corruptible, at least as the films begin. In *Marked For Death* he "had become what [he] most despised." In both *On Deadly Ground* and *Mercenary For Justice* he starts out as an admitted "whore." In *Pistol Whipped* he calls himself a "dirty cop," although there are few specifics of what he did. And in *Out For Justice*, even though he's the good guy, he is said to be taking advantage of his badge and has clearly crossed many, many lines past the original line that a police officer is not supposed to cross. He's a great movie character, but I wouldn't want any real cops taking those kind of liberties.

In a similar vein, several Seagal films (*Under Siege, Under Siege 2, Half Past Dead, Submerged, Attack Force, Flight of Fury*) show the concept of blowback – when the highly specialized training of government agents

---

78 Lord Acton, a British historian of the late nineteenth and early twentieth centuries.

comes flying back like a pissed off boomerang. There's also a similar warning about inanimate government assets: by creating deadly technologies and weapons for "defense" we are creating the opportunity for them to be used against us. This includes the nuclear submarine in *Under Siege*, the satellite in *Under Siege 2*, the chemical weapons in *The Patriot*, the mind control in *Submerged*, the suitcase bomb in *Black Dawn*, the drug in *Attack Force* and the invisible jet in *Flight of Fury*. (It could also apply, to some extent, to the Exploding Watermelon Fist in *Shadow Man* and the futuristic nanographite blades in *Attack Force*, so hopefully Seagal's characters will keep those methods from falling into the wrong hands.)

The politics of Seagalogy have evolved a little bit over the years. There's an annoying cliché that "9-11 changed everything," and believe it or not that could arguably apply to the films of Steven Seagal. Take a look at his filmography and you'll see that the permanent switch from theatrical movies to straight-to-DVD pretty much aligns with the attack on New York. *Half Past Dead* was Seagal's first movie after 9-11, it was his only PG-13 movie, it was not as big of a success as *Exit Wounds*, and it was his last movie released theatrically in the United States. (In fact, according to the director commentary, the PG-13 rating came in response to a general perception that people didn't want to see violent action movies after 9-11.)

As the world changed, so did Seagal's films. As recently as *The Patriot* in 1998, Seagal was playing the Nico Toscani type, the highly trained badass who's seen it all, saw through the corruption, tried to put it behind him but reluctantly became a whistleblower and used his old skills to save the day. But in the DTV/post 9-11 Era, Seagal usually played characters with murkier ethics. Jonathan Cold (his character from *The Foreigner* and *Black Dawn*) knows all the tricks in the book, but just sees double crosses and assassination as a reality of life. He doesn't have the same moral outrage as Nico or Forrest Taft. Most of his characters now stay out of politics, they only deal with the situations facing them (kidnapped daughter, kidnapped penpal, murdered fiancée, murdered son, murdered priest, etc.) The ad-libbed political statements are few and far between.

I supposed he's gotten his point across by now, but I think it would be a shame if he dropped those themes altogether like he did the fights in bars. I think I have demonstrated how his movies have been ahead of their time in calling attention to dangers that are going ignored in our country. It would also be interesting to see Seagal tackle environmental issues again. He really only addressed them in *On Deadly Ground* and *Fire Down Below*, and seemed to let it go after all the scorn he received for those. But he was clearly right, and many of the fringe issues he addressed in *On Deadly Ground* (the limited supply of oil, the possibility of alternative fuel sources, the inadequate legislation against businesses that abuse the environment, etc.) are mainstream political concerns today.

But those are just politics. While Seagal's films may be more consistently political than the ones made by many of his action hero peers, politics are not his purpose on this planet. "I prefer to be able to keep my mind, my heart on the path of mysticism and following the way of God and learning the teachings of all the great saints and buddhas and not to concern myself with politics," Seagal once claimed, "because I'm not a politician and I don't think I can make the world a better place by being in politics[79]."

With that in mind, the real message of Seagalogy may not be political, it might be more personal. We may need to look at the characters and determine what they represent as people. To find the meaning of Seagal and his movies – *the essence of a man* – I think we first need to go back to the very beginning, the first scene of the first movie. As discussed in Chapter One, the opening of *Above the Law* explains how a young Nico Toscani was taken to a baseball game and at half time there was a martial arts demonstration where, he says, "I saw this little old Japanese man doing things that I thought were *magical.*" In real life, Seagal's introduction to the martial arts was similar, except the demonstration took place at a school football game[80]. This must have been around the age of 7, when he began studying martial arts, later earning black belts

---

79 Moyer, "Steven Seagal: The State of the Martial Arts and the Relationship of Spiritualism" in *Martial Arts Legends Presents Shigemichi Take, Shihan Steven Seagal, The Spiritual Warrior Who Prospered on the Island of Budo*, p. 30.

80 Richman, "Black Belt, White Lies" in *GQ*, March 1991, p. 235.

in aikido, karate, judo and kendo. After college he moved to Japan with the girlfriend who would become his first wife. At this time it was unusual for an American to even live in Japan, let alone become prominent in the martial arts. Nevertheless, just like Nico he eventually operated his own aikido school in Tokyo, later returning to the States to found other dojos.

So the very beginning of Seagal's movies points us back to the very beginning of his life in aikido, the way of harmony. Nico's narration about the "little old Japanese man" is illustrated by three photos of aikido founder Morihei Ueshiba (1883-1969), who indeed was little, old and Japanese. It is often said that Seagal claimed to be taught aikido by Ueshiba (also known as O-sensei), but in fact what he has claimed is that he saw Ueshiba speak. Seagal didn't move to Japan until after Ueshiba's death, but he says that he went there many times as a young martial artist. Court TV's Crime Library reports that "At least one of Ueshiba's students remembers Seagal being around at the time," but does not explain who this student is[81].

Asked about Ueshiba by a student at the dojo he founded, Seagal only claims to have followed and emulated him. "I have very little experience with O-sensei," he said. "I was able to see him several times. I've seen him speak. I was very close to his spiritual teachers and I still am. I think I was the only white person to ever go exactly in the footsteps of O-sensei in terms of his mystical training. I became a priest in O'moto Kyo and went to all the aesthetic training with the priest that O-sensei was raised with. I never really knew him. I never got to butt heads with him on the mat or was thrown around by him or anything else.[82]"

Whatever Seagal's link to Ueshiba, we know he was the founder of aikido, Seagal's primary martial art and the one he has gone on to teach. When interviewed by martial arts magazines Seagal often quotes Ueshiba or mentions stories from his life. And we see here that he tried to "go exactly in the footsteps of O-sensei" in some ways. So Ueshiba would

---

81 It's not clear if they are paraphrasing a source of their own or one from someone else's article. Their entry has several inaccuracies. It says that aikido has no offensive moves (not true), that Seagal claims to have been taught by Ueshiba, and that Ueshiba died in 1968 (other sources say 1969).

82 *Off the Mat*, Tenshin Bugei Gakuen newsletter, November 1991.

have to be a hero to Seagal, and by looking at his parallels to his hero we can learn something about Seagal.

Like any teacher, Ueshiba started out as a student. He learned Daito-Ryu Aikijutsu under a guy named Sokaku Takeda. The combat system involved jujutsu, sumo, spear fighting and swords. Ueshiba also studied an obscure sect of the Shinto religion. He combined this spirituality with his martial arts to create aikido, and it was that spirituality that attracted Seagal to the art.

Like Ueshiba (but not as drastically), Seagal took what he learned from his teachers and developed it into his own system, which he then passed on to his own students. Teachers and gurus are very important to Seagal. He quotes one of his teachers as telling him, "Rather than spend ten years studying every day to perfect an art, spend ten years searching for the right teacher.[83]"

Seagal had many teachers in many different arts. The names of some of his aikido and karate senseis are on record, others are left up to the imagination. "There were high Buddhist monks," Seagal once said. "There were exalted Shinto priests, holy people, great sword masters, Jujitsu masters, Karate masters, Aikido masters; there were Judo masters.[84]" Surprisingly, Seagal's films rarely feature these sorts of masters, or any mentor for Seagal's character. *Above the Law*'s narration mentions "studying with the masters" in Japan, but does not feature those masters as characters. *Under Siege* has a sort of a career mentor in the Captain, but it's not really a master-student relationship. In *Mercenary For Justice* there's a guy who claims to have taught Seagal's character everything he knows, but this is not really explained. *Belly of the Beast* does have some of those "high Buddhist monks." But the only time he is really shown to have a master or a sifu is *Into the Sun*'s Master Cheung, who I assume is a mentor and not just an old friend, although it is not really specified. The Seagal character's training is always in the distant past, except in *Hard to Kill* where he is his own sensei retraining

---

83 Moyer, "Steven Seagal: The State of the Martial Arts and the Relationship of Spiritualism" in *Martial Arts Legends Presents Shigemichi Take, Shihan Steven Seagal, The Spiritual Warrior Who Prospered on the Island of Budo*, p. 14.

84 Same as 83, except this one's on page 21. (I don't want to retype all that shit.)

himself after a seven year coma.

Mentorship is a theme throughout the movies though, with Seagal being the mentor. In *Above the Law* and *Shadow Man* he has an aikido dojo. In both *Under Siege* films he teaches moves and weapon techniques to his sidekicks (and niece). In *Out For a Kill* he teaches Chinese archaeology at Yale. In *Black Dawn* he has an apprentice in the black ops arts. In *Into the Sun* he seems to have been Mai Ling's teacher in the past (unless he was just there when Master Cheung trained her). In *Attack Force* he is the leader and elder of the titular attack force, who regard him kind of like a den leader or cool social studies teacher. And in *Flight of Fury* he taught the bad guy pilot how to fly those jets.

Seagal thinks you should spend ten years searching for the right teacher, and in his movies he plays teachers. This supports the idea that the characters Seagal plays are offered as heroes, people to be admired, the kind of people we should aspire to be. I suppose this goes without saying anyway, since other than his alcoholic character in *Pistol Whipped* Seagal rarely plays characters that are presented as flawed (one possible exception being *Out For Justice*, where his vengeance is so fierce a mobster thinks he's sick in the head).

So through his movies we can figure out what makes the ideal Seagalian hero. Seagal's system of aikido is adapted for the realities of modern living, and so are his characters. Obviously he must be self-reliant and highly skilled in combat, including martial arts and automatic weapons. He must be able to unarm an opponent and use his weapon (or other inanimate object) against him. He must also be a master of tactics, knowing exactly how to track people, how to sneak around and take them out one-by-one, or when it is appropriate to go in through the front door. Seagal's character is always the leader of his group, rarely has a peer relationship with anyone, often is a loner.

Since Seagal's character has usually abandoned or semi-retired from his work as an intelligence agent or cop, he does not have access to the amenities of someone working from within the system. Therefore it's important for him to use his relationships to get what little outside help is necessary. Occasionally he needs someone to hack into a database, to look up a file for him, to tip him off to his enemy's plans. So he has to be good at networking.

But obviously these are qualities that are pretty standard for action heroes, they are not unique to Seagalogy. Another one that is fairly common, but that is strongly associated with Seagalogy, is his way of being an outsider on the inside, a rebel from within the system. The Seagalian hero is or has been a part of the system, an agent of The Man, but lives by his own code that maintains his individuality. Many of his characters are cops or former cops betrayed by their corrupt peers, and even more often they have a past in the CIA, military special ops or similar secret government work, but left (sometimes explicitly because they were disgusted by the activities of their peers). In *Above the Law* he quit the CIA after seeing drug smuggling and torture in Vietnam. In *Hard to Kill* he's framed and attacked by fellow officers who are down with the corrupt politician he plans to expose. In *Marked For Death* he quits the DEA because of disgust at his own corruption. In *Under Siege* he is shown as a rebel within the military who doesn't even have to wear a uniform, who once punched a commanding officer and who preaches individuality and questioning authority. In *On Deadly Ground* his reasons for leaving the CIA are unexplained, but it may have been a sellout move since he's now working for a corporation. However, even the authority and money of the corporation cannot ultimately overcome his code; he sees that what his boss is up to is wrong and becomes an outlaw to stop him. In *Fire Down Below* he works for the Environmental Protection Agency, and is serious about his mission, but it turns out the agency itself is not. In *The Patriot* he once designed chemical weapons, but quit when he saw what they were doing with them. In *Exit Wounds* he's another cop fighting his corrupt colleagues. In *Out of Reach* he clearly has some sort of intelligence agency past, but something caused him to abandon that life to become a hermit who lives in the woods and spends his time helping animals and children. In *Submerged* he is a military man who made the right decision to stop "another 9-11, except at sea" but had to take a fall for it due to politics. In many of the DTV films (*The Foreigner, Belly of the Beast, Into the Sun, Black Dawn, Mercenary For Justice, Shadow Man*) he plays a sort of rogue or freelance agent navigating a complicated maze of betrayal and deceit to achieve his mission. In these situations he has no choice but to follow his own code against so many other factions and interests.

Jurij Meden, a Seagal fan who grew up in the former Yugoslavia, tells me it is exactly this individuality from within the system that makes Seagal so popular internationally, particularly in ex-communist countries. Jurij describes Seagal as "the kind of proletarian hero an ordinary, small, often repressed man could perfectly identify with (unlike a lot of other action heroes from America who were often acting in the name of state or system)." In other words, Seagal can play cops, soldiers or agents, but these characters are acting on behalf of their own ethics, not just doing their job. When Jurij was growing up, Seagal's first three films were extremely popular on the pirate market under the titles *Nico*, *Nico II* and *Nico III*. But Yugoslavia at that time was not exactly welcoming of challenges to authority. "Indoctrination began at age seven," Jurij told me, referring to the *Pioniri* pledge made by many Yugoslavian children. But to him, Seagal represented an example of how one can stay true to a country or a system as long as they don't hold it up above their own code or sense of morality. "What matters is to remain an individual within the system, to proudly retain your personal code of ethics and act upon it. Even if it clashes against the system."

Perhaps part of the reason the Seagalian hero thinks for himself, and does not follow a strictly American ideology, is that he has been exposed to ways of thinking from many other parts of the world. That's the most important and distinctive quality of a Seagal hero: he is worldly. Like his movies themselves, Seagal travels all around the world. He has no trouble flying to other countries at a moment's notice, instantly adapting to the culture and language. He may be called "the American" by foes but will fit in anywhere despite his size and unusual appearance. He doesn't have a colonialist attitude. He is not xenophobic. He is knowledgeable and even experienced in the ancient arts and religions of many cultures. If you go up to him and start talking about a Chinese herbal remedy or a samurai sword technique, or even a Native American ritual, he will know what you're talking about and have some good insights to add.

And that brings us back to that little Japanese man and his magic. Looking back over Seagal's two decades on film, you only need to go one minute into *Above the Law* (and that's including the Warner Brothers studio logo) to find the DNA of Seagalogy, when Seagal has already "developed a crazy dream to go to the Far East" and ended up "there, studying with the masters." The movie tells the story of this self-proclaimed patriotic American cop who happens to have spent his formative years studying and teaching aikido in Japan before going to war for the United States. So there are two sides to Nico Toscani, and we can see now that there are two sides to Steven Seagal. There is the American side, and there is the Asian side.

The American side is the CIA agent, the cop, the Navy SEAL, the guy-who's-fascinated-with-the-mafia, the bluegrass guitarist, the bluesman. The Asian side is the aikido instructor, the antique sword expert, the Buddhist lama, the herbalist. The American side wears a black leather coat, maybe a beret. The Asian side wears embroidered silk shirts. The American side drinks Cherry Charge Lightning Bolt, the Asian side drinks Asian Experience.

Obviously Seagal isn't the only American action star to be fascinated with Asian culture. Chuck Norris's accomplishments in the martial arts brought him to the screen, and he has serious credibility just from facing Bruce Lee in *Way of the Dragon*. But over the years Norris has adopted a purely western persona, becoming far better known for wearing a cowboy hat in *Walker, Texas Ranger* than for being good at jujitsu. Not so with Seagal. Even with *Under Siege* (where he plays a regular old Navy SEAL) as one of his biggest hits, Seagal's public persona is always the holy warrior, the American guy with the ponytail who does martial arts, protects the environment, practices Buddhism.

As long as Seagal stays true to both sides, I think he will remain a unique and interesting figure in action cinema.

Although we'd all love to see an *Under Siege 3*, Seagal is not dependant on any franchises or characters. He's just dependant on being Seagal. To date he's only done two sequels, putting him on the low end of sequel-makers among his action star peers. Sylvester Stallone has done eight (*Rocky 2-6, First Blood 2-4*). Chuck Norris has done three (*Missing In Action 2-3, Delta Force 2*). Arnold Schwarzenegger has done three (*Conan the Destroyer, Terminator 2-3*). Only Jean-Claude Van Damme has gotten away with less, having only done *Universal Soldier: The Return*.

Still, a common knock on Seagal movies is that they're all, allegedly, the same. People look at the earlier, more famous films and make fun of the three-word titles, the CIA backgrounds, etc., and they think that's all there is to it. But they have no idea the degree to which these motifs have developed. And anyway, the repetitive nature of these types of stories is part of the appeal. Like a horror movie or a folk tale, you want to see variations on familiar themes. You want to be surprised sometimes by a left turn, or by the way the pieces fit together, but you also want to see the familiar elements. It's part of the ritual.

Throughout Seagal's films so far we've seen him speak English, Spanish, Japanese, Chinese, Italian, Inuit, Thai, Korean and some Native American dialect I'm not able to identify. He's taught aikido, practiced Chinese herbology, done acupuncture on himself, dabbled in Inuit spirituality, professed Tibetan Buddhism, performed bluegrass and collected and sold antique samurai swords. He's played seven cops, five intelligence agents, three soldiers, two mercenaries, a doctor, an EPA agent, a rogue corporate firefighter, a thief and a professor of Chinese archaeology at Yale. He's been ex-CIA, ex-DEA, ex-SEAL. He's visited 11 old agency or department buddies and girlfriends. He's made weapons out of a skewer, sand, a microwave, a pylon, a table saw, a sausage, a bar towel, a pool cue, a pan, a rolling pin, a corkscrew, a decorative rope, a tusk, a tree, an empty 2-liter bottle, a helicopter blade, a pipe, a cable, concentrated coconut oil, lighter fluid, a flare gun, a credit card, a bulldozer blade, a telephone, some lumber, a wine glass, a kerosene lamp, a CD, a phonograph, a chair leg, a ceremonial wooden club, a barber's smock, chopsticks, a faucet, urinals, a metal pole, a fork. He's had five fights in bars, two in liquor stores. He's broken countless windows, windshields, coolers, shelves of bottles, china cabinets, mirrors, a jewelry case, drinking glasses, a gun cabinet, two vending machines, fluorescent lights, a phone booth, a chandelier, a shower door… He's explored pollution two times, police corruption three times, CIA corruption nine times. He's avenged three murdered wives, a murdered fiancée, a murdered son, two murdered priests, a wounded niece and two kidnapped daughters. Through all this he's only died three times, and two of those times he was revived.

As I was finishing the first edition of this book the world of Seagalogy was in a dark place. Two of the most recent movies had left Seagal disappointed and feeling betrayed by the studio. Many of the fans felt the same, as they grew tired of the obvious dubbing, stunt doubles and shoddy production values of many of the recent DTV films. His music career, however, was at a peak. His tour for the *Mojo Priest* album had been very successful and earned him a certain amount of begrudging respect from those who had witnessed it. Promoting the tour he said in countless interviews that he saw himself more as a blues musician than as an actor. And who knows, maybe it was movies like *Flight of Fury* that had him singing the blues.

But there was a light at the end of the tunnel. I had hoped to end the book with *Prince of Pistols*, the Seagal movie set to be filmed in New Orleans, featuring an all-star cast of blues legends. It sounded like something closer to Seagal's heart, something he would really put his all into. Especially since he was supposed to direct – his first time since the seminal *On Deadly Ground.*

Unfortunately, *Prince of Pistols* has been postponed, and as of this writing still has not begun filming. Is it too good to be true? The way these things work you must be realistic, it may never happen. It could go either way. And even if it does happen, could it really fulfill my hopes? Or is it too late to return to the glory days?

I have no idea. With no *Prince of Pistols* to write about it looked as if the book would end like *Attack Force*: abrupt, unresolved, kind of a bummer. I figured maybe some day, when the filmography had grown longer, I would make a new edition of *Seagalogy*, and it would end in a better place, more of a *Marked For Death* ending. An ending where Seagal has killed his enemy six ways to Sunday and knows how to go out on a high note. Kill, one-liner, walk away, credits. I knew that day would come, but... *time*. Seagal needed time to change. And we did too, brother. We did too.

But as I said in that super-rare self-published edition, by being in a bad place Seagal was actually right where he needed to be. If Seagalogy is backed into a corner surrounded by enemies, then that's exactly where it belongs. In *The Path Beyond Thought*, a martial arts video about Seagal teaching his form of aikido, we learn about his black belt test *randori* – the three-man attack. It's a hell of a test that seems equal parts *36*[th]

Chamber of Shaolin and gang initiation. The student first goes through a full day's class, in order to be physically exhausted. Then he or she has a brief moment of peace facing three fellow students on their knees as Seagal says a few words. At any moment he could yell to begin, and the three will charge at the potential black belt full speed and attack. The four participants aren't supposed to hold back. They don't even necessarily need to use aikido moves, or follow any rules. Apparently they are even allowed to spit or bite, and to chase each other around the dojo knocking over furniture or banging heads against walls. Once Seagal feels the student is controlling the three attackers he or she passes the test. Very few pass on their first try, it is intended to seem impossible.

The idea of the test is to teach the student that they can overcome overwhelming odds, and to force them to internalize aikido. When there's three attackers there's no time to think. They just have to do it. That's the path beyond thought, that's Seagal's aikido, and it's also how he makes his movies. It's Seagalogy.

This book is obviously written from the point-of-view of someone who loves Seagal's movies and admires him for making them. There are many other fans and Seagalogists around the world, some of them even crazier and more forgiving than I am. But we are not the mainstream opinion. For the most part these days, pop culture treats Seagal as a joke, belittling his achievements, disowning even the hit movies from earlier in his career, writing off his fans as lowbrow idiots who don't know about film and just like to see punching and explosions. The press has never been a friend to Seagal, nor he to them, and they are especially cruel now that he has gained some weight and makes lower profile movies. You always need a so-called has-been to point at and call names. And it helps if there is a ponytail involved.

By 2006 or 2007 many of the fans were beginning to agree with those criticisms. Seagal was besieged on all sides. As Gene Shalit might say, he was under siege, he was marked for death. But fortunately he was also hard to kill. As demonstrated by the *randori*, the whole point of aikido is to even the odds, for one man or woman to be able to take on many. Aikido was created by a small man to take on bigger opponents, it is perfect for women to defend from men, because they can rely on their skills rather than strength. It teaches you to dodge and to turn, to always move to an enemy's side or back rather than in front of them, where they can do more damage. Which is exactly what Seagal did by suddenly appearing on stage wielding a guitar when people were expecting him to be in Hollywood begging Warner Brothers to do an *Under Siege 3*. In fact, the art form of the blues is itself a path beyond thought. You learn the basics, the foundation of the idiom. And then you can't think about it anymore. You can't just learn the notes for a blues solo, you have to internalize it, you have to project it from yourself, you have to feel it.

Obviously he already did *Exit Wounds*, but after that I knew not to expect Seagal to plan some PR strategy for a "comeback," like losing weight, teaming up with a popular younger co-star, doing a sequel to one of his hits and making the rounds on talk shows trying to show what a regular guy he is. That's thinking too hard, trying too hard. That's straying from the path beyond thought. Instead he needed to do what was inside him, what came instinctively. And that's exactly what he's done with *Urban Justice* and *Pistol Whipped*. Suddenly he's more invested in his movies than he's been in a while. More action, more solid fights, no dubbing, no obvious stunt doubles. The stories are sturdier, the acting is more accomplished, the overall product is more entertaining. Hopefully these two movies in a row are not just a lucky streak, but the beginning of a new and harder to kill Seagal.

And I think there's a good chance of that. Because that's what happens when a guy like this goes down: he gets back up. If you want to put him in a coma, be my guest. But some day he will wake up. And he will train. And he will come for you. Go ahead, back him into a corner. See how that works out for you. As Seagal himself narrates on *The Path Beyond Thought*, "Show me what you got when you got nothin' left. Show me what you got." There he was, exhausted after a long journey. But he was ready. He had internalized Seagalogy. And as those three metaphorical motherfuckers charged at him planning to beat the hell out of him, he didn't have to think about what to do.

"We're outgunned and undermanned, but you know something? We're gonna win. And I'll tell you why: superior attitude, superior state of mind. We'll get 'em, buddy. Believe me. Every fuckin' one of 'em."
– Mason Storm, *Hard to Kill*

appendix i:
OTHER APPEARANCES
AND PRODUCTIONS

This list is by no means complete, but it gives an overview of some of the Seagal works which were not fully explored in this book.

TELEVISION ADVERTISEMENTS:

DYNAMIC. In a short ad for this Japanese caffeine genki drink Seagal rides on top of a speeding car, then frets over back pain. There is an explosion of green liquid and then Seagal poses in a sleeveless shirt holding the Dynamic, which is so god damn dynamic that it has purple electricity popping off of it. In another spot he beats the fuck out of an aikido opponent before the explosion and the electrical what not. Good job Steven.

MOUNTAIN DEW. Suddenly in 2004 Seagal showed up out-of-the-blue in a comedic ad for Mountain Dew. A leather-jacketed Seagal sporting a George Hamilton style spray-on tan goes into a convenience store while a robbery is in progress. But Seagal is so focussed on the purchasing of Mountain Dew that he doesn't even notice. Opening the cooler he accidentally hits an armed robber in the head. This happens again when he pulls out his wallet to pay for the Mountain Dew (accidental wallet blows are the number one killer of armed robbers, by the way). When the clerk tries to thank him Seagal obliviously decides he is asking for an autograph, but when he bends down to sign it he headbutts the clerk, knocking him unconscious.

To be honest, I have no clue what the hell this commercial is about, but I believe it has something to do with *Mr. Magoo*-style slapstick comedy and a foul tasting soft drink colored similar to urine.

In a Japanese ad for NISSIN, Seagal kicks a door in and struts into a dark, dangerous looking room. His opponent turns out to be a bowl of noodles, and I'll give you one guess who wins. That's right, Seagal eats the shit out of those noodles, then says something in Japanese about it. I don't know the English translation but I get the impression he appreciated the quality of the noodles.

ORANGE. "Orange Film Funding: Steven Seagal pitch" is the title of a "turn off your cell phone before the movie" type ad Seagal did for the British company Orange. Seagal (playing himself) is on a golf course trying to pitch a romantic comedy to some Hollywood hot shot. As the guy tries to escape from Seagal's proposal it turns into a miniature action movie with Seagal fighting other golfers, a high speed golf cart chase (with explosion), and at the end Seagal uses a detonator to blow-up the big shot's escape helicopter.

GUEST APPEARANCES:

CELEBRITY GUIDE TO WINE. This 1990 VHS/laser disc release opens on a tense scene of Robert Loggia hosting a barbecue. When a guest asks to have ice in her red wine he obliges, sending his butler into a blind rage that results in a wacky swimming pool accident. Now, I never heard of anybody drinking wine on the rocks, so I was surprised to see that this was apparently a pretty controversial issue among celebrities back in '90. I don't know if they had a ribbon for it or anything but for a barbecue to erupt in violence over something you gotta figure it is a hot button issue of the day.

Fortunately our host, "international wine expert and maitre d' of world-famous Spago Restaurant" Bernard Erpicum is a man of peace, so he quickly interjects to tell us that if we like ice in our wine it's okay to do it, what matters is that you enjoy it. Then for almost an hour he uses his thick French accent to tell us about the different types of wine. He explains how French wines are named after their regions but California wines are named after their grapes. He gives us "Bernard's Picks" for wines in various price ranges, and smells a bowl of raspberries to compare it to the wine he's drinking. He doesn't seem like a snob like Paul Giamatti in *Sideways*, he's just some French guy trying to convince everybody of how awesome wine is.

But Bernard knows that not even laser disc collectors give a flying fuck what some dude says about wine unless he has celebrity friends like Peter Weller and Herbie Hancock to back him up. Fortunately, he does. I don't know if these guys all eat at Spago, or if they just like money. Either way, the movie occasionally cuts to Herbie at a picnic table with two women or Whoopi Goldberg holding a bottle of wine in front of her car in her driveway. Which I guess is where famous people keep their wine. Dudley Moore does a couple "hilarious" skits where he embarrasses himself by not knowing what wine to ask for, then literally puts his date to sleep by repeating Bernard's wine trivia, then educates us about the logic behind various wine glass shapes.

Seagal's role is only a few minutes long, and he doesn't do much, it's actually his then-wife Kelly LeBrock who does all the work. Seagal (looking like Mason Storm in his trademark black suit of the period) sits in a fancy living room with a fire going in the fireplace. LeBrock arrives wearing a lime green mini-skirt and apologizes for being late due to traffic. She then proceeds to put a bottle of wine between her legs and open it in a sexually suggestive manner. She pours herself a glass, smells it, tastes it, then pours him one.

Seagal spends most of his screen time sitting motionless, watching LeBrock and playing it cool, like a dude getting a lap dance. The one really unusual thing is seeing a close-up of Seagal "correctly" tasting the wine and smiling – not something he wastes our time with in his movies, so it's a novelty.

Once they've each tasted the wine they agree that it was a good liaison and LeBrock leaves, continuing the sexual innuendo to imply that LeBrock is some kind of kept woman who comes to Seagal only to pleasure him with quickie wine-opening sessions. After this there is a replay where LeBrock is seen opening the bottle in more detail so that you can I guess follow along at home.

It's an interesting curiosity, because Seagal and LeBrock didn't appear on screen together much outside of *Hard to Kill*. From their looks they could almost be the characters from that movie, but their rendezvous is more reminiscent of Mason Storm's romantic encounter with his wife right before she's murdered. Still, unless you want an educational video about wine I really wouldn't recommend searching this one out – it really contains no themes or motifs from other Seagal works and adds little to the understanding of Seagalogy.

The guide is written and directed by Daniel Helfgott, whose other works include *Hollywood's Amazing Animal Actors*, *Abbott and Costello Meet Jerry Seinfeld*, and the 1993 sequel *Celebrity Guide To Entertaining*, which recycles Seagal and LeBrock's wine-opening scene *Silent Night Deadly 2*-style.

THE FRIDAY NIGHT PROJECT. Seagal guest-hosted the February 9th, 2007 episode of this corny hour-long British comedy show. The format is a hybrid of many types of shows. Seagal does a short monologue and interacts with Justin Lee Collins and Alan Carr (the show's regular comedy duo) in front of a live audience. In between there is a video taped skit (a lame parody called *Blunder Siege*) a segment taped at a Thunderbox show, a few different wacky game shows involving audience participation and celebrity guest contestants, even a segment where Seagal does a *Candid Camera* style prank (a fake martial arts demonstration where he makes a guy believe he is moving objects with his mind, then that he does it wrong and causes the entire audience to bleed from their mouths and eyes). Probably the weirdest part is seeing Seagal sit at a news desk to participate in a *Weekend Update*-style segment.

Seagal does a decent job for the most part and seems humble and good-humored. For an American it's weird to see him on a TV show at this point in his career; here he hasn't done that type of promotion since the Golden Era. He uses his bluesman accent through most of the show and says "Lahd have mercy!" more than once. When referencing the movie *The Karate Kid* in a joke he uses the correct pronunciation of 'karate' rather than the Americanized one. He makes a reference to his song "Alligator Ass." He also makes some very questionable claims about being Deputy Chief of his "local community" of Jefferson Parish, indicating at the prompting of an audience member that he has been involved in shootouts there.

Politically he steps out on a couple limbs I've never seen him on before. In the monologue he jokes that "The Terminator has teamed up with someone even more determined than he is to destroy all human life," which of course is illustrated by a photo of Arnold Schwarzenegger standing with George W. Bush. It's an obvious joke and I'm sure they wrote it for him, but it's the only time I've ever seen him acknowledge the existence of that particular Bush, and I don't think he'd say it if he didn't agree with it. (I wonder why all those dipshits who wanted to kill the Dixie Chicks for shit-talking Bush in England haven't said peep about Seagal?) He also goofs around with cartoonishly gay co-host Alan Carr, even joking that he is thinking of "going gay," which suggests he's not homophobic or insecure about his sexuality.

It's not exactly a great comedy program, and the skits and jokes make it clear that their writers don't see the distinction between Seagal's movies and other American action movies of the '80s and early '90s. They make references to Schwarzenegger and Chuck Norris and incorrectly offer Seagal fighting a ninja as an example of a typical scene for a Seagal movie. But it's still enjoyable to see Seagal in this unusual setting, and it's nice that the co-hosts treat him as an awe-inspiring icon instead of making fun of him.

The show also was used as a lead-in to the network showing *Under Siege*.

GET BRUCE. Seagal appears briefly in this 1999 documentary about Bruce Vilanch, the oddly shaped and bearded writer of lame awards show jokes. Seagal is not interviewed, but is seen early on sitting with Vilanch and Salma Hayek in an empty auditorium, preparing the script for their presentation of an unnamed award. (It sounds like they're talking about the Oscars, but it must be something else because as far as I can tell Seagal and Hayek have not presented in the same year before.)

The documentary itself is not terrible, and Vilanch seems like a nice enough guy. But oh jesus is it painful to watch Whoopi Goldberg, Billy Crystal and friends go on and on about what a genius this guy is, while they show clip after clip of comedy that does not in any way support that claim. If your idea of cutting edge humor is those horrible medleys Crystal sings at the Oscars and fake-spontaneous one-liners on Hollywood Squares (both of which Vilanch is responsible for) then you will love this. There is even a part where they seriously talk about how edgy it was for Whoopi Goldberg to do a fart joke at the Oscars. And if that's not enough for you there's an interview with Robin Williams where instead of offering any sort of insight he does his complete cokehead spazz out thing where he spits out 700 wacky voices and references in 1 minute, and you don't know what the fuck his problem is so that's supposed to count as being a comic genius.

So really, watching this one is not necessary for a complete understanding of Seagal. In his scene he does appear to be an easy-going guy, seems to care about preparing his script and does not seem uncomfortable when Vilanch makes jokes about being gay. Seagal also uses the word "cocksucker" a couple times and mentions that he is a member of the Writer's Guild.

SATURDAY NIGHT LIVE. Seagal hosted the April 20, 1991 episode to promote *Out For Justice*, which at the time was #1 at the box office. You can practically hear the history books being typed out in the background. It was the day after Evander Holyfield beat George Foreman, the day before Johnny Carson announced his retirement. The Gulf War had ended earlier in the month, the Rodney King beating had happened less than two months earlier, apartheid would soon be ending in South Africa, and musical guest Michael Bolton still had his legendary mullet. Seagal wore an all black suit, looking for all the world like Nico Toscani. In fact, he parodied *Above the Law* in a skit called *Nico Tonelli: One Man Army* where he ended up working with Rob Schneider's copy machine guy and dangling him out a window. Playing himself, Seagal also tussled with the bodybuilder characters Hans and Franz, causing them to briefly fantasize about themselves in ponytails and calling themselves "Hans Seagal and Franz Seagal." He also played Andrew

"Dice" Clay interviewed by Chris Rock's character Nat X, doing a pretty decent impression.

A lot of the sketches didn't involve Seagal, though. A few of the more memorable moments from the episode include the *We Are the World*-style "Musicians For Free-Range Chickens" song and Adam Sandler's Weekend Update travel correspondent character who describes his trip to Greece where he just fucks around in the hotel the whole time.

Note: although I remember seeing the episode at the time, in recent years I've only seen it in a cable rerun, where they cut it down by a half an hour. In an event before their screening of *On Deadly Ground* at the 2002 Olympia Film Festival, *Mr. Show*'s Bob Odenkirk reminisced about being an *SNL* writer at the time of this episode. He described a closing skit insisted upon by Seagal where, he claimed, there was no joke, just Seagal beating up some sort of corporate bad guy for his environmental wrong-doing. Obviously I'd love to be able to see this sketch, which sounds like an interesting precursor to *On Deadly Ground*. But since I have not been able to get ahold of it I will have to settle for the monologue, where Seagal gives the most succinct ever description of what he's trying to do with his movies, then plays guitar and sings "Kung Fu Fighting."

NON-APPEARANCES:

HALF PAST DEAD 2 is the first Seagal-free sequel to a Seagal movie. But it's not completely terrible, and might be worth watching on a bored afternoon if you liked the first one. While many DTV sequels just rehash the original story with a different set of characters (*Wild Things 2* and *3*, *Cruel Intentions 2*, *Roadhouse 2*, etc.), this one actually continues the story, but from the point-of-view of one of the secondary characters, Twitch, played by the second-tier gangster rapper Kurupt.

You remember Twitch? He was the wacky guy always painting murals. I don't really understand why this type of character is supposed to be funny – he's a skinny wimp, but talks as if he's tough, and hilarity is supposed to ensue. As a rapper he's pretty respected for his appearance on early Snoop Dogg albums, and for a long solo career. But as a comic actor he's pretty much just channeling Martin Lawrence, who in my opinion isn't funny in the first place. So it's weird to turn this secondary character into the lead. It's kind of clever like a *Rosencrantz and Guildenstern* type gimmick but still, it almost makes you miss Ja Rule. Almost.

When the story begins Twitch is still in New Alcatraz, still painting murals. Tony Plana returns as the tough-lovin' warden with the neck tattoos, El Fuego. But we don't stay at New Alcatraz long enough to see the old pre-execution virtual reality room or find out how well they repaired the helicopter-sized hole in the skylight. Twitch purposely gets into trouble so he can get transferred to Creighton, a prison in *Missouri* "where society took a shit and built a forty foot wall around it."

Now, I'm not gonna claim there is great storytelling in this movie, but I do appreciate that they don't tell you at first why Twitch wants a transfer. They are smart enough to have characters do things that are unexplained until later, so that you have a reason to keep watching. This is a basic storytelling technique by normal movie standards, but by DTV standards it's sophisticated, almost futuristic. It's not until later that we find out that Twitch plans a jailbreak, but couldn't do it from New Alcatraz because he can't swim. Then we find out that the gold found at the end of part 1 was only half of Lester's stash. And finally we learn that only two people know where the gold is, the other is the guy Twitch got in a fight with at the beginning, who's getting out in a month. So it's a race to get the gold[85].

All that information is divvied out a piece at a time, and is on top of the larger story of a prison riot. That's another surprise. You would expect another guerilla attack on a prison (somebody trying to get the location of the gold from Twitch, maybe), but instead they have the more believable premise that two female visitors get taken hostage during a prison riot. One of the hostages is Twitch's fiancée Cherise (Angell Conwell). You may remember that the comedienne Mo'Nique came to visit Twitch in the first movie, but Cherise says that was just his "fatass girlfriend." The other hostage is Ellie (Alona Tal), the daughter of big, bald muscleman Burke (played by Bill Goldberg, who I would've figured was a WWE wrestler even if I didn't read it somewhere). So Burke and

---

85 Should be called *Half Past Dead 2: The Legend of Lester's Gold.*

Twitch team up to elude the black and Hispanic gangs that are after them and save their loved ones.

There is no mention of Sasha Petrosevich or Nick Frazier, even during the scenes where Twitch recalls what happened over flashback footage from the original. I guess Twitch didn't give a shit what was going on with them. The director is Art Camacho, who was action director for *Half Past Dead* and even played one of the invading 49ers, specifically 49er Eleven. The direction is more competent than you expect in DTV with one major exception: there's a scene that's absolutely crucial to the plot, but it doesn't make any sense. While Burke is on cafeteria duty, the leader of the Hispanic gang, Cortez, yells "Angel!" and then shoots Angel, the leader of the black gang. But immediately everyone decides Burke did it. I guess the idea is that Cortez was behind Burke, so people misunderstood what happened and thought he shot. But why would anybody think that? There are literally dozens of witnesses who saw Cortez with their own eyes, not only firing the gun but yelling out the name of his target, right there in the open. If by some chance somebody really was confused and thought Burke had done it, there would be probably 30 people who could correct him. Instead, *everybody* thinks Burke did it. They really should've shot that scene different.

One thing that's kind of weird: the first movie was called *Half Past Dead* because of Sasha's near death experience, only important because it's the reason Lester wants to talk to him. In this movie there is no reason why it should be called that. There is no near death element, no religious or spiritual element. But it does continue the story so I guess it's kind of like *Halloween II*. That took place on November 1ˢᵗ, but it was still *Halloween*.

Without Seagal it loses most of what was interesting about the first one, and – let's be honest – *Half Past Dead* is not exactly the most interesting Seagal movie anyway. Still, as far as DTV sequels go this one is way above average.

PRODUCED BY SEAGAL:

DRAGON SQUAD (aka *DRAGON HEAT*). Seagal is credited as producer of this Hong Kong crime film, which he invested over 40 million HK dollars in according to crienglish.com. Aside from some annoying text explanations of all the characters (both good guys and bad guys) and Seagalian special-ops backgrounds for all the bad guys there is very little that is reminiscent of Seagal. The story involves a group of young pretty boy cops (and one girl) with various specialties who don't know each other until they come together to testify against a major crime figure. But when their guy is kidnapped by a rival gang while being transferred, they realize that they should team up and work together. Eventually they are able to recruit the days-away-from-retirement Sammo Hung to become their reluctant cigar-chewing leader.

It's not a bad movie, but it's not as fun as it ought to be. The specialties of the various squad members are not fully utilized. The action is almost entirely gun-related, the only martial arts being in Sammo's two fights. There is a lot of emotion and crying, and the villains are shown to be somewhat human, two things that are very Hong Kong and not very Seagal. Some of the movie is in English because one of the lead villains is played by Michael Biehn (*Terminator, Aliens*), who kind of talks like Dennis Hopper in this one.

The film is directed by Daniel Lee (*Black Mask*) and also features Maggie Q (*Mission: Impossible 3, Live Free or Die Hard*) as a bad guy sniper who blows the back of the pretty good girl's head off, but still gets a somewhat sad death after a cool shootout swinging around on a cable hanging from a tree in the middle of a graveyard.

NOT EVEN THE TREES. This never distributed drama about a drug-addicted model was Seagal/Nasso's first attempt at producing a Seagal-free movie. Since it hasn't been released on video I haven't seen it, but one of its co-stars, Chris Lawford (the same guy who played the Vice President in the opening of *Exit Wounds*) does not recommend it. "Have you seen *Not Even The Trees*?" he once asked an interviewer. "Terrible title, and guess what? Terrible film[86]."

THE PATH BEYOND THOUGHT. Seagal's company Steamroller Productions produced this hour-long 2001 documentary about Seagal's

---

86 Aidan Smith, "Jack's the hardest act to follow" from *Scotland on Sunday*, 26 February 2006.

aikido. The director is Binh Dang, who went on to produce many of the Seagal DTV pictures starting with *The Foreigner*. This movie was sold as a VHS tape on his official web site; a DVD version was scheduled to be used as a premium with Lightning Bolt Energy Drink, but as of this writing that offer has never actually appeared.

Illustrated with home video footage of Seagal teaching aikido throughout the years, both in Japan and in the U.S., the story is told through interviews with several of Seagal's students. They describe his "severe" form of aikido, his teaching style, and what it was like to be his student. The hotshots who claim Seagal has no skills ought to watch this video and try to rationalize it. You see him demonstrating moves about ten thousand times, and it's pretty clear he knows what he's doing. Of course, a lot of it is sparring designed to show how the move works, with the student flipping to the mat to practice their falls. But there are also many passages where they're clearly going for it. The students praise Seagal for using real punches and chokes in his training, so students can learn a "realistic" and "practical" defense method, instead of just learning how to avoid pulled punches.

With beginners, they say, Seagal is very gentle, friendly and surprisingly approachable. As they get more advanced he gets into the tough love. In some footage he is seen yelling at students for their mistakes, and here he starts to seem like his onscreen persona. One in particular, where he's telling a guy what to do as three other students attack him (part of the black belt test), sounds just like in *On Deadly Ground* when he's yelling "You're a man, right?" at Big Mike. He even seems to pick up a little bit of his *Out For Justice* Brooklyn accent at one point.

This is not an instructional video, and you don't hear anything from Seagal's point-of-view other than an *Above the Law* style opening bit of narration over a photo montage. But it is far and away the clearest look at Seagal as a martial artist and instructor.

PRINCE OF CENTRAL PARK. In 2000 (between *The Patriot* and *Exit Wounds*) Seagal/Nasso Productions put together this independent family drama about an orphan living in Central Park. The movie stars 13-year-old Frankie Nasso, Julius Nasso's son who played Mason Storm's son in

Hard to Kill. Frankie is actually pretty good in this movie, but you still have to laugh at the cast and crew notes on the DVD where the director talks about why he chose Frankie over all the other kids that auditioned, and it never mentions that his dad was the producer of the movie.

The movie has very little Seagalogy in it. Frankie's character J.J. does open the movie with narration (like *Above the Law*) and music is very important to him – he carries around a keyboard which he plays even when it has no batteries. But he doesn't speak different languages (he can barely even read English), his shadowy past just has to do with not knowing what happened to his mother, and he gets beat up more than once. He does not have a sword.

Jerry Orbach (*Out For Justice*) does have a bit part. And the DVD cover has a Seagal-esque lack of accuracy, depicting Harvey Keitel clean-shaven and normal even though in the movie he's a crazy homeless man with a pointy goatee and a hat covered in buttons. He plays one of those lovable, magical homeless people you see in movies who live life as a fairy tale and dispense wisdom to children. As far as we can tell he is not addicted to drugs, is more "eccentric" than mentally ill, and doesn't smell like piss.

The director is John Leekley, a TV veteran who wrote pilots for a *The Omen* TV series and *Knight Rider 2010*. Strangely enough he is also the co-author of two books about the Civil War, including *The Blue and the Gray*, which was turned into a famous mini-series. He had not directed before this, but according to the cast and crew notes he had been friends with Seagal and Nasso for over ten years. His direction here is mostly competent other than a few awkward reaction shots early on. Leekley also wrote the script, which on the end credits is said to be adapted from a particular production of a "musical play." Wherever he got it from, the story originated as a book by an author named Evan Rhodes. It was also adapted into a 1977 TV movie starring Ruth Gordon (once available on VHS, but not on DVD).

Seagal is not listed in the credits, but the production notes on the DVD make a big deal about his involvement. If he had any creative input it's hard to notice. He is described as being "involved in the development, production and financing of motion pictures" and said to have helped "by assembling an impressive team of financiers and filmmakers." The notes also say that he "dazzled audiences with his lifelong practice of material [sic] arts." Later they say that "The film offers a chance to try something that Seagal/Nasso Productions is not known for, since Steven Seagal typically conjures up thoughts of 'action.'" Yes, they put action in quotes.

I've seen worse movies, but I don't really see a reason to recommend this one, not even to Seagal completists.

HARD TO FILM: THE ONES THAT NEVER MADE IT

A selected unfilmography of movies Seagal developed but did not film.

THE BIRDMAN OF ALCATRAZ. This was not an actual project, but in an interview with PETA Seagal said, "*The Birdman of Alcatraz* is a true story. I'd like to remake that movie."

BLOOD ON THE MOON (aka *CRUISE*). One of the movies Julius Nasso had lined up for Seagal before they had their falling out. Seagal would've played a businessman hunting down a "pirate gang" who murdered his family during a cruise. Planned to shoot after *On Deadly Ground*, it was going to be made in Hong Kong. The director would've been Steve Wang, who directed the above average Mark Dacascos/Kadeem Hardison teamup *Drive*. The script was by Wang and Scott Phillips. In a lawsuit, former Seagal student Ahnume Guerios claimed he shot footage of "200 Brazilian Indian" extras for this picture, but that Seagal scrapped the footage because he thought the women in it were "too fat."

BLUE BAYOU. Guerios also claimed to have helped Seagal develop this intriguing movie which would "combine action and music, so that Seagal would be able to show his musical talent." This may or may not have evolved into *Prince of Pistols*.

THE FINAL OPTION. This was not actually a movie, but an unreleased video game. These days video games are real elaborate and cinematic, but this was developed in the days of the "Super Nintendo" which, in retrospect, was not very super. A crude 2-dimensional animation of Seagal would've gone sideways across the screen, jumping over crates and shooting at bad guys.

GENGHIS KHAN. For many years it has been Seagal's dream to play Genghis Khan. Not some freelance black ops dude named Genghis Khan, but the actual Genghis Khan. The biopic was another one Seagal had developed with Nasso before they split. Seagal even went to Beijing to scout locations and cast the martial artists who would play Khan's sons and grandsons. Reportedly he met with director Chen Kaige (*Farewell My Concubine*).

MAN OF HONOR. After the success of *Under Siege*, Seagal first planned this as his directorial debut, but financing fell through just days before filming so he moved on to *On Deadly Ground*. Seagal would've played the son of a mafia kingpin who protects a female informant. The screenplay was by Seagal and Jim Carabatsos (*Hamburger Hill*).

THE ONION MOVIE. Seagal stars in a fake movie trailer that's part of this sketch comedy compilation from the creators of the satirical newspaper *The Onion*. The movie was filmed in 2003 but shelved by Fox Searchlight, so for years it's plagued Seagal's IMDb filmography. The entry disappeared for a while and then returned in February 2008 when a trailer was included on the DVD for *The Darjeeling Limited*. The director and writers have long since disavowed the project and reports from test screenings have been dire. A reviewer calling himself "MovieManManzels" told Joblo.com, "Also Steven Seagal makes the only known celebrity appearance as Cock Puncher so if you think Steven Seagal hitting people in the nuts over and over again is funny then this goes to prove that American society is getting dumber." Actually, that does sound pretty funny. If it never comes out, at least Seagal's part is featured heavily in the trailer.

SECRET SMILE. Would've been directed by Dean Semler (who later did *The Patriot*) as the follow-up to *Under Siege 2*. Seagal was supposed to play an agent who takes "smart-drugs" to help him track down a criminal genius of some kind. Keep in mind, this was years before the formulation of Lightning Bolt.

SHADOWS ON THE SUN aka *SHADOWS OF THE PAST*. This different sort of Seagal movie was to be written by Bey Logan, the Asian cinema expert and editor of *Impact Magazine*. A 2005 Variety story said that Seagal would be playing "a burned out former intelligence officer who runs a medical clinic in Japan just after WWII." The IMDb listing for this project eventually became *Shadow Man*, leading myself and others to believe that the Japanese medical clinic period piece had somehow evolved into the modern day kidnapping and deadly virus thriller. However, according to *Shadow Man* writer Joe Halpin, the two were completely unrelated projects. Seagal briefly considered *Shadows of the Past*, but it never had financing. Meanwhile, the studio had this spec script they wanted him to do called *Shadow Man*. Nothing against the Exploding Watermelon Fist, but it might've been more exciting if he had been able to do the other one since it sounds more off the beaten path.

SMASH AND GRAB. Another one that fell apart when Seagal and Nasso's relationship ended.

UNKNOWN DAVID ZUCKER PROJECT. In 2006 Variety reported a deal between Seagal, Fox Searchlight, and producers David Zucker and Gil Netter. Zucker (formerly of *Airplane!* fame, now unfortunately the guy who did *Scary Movie 3*) was supposed to direct a comedy where Seagal would parody his persona, an idea they got after Seagal's role in *The Onion Movie*.

MY REVIEW OF STEVEN SEAGAL AND THUNDERBOX LIVE IN SEATTLE

as originally published in my column VERN TELL'S IT LIKE IT IS the day after the concert

THE STEVEN SEAGAL BLUES BAND
May 27th, 2006 at the Tractor Tavern, Seattle

I'm not about to start writing concert reviews, but I think the Steven Seagal Blues Band tour is worth an explanation. From the moment I first heard about the show to the second I got there, I really had no clue what the hell was gonna happen. And I had many discussions with people about who was gonna show up, if anybody. Wouldn't it just be young people going to laugh at him? Would it be embarassing? Would he have to break a dude's wrist and throw him through a window? Or pull a decorative lasso or samurai sword off the wall and go to work? I even had an elaborate notion of how he could bring along a stuntman to pose as a heckler, then do a couple moves on the guy and throw him through sugar glass. That would be one hell of a show.

I know because of steven-seagal.net that there are some crazy female fans whose Seagal fandom is purely about lust. But the internet is a worldwide medium. The question is how many of these women there really are in the world and how many are within driving distance of Seattle. I figured 1 or 2 tops, probaly none. But I figured wrong.

The show sold out, and there were people outside with signs begging for extra tickets. It was a mostly older crowd inside. Lots of grey hair, also lots of bald heads and tattoos. Some tough guys, some ponytails, some nerdy old guys in leather jackets. I wondered if anybody was a serious blues fan. Was anyone here to genuinely examine his chops? There was a pack of crew-cutted frat boys hooting in the back, some young hipster types here and there, possibly for ironic purposes, possibly for Seagalogical study. Probaly more men than women but not much, seemed like lots of husbands and wives. Mostly white people, but all races were represented. I noticed a decent percentage of Native Americans, and a woman wearing a fringed jacket with beadwork like Seagal wears in ON DEADLY GROUND. That made my day. I figured if there was ever a Seagalogy convention you'd be seeing alot of those.

I never been to this place, the Tractor Tavern. There are cowboy boots, some tractor tires and a few farming type tools decorating the place, lots of things that could become improvised weapons if a fight were to break out. Unfortunately there's no pool table so we're not gonna see the legendary pool balls in the napkin move from OUT FOR JUSTICE. This is Seattle, so the country theme is a put-on. It's not an authentic tough joint but it is an approximation of a bar where a fight might occur in a Seagal picture. The bathroom is ridiculously narrow and has a piss trough instead of urinals. But there's a sign on the wall that says "Be nice or leave," and I was immediately struck by how nice everybody was. People apologizing for bumping into each other, letting ladies go first in line, bartenders replacing spilled drinks for free. I saw a woman trying to buy a ticket even though the show was long sold old. She said she had driven all the way from Oregon. The ticket girl thought about it for a moment, stamped the lady's wrist and let her in.

This type of courtesy was also extended by the acts. The show time on the tickets was 8:00, which in Seattle usually means "doors at 8:30, endless shitty opening acts at 10ish." For this show though the opening act started at 8:05. It was J.J. Gilmour, a likeable Scottish singer and guitar strummer. The crowd seemed to like him so it was sad later on to see him having to sell Seagal's t-shirts.

Oh yeah if you're going to this tour you should know that yes, there is merchandise. They got the new CD "Mojo Priest" by Steven Seagal & Thunderbox, and they got a t-shirt with the album cover on it (Seagal sitting on a porch playing an unplugged electric guitar). The shirt comes in grey or black and various sizes, both items cost a reasonable $15.

The band came out promptly and professionally at 9:05. Although they were advertised as "The Steven Seagal Blues Band," some other dates on the tour call them Thunderbox, and I think Seagal called them "Memphis Thunderbox" at one point. Now, I have noticed before that Seagal is a white man, and I am not a particular fan of the white man's blues. So I was pleasantly surprised to discover that Thunderbox is an all black, super fuckin tight young blues band. I vouch for these guys 100%. I'm no expert on the blues, I got "Electric Mud" and I like some Howlin' Wolf and what not when I hear it. Also I've been sad before and I'm pretty broke right now. That's the extent of my expertise. But I'm very confident in my claim that this band is topnotch.

Here's how it lays out: 3 backup guitarists, the most noticeable being Bernard Allison (son of Luther Allison it turns out) because he has two rattlesnake heads on his hat. Then you got a drummer of course, a bass player, a guy on Hammond B-3 (really good) and two very attractive backup singers, one female one male. They jam for a minute and warm up the crowd and then somebody says, "Ladies and gentlemen, Mr. Steven Seagal" and the motherfucker climbs up on stage with a flying-V guitar and one of those shiny Asian numbers he loves, orange and sleeveless. He betrays no emotion as he strolls up and starts bluesin it up on the guitar. And the crowd goes fuckin NUTS. His opening salvos are choice but there's no question, they are not cheering for the blues. They are cheering for Casey Ryback. They are cheering for Nico Toscani. They are cheering for the fucking ponytail.

I know because I was one of these people. How often do you get a chance to cheer for a dude you saw throwing people through windows in a couple dozen movies? I know my bud Telf over on the Ain't It Cool talkbacks saw Bruce Willis on stage, but most people have not had that experience. You see them in movies, you don't expect to ever see them in the same room as you. But there he is, towering over everybody else, squinting those eyes, looking exactly like always, except right there in front of me, in person. AND PLAYING A FUCKING GUITAR.

Another thing I wondered when I realized I had a chance to see Steven Seagal playing music was whether or not he would have guitar face. I don't know if anybody else is as fascinated by this as me, but alot of guitarists make goofy faces while they play. They bob their head around and mouth the sounds they're trying to make. Or sometimes they scrunch up like somebody just farted in their face. With somebody like Jimi or some of the traditional blues guys it might be cool. With alot of people, especially white people, it looks ridiculous. And when you are better known as a movie star, like say if you were Al Pacino or Patrick Stewart, you would look even funnier making guitar face. So this was an important question in my mind.

The answer is that Seagal has a very powerful and unique guitar face that is entirely contained within his brow. For most of his playing his face was completely motionless. His mouth just looked like a bracket tipped over. Like in his movies, his eyes were so narrow that you couldn't tell if they were open or closed. But his eyebrows would tilt in and out of a concerned upside down V and he'd shake his head slightly side to side. This is an entirely respectable guitar face that in no way compromises his tough guy screen persona. In fact it emphasizes it, using my Theory of Badass Juxtaposition. Blues guitar is pretty manly so it's not as strong of a juxtaposition as jazz piano (Clint Eastwood) but personally I believe any expressive art counts.

How good is Seagal? I would say he's pretty good, definitely above expectations. With the extreme tightness of his band, I could tell he was a little sloppy on the guitar. At one point I thought one of the backup guitarists might have winced at his playing, but that was probaly my imagination. I don't think his performance was embarassing at all. He could've gotten away with strumming and singing, but he took almost all of the solos. We're not talking about memorizing some chords, he has to know the idiom of blues soloing in order to be able to play these songs, so I think he's serious, not just going through a phase. He did well.

You might've heard some of his singing on his movies. It's funny because you can tell it's him. Like alot of blues I'm sure, the whole production sounds way better live than on CD, including the singing. I couldn't make out all the lyrics, but he's definitely following blues traditions more than putting his unique Seagalian spin on them. A lot of "Well I woke up this morning" and "I went to bed last night" and that kind of stuff. I noticed in one song he mentioned seeing Jesus and the Devil walking down a road together, which seemed like an unusual thing for a Buddhist lama to be singing about. But it's an acceptable use of symbolism. One song they played turns out to be called "Talk To My Ass," but the lyrics never say that as far as I can tell. Another one was called "Alligator Ass" because of the punchline at the end where he says he ordered some chicken but they gave him alligator ass. The bastards.

Every song or two a guy would come out and hand Seagal a different guitar. One of them had a snakeskin strap that looked like it had part of the head still on there. Despite that, Seagal's presence was serious and humble, mostly expressionless but occasionally he would look at his bandmates and break into a wide, boyish smile. Some of the crowd were yelling things like "UNDER SIEGE!" but instead of getting mad he smiled and nodded and a couple times shook people's hands. There was very little between songs banter (I would've liked a speech on alternative fuel resources) but he did go around and introduce the band, telling where they were from, what they did (this guy tours with Alicia Keys, this guy plays with "everyone from the Rolling Stone on down"), and invariably describing them as "amazing." Bernard Allison for example is "The son of an amazing blues legend, and he himself is an amazing... blues legend." After he'd introduced everybody in detail, almost as an afterthought he said, "Oh, and I'm Steven Seagal," and the band busted immediately into the next song as the crowd went nuts again. Because it's true, he was Steven Seagal.

The show was pretty short, just about an hour before the encore. But at least they didn't wear out their welcome. The last song before the encore was "Feet Don't Fail Me Now," which he doesn't have on the CD. I think it's a traditional zydeco song, but they played it as funk, even throwing in a little "Fire!" from the Ohio Players. Now, I don't know blues but I do know a thing or two about funk. I've seen James Brown a couple times, I've seen Parliament-Funkadelic, I've seen the other Parliament where they don't have George Clinton but they have all the other original members. I've seen the Meters (without Zigaboo unfortunately), I've seen War. One time I saw the original JBs opening for James Brown – Bootsy, Fred Wesley and everybody. I saw Herbie Hancock's reunion with the original Headhunters. I even saw Dolemite once. I've also seen shitty funk bands and you can tell when it's bad. You do it wrong and it's cheesy as hell. And you have to be tight or it doesn't seem funky. Funk to me is what X-Men is to nerds, so believe me when I say that this was scorchin. The Hammond somehow sounded like a funky ass horn section, but distorted like a dusty old record from a low budget session. I couldn't fuckin believe what I was experiencing here. The crowd was dancing. The band was burning up. And Steven Seagal was standing there in his orange shirt wailing away. What the fuck is this, is this a dream or is this real life? Did my love for OUT FOR JUSTICE and old school funk seriously just intersect right before my eyes?

I'm not lying people, this was one of the most amazing things I've seen in my life. It was a genuinely entertaining concert, and every song got an explosive applause from the audience. There was never a point where the appreciation, or the novelty, or whatever you think it was, seemed to be wearing thin. Some of those crazy women were yelling "I love you Steven!" and dudes were yelling things about his movies, but with few exceptions I got the feeling these were sincere fans. A lot of them knew that it was funny what they were seeing but they were genuinely appreciative of Seagal. Now that I think of it it's kind of a relief because these are the people I'm trying to write *Seagalogy* for. Now I know there are lots of them.

Now don't get me wrong, if this great band had had some "amazing blues legend" as the leader instead of an aikido instructor turned movie star turned lama turned bluesman, you would've had some more all-around technically proficient and authentic blues. But it might not have been as good. Because the sight of a genuinely awesome band fronted by the guy from BELLY OF THE BEAST is surreal and beautiful. A once in a lifetime dream. I had that constant "this is too good to be true" feeling pretty much from start to finish.

As "Feet Don't Fail Me Now" was ending, Seagal left the stage, followed by the band, and the crowd chanted, "RYBACK! RYBACK!

RYBACK!" until they came back for one more. After the encore, everybody had huge smiles threatening to break off of their faces. Most people were in too much of a daze to leave. Some people crowded at the corner of the stage hoping to catch another glimpse of Seagal. Sure enough he came out and shook some hands. Suddenly it threatened to turn into mayhem as people rushed the corner trying to get a piece of the action. After a few minutes Seagal climbed on stage and tried to find a live mic.

Holy shit, I thought. Is he gonna do it? Is he gonna make the speech from the end of ON DEADLY GROUND? Or maybe the sermon from FIRE DOWN BELOW? Is he gonna take questions? Instead he said that he was going to find a place to sign things and "spend some time with you." This, of course, resulted in a burst of Beatlemania-esque hysteria.

Eventually Seagal was seated behind a little table and everyone tried to crush each other to get to him. This was when you really got a feel for the type of fandom you had attending the show. There were definitely obsessed women, including two feisty plus-sized ladies who had managed to score a sweaty hand towel Seagal had used. They explained that it was the one he used when he lifted up his ponytail and wiped the sweat off the back of his neck. They were honorable though so they found a man with a pocket-knife to cut it in half so they could each have a piece. There were plenty of admiring middle aged women who were not crazy, and some of them decided that an autograph was not worth being crushed and just left. Another one kept saying she was going to touch his hair.

I guess I'm not as much of a superfan as you'd think, because I didn't bring a DVD to autograph or a camera. But I was amazed at the memorabilia that seemed to appear out of nowhere. Posters, huge blow up glossies, laser discs of OUT FOR JUSTICE and UNDER SIEGE. Some young Seagalogists were obviously amused by the whole thing but I was happy that they weren't just being ironic. I heard discussions of INTO THE SUN and how PRINCE OF PISTOLS is gonna be about the blues. People were calling their friends to brag that they were ten feet away from Steven Seagal. "Oh my god, I can't believe it, that's Casey Ryback right there." There was a real camaraderie here. Strangers crammed together, talking about their favorite Seagal movies, making jokes about the titles. Somehow word had spread throughout the neighborhood, so some kids were gathering outside begging to get in, but they didn't have IDs.

Watching Seagal sign was almost as good as watching him play. He spoke quietly so you couldn't tell what he was saying to people. But he would put on these little reading glasses (perhaps the same ones he uses to examine antique samurai swords for museums) and then he'd take them off to pose for pictures with people. For every picture he would assume his dead-eyed badass face. No smile at all. I saw people posing for what must've been some hilarious pictures – groups of college kids with gigantic smiles surrounding Seagal with the look of a stone cold killer on his face. (If any of these show up on the internet here let me know and I'll link to them.)

Now, I haven't met too many famous people or gotten too many books signed or anything, but when it happens I got a rule. Don't assume you are the one cool guy who can relate to your hero and ask a question he hasn't heard a million times before. Just be polite, say thank you or whatever. Make it simple. So when I got up to the front I just shook the man's hand and said "Thank you very much, I'm a huge fan, it was a wonderful show." Usually I'd probaly just say "thank you" but how often are you gonna meet Steven fucking Seagal? So I splurged and threw in that extra "wonderful" part.

I didn't feel like I made a personal connection with the man. Not that he was unfriendly, but he's been sitting there signing autographs for a bunch of crazy people, not sure who's sincere and who's gonna try to sell it on ebay. You can't blame him for not seeming like he's your best friend. I can't even remember what he said back to me. I was probaly too busy wondering how the hell I was standing there shaking Steven Seagal's hand to actually experience the moment.

As I walked away from the tavern I just started laughing at my luck. I've done well with this hand. It's worked out pretty good for typing, it's flipped off Dick Cheney to his face, and it's shaken Steven Seagal's hand. If I ever get horribly maimed, now I got another reason to hope it happens on the left side.

Some kind of jug band was playing on the sidewalk next to a hot dog stand. Other people were floating to their cars or bus stops powered by post-Seagal highs. That movie didn't lie, life is beautiful. The problems of the world might go away if everybody could get a chance to see Steven Seagal with a flying-V. I figure no matter how down in the dumps you are, try to always live your life as if you might shake Steven Seagal's hand later that night. Because who knows, you might.

As I got further away I began to run into people from the outside world, people who may not have even been aware that the star of THE GLIMMER MAN was sitting in a tavern nearby. And everybody I passed I had to fight the urge to say, "Excuse me, I just shook Steven Seagal's hand."

Nah, they wouldn't understand. It's something you have to live.

—VERN

special thanks:

Joe Halpin and mink for their openness and sportsmanship, Harry Knowles and Drew McWeeny for posting some of my earliest Seagal writings and creating a forum for open Seagalogical discussion, David Gordon Green for the introduction, David Wingo for hooking up the introduction, J. Koogler for editorial assistance, Brian Thiess for artwork, Neil Young U.K. for sending me *The Friday Night Project*, Richard Grendzinski for the *Celebrity Wine Tasting* laser disc, Matthew Lynch for transferring it to VHS, Bruce Willis for posting in my talkback that one time, David DeFalco for challenging me to that wrestling match, and most of all I want to thank everyone who has corresponded with me over the years about Badass Cinema, Seagalogy or other topics. *Strive for excellence.*